PSYCHOLOGICAL SCIENCE IN THE COURTROOM

Psychological Science in the Courtroom

CONSENSUS AND CONTROVERSY

edited by
Jennifer L. Skeem
Kevin S. Douglas
Scott O. Lilienfeld

THE GUILFORD PRESS
New York   London

Library of Congress Cataloging-in-Publication Data

Psychological science in the courtroom : consensus and controversy / edited by
Jennifer L. Skeem, Kevin S. Douglas, Scott O. Lilienfeld.
    p. cm.
  Includes bibliographical references and index.
  ISBN 978-1-60623-251-4 (hardcover)
    1. Law—Psychological aspects.   2. Law—United States—Psychological
aspects.   3. Forensic psychology.   I. Skeem, Jennifer L.   II. Douglas, Kevin S.
III. Lilienfeld, Scott O., 1960–
  K346.P7894 2009
  614.'1—dc22

                                                                2008047686

About the Editors

Jennifer L. Skeem, PhD, is Associate Professor of Psychology and Social Behavior at the University of California, Irvine, where she is also a member of the MacArthur Research Network on Mandated Community Treatment, the Center for Psychology and Law, and the Center for Evidence-Based Corrections. Dr. Skeem conducts research on such topics as psychopathic personality disorder, violence risks, and psychiatric treatment outcomes of offenders. She is a recipient of the Saleem Shah Award for Early Career Excellence in Psychology and Law, awarded jointly by the American Psychology-Law Society (Division 41 of the American Psychological Association) and the American Academy of Forensic Psychology.

Kevin S. Douglas, LLB, PhD, is Associate Professor and Coordinator of the Law and Forensic Psychology Program in the Department of Psychology, Simon Fraser University, Canada. He conducts research on forensic assessment and violence, with a specific focus on violence risk assessment. Dr. Douglas is a Michael Smith Foundation for Health Research Career Scholar and a recipient of the Saleem Shah Award for Early Career Excellence in Psychology and Law.

Scott O. Lilienfeld, PhD, is Professor of Psychology at Emory University. His research focuses on the causes of personality disorders, particularly psychopathic personality; psychiatric classification and diagnosis; and evidence-based practice in clinical psychology. Dr. Lilienfeld is a fellow of the American Psychological Society and a recipient of the David Shakow Early Career Award from Division 12 (Clinical Psychology) of the American Psychological Association. He is editor of the *Scientific Review of Mental Health Practice*.

Contributors

Kendra Beitz, PhD, Department of Psychology, University of Nevada Reno, Reno, Nevada

Elza Boycheva, MS, Department of Psychology, Binghamton University, Binghamton, New York

Maggie Bruck, PhD, Department of Psychiatry and Behavioral Sciences, Johns Hopkins University, Baltimore, Maryland

Stephen J. Ceci, PhD, Department of Psychology, Cornell University, Ithaca, New York

Brian L. Cutler, PhD, Faculty of Criminology, Justice, and Policy Studies, University of Ontario Institute of Technology, Oshawa, Ontario, Canada

Deborah Davis, PhD, Department of Psychology, University of Nevada Reno, Reno, Nevada

Amanda Deming, MS, Department of Psychology, Binghamton University, Binghamton, New York

Kevin S. Douglas, PhD, Department of Psychology, Simon Fraser University, Vancouver, British Columbia, Canada

John F. Edens, PhD, Department of Psychology, Texas A&M University, College Station, Texas

David L. Faigman, JD, MA, Hastings College of Law, University of California San Francisco, San Francisco, California

Howard N. Garb, PhD, Wilford Hall Medical Center, Lackland Air Force Base, San Antonio, Texas

Jennifer L. Groscup, JD, PhD, Department of Psychology, Scripps College, Claremont, California

Michael N. Hallquist, MS, Department of Psychology, Binghamton University, Binghamton, New York

Michelle Haring, PhD, North Shore Stress and Anxiety Clinic and British Columbia Women's Hospital, Vancouver, British Columbia, Canada

Kirk Heilbrun, PhD, Department of Psychology, Drexel University, Philadelphia, Pennsylvania

William G. Iacono, PhD, Department of Psychology, University of Minnesota Twin Cities, Minneapolis, Minnesota

Patrick J. Kennealy, MA, Department of Psychology and Social Behavior, University of California Irvine, Irvine, California

William J. Koch, PhD, Departments of Psychiatry and Psychology, University of British Columbia, and Department of Psychology, Simon Fraser University, Vancouver, British Columbia, Canada

Richard N. Kocsis, PhD, forensic psychologist in private practice, Sydney, Australia

Scott O. Lilienfeld, PhD, Department of Psychology, Emory University, Atlanta, Georgia

Elizabeth F. Loftus, PhD, Department of Psychology and Social Behavior, University of California Irvine, Irvine, California

Steven Jay Lynn, PhD, Department of Psychology, Binghamton University, Binghamton, New York

Sarah Manchak, MA, Department of Psychology and Social Behavior, University of California Irvine, Irvine, California

Bradley D. McAuliff, JD, PhD, Department of Psychology, California State University Northridge, Northridge, California

Christian A. Meissner, PhD, Departments of Psychology and Criminal Justice, University of Texas El Paso, El Paso, Texas

John Monahan, PhD, School of Law, University of Virginia, Charlottesville, Virginia

Rami Nader, PhD, North Shore Stress and Anxiety Clinic and Department of Psychology, University of British Columbia, Vancouver, British Columbia, Canada

M. Teresa Nezworski, PhD, Wilford Hall Medical Center, Lackland Air Force Base, San Antonio, Texas

William T. O'Donohue, PhD, Department of Psychology, University of Nevada Reno, Reno, Nevada

John P. Petrila, JD, Louis de la Parte Florida Mental Health Institute and Department of Health Policy and Management, College of Public Health, University of South Florida, Tampa, Florida

Devon L. L. Polaschek, PhD, Department of Psychology, Victoria University of Wellington, Wellington, New Zealand

Norman G. Poythress, PhD, Louis de la Parte Florida Mental Health Institute and Department of Mental Health Law and Policy, University of South Florida, Tampa, Florida

Allison D. Redlich, PhD, School of Criminal Justice, State University of New York Albany, Albany, New York

Jennifer L. Skeem, PhD, Department of Psychology and Social Behavior, University of California Irvine, Irvine, California

Lauren Tolle, MA, Department of Psychology, University of Nevada Reno, Reno, Nevada

Gary L. Wells, PhD, Department of Psychology, Iowa State University, Ames, Iowa

James M. Wood, PhD, Department of Psychology, University of Texas El Paso, El Paso, Texas

Kento Yasuhara, BA, Department of Psychology, Drexel University, Philadelphia, Pennsylvania

Patricia A. Zapf, PhD, John Jay College of Criminal Justice, The City University of New York, New York, New York

Preface

The past several decades have witnessed exponential growth in clinical, cognitive, developmental, and social psychological research relevant to legal decision making. Yet much of this research has yet to exert a tangible impact within the courtroom. Many legal decisions are still based on inadequate psychological science or, worse, no psychological science at all.

In part, this chasm exists because the worlds of psychology and law—despite sharing the subject matter of human behavior—differ in their core assumptions about what drives human behavior. Scientific psychology views behavior as determined, or strongly influenced, by antecedent causes. Although the law sometimes recognizes such influences, it generally assumes that behavior is freely chosen. More important, the two worlds differ in their fundamental methods for acquiring knowledge. Psychology aims to ascertain the "truth" by encouraging the open dissemination and evaluation of all scientific evidence; the legal system aims to fairly resolve disputes by means of an adversarial framework that often relies on experts and implicitly encourages the suppression of contrary evidence. Of course, these are primarily differences of degree rather than of kind. For example, some psychologists ignore or downplay evidence that runs counter to their pet theories, and some lawyers honorably acknowledge evidence that weakens their case. Despite these occasional areas of overlap, the worlds of psychology and the law remain divided by a yawning chasm, one often marked by mutual misunderstanding and mistrust.

Although little can be done about the fields' underlying differences in philosophy and method, we can target two barriers to the use of psychological science in the courtroom for change. First, many psychological experts rely on what they "know" rather than keeping abreast of evolving and highly technical research. This reliance on the familiar is problematic because such "knowledge" may often reflect clinical lore, urban legends, or outdated research findings rather than state-of-the-art scientific evidence. Because the body of research bearing on legal decision making has become vast and increasingly specialized, even forensic psychologists find it difficult to keep up with scientific developments within their own domains of expertise, let alone across domains. General clinicians and researchers who occasionally testify in court may be unfamiliar with these developments or uncertain about how to evaluate and clearly present scientific evidence pertaining to legal issues.

Second, numerous domains lying at the intersection of psychology and the law are rife with myths, misconceptions, and controversies. In part, these are fueled by pseudoscience. Many practitioners are poorly acquainted with the mixed or weak research evidence for such techniques as criminal profiling, polygraph testing and other methods for detecting deception, forensic hypnosis, suggestive interviews with children, and projective testing. Even practitioners who specialize in such heavily researched areas as forensic assessment may be unaware of crucial nuances and gaps in the scientific evidence and, for example, unknowingly perpetuate the misconceptions that "adjudicative competence can be tested" or that "treatment makes psychopaths more dangerous." At best, experts' inadequate knowledge of scientific evidence pertaining to legal issues prevents psychological science from informing legal decisions; at worst, it has the potential to mislead triers of fact.

This edited volume attempts to shatter these barriers to the effective use of psychological science in the courtroom. Its goal is to bridge the wide chasm between psychological science and the legal system by addressing one overarching question: *"What does the best available scientific evidence tell us about how to evaluate legal issues relevant to psychology?"* The recent surge of interest and activity in the fields of psychology and law has advanced our understanding of a variety of psycholegal issues, but also has highlighted critical challenges that have yet to be addressed. This volume provides an overview of where the field stands now, particularly with respect to core controversies in psychology and law, and where it should be headed in the future. It includes contributions from the world's foremost experts across a number of areas of psycholegal research, which we define as the application of psychological research to legal issues.

We have organized chapters into five broad thematic sections focused on (1) standards of legal admissibility and the trier of fact's ability to distinguish psychological science from nonscience; (2) memory and suggestibility, including the scientific status of "repressed" and "recovered" memories of trauma, testimony elicited from eyewitnesses and child witnesses, forensic hypnosis, and police interrogation and confessions; (3) use of specific tests and techniques in the courtroom, including projective techniques, the leading measure of psychopathy, and the polygraph test; (4) forensic evaluation of specific psycholegal issues, including criminal profiling, psychological injuries, child custody, and competence to stand trial; and (5) issues related to courtroom sentencing, including violence risk assessment and the potential for rehabilitation. In the final integrative chapter, John P. Petrila comments on key themes emerging from the volume and highlights priorities for finding future common ground between psychological science and the law.

Across domains, we focus on scientific research that can assist professionals in accurately and effectively applying scientific evidence to legal issues. This volume is coordinated by this overarching goal, as well as chapter authors' achievement of six specific objectives. That is, in Chapters 3–16, our distinguished authors (1) describe key controversies about the forensic techniques or issues of focus; (2) review the science that supports, and does not support, the techniques; (3) outline gaps in our present knowledge about the techniques; (4) dispel widespread myths and misconceptions about the techniques; (5) arrive at a balanced conclusion about the state of the science on the techniques, referencing standards of legal admissibility to delineate scientifically supported uses, scientifically unsupported uses, and scientifically controversial or still largely untested uses; and (6) explain how the science can be accurately, fairly, and clearly presented in courtroom testimony and in written reports. These six objectives, we believe, will help readers to bridge the wide gap between psychological science and its application in the courtroom and other legal settings.

Compared with other books on psychology and law, the current volume is distinctive in its integrative structure, its focus on distinguishing science from nonscience on controversial issues, and the currency of its coverage. Its basic objective is to help forensic psychologists, lawyers, judges, and other professionals with the complex task of evaluating conflicting and often confusing research evidence to arrive at clear conclusions about the state of the science and how it applies to legal issues. In essence, this book is intended to serve as an indispensable "practitioner's field guide" on contemporary scientific thinking regarding legal decision making. Given this applied objective, the book is an invaluable resource for forensic psychologists, clinical psychologists, and other mental health professionals who testify in court or work with criminal offenders. Because the book focuses on contemporary research findings relevant to key controversies in psychology and law, it will also be of particular interest to academics, their students, and other researchers in psychology, law, and criminology. The book should also be of considerable value to lawyers, judges, and other legal professionals, given its nontechnical but comprehensive coverage of research and clear statement of the state of the science on key legal issues.

This volume reflects considerable investment of effort over a lengthy period of time. We are profoundly grateful to our authors for their scholarly contributions and their patience in making any revisions necessary to fit the book's framework and produce a coherent whole. We thank Jim Nageotte, our editor at The Guilford Press, for his wise guidance and consistent support throughout the process—from prospectus to product. We also greatly appreciate the efforts of Sarah Manchak and Jillian Peterson—fantastic doctoral students at the University of California, Irvine—who helped us to finalize the drafts. Finally, we thank Margaret Ryan, copy editor, and Laura Specht Patchkofsky, Senior Production Editor, at The Guilford Press for their valuable assistance in editing and production.

When we initiated this edited book, we were both energized by the recent accumulation of psychological research with clear relevance to improving legal decision making and disheartened by the nonuse, misuse, or misunderstanding of this research in the courtroom. We gathered the strongest group of scholars possible and asked them to provide the field with a concise, clear, and comprehensive consolidation of science relevant to controversies in their areas of psycholegal expertise. We wished to know what, precisely, could and could not be concluded about these controversies based on research. We asked authors to dispel possibly harmful myths, offer direction for filling gaps in knowledge, and provide scientifically and legally informed advice on how practitioners should best represent the state of the science in legal arenas. Our chapter authors did not disappoint. In fact, they have done more than we could have ever hoped: provide the field with cogent integrations of research in the most important areas within psychology and law, and chart a course for the future of psychology and law.

Contents

PART I. PSYCHOLOGICAL SCIENCE AND ITS APPLICATION IN COURTS OF LAW

1. Standards of Legal Admissibility and Their Implications
for Psychological Science
David L. Faigman and John Monahan   3

2. *Daubert* and Psychological Science in Court: Judging Validity
from the Bench, Bar, and Jury Box
Bradley D. McAuliff and Jennifer L. Groscup   26

PART II. MEMORY AND SUGGESTIBILITY

3. The Scientific Status of "Repressed" and "Recovered" Memories
of Sexual Abuse
Deborah Davis and Elizabeth F. Loftus   55

4. Forensic Hypnosis: The State of the Science
Steven Jay Lynn, Elza Boycheva, Amanda Deming,
Scott O. Lilienfeld, and Michael N. Hallquist   80

5. Expert Testimony Regarding Eyewitness Identification
Brian L. Cutler and Gary L. Wells   100

6. Techniques and Controversies in the Interrogation of Suspects:
The Artful Practice versus the Scientific Study
Allison D. Redlich and Christian A. Meissner   124

7. Reliability of Child Witnesses' Reports
Maggie Bruck and Stephen J. Ceci   149

PART III. SPECIFIC TESTS AND TECHNIQUES

8. The Psychopathy Checklist in the Courtroom: 175
Consensus and Controversies
John F. Edens, Jennifer L. Skeem, and Patrick J. Kennealy

9. Projective Techniques in the Courtroom   202
James M. Wood, M. Teresa Nezworski, Scott O. Lilienfeld,
and Howard N. Garb

10. Psychophysiological Detection of Deception and Guilty Knowledge   224
William G. Iacono

PART IV. FORENSIC EVALUATION OF PSYCHOLEGAL ISSUES

11. Criminal Profiling: Facts, Fictions, and Courtroom Admissibility   245
Richard N. Kocsis

12. The Science and Pseudoscience of Assessing Psychological Injuries   263
William J. Koch, Rami Nader, and Michelle Haring

13. Controversies in Child Custody Evaluations   284
William T. O'Donohue, Kendra Beitz, and Lauren Tolle

14. Controversies in Evaluating Competence to Stand Trial   309
Norman G. Poythress and Patricia A. Zapf

PART V. COURTROOM SENTENCING: RISK AND REHABILITATION

15. Violence Risk Assessment: Core Controversies   333
Kirk Heilbrun, Kevin S. Douglas, and Kento Yasuhara

16. Appropriate Treatment Works, but How?: Rehabilitating General,   358
Psychopathic, and High-Risk Offenders
Jennifer L. Skeem, Devon L. L. Polaschek, and Sarah Manchak

PART VI. CONCLUDING THOUGHTS AND FUTURE DIRECTIONS

17. Finding Common Ground between Scientific Psychology and the Law   387
John P. Petrila

Index   408

PART I

PSYCHOLOGICAL SCIENCE AND ITS APPLICATION IN COURTS OF LAW

Standards of Legal Admissibility and Their Implications for Psychological Science

David L. Faigman and John Monahan

Although jurisdictions employ a dizzying array of admissibility standards to assess the value of expert evidence, most of these are variants of three basic tests. The first originated in *Frye v. United States* (1923) and inquires whether the expert opinion is based on knowledge or a technique that is generally accepted in the particular field from which it comes. The second test, which has largely become predominant today, originated in *Daubert v. Merrell Dow Pharmaceuticals, Inc.* (1993), and inquires whether the expert testimony is based on methods and principles that are likely to produce valid opinions. The third test, used by sporadic jurisdictions and sporadically by *Frye* and *Daubert* jurisdictions as an exception to their usually applicable admissibility standards, is referred to as the "relevancy test." This test is not much of a test at all, however, since it inquires only whether the expert opinion is relevant and the witness is competent (i.e., qualified), conditions that are prerequisites for the admission of all evidence. In one form or another, and either alone or in combination, these three tests are used by virtually all U.S. jurisdictions today to measure psychological expert testimony.

It must be noted at the outset, however, that these tests represent archetypes and that few jurisdictions use a pure form of any one of them. Indeed, *Daubert* itself advanced the general acceptance criterion as one of several that might be used to measure the validity of the underlying basis for proffered expertise. Moreover, some states use the *Frye* or *Daubert* test for scientifically derived expert testimony, but employ the relevancy test for expert opinion based on personal experience. In California and Arizona, for example, this exception exempts from serious threshold review psychological expert opinion that is deemed "experience-based." Scientifically grounded psychological expertise, in contrast, is evaluated under a rigorous threshold test in these states. In this chapter we consider the implications of these basic admissibility standards, in their pure and hybrid forms, for psychological science.

In the next section we begin by exploring the time before *Daubert,* when the "general acceptance" test of *Frye* provided the lodestar that guided the introduction of scientific evidence in court. The *Frye* test remains highly relevant today, though it has changed fundamentally due to the new understanding brought about by *Daubert*. Later, we turn more fully to the *Daubert* decision and subsequent developments in case law and in amendments to the Federal Rules of Evidence. *Daubert* brings fairly high expectations to expertise based on psychological science, and this section explores the implications of these demands on the psychology and law connection. Increasingly, however, courts exempt aspects of psychological expertise from review under admissibility tests. For example, states such as California and Arizona explicitly exempt experience-based expert opinion and apply the weak relevancy test to this testimony. We also consider the justification for this practice of exempting experience-based expert opinion and critically assess the wisdom of this practice. Finally, in conclusion, we consider the future prospects for psychology and psychologists under these admissibility standards.

FRYE'S GENERAL ACCEPTANCE TEST

All rules of admissibility are constructed on the premise that, although U.S. courts employ the adversarial process, the parties do not fully control what evidence reaches the trier of fact. In the realm of expert evidence, this means that some principle must control what sorts of evidence are admitted and what sorts are excluded. Prior to *Daubert*'s validity test, and still the most often posited alternative to that test, the general acceptance standard of *Frye* provided the basic procedure for handling scientific and technical evidence. Under this standard, novel expert testimony is admissible only once it has reached general acceptance in the particular field from which it comes. Although few courts cited *Frye* immediately after it was decided, general acceptance eventually became the standard to which all subsequent tests of admissibility have been compared (Faigman, Porter, & Saks, 1994).

Courts'—and scholars'—views of *Frye* are decidedly mixed. *Frye* plainly possesses an assortment of positive attributes. Foremost, perhaps, the general acceptance test does not require judges and lawyers to have any substantive knowledge of the science underlying proffered expertise. Lawyers are not generally known for their proficiency with science (Gatowski et al., 2001). The *Frye* test puts little pressure on them to learn any. General acceptance employs the logical proposition that the best groups to ask about a technology or set of research findings are the very scientists who specialize in the subject. Waiting for a consensus to develop also operates to insulate courts from changing fads and fashions. The law is principally a conservative discipline and, on the whole, judges would prefer not to amend or overrule settled law with the publication of each new study or each new edited volume. *Frye* seemed to ensure an orderly and accurate, albeit gradual, development of the jurisprudence of scientific evidence.

But *Frye* also has more than its share of detractors. First of all, *Frye*'s perceived strength of not requiring judges and lawyers to know much about science also means that the law effectively abdicates review authority to others. *Frye* also can be readily manipulated in order to obtain preordained outcomes, and for that reason has been labeled both too conservative and too liberal. It is too conservative because it can lead courts to exclude cutting-edge research until the respective fields embrace the new work. True consensus can take years to develop, even for the best science. For example, despite the general acclaim among psychologists for eyewitness identification research (Kassin, Tubb, Hosch, & Memon, 2001), courts sometimes exclude expert opinion on this subject because it continues to attract significant detractors (*People v. Smith*, 2004). At the same time, however, *Frye* is sometimes criticized for being too liberal, in that it might permit experts to testify to opinions based on little or no research. Because *Frye* only consults the pertinent field, findings from scientific disciplines that bring little rigor to their claims might pass legal muster quite readily despite the absence of adequate data or poor research methods. Although many examples might be cited, perhaps the most notorious is the battered woman syndrome. It has achieved widespread judicial acceptance based largely on a consensus of experts who are devoted to the subject, despite a research foundation that is very thin (Faigman, Kaye, Saks, Sanders, & Cheng, 2007). In this way, *Frye* effectively constitutes deference to established professional fields, and admissibility becomes a guild issue (Faigman, 1989).

Moreover, the *Frye* inquiry contains an inherent ambiguity. Judges are prompted to ask whether particular findings or techniques are generally accepted among researchers and practitioners in the field. But the relevance of the science may be very different for the law than it is for the researchers and practitioners who are asked about general acceptance. Consider, for example, polygraphs. Polygraph utility for the courts depends wholly on the test's power to distinguish between truthful answers and those that are deceptive for particular questions asked. Use in the field includes this utility, but may also include many others, including as a prop to interrogations, deterrence in national security screening, and detection of general nervousness to a line of questioning. Inquiring about the general acceptance of a technique without being specific regarding what it is generally accepted to do is a source of great confusion under *Frye*. There is little question that polygraphs are generally accepted among police, government security agencies, and professional polygraphers. But the acceptance of the polygraph as a tool of interrogation says little about its scientific validity (National Research Council, 2003). Psychology, perhaps more than most sciences, is rife with examples of this phenomenon. A diagnosis may be generally accepted for therapeutic purposes, for example, but not for forensic purposes. Rape trauma syndrome illustrates this therapeutic/forensic divide, since the underlying trauma associated with the syndrome is largely unquestioned in therapy but is the operative issue in the courtroom. Judges must ask the right questions under *Frye* in order to get useful answers.

THE *DAUBERT* TRILOGY AND THE FEDERAL RULES OF EVIDENCE

In *Daubert v. Merrell Dow Pharmaceuticals, Inc.* (1993), the Supreme Court considered the question of the proper interpretation of Federal Rule of Evidence 702 (see p. 12), the principal rule that governs expert testimony. As an initial matter, the Court held that Rule 702 had not incorporated the *Frye* test into the federal practice. The *Daubert* Court held that, unlike under *Frye*, judges could not simply defer to respective fields when assessing the validity of proffered expert testimony. Trial judges are gatekeepers who have the responsibility to assess for themselves the reliability and validity of the methods and principles underlying expert evidence. A judge's responsibility thus changed from merely assessing agreement in a field—the test under *Frye*—to evaluating the research methods and statistics that lay behind expert opinion. Therein lay the revolution of *Daubert*.

The Operating Premises of *Daubert*

Like many Supreme Court decisions, *Daubert* established a foundation upon which a new edifice could be built. *Daubert*, in time, is likely to become more important for the principle it represents than for what it actually says. That principle, in short, is that the law must join the scientific age.

The very first question raised by scholars following the *Daubert* decision was whether the opinion would lead to more expert testimony or less (Chesebro, 1994). This is a debate that has not fully disappeared (Owen, 2002), though most observers find *Daubert* to be fairly restrictive in practice. But if there remained any doubt about the philosophical tenor of *Daubert*, three subsequent Supreme Court decisions dispelled it. The first two join *Daubert* to make up the often-cited "trilogy" of scientific evidence cases. The third is a sometimes-overlooked decision interpreting the scope and import of *Daubert*.

In 1997 the Court ruled in *General Electric Co. v. Joiner* that the Eleventh Circuit Court of Appeals had erred in reversing a trial court's exclusion of expert testimony. Chief Justice Rehnquist wrote for a unanimous Court, holding that appellate courts owe deference to a trial court's admissibility rulings. The Eleventh Circuit had thus erred in second-guessing the trial court's determination that the proffered expert testimony was unreliable. Of great significance, Rehnquist, who had worried over judges playing amateur scientists in *Daubert*, now carefully scrutinized the proffered expertise and, in some detail, pointed out its many deficiencies. Moreover, the Court revised Justice Blackmun's statement that the trial court's obligations were restricted to methods and principles and now made clear that conclusions, too, were part of the court's gatekeeping duties. As Rehnquist put it, "nothing in either *Daubert* or the Federal Rules of Evidence requires a district court to admit opinion evidence that is connected to existing data only by the ipse dixit of the expert" (p. 146), that is, by the expert's unsupported assertion.

Two years later, in *Kumho Tire Ltd. v. Carmichael* (1999), the Court closed the biggest loophole left from *Daubert*. Justice Stephen Breyer held that a court's gatekeeping responsibilities extended to all expert opinion, not just the scientific variety. According to the Court, therefore, a judge's gatekeeping responsibility includes assessing the validity of experience-based experts as well. The *Kumho Tire* opinion is replete with statements regarding a trial court's abilities to become sophisticated consumers of science and the resources available, such as court-appointed experts, who could assist them in their assigned task.

Finally, in *Weisgram v. Marley* (2000), the Court affirmed an Eighth Circuit opinion that reversed a district court's admission of expert testimony and then held that the expert testimony was not admissible as a matter of law and dismissed the suit. The district court had admitted the testimony of a fire captain, a fire investigator, and a metallurgist in a civil action involving whether a home heater had been defective and had caused the fire. The Court of Appeals reversed. Instead of remanding for a new trial, however, the Eighth Circuit held, as a matter of law, that the expert opinion was inadmissible and then remanded and ordered the district court to enter judgment for the defendant. The Supreme Court affirmed the dismissal of the suit. The Court thus sustained the remarkable power of appellate courts to find expert testimony inadmissible as a matter of law and to direct a verdict accordingly. In agreeing that the plaintiffs should not be given a second chance to find an admissible expert, Justice Ruth Bader Ginsburg stated (pp. 456–457):

> Since *Daubert*, ... parties relying on expert evidence have had notice of the exacting standards of reliability such evidence must meet. It is implausible to suggest, post-*Daubert*, that parties will initially present less than their best expert evidence in the expectation of a second chance should their first try fail. We therefore find unconvincing [the plaintiff's] fears that allowing courts of appeals to direct the entry of judgment for defendants will punish plaintiffs who could have shored up their cases by other means had they known their expert testimony would be found inadmissible.

Daubert in Practice

The *Daubert* test applies to all types of psychological knowledge, whether based on clinical experience or on extensive empirical testing in the laboratory or in the field. A basic lesson of *Kumho Tire* is that *all* expert evidence— whether it is described as "scientific" or otherwise—must pass a basic threshold test of validity. This is not to say that all expertise is, or is expected to be, comparable. But under *Daubert*, the courts need not make bright-line distinctions among kinds of knowledge. Federal Rule of Evidence 702 speaks in terms of scientific, technical, or specialized knowledge, with all three being subject to the *Daubert* requirement that the judge act as a gate-keeper. But, as the *Kumho Tire* Court recognized, no bright lines divide these three kinds of expert opinions. In fact, all expert opinion is actually based on specialized knowledge (Faigman, 2002). *Daubert* requires judges to assess the worth of such knowledge.

In light of the multitude of contexts in which *Daubert* is employed, from accident reconstruction to nuclear physics, it is not surprising that commentators' views about how the rule applies should vary widely. Nonetheless, there are certain principles that virtually all *Daubert* watchers, whether as supporters or detractors, would agree upon. At its most basic, *Daubert* requires the proponent of expert testimony to bear the burden of proof to show that his or her expert is qualified, that the proffered testimony is relevant to a fact in dispute, and that the basis for the expert's opinion is reliable and valid. In this section we consider these three criteria in regard to psychological expertise.

Qualifications

Rule 702 of the Federal Rules of Evidence speaks of expertise in broad terms. The rule contemplates a wide assortment of potential experts and does not contain degree requirements. An expert must be qualified only by virtue of knowledge, skill, experience, training, or education. The case law, therefore, is replete with statements of deference to proffered expert's qualifications, recognizing the value of experience and practical training.

Cases that exclude experts based on qualifications fall generally into two overlapping camps. In one, the expert lacks the basic credentials or experience to testify on the subject for which he or she is offered. An example might be a nonlicensed therapist seeking to testify regarding the competence of a defendant to stand trial. In the second category, the expert may be well qualified in one area or as a generalist, but has insufficient expertise to testify on the specific subject in dispute. This latter category is by far the more prevalent and also the more controversial.

Some courts adopt a permissive approach to qualifying experts and hold that once the proponent demonstrates the expert's general competency to testify, questions regarding expertise in a specific subdiscipline are a matter of weight and not admissibility. In *Zemaitatis v. Innovasive Devices, Inc.* (2000, p. 633), for example, the court permitted the testimony of a physician who was a jack-of-all-trades. However, a large number of courts agree that a witness may be qualified as an expert on certain matters and not others (*United States v. Roldan-Zapata,* 1990, p. 805). These courts require that the expert display the knowledge or skill necessary to address the specific subarea that is the subject of the litigation (Faigman et al., 2007). Although examples can be found in many areas, courts have particularly frowned upon medical doctors who are offered to testify on every conceivable medical question (e.g., *Alexander v. Smith & Nephew,* 2000).

Psychology presents a similar situation to medical science, in that many practitioners are trained as generalists but there are a number of subdisciplines in which psychologists can specialize. On the whole, however, this issue appears to arise in the courts less frequently in regard to psychologists. One reason may be that in medicine, doctors typically specialize as a matter of residency training, and they rarely jump specialties. An oncologist is likely to have little claim to be an expert on podiatry. If one does make such a claim, courts notice. In psychology, in contrast, specialty areas tend to be less rigidly defined, and generalists often engage in a variety of specialties. Contemporary psychology is primarily defined by either theoretical orientation or developmental stage of the subjects of study—categories that tend to cut across legal issues. Thus, it would not be unusual to see the same behavioral clinician testify in both a competency hearing and a parole determination.

As psychology continues to mature as a discipline, it might very well follow the medical profession in establishing areas of specialization with accompanying certification. This may be especially the case in forensic psychology, which the American Board of Professional Psychology now recognizes as a specialty area of practice and designates educational and training prerequisites. Over time, courts should be expected to become more demanding of the experts who appear before them, insisting on expertise in the specific area of their proposed testimony. In Virginia, for example, an expert may assist a defendant in civil commitment proceedings under the state's Sexually Violent Predators Act on subjects relating to the defendant's mental health (Va. Code § 37.2-907[A], 1999). Under the law, such an expert "shall be a licensed psychiatrist or a licensed clinical psychologist who is skilled in the diagnosis and treatment of mental abnormalities and disorders associated with sex offenders." The Virginia Supreme Court, in fact, recently found that the trial court erred when it admitted the testimony of a psychiatrist who did not treat sex offenders (*Commonwealth v. Miller*, 2007).

The more likely qualifications debate to be heard in courtrooms today involves what credentials should qualify someone to testify as a psychologist. A wide assortment of psychology-related degrees are available, including (but not limited to) the PhD, EdD, PsyD, MS, and MA. Complicating matters further, state certification standards vary widely and often depend on supervised training more than academic education. In general, courts have been permissive in allowing specialists in human behavior to testify. Experience alone often appears to be sufficient to qualify an expert. This has been true, for example, for therapists seeking to testify on the rape trauma syndrome and the battered woman syndrome (Faigman et al., 2007). It is important to note, however, that qualifying an expert is merely the first step in determining admissibility. Whereas experience alone may be enough to meet the qualifications requirement, it may not be sufficient to validate the substantive aspects of the proposed testimony.

Relevance or Fit

A prerequisite for all admitted evidence is that it must be relevant to some fact in dispute. Although no single piece of evidence is expected to create the chain of inferences necessary to construct a case, every piece of evidence must at least constitute a link in the chain. The same is true for expert testimony. The *Daubert* Court described this requirement as an issue of "fit." The methodological basis underlying an expert's testimony must allow him or her to offer an opinion on a subject in dispute at trial.

The most basic query concerning relevance asks whether the evidence permits an inference to be drawn regarding some fact in dispute. For instance, expert testimony that a defendant lacks volitional control over his or her behavior is relevant in a state employing the American Law Institute (ALI) test of insanity but is irrelevant in states using the M'Naughten test, under which the defendant must prove that he or she cannot distinguish right from wrong. Relevance ordinarily is a basic logical proposition that asks whether knowing X makes Y more or less likely, where Y is a fact that is material to the law that applies to the case. Under the ALI test for insanity, lack of volitional control is an element of the defense, but under M'Naughten, it is not.

In the realm of expert evidence, the fit inquiry raises methodological issues regarding whether the methods used in the research underlying the disputed expert evidence are sufficient to support the opinion offered in a particular case. This is primarily an issue of external validity. A classic instance of this point concerns whether research on the toxicity of certain substances generalizes from animal research to humans. Psychological research is replete with such issues. Does jury research on undergraduates generalize to real jurors? Would a finding of discrimination in one state's capital sentencing system permit inferences about another state's process? Does research on children's competency in one legal context generalize to other legal contexts? Because so much psychological research uses subjects or situations that depart widely from the legal realities, this aspect of relevancy can present substantial obstacles to the admission of psychological opinion.

Reliability and Validity

The core holding of *Daubert* was the Court's interpretation of Federal Rule of Evidence 702 that the proponent of expert testimony has the burden to demonstrate by a preponderance of the evidence that the basis for the proffered opinion is valid. Although the *Daubert* Court stated that it was merely interpreting the plain meaning of the Federal Rules, the rules themselves were amended in 2000 to reflect the meaning the Court had found in them 7 years before. The new Rule 702 essentially codified *Daubert*:

> If scientific, technical, or other specialized knowledge will assist the trier of fact to understand the evidence or to determine a fact in issue, a witness qualified as an expert by knowledge, skill, experience, training, or education, may testify thereto in the form of an opinion or otherwise, if (1) the testimony is based upon sufficient facts or data, (2) the testimony is the product of reliable principles and methods, and (3) the witness has applied the principles and methods reliably to the facts of the case.

The *Daubert* Court suggested four factors that courts might use to assess the scientific validity underlying expert testimony. These were (1) testing, (2) error rate, (3) peer review and publication, and (4) general acceptance. In addition, courts and commentators have usefully suggested additional factors that might be employed to complete the assigned task (Faigman et al. 2007). Most importantly, courts have increasingly recognized that the myriad kinds of expertise they confront require a flexible and nuanced approach. Hence, peer review and publication may be an appropriate criterion for both histologists and historians, but error rate is not. *Daubert* mandates that trial courts determine whether the basis for proffered expert opinion is reliable and valid. The process trial courts use to reach this determination can be adjusted for each category of expertise and is largely within each court's discretion. At the same time, it is clear that some process and some factors must be employed to make this judgment. Justice Antonin Scalia emphasized this point in his *Kumho Tire* (1999) concurrence. He stated, "Although, as the Court makes clear today, the *Daubert* factors are not holy writ, in a particular case the failure to apply one or another of them may be unreasonable and hence an abuse of discretion" (p. 159).

Since psychological testimony is ostensibly based on scientific knowledge, the *Daubert* factors are a reasonable starting point in most cases. We therefore use the *Daubert* factors below to frame our discussion of psychological expertise.

TESTING

Although the *Daubert* Court listed testability as one of its four basic factors, it is almost certainly a prerequisite to all that follows. In psychology, as in all science, without testing, error rates could not be ascertained, peer-reviewed journals ordinarily would not publish the work, and general acceptance would not be forthcoming. It is important to remember that *Daubert* requires not merely that the basis for the opinion be testable, but that it has been adequately tested (Black, Ayala, & Saffran, 1994). Ultimately, the challenge of *Daubert* lies in measuring this adequacy.

Properly understood, the *Daubert* factors represent a set of criteria by which fairly traditional scientific evidence might be tested. Although the actual inquiry might be significantly more robust, scientists themselves would consider whether and how a hypothesis had been tested, the degree and type of error associated with the science or technology, whether the report of the research was published in a high-quality, peer-reviewed journal, and what scientists in the respective or associated fields thought about the work. When an expert proposes to testify regarding knowledge that is amenable to evaluation by those criteria, courts should use those criteria to assess the success of that knowledge.

ERROR RATE

The *Daubert* Court's use of error rates is at once completely understandable and quite perplexing. Error, of course, is a core component of all science, and it comes in an assortment of varieties. Moreover, from the judicial perspective, the amount of potential error expert evidence poses ought to affect judgments about its admissibility. The cost of making a mistake, whether of the false-positive or false-negative variety, is an integral component of the policy implications of any admissibility determination. Yet Justice Blackmun's mention of error rate was perfunctory and not well designed to give most experts substantial guidance. He merely stated that, "in the case of a particular scientific technique, the court ordinarily should consider the known or potential rate of error" (*Daubert*, p. 594). He thus appeared to limit his concern with error to techniques such as DNA profiling or polygraph tests, which might have an identifiable error rate with repeated applications. Lower courts since *Daubert* have done little to remedy the deficiencies in Blackmun's analysis of error rates. For instance, courts rarely distinguish between Type I and Type II error when they discuss this factor. Error is a multidimensional construct with widely varying implications for the law. It is worthy of much more attention than it has so far received from the courts and, indeed, is a subject deserving of sustained scholarly attention.

PEER REVIEW AND PUBLICATION

In *Daubert*, the Court cited peer review and publication as a helpful proxy of good-quality research, but emphasized that it should not be considered the sine qua non of validity. Although publication in peer-reviewed journals is the hallmark of the successful completion of research, the process does not guarantee quality data. Much that is published in the very best journals can be criticized, is impervious to replication, or turns out to be invalid (Jasanoff, 1996). Also, some work that appears outside the strict scientific peer-review process is well done and well worth relying on. Nonetheless, the ordinary culmination of most scientific research is publication in a peer-reviewed journal, and, as implied in *Daubert*, expert opinion that comes without this imprimatur is suspect.

Also, a somewhat less noticed aspect of the peer-review and publication factor is the more general dynamic present in healthy scientific communities. Psychology is somewhat less successful at this more general checking function than many sciences. The single most effective checking tool in science is replication. If one laboratory announces the discovery of cold fusion, for instance, others inevitably follow fast on its heels to assess the validity of the claim. This is true even with many complex applied phenomena, such as the epidemiology of the effects of some alleged toxic substance or product. One or two studies of a phenomenon from one or two laboratories are ordinarily not enough to recommend policy. In psychology, in contrast, it is not unusual for one or two studies to serve as the substantive foundation for policy recommendations.

GENERAL ACCEPTANCE

Like peer review and publication, the use of widespread or general acceptance as a criterion of validity depends on the quality of the field from which the findings come. Unlike the testing and error-rate factors, general acceptance is merely a proxy for validity and is only as good as those doing the accepting or rejecting. The biggest danger associated with this factor from the law's standpoint is that consensus might replace critical assessment. This has largely occurred, for example, in the forensic specialties, such as bitemark and handwriting identification analysis, where the main community involved is law enforcement and dissent is strongly frowned upon. Although psychology, as a field, demonstrates much greater critical judgment than many forensic areas, it nevertheless shares some of the difficulties that are endemic in the forensic specialties. Especially deleterious to self-criticism is that some psychologists measure the success of their work by whether courts accept or reject it.

The *Daubert* and *Frye* tests both create fairly substantial hurdles for expert evidence to overcome. Many states, however, create an exception to their applicable expert testimony rule for expert opinion that is not scientifically derived. In these jurisdictions, experience-based expert opinion must pass only a stunted relevancy inquiry.

THE RELEVANCY TEST

The relevancy test in many respects constitutes the foundational requirement for all evidence under virtually every evidence code. Under the test, the proponent is first obligated to demonstrate that the evidence has probative value regarding an issue in dispute under the substantive law that applies in the case. Typically, this simply means that the evidence makes a material fact in the case more likely or less likely to be true. It is a modest requirement. In addition, the use of the relevancy test in the context of expert testimony ordinarily incorporates a competency of the witness requirement. In the case of experts, this involves the question whether the expert is qualified. Where the relevancy test is employed, however, qualifications are usually interpreted broadly, and doubts about an expert's credentials are typically left to the jurors to resolve in evaluating the weight of the evidence.

Although a few states, such as Wisconsin, use a relevancy test exclusively for expert testimony, it is widely employed as an exception to the prevailing rule for expert testimony. California and Arizona, for example, both exempt nonscientific, experience-based, expert opinion from their *Frye*-based tests. This practice disproportionately affects medical and psychological expert testimony. For instance, such prominent subjects as repressed memories, predictions of violence, posttraumatic stress disorder, and child abuse accommodation syndrome are not subject to a *Frye* analysis (Faigman et al., 2007). This section considers whether the basis for this exception is well founded.

California divides the world of expert evidence into two basic categories. On the one hand, experts sometimes offer opinions that are based on scientific or technical processes or tests, whereas, on the other hand, experts sometimes offer opinions based on professional experience. The former tes-

timony is thought to be particularly worrisome because of the aura of certainty that might surround opinion based on the seeming wizardry of science. Using *Frye*, California erects evidentiary barriers to this sort of expert
opinion, fearing that it might overwhelm the tender sensitivities of fact-
finders. In contrast, expert opinion that is based on experience and claims
no pretensions to scientific exactitude does not receive this close evidentiary
review. In effect, California exempts experiential expert opinion—or nonscientifically derived opinions—from the rigors of evidentiary review. This
practice, one employed explicitly or implicitly in many jurisdictions, is often
referred to as the "opinion rule." The opinion rule is supported neither by
jurisprudential nor empirical considerations.

Consider the case of *People v. Miller* (2005), in which a California appellate court applied the opinion rule and held that psychiatric and psychological testimony predicting future violence under the state's Sexually Violent Predator Act is not scientific evidence subject to California's version of
the *Frye* test, termed *Kelly–Frye* (*People v. Kelly*, 1976). The defendant had
complained that the state's expert had relied on statistical tests that should
have been demonstrated to be generally accepted by the relevant scientific
community. The *Miller* court, however, rejected this argument, pointing
out that the expert's opinion was clinically based and the statistical tests
were used, at most, to support an experience-based clinical judgment. The
court explained "that since the expert's opinion testimony was not based
solely on the actuarial evidence, but rather on a variety of factors and the
expert indicated such evidence was not infallible, a *Kelly* hearing was not
required" (p. 1). The California court, therefore, sought to draw a bright-line
distinction between actuarial techniques, which are derived from extensive
research programs, and clinical judgments, which are primarily experience-
based determinations. In practice, risk assessments exist on a continuum of
structure, with completely unstructured (corresponding to "clinical") assessment occupying one end of the continuum and completely structured assessment (corresponding to "actuarial") occupying the other, but with additional forms of more-than-unstructured-but-less-than-fully-structured risk
assessments lying between these poles (Monahan, 2008).

Under the California approach to expert testimony, therefore, clinical
psychological opinion that is not primarily based on statistical techniques
is admitted with no *Kelly–Frye* threshold check, but psychological opinion
that *is* premised on such technology confronts the formidable barriers of
that test. In effect, the California rule means that expert opinion with little
or no scientific basis is readily admitted, but opinion that is based on scientific test must survive the *Kelly–Frye* gauntlet. This approach is particularly

perverse in the context of violence risk assessment, since research has consistently demonstrated over the last five decades that well-validated empirically structured risk assessments are much more accurate than unstructured clinical judgment (Meehl, 1954; Monahan, 2007b). Moreover, research in the last decade is leading to the development of ever more powerful actuarial technology, so the gap between clinical judgment and actuarial methods is likely to further widen (Monahan, 2007a). Yet the California approach effectively gives a free pass to experience-based clinical judgment and erects substantial barriers to the introduction of science-based actuarial techniques.

California and other jurisdictions advance two basic arguments in support of the rule that relaxes evidentiary standards for experience-based expert opinion. The first is not always spelled out, but such a regime must presume that a dividing line can be identified between scientific and nonscientific evidence. The second argument advanced to support the California rule is the belief that jurors are more likely to be impressed by the aura of infallibility that surrounds scientific opinion, but can critically assess nonscientific opinion readily enough.

DISTINGUISHING SCIENCE FROM NONSCIENCE

Although there is certainly a distinction to be drawn between science and nonscience, logic does not recommend its use to support a rule that would allow nonscientific opinion easy admission and enact substantial hurdles to the admission of science-based evidence. That something is not science is hardly reason to admit it for the jury's consideration. The California courts have not explored this issue in any depth, but have merely assumed that a line dividing science and nonscience is readily identifiable. Other courts applying the opinion rule have sought to define the parameters of the boundary between science and nonscience.

The most ambitious attempt to set forth the premises underlying the opinion rule was advanced by the Arizona Supreme Court in *Logerquist v. McVey* (2000). The court held that the *Frye* test—the state's ordinary rule of admissibility for scientific evidence—did not apply to nonscientific expert opinion. The court explained, "*Frye* is applicable when an expert witness reaches a conclusion by deduction from the application of novel scientific principles, formulae, or procedures developed by others" (p. 133). However, the court argued, *Frye* "is inapplicable when a witness reaches a conclusion by inductive reasoning based on his or her own experience, observation, or research" (p. 133). Hence, for the *Logerquist* court, opinion based on inductive reasoning is not subjected to any substantial threshold test, but opinion that stems from deductive reasoning receives close scrutiny.

The error the *Logerquist* court makes is believing that scientific knowledge is discrete or categorical. It is not. The scientific method is a process. Indeed, it is a process that invariably begins with experience. Consider the example of repressed memories, the subject of the *Logerquist* decision. A doctor might have examined one or more people who claim to have begun remembering things of a disturbing nature and of which they had been previously unaware. A scientist's approach to this observation would be at least twofold. On the one hand, employing inductive reasoning, a scientist might look for further instances of this phenomenon. The initial observation could have been an anomaly or not accurate for a variety of reasons. In seeking confirmation, the wise researcher would want to ensure that the underlying traumas occurred, that the amnesia was not explainable by other factors— such as biological amnesia—and that the reports of repression were not spurious products of expectations of either the subjects or researchers. At the same time, using deductive reasoning, the scientist would seek to integrate his or her observations into what is generally known about human memory and the brain. Does this observation conform to theory? Perhaps theory suggests another explanation for the recalled memories other than repression. Or possibly—and of potentially great excitement for the scientist—the theory itself needs to be adjusted to account for these newly discovered facts.

Given the structure of science, the distinction the *Logerquist* court makes between deductive and inductive reasoning, for purposes of admissibility standards, is chimerical. What the court called inductive reasoning is simply hypothesis formation through anecdotal experience. The subject of repressed memories well illustrates the point. In *Logerquist*, the plaintiff's expert, Dr. van der Kolk, said that he had treated "hundreds of survivors of childhood sexual abuse" and that he was prepared to testify that some of these "victims do have delayed memories, that their memories are as reasonably accurate as normal memories, if not better" (p. 117). How would he know something like this? Even more arrogant is the doctor's claim that "delayed memories" are as "accurate as normal memories, if not better" (p. 117). Better? He thus claims experience with repressed memory and normal memory formation, comparisons of the two, as well as the investigatory capacity to check claims of abuse several decades old. That is some very impressive experience.

The basic error of *Logerquist* lies in the court's failure to critically assess the proffered evidence in a scientifically sophisticated way. It is not simply that repression is not yet science, it is that repression has repeatedly failed scientific attempts to validate it (Faigman et al., 2007).

JUROR CREDULITY

Even if a realm of nonscientific expert opinion could be identified reliably, is it reasonable to assume that no substantial threshold test is necessary because jurors can readily assess its validity and weight? According to the California Supreme Court, the primary concern with scientific opinion is the possibly overwhelming influence complex scientific evidence has on jurors (*People v. Kelly*, 1976). The court observed that "lay jurors tend to give considerable weight to 'scientific' evidence when presented by 'experts' with impressive credentials" (p. 1244). The *Frye* threshold, therefore, establishes a barrier in order to protect against juror credulity. Nonscientific expert opinion, according to the California high court, does not present a similar danger: "When a witness gives his personal opinion on the stand—even if he qualifies as an expert—the jurors may temper their acceptance of his testimony with a healthy skepticism born of their knowledge that all human beings are fallible" (*People v. McDonald*, 1984, p. 724).

A basic premise implicit in the California approach is the apparent belief that jurors are better able to parse personal opinion than they are able to critique scientific opinion. The court in *People v. Venegas* (1998) summarized this argument:

> The *Kelly* test is intended to forestall the jury's uncritical acceptance of scientific evidence or technology that is so foreign to everyday experience as to be unusually difficult for laypersons to evaluate. In most other instances, the jurors are permitted to rely on their own common sense and good judgment in evaluating the weight of the evidence presented to them. (p. 546)

Although it might indeed challenge jurors to critically assess scientific opinion, it is not clear that they are likely to do considerably better with nonscientific opinion. How, in fact, should a juror evaluate experience-based expert opinion? The California Supreme Court advances common sense and good judgment as if these characteristics were self-defining and obviously applicable to the task at hand.

Consider again the issue of repressed memories, a subject generally thought to be exempt under the opinion rule (*Wilson v. Phillips*, 1999). An expert might testify that the plaintiff repressed her memory from a young age until adulthood, that such a phenomenon has occurred in other cases, and that the memories recalled are reliable. If you are a commonsensical juror with good judgment, how do you assess this claim? There are an assortment of possibilities, such as demeanor, the prospect of bias due to expert witness fees, credentials, and admissions or inconsistent statements elicited on cross-examination. Of course, all of these commonsense good judgments are available to critically assess scientific opinion as well. Other than these standard indicia of reliability, all with questionable value, there is nothing more. Nonscientific expert opinion is, in fact, little more than *ipse dixit*. Repressed memories are so because an expert with 20 years of experience with the subject says that they are so. By this measure, bloodletting and alchemy were valid too.

Cross-examination is unlikely to be particularly effective with well-credentialed experts for another reason. Most of these witnesses believe the content of their testimony. A lying witness may have sweaty palms, avoid eye contact, and stutter. A lying witness might also be caught in a contradiction or be unable to explain prior inconsistent statements. But many experience-based experts are fully convinced of the validity of their judgment. Experience, after all, has failed to falsify their beliefs. The weakness of their testimony does not lie with the witness, it lies with the content of their opinion and the methods they used to form it.

California's practice of employing a restrictive test for science-based expert opinion and a permissive test for experience-based expert opinion is arguably the opposite of what good scientific common sense would recommend. At the very least, however, there is no compelling basis for California's approach of using two different tests for expert opinion evidence. Expert opinion, whatever the ostensible foundation it rests upon, presents similar dangers to jurors. Moreover, the factors that are likely to be relevant to determining the weight of proffered expert opinion are generally the same, whether the evidence is scientifically or experientially based.

Perhaps the strongest argument against the exception for experience-based opinions is practical. In *Miller* itself, the expert purported to rely on a combination of actuarial and clinical indicia to reach an opinion. It was the fact that the expert did not rely "solely on the actuarial evidence" that was determinative for the court. In the context of risk assessment, this integration of structured test and clinical experience is generally standard operating procedure. Indeed, it would be difficult to identify any area of applied science in which experience did not buttress an expert's opinion that was ostensibly based on a structured or mechanical test. No expert comes into court and simply recites the outcome of some test, whether it is a radiologist "interpreting" an x-ray or a polygrapher reporting the "results" of a polygraph. Moreover, even if a scientific test provided "the" answer, inevitably some experience-based judgments would have been built into the test. Every test has a decision threshold that is associated with human judgment somewhere along the way (Swets, Dawes, & Monahan, 2000). California's attempt to draw distinctions between "science" and "nonscience" is doomed to fail. The rational approach in the risk assessment area, therefore, would be to hold *Kelly–Frye* hearings for (1) purely actuarial prediction, (2) clinically reviewed actuarial prediction, and (3) purely clinical prediction.

FUTURE PROSPECTS

Greater Legal Sophistication through Court-Appointed Experts

As we noted at the start of this chapter, the revolution sparked by *Daubert* primarily involved a changed perspective. Under *Frye's* general acceptance test, admissibility determinations consisted of little more than counting noses of professionals in a particular field. *Daubert* demands that judges evaluate the research methods supporting expert evidence and the principles used to extrapolate from that research to the task at hand (Risinger, 2007). This is a daunting task, especially for judges who, on average, have little formal training in statistics and research methods. How, it may reasonably be asked, are judges to become sophisticated consumers of psychological and other expertise, as *Daubert* requires?

One proposed solution to this question is greater use of court-appointed, rather than party-retained, experts. Scholars have actively advocated this device (Berger, 1994; Gross, 1991). Although research indicates that courts are disinclined to appoint experts for themselves, there are signs that this reluctance is slowly changing (Faigman et al., 2007). Cecil and Willging (1994) found that judges relied little on this appointment power and, moreover, most (62%) of those surveyed thought that the "appointment of an expert [is] an extraordinary action" (pp. 1015–1018). The principal reason for this view was judges' belief that court-appointed experts undermine the adversarial process. Yet, as experience with the challenges of implementing *Daubert* has been gained, courts appear increasingly sympathetic to the possibility of appointing experts (*Hall v. Baxter Healthcare Corp.*, 1996). Indeed, Justice Breyer, concurring in *General Electric Co. v. Joiner* (1997), quoted approvingly the *New England Journal of Medicine's* amicus brief calling for greater use of court-appointed experts:

> [A] judge could better fulfill this gatekeeper function if he or she had help from scientists. Judges should be strongly encouraged to make greater use of their inherent authority ... to appoint experts .... Reputable experts could be recommended to courts by established scientific organizations, such as the

National Academy of Sciences or the American Association for the Advancement of Science. (p. 149)

In federal cases, court experts assume primarily one of two forms. The first, properly termed court-appointed experts, are selected mainly to assist jurors determine what weight to give the expert evidence that is presented by the parties. These experts give testimony in court, are subject to the ordinary procedures of discovery, and may be cross-examined by one or both parties. The second type of court expert, increasingly prevalent in the case law, is the technical adviser. These experts' primary function is to assist judges rather than juries. They typically are not subject to adversarial processes such as discovery or cross-examination. In effect, technical advisers sit at judges' sides, like law clerks, assisting them to understand the expert evidence that the parties seek to have admitted at trial. In the future, greater use of psychologists as court-appointed experts or as technical advisors could go far in educating juries and judges to be sophisticated consumers of psychological evidence.

Greater Psychological Sophistication through Evidence-Based Practice

We write at a time when a debate rages in clinical psychology around what is being termed "empirically validated treatment" or, more broadly, "evidence-based practice." On one side of this debate are Scott Lilienfeld (2002), David Barlow and colleagues (Barlow, Levitt, & Bufka, 1999), and Richard McFall (1991), clinicians themselves, who take the view that clinical psychologists should restrict their professional activities to those that have ample support in the scientific literature. As Lilienfeld has stated:

> Once we abdicate our responsibility to uphold scientific standards in administering treatments, our scientific credibility and influence are badly damaged.... Our students will most likely follow in our footsteps and continue to turn a blind eye to the widening gap between scientist and practitioner, and between research evidence and clinical work. (p. 9)

On the other side of this debate are Ronald Fox (2000) and Ronald Levant (2004), both of whom are past presidents of the American Psychological Association. Fox (pp. 1–2) has written, "Psychologists do not have to apologize for their treatments. Nor is there any actual need to prove their effectiveness." Levant has taken the position that in clinical psychology "many treatments have not been empirically studied, and that there is a big difference between a treatment that has not been tested empirically and one that has not been supported by the empirical evidence" (p. 221). An emphasis on evidence-based practice, Levant believes, has already hurt practitioners by restricting the interventions that are reimbursed by insurance companies, and this emphasis "could create additional hazards for practitioners in the courtroom if empirically-validated treatments are held up as the standard of care in our field" (p. 221). Rather than reliance on evidence-based practice, Levant has called for "a broad perspective that allows the integration of the research (including that on empirically validated treatments ...) with clinical expertise and, finally, brings the topic of patient values into the equation. Such a model, which values all three components equally, will better advance knowledge related to best treatment and provide better accountability" (p. 223).

We would agree with the views of another clinician, however. As Larry Beutler (2004) has stated, "To elevate even the best clinical judgment to the status of knowledge, rather than hunch ... is the point at which we will both jeopardize our status among learned professions and harm our patients.... Contrary to Levant, research, experience, and patient values are not equivalently valid. Scientific research is more likely to produce valid conclusions than sincere clinical opinion based on unsystematic experience" (p. 228).

Rarely has the law come down so forcefully on what might be seen as an intraprofessional dispute (Appelbaum, 2002). *Daubert* unequivocally endorses "empirically validated treatments" and "evidence-based practices." Under *Daubert*, there is, in fact, *no difference* "between a treatment that has not been tested empirically, and one that has not been supported by the empirical evidence" (Levant, 2004, p. 221). Neither is admitted. Whatever clinical value unvalidated psychological assessment or treatment techniques may or may not have in the consultation room, *Daubert* makes plain that testimony employing such techniques has no place on the witness stand.

REFERENCES

Alexander v. Smith & Nephew, 90 F.Supp.2d 1310 (N.D. Okla. 2000).

Appelbaum, P. S. (2002). Policing expert testimony: The role of professional organizations. *Psychiatric Services, 53*(4), 389–399.

Barlow, D., Levitt, J., & Bufka, L. (1999). The dissemination of empirically supported treatments: A view to the future. *Behavioral Research and Therapy, 37,* 147–162.

Berger, M. (1994). Novel forensic evidence: The need for court-appointed experts after *Daubert*. *Shepard's Expert and Scientific Evidence, 1,* 487–512.

Beutler, L. E. (2004). The empirically supported treatments movement: A scientist-practitioner's response. *Clinical Psychology: Science and Practice, 11*(3), 225–229.

Black, B., Ayala, J., & Saffran, C. (1994). Science and the law in the wake of *Daubert*: A new search for scientific knowledge. *Texas Law Review, 72,* 715–802.

Cecil, J., & Willging, T. (1994). Accepting *Daubert's* invitation: Defining a role for court-appointed experts in assessing scientific validity. *Emory Law Journal, 43,* 995–1070.

Chesebro, K. J. (1994). Taking *Daubert's* "focus" seriously: The methodology/conclusion distinction. *Cardozo Law Review, 15,* 1745–1753.

Commonwealth v. Miller, 643 S.E.2d 208 (Va. 2007).

Daubert v. Merrell Dow Pharmaceuticals, Inc., 509 U.S. 579 (1993).

Faigman, D. L. (1989). To have and have not: Assessing the value of social science to the law as science and policy. *Emory Law Journal, 38,* 1005–1095.

Faigman, D. L. (2002). Is science different for lawyers? *Science, 197,* 339–340.

Faigman, D. L., Kaye, D. H., Saks, M. J., Sanders, J., & Cheng, E. K. (2007). *Modern scientific evidence: The law and science of expert testimony* (2d ed.). Minneapolis, MN: West/Thompson.

Faigman, D. L., Porter, E., & Saks, M. J. (1994). Check your crystal ball at the courthouse door, please: Exploring the past, understanding the present, and worrying about the future of scientific evidence. *Cardozo Law Review, 15,* 1799–1835.

Fox, R. E. (2000). The dark side of evidence-based treatment. *Practitioner Focus.* Retrieved April 27, 2008, from *www.apa.org/practice/pf/jan00/cappchair.html*.

Frye v. United States, 293 F. 1013 (D.C. Cir. 1923).

Gatowski, S. I., Dobbin, S. A., Richardson, J. T., Ginsburg, G. P., Merlino, M. L., & Dahir, V. (2001). Asking the gatekeepers: A national survey of judges on judging expert evidence in a post-*Daubert* world. *Law and Human Behavior, 25,* 433–458.

General Electric Co. v. Joiner, 522 U.S. 136 (1997).

Gross, S. (1991). Expert evidence. *Wisconsin Law Review,* pp. 1113–1232.

Hall v. Baxter Healthcare Corp., 947 F.Supp. 1387 (D.Or. 1996).

Jasanoff, S. (1996). *Science at the bar: Law, science, and technology in America.* Cambridge, MA: Harvard University Press.

Kassin, S. M., Tubb, V. A., Hosch, H. M., & Memon, A. (2001). On the "general acceptance" of eyewitness testimony research: A new survey of the experts. *American Psychologist, 56,* 405–416.

Kumho Tire v. Carmichael, 526 U.S. 137 (1999).

Levant, R. (2004). The empirically validated treatments movement: A practitioner/educator perspective. *Clinical Psychology: Science and Practice, 11,* 219–224.

Lilienfeld, S. O. (2002). The scientific review of mental health practice: Our raison d'etre. *Scientific Review of Mental Health Practice, 1,* 5–10.

Logerquist v. McVey, 1 P.3d 113 (2000).

McFall, R. M. (1991). Manifesto for a science of clinical psychology. *The Clinical Psychologist, 44*, 75–88.

Meehl, P. (1954). *Clinical versus statistical prediction: A theoretical analysis and a review of the evidence.* Minneapolis: University of Minnesota Press.

Monahan, J. (2007a). The scientific status of research on clinical and actuarial predictions of violence. In D. L. Faigman, D. H. Kaye, M. J. Saks, J. Sanders, & E. K. Cheng (Eds.), *Modern scientific evidence: The law and science of expert testimony* (2nd ed., pp. 124–149). Minneapolis, MN: West/Thompson.

Monahan, J. (2007b). *Tarasoff* at thirty: How developments in science and policy shape the common law. *University of Cincinnati Law Review, 75*, 497–521.

Monahan, J. (2008). Structured violence risk assessment. In R. Simon & K. Tardiff (Eds.), *American Psychiatric Publishing textbook on violence assessment and management* (pp. 17–33). Washington, DC: American Psychiatric Publishing.

National Research Council. (2003). *The polygraph and lie detection.* Washington, DC: National Academies Press.

Owen, D. G. (2002). A decade of *Daubert. Denver University Law Review, 80*, 345–372.

People v. Kelly, 549 P.2d 1240 (1976).

People v. McDonald, 690 P.2d 709 (1984).

People v. Miller, 2005 WL 768749 (Cal.App.4 Dist. 2005).

People v. Smith, 784 N.Y.S.2d 923 (Table), 2004 WL 690321 (N.Y. Supp. 2004).

People v. Venegas, 954 P.2d 525 (1998).

Risinger, D. M. (2007). Preliminary thoughts on a functional taxonomy of expertise for the post-*Kumho* world. In D. L. Faigman, D. H. Kaye, M. J. Saks, J. Sanders, & E. K. Cheng (Eds.), *Modern scientific evidence: The law and science of expert testimony* (2nd ed., pp. 119–151). Minneapolis, MN: West/Thompson.

Sexually Violent Predator Act, VA. Code § 37.2-907 A (1999).

Swets, J. A., Dawes, R. M., & Monahan, J. (2000). Psychological science can improve diagnostic decision. *Psychological Science in the Public Interest, 1*, 1–26.

United States v. Roldan-Zapata, 916 F.2d 795 (2d Cir. 1990).

Weisgram v. Marley Co., 528 U.S. 440 (2000).

Wilson v. Phillips, 86 Cal.Rptr.2d 204 (4th Dist. 1999).

Zemaitatis v. Innovasive Devices, Inc., 90 F.Supp.2d 631 (E.D.Pa. 2000).

CHAPTER 2

Daubert and Psychological Science in Court

JUDGING VALIDITY
FROM THE BENCH, BAR, AND JURY BOX

Bradley D. McAuliff and Jennifer L. Groscup

In *Daubert v. Merrell Dow Pharmaceuticals, Inc.* (1993), the U.S. Supreme Court put to rest the long-standing controversy of whether the Federal Rules of Evidence (FRE) or *Frye* standard governs the admissibility of expert evidence in federal court. The Court's holding that the FRE superseded *Frye* essentially shifted determinations of scientific validity from a consensus of experts in the relevant field of inquiry to individual judges in court. Many legal scholars and social scientists have questioned whether judges are up to the challenges inherent in *Daubert*. Namely, can judges act as amateur scientists and successfully distinguish between valid and junk science?

Fifteen years later, we are privy to a wealth of social scientific research and legal commentary that shed light on this fundamental concern. Our goal in writing this chapter is to synthesize the existing literature with an eye toward answering three related questions: Can judges evaluate psychological science effectively? If not, and methodologically flawed evidence is admitted, are attorneys and jurors able to detect those flaws? And finally, how successful are traditional legal safeguards and other strategies at enhancing the quality of psychological science in court?

THE *DAUBERT* TRILOGY AND ITS LEGACY

Concern in the United States regarding judges' ability to evaluate scientific evidence effectively has increased in the wake of several recent Supreme Court rulings on the admissibility of expert evidence (*Daubert*, 1993; *General Electric Co. v. Joiner*, 1997; *Kumho Tire Ltd. v. Carmichael*, 1999). The *Daubert* decision entrusted judges with a gatekeeping role in which they should base their admissibility decisions on the relevance and reliability of the proffered expert evidence. According to the Court, judges should consider certain nonexclusive factors (falsifiability, known or potential rate of error, peer review and publication, and general acceptance) when determining evidentiary reliability. The significance of judges' initial determinations was later realized in *Joiner* when the Court held that an abuse of discretion was the appropriate standard for review on appeal and that an appellate court should defer to the trial court's admissibility ruling unless it was clearly in error. In *Kumho*, the Court clarified that judges' gatekeeping role applies to all expert evidence covered under FRE 702 (i.e., scientific, technical, or other specialized knowledge) and not just expert scientific evidence. The cumulative result of *Daubert, Joiner*, and *Kumho* can be succinctly stated as follows: Federal judges are expected to apply fairly sophisticated scientific concepts when evaluating evidentiary reliability to make admissibility decisions about a wide range of expert evidence that will be upheld on appeal unless clearly in error.

Recent surveys and case reviews reveal that the *Daubert* trilogy has influenced the practice of law in civil and criminal cases. From the bar, attorneys are more likely to challenge expert testimony by filing more motions *in limine* and objecting more often at trial to limit or exclude testimony from an opposing expert (Dixon & Gill, 2002; Krafka, Dunn, Johnson, Cecil, & Miletich, 2002). When successful, these efforts often lead to motions for summary judgment. Attorneys also report that *Daubert* has prompted them to take a more proactive approach in selecting their own experts and preparing for trial testimony (Krafka et al., 2002).

On the bench, judges are more likely to exclude evidence now than before *Daubert* (Dixon & Gill, 2002; Krafka et al., 2002). Judges' discussion of *Daubert* has increased over time (Groscup et al., 2005); however, they rarely mention its specific reliability factors (Groscup, Penrod, Studebaker, Huss, & O'Neil, 2002; Krafka et al., 2002), and the number of evidence characteristics evaluated by judges has remained steady (Merlino, Murray, & Richardson, 2008). Instead, what has changed is that judges have begun to expand the scope of their reliability analysis beyond the *Daubert* factors

(Dixon & Gill, 2002) and increasingly evaluate expert characteristics such as skill or subject matter knowledge, experience, and education when determining admissibility (Merlino et al., 2008). In other words, even though judges are discussing *Daubert* and excluding evidence more frequently, these actions appear to be based more on characteristics of the expert than on those of the evidence.

The fact that judges are scrutinizing expert testimony more carefully and excluding it more frequently after *Daubert* says nothing about the accuracy of their decisions. None of the research we have reviewed has provided any evidence that judges are admitting valid science and excluding junk science. The same can be said for attorneys: Just because they are filing more motions to exclude expert testimony or are more selective when choosing experts does not mean that they are doing so effectively. This being the case, several critical questions remain unanswered, perhaps the most important of which is whether judges can, in fact, fulfill the role of amateur scientist thrust upon them by *Daubert*. If judges are unable to differentiate between valid and junk science, the ability of attorneys and jurors to do so becomes increasingly critical.

SCIENTIFIC REASONING ABILITY

Previous psychological research has identified deficits in laypeople's understanding and use of statistical, probabilistic, and methodological information. When judging the probability of certain outcomes, laypeople prefer anecdotal information and underutilize base-rate information (Bar-Hillel, 1980; Kahneman & Tversky, 1973). People often are insensitive to sample bias (Hamill, Wilson, & Nisbett, 1980) and fail to recognize the unreliability of results obtained from small or atypical samples (Fong, Krantz, & Nisbett, 1986). Participants in one study who completed a series of inductive reasoning problems varied considerably in their use of certain statistical reasoning skills (e.g., the law of large numbers, regression, and base-rate principles; Jepson, Krantz, & Nisbett, 1983). Participants in other studies have failed to recognize missing comparative or control-group information when evaluating certain scientific claims, such as the relation between fluoride use and tooth decay (Gray & Mill, 1990; Mill, Gray, & Mandel, 1994).

To what extent is this research relevant to legal decision making and *Daubert?* The answer to this question depends first on how broadly or narrowly one defines the concept of validity and second on the exact nature of expert testimony at issue. The *Daubert* Court faced the daunting task of describing validity in such a way that would encompass all "scientific, technical, or other specialized knowledge" set forth by FRE 702. From this perspective, the Court's treatment of validity was at best generic and superficial, and at worst, specious and uninformed. True, the Court did outline certain concepts fundamental to any form of science—namely, falsifiability, error rate, peer review, publication, and general acceptance—but at the same time it was extremely careful to steer clear of more definitive descriptions of validity.

At the broadest, most conceptual level the Court's treatment of validity can be understood as the ability of a particular theory, test, or methodology to produce accurate results. Still one cannot deny that a narrower, more literal interpretation of validity is also possible. From this perspective we realize the multidimensional nature of validity. In essence, there are many rooms in the house of validity, and the significance of one particular type versus another will vary as a function of the expert testimony proffered at trial. Evaluating one type of psychological expert evidence such as experimental research on the effects of misleading information on witness accuracy will emphasize certain types of validity and methodological skills that are quite different from those required to evaluate another, such as a psychopathy measure used to predict future violence. With respect to the first example, certainly the concepts of *internal validity* (the ability to conclude that any observed changes in the dependent variable were caused by the manipulated independent variable), *external validity* (the extent to which the observed results hold across different experimental settings, procedures, and participants), and *ecological validity* (the degree to which the methods, materials, and setting of the experiment approximate the real-life situation under examination) will be of paramount interest to judges, attorneys, and jurors. However, with respect to the second example, the concepts of *construct validity* (the extent to which a scale measures that which it purports to measure) and *predictive validity* (the extent to which a score predicts performance or some outcome on an additional measure) may be more relevant.

Our point here is simply this: The myriad conceptualizations of validity and forms of expert testimony that fall under the umbrella of *Daubert* present formidable hurdles for legal decision makers charged with evaluating this complex information. The same is true for social scientists who wish to examine the accuracy of these individuals' evaluations, which brings us full circle to our original question of whether basic research on laypeople's scientific reasoning ability is relevant to legal decision making and *Daubert*. It would appear that understanding certain basic concepts such as the significance of control groups, the unreliability of results obtained from small or biased samples, and the utility of base rates when evaluating probabilistic information would benefit decision makers in legal settings. Because the research reviewed indicates that laypeople struggle with these tasks, we expect that judges, attorneys, and jurors will as well. However, experiments more applied in nature are needed to better answer this question.

JUDGING VALIDITY FROM THE BENCH, BAR, AND JURY BOX

Judges

Recent research suggests that the *Daubert* Court may have been overly optimistic of judges' ability to fulfill their gatekeeping role. Gatowski and colleagues (2001) used a two-part survey that yielded impressive response rates (71% and 81%, respectively) to determine state court judges' opinions about *Daubert* and their ability to operationalize the reliability factors promulgated in that decision. Overall, judges were extremely positive about *Daubert* and believed that their role of gatekeeper was appropriate. Fifty-five percent reported that *Daubert* had a "great deal of value," and a sizeable 91% believed that the gatekeeping role was appropriate for judges. Nearly two-thirds of judges (62%) surveyed indicated that they took an "active role" in the admissibility process. Judges were more mixed in their beliefs as to whether their education had prepared them adequately to deal with the range of expert evidence they encountered in court, with just over half (52%) stating that they felt adequately prepared.

Gatowski and colleagues (2001) also asked judges whether each of the reliability factors articulated by the Court (falsifiability, error rate, peer review and publication, general acceptance) was useful in determining the merits of expert evidence and then prompted judges to discuss how they would apply each of the reliability factors to determine admissibility. The vast majority of judges believed that falsifiability (88%), error rate (91%), peer review and publication (92%), and general acceptance (93%) were useful in determining the merits of proffered scientific evidence. In stark contrast, however, judges' responses to the application prompt revealed an extremely limited understanding of these reliability concepts. Only 6% of judges' responses were reliably coded by multiple coders as possessing an accurate understanding of falsifiability (i.e., made explicit reference to testability, test and disproof, prove wrong a theory or hypothesis, or proof–disproof), and similar deficits were observed for error rate as well, with only 4% demonstrating a true understanding of that concept. Judges fared better on peer review and general acceptance, with 71% and 82% of their responses indicating an accurate understanding of these factors, respectively.

Kovera and McAuliff (2000) conducted an experiment to determine whether judges can effectively evaluate expert evidence as required by *Daubert*. Florida circuit court judges were asked to role-play that they were presiding over a hostile work environment case in which the defense attorney had filed a standard motion to bar expert testimony proffered by the plaintiff. After reading a brief description of the expert's testimony, judges were asked to rule on that motion and to answer a series of open- and close-ended questions in which they provided the rationale for their admissibility decisions and evaluated the expert's testimony. Within the description of the expert's study, Kovera and McAuliff manipulated its internal validity (valid, missing control group, confound, or experimenter bias) and peer-review status (published in a peer-reviewed journal or not).

Judges were extremely reluctant to admit the expert's testimony, and this response did not vary as a function of peer-review status or internal validity. Even the internally valid version of the study was rarely admitted by judges (17%) and did not significantly differ from admissibility rates in the other internal validity conditions: missing control group (11%), confound (17%), and experimenter bias (24%). In their admissibility decision rationales, judges who admitted the expert testimony were more likely to state that the evidence would assist jurors and that the expert was highly qualified, compared to judges who refused to admit the testimony. Conversely, judges who did not admit the expert's testimony mentioned *Frye* or general acceptance more frequently than those who admitted the testimony. Judges were more likely to mention some aspect of scientific validity when they refused to admit the expert's testimony than when they admitted it; however, very few judges in either group mentioned the internal validity threats when they were present. Only 8% of judges who read the missing control group study mentioned this flaw, and similarly only 13% and 9% mentioned the confound and experimenter bias when these internal validity threats were present. Finally, judges believed that they, along with attorneys, were better able to recognize flaws in scientific research than jurors.

With only two studies to date, it is clear that the empirical literature on judges' gatekeeping abilities is still in its infancy. Nevertheless, we would like to offer some general conclusions based on this work. First, judges appear to lack the scientific literacy necessary to scrutinize expert evidence as required by *Daubert*. Almost all judges did not sufficiently understand the reliability-related concepts of falsifiability and error rate, despite believing that these concepts are useful when deciding whether to admit expert evidence. Almost half of judges surveyed believed that their education had not adequately prepared them to confront the wide range of scientific evidence they encounter in court. Second, judges were largely unable to detect specific threats to internal validity when present in expert testimony. Judges' admissibility decisions did not vary as function of whether an expert's study was valid, lacked an appropriate control group, included a confound, or contained experimenter bias.

Judges were quite reluctant to admit expert testimony in Kovera and McAuliff's study, in keeping with trends reported by Krafka and colleagues (2002) and Dixon and Gill (2002). Given these low rates of admissibility, it would appear that judges are more likely to exclude valid expert evidence (a false-negative error) than to admit invalid expert evidence (a false-positive error). The potential for a high rate of false-negative errors is troubling in two respects: First, it is at odds with the liberal thrust of the FRE, which has been described by the U.S. Supreme Court as "relaxing traditional barriers to opinion testimony" (*Beech Aircraft Corp v. Rainey*, 1988, p. 163) and second, psychological science that can assist triers of fact as required by FRE 702 is not being admitted at trial. Recall that judges were more likely to cite scientific validity issues when denying versus admitting expert evidence, even though their ability to recognize the specific internal validity threats included in Kovera and McAuliff's study was extremely limited.

Despite these concerns, judges overwhelmingly support their role as gatekeepers and believe that they are better able to evaluate scientific evidence than jurors. When judges fail to recognize their limited scientific literacy, they may admit invalid expert testimony (even if this occurs less frequently than excluding valid expert testimony). As such, the ability of attorneys and jurors to evaluate scientific evidence effectively becomes increasingly critical. Attorneys, in particular, must be able to identify invalid research, file a motion to exclude that research, and successfully argue the basis for their motion before the court.

Attorneys

Kovera and McAuliff (2009) conducted a second study in which they presented the same basic fact pattern and expert testimony to attorneys instead of judges. Similar to judges' admissibility decisions in Kovera and McAuliff's study, attorneys' decisions to file a motion to exclude the expert's testimony were not influenced by the study's internal validity or peer-review status. Almost all of the attorneys indicated they would file such a motion irrespective of whether the study was internally valid or peer-reviewed/published. In contrast, however, attorneys were sensitive to peer-review status when rating the scientific reliability of the expert's research. They rated the peer-reviewed and published study to be more scientifically reliable than the study that lacked these qualities. Internal validity did not affect attorneys' ratings of scientific reliability, and none of the manipulated variables influenced attorneys' ratings of whether they would consult their own expert in preparation for trial in the case.

When asked what topics they would address during cross-examination, attorneys focused more on the expert's potential bias (e.g., history of testifying for plaintiff or defense, compensation) when the research was peer-reviewed/published than when it was not. However, the internal validity and peer-review manipulations did not influence the extent to which attorneys' cross-examination focused on the study's internal validity, external validity, or the pervasiveness of the media priming effects demonstrated in the research. Attorneys also believed that judges and attorneys were better able to spot invalid research than jurors.

These findings bear a striking resemblance to those from Kovera and McAuliff's (2000) judge study. Like judges, attorneys failed to identify specific threats to internal validity present in proffered expert evidence, and they shared judges' optimism that they are better able to identify flawed expert evidence than jurors. Unlike judges, however, attorneys rated the peer-reviewed and published study to be more scientifically reliable than when it was not peer reviewed or published. Attorneys' reliance on a study's publication status is reassuring if we assume that the peer-review process effectively screens out invalid psychological science. At the same time, however, using a study's publication status as a proxy for its scientific validity can be misleading because undoubtedly invalid research has been published in peer-reviewed outlets and likewise valid research might not yet have been published. Looking beyond this study, it seems reasonable to expect that legal professionals (and laypeople, for that matter) who rely on a study's peer-review and publication status when evaluating its validity will render sounder, albeit imperfect, judgments than those who do not rely on these features.

Jurors

Jurors may encounter flawed psychological science at trial if judges and attorneys are unable to identify internal validity threats such as those included in the Kovera and McAuliff studies. Can jurors detect these threats even if judges and attorneys cannot? What about variations in other types of validity, such as whether the expert adequately measured the construct under examination?

McAuliff and Kovera (in press) discovered that, unlike judges and attorneys, jurors appear to be sensitive to at least one internal validity threat: a missing control group. Those researchers presented jury-eligible citizens with a written summary of a hostile work environment case in which an expert testified about a study on the effects of viewing sexualized materials on men's behavior toward women. They varied the study's internal validity (valid, missing control group, confound, and experimenter bias) and ecological validity (whether the study included college students or trucking company employees similar to those at the plaintiff's workplace). Jurors' evaluations of expert evidence quality and expert credibility were higher for the valid versus missing control group study only, and no differences emerged on the verdict and plaintiff credibility dependent measures. Ecological validity had virtually no effect jurors' decisions.

These findings are similar to an earlier study in which McAuliff and Kovera (2008) observed that jurors high in the need for cognition (NC; individuals who naturally engage in and enjoy effortful cognitive endeavors) (Cacioppo & Petty, 1982) found the defendant liable more often and evaluated the quality of the expert's study more favorably when it contained an appropriate control group than when it did not. When asked in that study whether judges, attorneys, and jurors were able to identify internal validity threats in expert evidence, jurors believed that judges and attorneys were best able to do so, followed by jurors.

A final experiment from the Kovera and McAuliff research program shifted the focus from internal validity threats to whether jurors detect variations in the construct validity of an expert's study. Using the same basic hostile work environment case and expert testimony described earlier, Kovera, McAuliff, and Hebert (1999) filmed a trial simulation in which third-year law students played the role of attorneys and professional actors served as the other trial participants. Kovera and colleagues varied the study's peer-review/publication status and ecological validity in addition to whether the study was high or low in construct validity (i.e., included multiple measures that triangulated on the construct of sexual harassment versus a single measure). Jury-eligible university students serving as mock jurors were insensitive to variations in the study's construct validity. Instead, they relied on the study's peer-review/publication status and ecological validity when making trial-related judgments. They rated the expert's trustworthiness and the validity of her study more favorably when it was peer-reviewed and published than when it was not.

Comparing these results with Kovera and McAuliff's earlier research involving legal professionals, we see that jurors, like judges and attorneys, have difficulty evaluating the validity of psychological science presented by an expert in court. One exception to this general rule was jurors' sensitivity to the inclusion of an appropriate control group. Jurors, like attorneys, also relied on the study's peer-review and publication status when forming judgments related to the expert evidence. Both jurors and attorneys found the expert's study to be more valid when it was peer-reviewed and published than when it was not, and jurors believed the expert was more trustworthy in this condition as well. The effects of ecological validity on jurors' decisions were mixed across studies. Finally, jurors agreed with judges and attorneys that these two groups of legal professionals were better able to identify flawed psychological science than jurors at trial.

These findings raise the question: Who performed best among the three groups included in Kovera and McAuliff's research program? Recall that validity is a multidimensional construct and that the significance of one particular type versus another under a *Daubert* analysis will vary according to the exact nature of expert testimony in question. Given the experimental methodology used by the expert in Kovera and McAuliff's studies, internal validity should be the criterion of utmost concern. In other words, how can an expert conclude that exposure to sexualized materials causes men to sexually harass women if there is no comparison group of nonexposed men or the presence of a confound or experimenter bias introduces an alternate explanation for the observed differences? Unlike these fatal flaws, a study containing college students versus trucking company employees (ecological validity) can still be internally valid, thus allowing the expert to accurately conclude that viewing sexualized materials increases the likelihood of sexual harassment. Of the four experiments that tested respondents' sensitivity to internal validity variations, only jurors recognized one threat to internal validity: a missing control group. True, the primary dependent measures included in each study varied slightly: Judges indicated whether they would admit the expert's testimony, attorneys whether they would object to the evidence by filing a pretrial motion, and jurors whether they believed the defendant was liable; however, participants in all four studies rated the validity of the expert's evidence, and only jurors were sensitive to the presence or absence of the control group. In this sense, jurors outperformed judges and attorneys.

This conclusion and the findings on which it is based are subject to certain limitations that cannot be overlooked. With the exception of Gatowski and colleagues' (2001) survey of judicial decision making, the program of research we have described was conducted by one pair of researchers. Kovera and McAuliff's experiments all used the same basic fact pattern and focused exclusively on three types of validity (internal validity, ecological validity, and construct validity) in addition to peer-review and publication status. As is typical with research involving professional samples, the studies that surveyed judges and attorneys had low response rates and may have been influenced by a self-selection bias. Clearly additional research that uses different trial stimuli, includes other types of expert testimony, focuses on alternative conceptualizations of validity, and includes more representative samples is needed before we can truly understand the complex question at hand. That said, the Kovera and McAuliff program of research represents the most current and on-point assessment of whether judges are up to the challenge born by *Daubert* and, if not, whether attorneys and jurors can evaluate expert evidence effectively.

IMPROVING JUDGMENTS OF VALIDITY IN COURT: TRADITIONAL SAFEGUARDS AND BEYOND

Daubert and Traditional Safeguards against Junk Science

Given the great concern over admitting junk science in court that formed the basis for the *Daubert* and *Kumho* opinions, the *Daubert* Court discussed several safeguards already available in the legal system that might prevent jurors from giving improper weight to lower quality scientific evidence. The Court specifically stated that "vigorous cross-examination, presentation of contrary evidence, and careful instruction on the burden of proof are the traditional and appropriate means of attacking shaky but admissible evidence" (*Daubert*, 1993, p. 576). The Court also suggested that the judicial power to direct a verdict or grant summary judgment could also serve as a safeguard against the admission of unreliable expert evidence. The Court claimed that the use of these safeguards would be a more appropriate under FRE 702 than the overly inflexible general acceptance standard alone, which may result in total exclusion. No empirical research has been conducted on the effectiveness of summary judgment or directed verdict, which would be difficult to study in actual cases and even more difficult to study experimentally. However, some studies have examined the effectiveness of opposing expert testimony, cross-examination, and jury instructions.

Opposing Experts

One of the concerns raised by the presentation of expert testimony is the potential for a "battle of the experts" and the effect this might have on jury decision making. The *Daubert* Court suggested the presentation of contrary evidence as a safeguard against unreliability. One way to present contrary testimony is via an opposing expert. Several studies have manipulated the party presenting the expert testimony and whether or not there is an opposing expert testimony (Cutler, Dexter, & Penrod, 1989; Greene, Downey, & Goodman-Delahunty, 1999). Overall, these studies have found that opposing experts weakly affect jurors' ultimate verdicts in criminal cases or damage awards in civil cases. However, the presence of opposing expert opinions has sometimes affected the manner in which jurors evaluate evidence.

Krauss and Sales (2001) examined the effects of opposing expert testimony on jurors' evaluations of the reliability of expert testimony in capital cases that required determination of the defendant's future dangerousness. They manipulated the type of opposing expert testimony, the scientific reliability of the testimony offered (low—unaided clinical judgment—versus high—actuarial risk estimate), and the effectiveness of cross-examination (see the next section). The opposing expert was either the same type as the primary expert (clinical or actuarial) and disagreed with the primary expert's conclusions or was the opposite type (i.e., clinical when the primary expert was actuarial) and disagreed with the primary expert's methods and conclusions. Clinical expert testimony had a larger main effect on dangerousness judgments than actuarial testimony. Opposing expert testimony exerted less of a negative effect on clinical testimony compared to actuarial testimony. Opposing experts' attacks on the primary expert's methods were no more effective than simple attacks on the primary expert's conclusions. What do these results mean in light of our focus? First, jurors may resonate more with experts who have clinical- than science-based opinions. Second, the safeguard of an opposing expert is less effective for clinical- than science-based opinions. Krauss and Sales argued that opposing experts may not be effective because the two experts essentially cancel each other out.

Recent research by Groscup and her colleagues has investigated the use of opposing expert testimony as a safeguard against unreliable expert testimony. Brown, Tallon, and Groscup (2008) varied the quality of the research relied on by an expert in a mock trial. They also manipulated the presence and type (either disagreeing with the conclusions of the primary expert or attempting to educate the jurors about the quality of the methods used by the primary expert) of opposing expert testimony to determine if such testimony would prevent mock jurors' reliance on questionable expert testimony. Minimal improvements in participants' actual understanding of the science arose from the presentation of either type of opposing expert. The opposing expert who attempted to educate jurors sometimes increased their ability to appropriately evaluate the expert based on the quality of his or her research. These results indicate that there may be some potential for sensitizing jurors to the quality of the science relied on by the expert via opposing expert testimony, but additional research is needed.

Cross-Examination

Several experiments have manipulated the presence and content of cross-examination on verdicts and on expert credibility, but only a few have examined cross-examination in conjunction with reliability. Kovera and colleagues (1999) explored the potential of cross-examination to be an educational tool for the jury. They varied the quality of the science used by the expert on a number of dimensions (ecological validity, construct validity, and general acceptance), and they manipulated whether the expert was cross-examined with scientific questions or nonscientific questions. Scientific questions concerned the methodology used by the expert. No effect from the type of cross-examination of the expert emerged. Jurors did not discriminate between the expert with good methodology and the expert with poor methodology, even with the educational cross-examination questions. Based on those results, the authors argued that cross-examination may not be a particularly effective safeguard against the use of junk science by the jury and suggested that future research include a longer, more involved cross-examination.

Krauss and Sales (2001), as noted above, tested the effect of clinical and actuarial testimony about future dangerousness on juror assessments of dangerousness. They also tested the tempering effect of cross-examination on these assessments and on the perceptions of the expert, in addition to testing the effectiveness of opposing expert testimony, as described earlier. Cross-examination was either general (attacking the general credibility of the expert) or reliability based (attacking the content of the testimony, including its reliability). Cross-examination reduced ratings of dangerousness, as would be expected if cross-examination reduces the persuasiveness of the expert, and cross-examination also negatively influenced perceptions of the expert. In addition, they observed that cross-examination had fewer negative effects on clinical testimony than on actuarial testimony. There were few significant differences between the two types of cross-examination.

Overall, cross-examination reduced the credibility of the expert regardless of methodology, which is what we would expect of this adversarial technique. However, the jurors were not affected by it in the hypothesized way. Cross-examination had less negative impact on the low-science, clinically based testimony when the opposite would be true if it were entirely effective at educating jurors about science.

Krauss and Lee (2003) again investigated cross-examination as a safeguard against unreliable expert testimony but expanded the research to include deliberations. Using the same paradigm, either a clinically based or an actuarially based psychological expert in risk assessment testified at the sentencing phase of a death penalty trial. The expert was given either what the authors termed "ineffective" cross-examination, which attacked the expert's qualifications and general credibility, or "effective" cross-examination, which targeted the quality of the science relied on by the expert. Kraus and Lee did observe some differences between the two types of cross-examination. Participants were less confident in their own dangerousness ratings after the effective, as compared with the ineffective, cross-examination. In addition, cross-examination influenced mock jurors' ratings of the expert. The expert was perceived as less influential, lower in scientific quality, and less credible after cross-examination, but these effects were strongest for the clinical expert especially after the effective cross-examination. These results indicate that it may be possible to educate jurors and improve their evaluations of expert evidence with cross-examinations and deliberations.

Finally, Groscup and her colleagues (Monier, Tallon, Giresi-Ficarra, Jacobs, & Groscup, 2008; Tallon, Brown, Giresi-Ficarra, & Groscup, 2008) have studied the use of cross-examination as a safeguard against unreliable expert testimony. As previously described, they varied the quality of the research relied on by an expert in a mock trial. Following the *Daubert* Court's suggestion that cross-examination would help jurors properly evaluate scientific expert testimony, they manipulated the presence and type of cross-examination (a general attack on credibility or an educational cross-examination about his research methods) to determine whether cross-examination would prevent reliance on questionable expert testimony. Consistent with other research; cross-examination decreased credibility assessments of the expert and had a limited educational effect on jurors. It did not always improve jurors' ability to distinguish between good and bad science, and unfortunately it sometimes made jurors evaluate the expert's reliability incorrectly. Given that some improvements in jurors' actual understanding of science and in their ability to appropriately evaluate the quality of the expert's research were observed, cross-examination may have some potential for sensitizing jurors to the quality of the science relied on by the expert.

Jury Instructions

The *Daubert* Court suggested "careful instruction on the burden of proof" as a potential safeguard against the reliance on unreliable expert testimony (*Daubert*, 1993, p. 576). Commentators have suggested instructions as a means to assist the jury in evaluating and weighing expert testimony (Beyea & Berger, 2001). However, research indicates that jurors have difficulty understanding and applying jury instructions. Across a large number of studies, some estimate that jurors understand 70% of instruction content at most (Lieberman & Sales, 1997). Burden-of-proof instructions are particularly poorly understood and can create confusion in how they should be applied to determine whether reasonable doubt exists, which is the intent of the instruction (see Horowitz & Kirkpatrick, 1996; Kagehiro, 1990; Lieberman & Sales, 1997). Given that jurors have difficulty with the actual target of burden-of-proof instructions, it is unlikely that such instructions will help jurors evaluate expert reliability, which they are not intended to do. However, it is possible that instructions aimed at educating the jury about scientific reliability may prove more effective than the suggested instruction on the burden of proof. Scant systematic research has been conducted on the effectiveness of educational instructions and expert testimony.

Studies that have evaluated the use of educational instructions indicate that they may have little positive impact on jurors' ability to appropriately weigh expert credibility. One such type of educational instruction is known as the *Telfaire* instruction (*United States v. Telfaire*, 1972), a model instruction that was intended to educate the jury about eyewitness reliability and provide information similar to expert testimony. The instruction encourages the jury to consider the eyewitness's opportunity to observe the crime, the likelihood that the identification resulted from the eyewitness's memory and not a faulty procedure, the consistency of the identification across time, and the personal credibility of the eyewitness when evaluating the credibility of the eyewitness identification. Research conducted on the effectiveness of the *Telfaire* instruction has shown little educational effect on the jury. Cutler, Dexter, and Penrod (1990) presented participants with either expert testimony, *Telfaire* instructions, or no expert/instruction information. Instructions had no effect on jurors' sensitivity to eyewitness reliability, their skepticism about eyewitness identification, or their verdict in the mock trial. In slight contrast, Ramirez, Zemba, and Geiselman (1996) found that the *Telfaire* instruction increased skepticism of eyewitness evidence but not sensitivity to its quality. Ramirez and colleagues also examined a revised instruction that did not increase skepticism toward eyewitness evidence, but it also did not increase juror sensitivity to eyewitness reliability. These studies indicate that the educational impact of instructions about expert testimony topics might be negligible, but they do not address whether instructions could educate jurors about expert evidence quality.

More recent research has examined the effectiveness of instructions as a safeguard against unreliable expert testimony. Groscup and her colleagues (Giresi, Brown, Chrzanowski, Henriquez, & Groscup, 2006) varied the quality of the research relied on by an expert and the presence of burden-of-proof instructions to determine whether the instructions would prevent mock jurors' reliance on questionable expert testimony. They hypothesized that the burden-of-proof instructions would be an ineffective educational tool for the jury regarding the scientific quality of the expert. Instructions intended to educate jurors about scientific reliability and validity were also created, and their presence was manipulated to determine if specialized educational instructions might be more effective than traditional jury instructions. They hypothesized that these educational instructions would be more likely to increase jurors' sensitivity to the expert's scientific quality. Generally, participants felt the instructions were helpful and that the educational instructions increased their understanding of science. However, all of the instructions had a limited impact on decision making. Minimal improvements in participants' actual understanding of science and in their ability to appropriately evaluate the quality of the expert's research were observed, indicating there may be some potential for sensitizing jurors to the quality of the science relied on by the expert via instructions.

SUMMARY AND CONCLUSIONS ABOUT OPPOSING EXPERTS, CROSS-EXAMINATION, AND JURY INSTRUCTIONS

The implications of the research regarding the potential for using opposing expert testimony, cross-examination, and jury instructions as safeguards against jurors' use of unreliable evidence are unclear. Although the Court reasoned that these options would help jurors better evaluate scientific evidence, the research conducted thus far indicates that their educational value may be limited. All three safeguards individually had some effect on sensitizing jurors to science, but none had the broad impact we would expect from a truly effective jury aid. Opposing expert testimony had some educational effects, but it may more likely result in the jurors discounting all expert testimony. Cross-examination also exerted some positive effects on jurors' understanding of science. It helped jurors better understand some aspects of validity and showed some promise for increasing jurors' abilities to properly evaluate the scientific quality of clinical and actuarial risk assessment testimony. However, it also had the effect of reducing the expert's credibility, regardless of scientific quality, due to its adversarial nature. Educational jury instructions had the fewest effects on jurors' evaluations of scientific reliability. Perhaps given jurors' limited understanding of instructions, such instructions appear only minimally effective as a safeguard against an unreliable expert. These negative outcomes may make opposing expert testimony, cross-examination, and jury instructions less effective than the Court reasoned.

To date there has been little published research that combines the manipulation of expert evidence quality and the presence of any of these three safeguards. Because the research that has been conducted is minimal, the range of stimulus materials used to address these research questions has also been limited in scope. It may be that the safeguards have limited effectiveness for the types of experts presented in the mock trials used (e.g., sexual harassment, risk assessment, and eyewitness reliability), but they may have a greater impact when used with a different type of expert (e.g., a medical doctor, engineer, or economist). Social scientists should expand this line of scientific inquiry to incorporate a wider variety of trial contexts and different types of expert testimony before we can draw any final conclusions about safeguard effectiveness. Similarly, future studies should operationalize safeguards in different ways to determine if other safeguards might be more effective than those tested in past research. It may also be possible that the safeguards are less effective when introduced individually. In an actual trial, it is likely that more than one if not all safeguards would be present. The combined effect may provide the assistance indicated by the Court. In terms of research design, the studies conducted on these safeguards have all been experimental in nature. An examination of safeguard effectiveness in the field would greatly inform our understanding of how they may affect jury decision making in actual cases. If the suggested safeguards do not sensitize jurors to science as much as we would like, other aids to juror processing, which have thus far not been widely studied in relation to expert testimony, might also be used to sensitize jurors to reliability.

Other Potential Aids to Jurors' Scientific Reasoning

Many aids to jurors' processing of evidence have been implemented by courts, including allowing jurors to take notes, ask questions, and discuss the case prior to deliberations (see Robbenolt, Penrod, & Groscup, 2006, for a review). Many of these procedures could be used by courts to increase jurors' ability to understand and evaluate scientific expert testimony. One potential aid to jurors might be allowing them to ask the expert questions during or after his or her testimony. Although research on the use of juror questions has not focused specifically on expert testimony, results from field research on juror questions indicates that they might be a useful aid to jurors' understanding of expert testimony. Diamond, Rose, and Murphy (2004) compiled a list of questions asked by jurors in real cases in Arizona. Approximately half of the questions asked pertained to the expert. These questions asked for clarification of the experts' testimony and asked about the bases for the experts' opinions. The questions did not focus on irrelevant details such as pay, indicating that the jurors had a legitimate need for more information and that they were using the questions to obtain it. Another field study found that jurors posed questions to approximately half of the experts who testified (Diamond, Rose, Murphy, & Smith, 2006). Although not all of these questions were answered, the answers provided were sometimes later discussed in deliberations. The fact that the jurors in these studies asked questions to help them better understand expert testimony and that they used this information in deliberations indicates that juror questions might be an effective aid to jurors' processing of expert evidence. However, the effectiveness of questions as an aid to understanding scientific reliability has not been tested empirically, and questions may prove to be ineffective for aiding jurors in this particular task. Therefore, more research should be conducted that targets this specific aspect of juror questions using a wider variety of methods.

Juror note taking is another potential aid to jurors in understanding expert testimony. As with juror questions, most research on juror note taking has not focused specifically on its ability to improve jurors' comprehension and use of expert testimony. However, research does indicate that it might be a useful aid to jurors for expert testimony. Although some research has found few positive effects resulting from note taking (Heuer & Penrod, 1988, 1994), other research has found that allowing jurors to take notes increases the amount of probative evidence they remember and their satisfaction with performing the duries of a juror (ForsterLee & Horowitz, 1997; ForsterLee, Horowitz, & Bourgeois, 1994; Rosenhan, Eisner, & Robinson, 1994). Even though most of this research did not specifically focus on experts, some results regarding experts are encouraging for the use of note taking. For example, ForsterLee and Horowitz (1997) found that experts were mentioned in the more detailed jurors' notes. The volume of notes taken about the expert increased when the jurors were preinstructed about the law, giving them an idea of what evidence might be important (ForsterLee & Horowitz, 1997). If the topics on which jurors take notes are better understood, then these results could indicate that jurors' processing of scientific evidence might be improved with note taking, Indeed, several researchers concluded that note taking might be most helpful in complex trials or for complex evidence, such as expert testimony (ForsterLee & Horowitz, 1997; Heuer & Penrod, 1994; Rosenhan et al., 1994). As with juror questions, the effectiveness of note taking in sensitizing jurors to scientific reliability is untested to date and should be examined using controlled research.

Another procedure that could assist jurors in evaluating scientific expert evidence is providing them with a written summary of the expert's testimony. This approach could help to create a schema that would improve processing of this complex form of trial evidence (ForsterLee, Horowitz, Athaide-Victor, & Brown, 2000). Research on expert summary statements demonstrates that they might be helpful to jurors in processing expert evidence generally. One study found that written summaries of an expert's testimony, given to the jury prior to the expert's actual testimony, improved recall of the expert information, processing of the expert information, and appropriate application of the expert information to the case facts (Forster-Lee et al., 2000). A second experiment then examined the combined effects of providing jurors with written summaries of the expert's testimony and of permitting them to take notes (ForsterLee, Kent, & Horowitz, 2005). This research confirmed that providing summary statements prior to hearing expert testimony helped jurors to appropriately distinguish between differentially worthy plaintiffs in their compensatory awards. This differentiation was performed better when jurors with access to written summaries were also permitted to take notes. Jurors with access to summary statements and jurors who were allowed to take notes recalled more relevant evidence and rated the evidence as less complex than their no-access, no-note-taking counterparts (ForsterLee et al., 2005).

Conclusions about Other Potential Aids

Several jury reforms and aids that were not suggested by the Court in *Daubert* may also improve jurors' abilities to properly evaluate expert science.

Improvements in the processing of case information presented via expert testimony, resulting from the presentation of summary statements, indicate that, if they were routinely allowed in court, they might aid jurors in evaluating scientific expert testimony, including its reliability. Other research on juror questions indicates that when they are allowed, jurors use them to better understand the content and underlying bases of expert testimony. This finding may also apply to their understanding of the science underlying expert testimony. However, research on these aids did not focus specifically on assisting jurors in the task of evaluating science. Future research could address this question more directly, as these techniques may prove equally or less effective than the safeguards suggested by the *Daubert* Court. It is also possible that these aids may increase the effectiveness of the suggested safeguards when used in conjunction with them. Research addressing these questions would help us better understand how best to maximize jurors' understanding of scientific evidence.

Assisting Judges with Scientific Gatekeeping

Because judges may lack the skills necessary to evaluate the reliability of scientific expert testimony, alternative presentations for this type of evidence and aids for judges in dealing with this type of evidence have been suggested. In general, the alternatives that have received attention in the legal commentary can be divided into three general types: court-appointed experts, scientific advisors, and specialized training.

Court-Appointed Experts

The first type of alternative is the appointment of expert witnesses by the court under FRE 706 or its state counterpart (see Faigman & Monahan, Chapter 1, this volume, for additional information). Court-appointed experts are viewed as neutral and therefore potentially more reliable and less risky for admission. In surveys of judges, the judges indicated willingness to appoint an expert only under special circumstances. Judges also believed that the presence of court-appointed experts interferes with the adversarial process, as evidenced by their observations that juries typically followed the experts' recommendations when they were used (see, e.g., Cecil & Willging, 1994). The Advisory Committee to the FRE also raised concerns about the fact-finder ascribing increased credibility to a court-appointed expert relative to the credibility that might be ascribed to an adversarial expert. Results from controlled research on court-appointed experts and juries are conflicting. Some studies indicate that court-appointed experts can help juries and that juries are not overly influenced by their opinions (Brekke, Enko, Clavet, & Seelau, 1991; Crowley, O'Callaghan, & Ball, 1994), whereas other studies demonstrate a tendency for juries to follow the recommendations of a court-appointed expert, as feared (Cooper & Hall, 2000; Cutler et al., 1989, 1990).

Appointment of Scientific Advisors

Judges also have the authority to appoint persons to serve as advisors to them or as the decision makers about expert testimony. Individual scientific or technical advisors or a panel of advisors can be appointed to advise the judge on issues of scientific evidence (Black, Ayala, & Saffran-Brinks, 1994). Advisors are most often experts in the field of the scientific evidence in question. Advisors provide assistance, but they do not make decisions for the judge. Judges can also appoint either Special Masters or U.S. Magistrates, who can evaluate evidence, make recommendations, and make some evidentiary determinations for the judge. Another proposed alternative is the institution of a "science court." The science court is a panel of scientists or experts in the field at issue who are charged with the duty of deciding the quality of the science presented to them. To our knowledge, no systematic research testing the effectiveness of these alternatives exists.

Scientific Training

A final alternative is to provide specialized training for judges and attorneys. This training could help alleviate their difficulty in evaluating the quality of scientific evidence (Merlino, Dillehay, Dahir, & Maxwell, 2003). In general, various forms of scientific training can improve the ability of laypeople to reason about statistical and methodological issues related to everyday problems. Statistical training involving the law of large numbers improved both the frequency and quality of participants' statistical reasoning skills in a study by Fong and colleagues (1986). Undergraduates majoring in the social sciences (e.g., psychology) showed greater improvement in their ability to apply statistical and methodological skills to a wide variety of problems, compared to students majoring in the natural sciences (e.g., chemistry) and humanities (e.g., history; Lehman & Nisbett, 1990). Similar findings emerged when researchers tested the reasoning skills of graduate students who were majoring in law, medicine, psychology, and chemistry (Lehman, Lempert, & Nisbett, 1988). However, specialized tutoring, in addition to statistics and research methodology coursework, may be necessary to increase students' ability to identify certain methodological flaws, such as a missing control group (Mill et al., 1994).

Scientific training specifically for attorneys and judges could occur as early as law school. Indeed, courses targeting the understanding of science have become more common in law school curricula nationwide (Merlino et al., 2003). Merlino and colleagues (2003) surveyed law schools about the inclusion of science and scientific methods in their overall curricula, courses, and instructional methods and found that some law schools include up to as many as 15 science-related courses in their curricula. Of the schools that offered science-related courses, many targeted environmental law, medicine, and psychiatry/psychology. At least one school offered training to prepare students to examine scientific experts by having them interact with actual scientific experts. In addition to law school training, several universities offer master's degrees and doctorates to judges that include scientific training, such as the University of Nevada–Reno and the University of Virginia (Merlino et al., 2003).

Training for currently presiding judges could occur in a variety of ways. Continuing education seminars for judges, precisely tailored to the education of judges in empirical methods, might be helpful (Black et al., 1994). Seminars would be particularly helpful if the information were related to the criteria with which judges are intended to make admissibility determinations. For federal judges and some state judges this would include the *Daubert* factors. Merlino and colleagues (2003) researched the availability and sources of continuing judicial education programs on science; they found many programs offered by national agencies and individual states and concluded that these programs are widely available and increasing in number.

Although this is an oft-suggested aid for judges, there is little controlled research testing the effectiveness of either scientific training during law school or continuing judicial education on science. This reality raises the question of whether judges who have scientific training of any type are better able to judge the quality of science. Kovera and McAuliff (2000) provide us with some information about decision making by trained versus untrained judges. They found that scientifically trained judges (i.e., those with undergraduate majors in the natural sciences or psychology, had graduate training in psychology, or took at least one continuing legal education class on the scientific method) were better able to distinguish between good and questionable scientific evidence. Trained judges gave higher admissibility ratings to an internally valid study than did those with no scientific training. In contrast, scientifically untrained judges rated a confounded study more favorably than did scientifically trained judges. However, scientific training did not affect judges' admissibility ratings for a study that lacked an appropriate control group or contained experimenter bias (Kovera & McAuliff, 2002). These results indicate that training programs, such as those previously discussed, might assist judges in appropriately evaluating the reliability of scientific evidence.

An alternative to training would make available to judges information on science and scientific methods, allowing them to conduct their own research when a scientific issue is raised in their courtroom (Tomkins & Cecil, 1994). This information could come in the form of specially tailored databases that could be established for judges to use when a case involving scientific evidence arises. These databases could include indexes of topics upon which articles have been written and the specific empirical methodology utilized by different areas of science. One such resource already exists in a format familiar to judges: a treatise on scientific evidence edited by Faigman, Kaye, Saks, and Sanders (1997). There are also no published experiments on the use or effectiveness of providing judges with this type of information.

CONCLUSIONS

Without a doubt, the *Daubert* trilogy presents formidable challenges to judges, attorneys, jurors, and social scientists alike. The past 15 years of social scientific research and legal commentary have revealed critical limitations in the ability of legal professionals and laypeople to identify flawed psychological science in court. Moreover, this literature has raised serious concerns about the effectiveness of traditional methods used to safeguard courts against junk science. Looking ahead to the next 15 years, we are confident that continued efforts to better understand these limitations, coupled with new research on maximizing the effectiveness of traditional safeguards and evaluating innovative alternatives, ultimately will improve the quality of psychological science admitted and relied on at trial.

REFERENCES

Bar-Hillel, M. (1980). The base-rate fallacy in probability judgments. *Acta Psychologica, 44,* 211–233.
Beech Aircraft Corp. v. Rainey, 488 U.S. 153 (1988).

Beyea, J., & Berger, D. (2001). Complex litigation at the millennium: Scientific misconceptions among *Daubert* gatekeepers: The need for reform of expert testimony procedures. *Law and Contemporary Problems, 64,* 327–372.

Black, B., Ayala, F. J., & Saffran-Brinks, C. (1994). Science and the law in the wake of *Daubert*: A new search for scientific knowledge. *Texas Law Review, 72,* 715–802.

Brekke, N., Enko, P., Clavet, G., & Seelau, E. (1991). Of juries and court-appointed experts: The impact of nonadversarial versus adversarial expert testimony. *Law and Human Behavior, 15,* 451–475.

Brown, M., Tallon, J., & Groscup, J. (2008, March). The effectiveness of opposing expert testimony as an expert reliability safeguard. In J. Groscup (Chair), *Scientific reliability in the courtroom: Jurors' assessments of scientific evidence and legal safeguards.* Symposium conducted at the annual meeting of the American Psychology-Law Society, Jacksonville, FL.

Cacioppo, J. T., & Petty, R. E. (1982). The need for cognition. *Journal of Personality and Social Psychology, 42,* 116–131.

Cecil, J. S., & Willging, T. E. (1994). Court-appointed experts. In *Reference manual on scientific evidence* (pp. 525–572). Washington, DC: Federal Judicial Center.

Cooper, J., & Hall, J. (2000). Reactions of mock jurors to testimony of a court-appointed expert. *Behavioral Sciences and the Law, 18,* 719–729.

Crowley, M. J., O'Callaghan, G. M., & Ball, P. J. (1994). The juridical impact of psychological expert testimony in a simulated child sexual abuse trial. *Law and Human Behavior, 18,* 89–105.

Cutler, B. L., Dexter, H. R., & Penrod, S. D. (1989). Expert testimony and jury decision making: An empirical analysis. *Behavioral Sciences and the Law, 7,* 215–225.

Cutler, B. L., Dexter, H. R., & Penrod, S. D. (1990). Nonadversarial methods for sensitizing jurors to eyewitness evidence. *Journal of Applied Social Psychology, 20,* 1197–1207.

Daubert v. Merrell Dow Pharmaceuticals, Inc., 113 S.Ct. 2786 (1993).

Diamond, S. S., Rose, M. R., & Murphy, B. (2004). Jurors' unanswered questions. *Court Review, 40,* 20–29.

Diamond, S. S., Rose, M. R., Murphy, B., & Smith, S. (2006). Juror questions during trial: A window into juror thinking. *Vanderbilt Law Review, 59,* 1927–1972.

Dixon, L., & Gill, B. (2002). Changes in the standards for admitting expert evidence in federal civil cases since the *Daubert* decision. *Psychology, Public Policy, and Law, 8,* 251–308.

Faigman, D. L., Kaye, D. H., Saks, M. J., & Sanders, J. (1997). *Modern scientific evidence: The law and science of expert testimony* (Vol. 1, sections 1–3.4, 29–37). St. Paul, MN: West.

Fong, G. T., Krantz, D. H., & Nisbett, R. E. (1986). The effects of statistical training on thinking about everyday problems. *Cognitive Psychology, 18,* 253–292.

ForsterLee, L., & Horowitz, I. (1997). Enhancing juror competence in a complex trial. *Applied Cognitive Psychology, 11*, 305–319.

ForsterLee, L., Horowitz, I., Athaide-Victor, E., & Brown, N. (2000). The bottom line: The effect of written expert witness statements on juror verdict and information processing. *Law and Human Behavior, 24*, 259–270.

ForsterLee, L., Horowitz, I., & Bourgeois, M. (1994). Effects of note taking on verdicts and evidence processing in a civil trial. *Law and Human Behavior, 18*, 567–578.

ForsterLee, L., Kent, L., & Horowitz, I. (2005). The cognitive effects of jury aids on decision-making in complex civil litigation. *Applied Cognitive Psychology, 19*, 867–884.

Frye v. United States, 293 F. 1013 (D.C. Cir. 1923).

Gatowski, S. I., Dobbin, S. A., Richardson, J. T., Ginsburg, G. P., Merlino, M. L., & Dahir, V. (2001). Asking the gatekeepers: A national survey of judges on judging expert evidence in a post-*Daubert* World. *Law and Human Behavior, 25*, 433–458.

General Electric Co., et al., v. Joiner et ux., 522 U.S. 136 (1997).

Giresi, M., Brown, M., Chrzanowski, L., Henriquez, E., & Groscup, J. (2006, March). *The effects of instructions on jurors' evaluations of scientific validity.* Paper presented at the annual meeting of the American Psychology-Law Society, St. Petersburg, FL.

Gray, T., & Mill, D. (1990). Critical abilities, graduate education (biology versus English), and belief in unsubstantiated phenomena. *Canadian Journal of Behavioural Science, 22*, 162–172.

Greene, E., Downey, C., & Goodman-Delahunty, J. (1999). Juror decisions about damages in employment discrimination cases. *Behavioral Sciences and the Law, 17*, 107–121.

Groscup, J. L., Penrod, S. D., Studebaker, C. A., Huss, M. T., & O'Neil, K. M. (2002). The effects of *Daubert* on the admissibility of expert testimony in state and federal criminal cases. *Psychology, Public Policy, and Law, 8*, 339–372.

Hamill, R., Wilson, T. D., & Nisbett, R. E. (1980). Insensitivity to sample bias: Generalizing from atypical cases. *Journal of Personality and Social Psychology, 39*, 578–589.

Heuer, L., & Penrod, S. (1988). Increasing jurors' participation in trials: A field experiment with note taking and question asking. *Law and Human Behavior, 12*, 131–161.

Heuer, L., & Penrod, S. (1994). Juror note taking and question asking during trials: A national field experiment. *Law and Human Behavior, 18*, 121–150.

Horowitz, I. A., & Kirkpatrick, L. (1996). A concept in search of a definition: The effects of reasonable doubt instructions on certainty of guilt standards and jury verdicts. *Law and Human Behavior, 20*, 671–670.

Jepson, C., Krantz, D. H., & Nisbett, R. E. (1983). Inductive reasoning: Competence or skill? *Behavioral and Brain Sciences, 6*, 494–501.

Kagehiro, D. (1990). Defining the standard of proof in jury instructions. *Psychological Science, 1*, 194–200.

Kahneman, D., & Tversky, A. (1973). On the psychology of prediction. *Psychological Review, 80,* 237–251.

Kovera, M. B., & McAuliff, B. D. (2000). The effects of peer review and evidence quality on judge evaluations of psychological science: Are judges effective gatekeepers? *Journal of Applied Psychology, 85,* 574–586.

Kovera, M. B., & McAuliff, B. D. (2009). *Attorneys' evaluations of psychological science: Does evidence quality matter?* Manuscript submitted for publication.

Kovera, M. B., McAuliff, B. D., & Hebert, K. S. (1999). Reasoning about scientific evidence: Effects of juror gender and evidence quality on juror decisions in a hostile work environment case. *Journal of Applied Psychology, 84,* 362–375.

Krafka, C., Dunn, M. A., Johnson, M. T., Cecil, J. S., & Miletich, D. (2002). Judge and attorney experiences, practices, and concerns regarding expert testimony in federal civil trials. *Psychology, Public Policy, and Law, 8,* 309–332.

Krauss, D. A., & Lee, D. H. (2003). Deliberating on dangerousness and death: Jurors' ability to differentiate between expert actuarial and clinical predictions of dangerousness. *International Journal of Law and Psychiatry, 26,* 113–137.

Krauss, D. A., & Sales, B. D. (2001). The effects of clinical and scientific expert testimony on juror decision making in capital sentencing. *Psychology, Public Policy, and Law, 7,* 267–310.

Kumho Tire Co., Ltd., et al. v. Carmichael et al., 526 U.S. 137 (1999).

Lehman, D. R., Lempert, R. O., & Nisbett, R. E. (1988). The effects of graduate training on reasoning: Formal discipline and thinking about everyday life events. *American Psychologist, 43,* 431–443.

Lehman, D. R., & Nisbett, R. E. (1990). A longitudinal study of the effects of undergraduate training on reasoning. *Developmental Psychology, 26,* 952–960.

Lieberman, J., & Sales, B. (1997). What social science teaches us about the jury instruction process. *Psychology, Public Policy, and Law, 4,* 589–644.

McAuliff, B. D., & Kovera, M. B. (2008). Juror need for cognition and sensitivity to methodological flaws in expert evidence. *Journal of Applied Social Psychology, 38,* 385–408.

McAuliff, B. D., & Kovera, M. B. (in press). Can jurors recognize missing control groups, confounds, and experimenter bias in psychological science? *Law and Human Behavior.*

Merlino, M. L., Dillehey, R., Dahir, V., & Maxwell, D. (2003). Science education for judges: What, where, and by whom? *Judicature, 86,* 210–213.

Merlino, M. L., Murray, C. I., & Richardson, J. T. (2008). Judicial gatekeeping and the social construction of the admissibility of expert testimony. *Behavioral Sciences and the Law, 26,* 187–206.

Mill, D., Gray, T., & Mandel, D. R. (1994). Influence of research methods and statistics courses on everyday reasoning, critical abilities, and belief in unsubstantiated phenomena. *Canadian Journal of Behavioural Science, 26,* 246–258.

Monier, A., Tallon, J., Giresi-Ficarra, M., Jacobs, M., & Groscup, J. (2008, March). The effects of cross-examination on understanding scientific validity. In J. Groscup (Chair), *Scientific reliability in the courtroom: Jurors' assessments of scientific evidence and legal safeguards*. Symposium conducted at the annual meeting of the American Psychology-Law Society, Jacksonville, FL.

Ramirez, G., Zemba, D., & Geiselman, R. E. (1996). Judges' cautionary instructions on eyewitness testimony. *American Journal of Forensic Psychology, 14*, 31–66.

Robbenolt, J. K., Groscup, J. L., & Penrod, S. (2006). Evaluating and assisting jury competence in civil cases. In I. B. Weiner & A. K. Hess (Eds.), *Handbook of forensic psychology* (3rd ed., pp. 392–425). New York: Wiley.

Rosenhan, D., Eisner, S., & Robinson, R. (1994). Notetaking can aid juror recall. *Law and Human Behavior, 18*, 53–61.

Tallon, J., Brown, M., Giresi-Ficarra, M., & Groscup, J. (2008, March). Cross-examination effects on jurors' perceptions of expert reliability. In J. Groscup (Chair), *Scientific reliability in the courtroom: Jurors' assessments of scientific evidence and legal safeguards*. Symposium conducted at the annual meeting of the American Psychology-Law Society, Jacksonville, FL.

Tomkins, A. J., & Cecil, J. S. (1994). Treating social science like law: An assessment of Monahan and Walker's social authority proposal. *Shepard's Expert and Scientific Evidence Quarterly, 2*, 343.

United States v. Telfaire, 469 F.2d 552 (1972).

PART II
MEMORY AND SUGGESTIBILITY

The Scientific Status of "Repressed" and "Recovered" Memories of Sexual Abuse

Deborah Davis and Elizabeth F. Loftus

Over the last two decades, hundreds of alleged victims have filed civil actions reporting "recovery" of long-repressed memories of sexual abuse. Based on such claims, many individuals have also been prosecuted for "crimes" that allegedly occurred at the hands of parties ranging from Satan himself to strangers, neighbors, family, or other trusted authority figures, most recently including the host of accusations against Catholic priests (e.g., *Boston Globe* Investigative Staff, 2003). These claims have provoked a firestorm of controversy in the psychological, psychiatric, and legal communities—so vitriolic as to often be referred to as the "memory wars" (e.g., Ost, 2003)—over the question of whether such repression and later recovery of memories for traumatic events is likely, or even possible.

One side, consisting primarily of practicing therapists, has contended that there is overwhelming support for the claims that memory for traumatic events can be, and often is, repressed; and furthermore, that such repression is *more* likely for child sexual abuse relative to other traumatic events, for abuse committed by trusted adults, for more traumatic forms of abuse, and for abuse repeated over time (e.g., Brown, Scheflin, & Hammond, 1998; Dalenberg, 2006; Freyd, 1996). The other side, consisting primarily of academic clinical, cognitive, and social psychologists (e.g., Loftus, 1994; Loftus & Davis, 2006; McNally, 2003b, 2007; Ofshe & Watters, 1994; Piper,

55

-Lillevick, & Kritzer, 2008; Pope, Oliva, & Hudson, 2002), contends that there is virtually no credible support for the psychoanalytic notion of repression, and furthermore, that there is overwhelming support for the proposition that the occurrence of traumatic events, including sexual abuse, is remembered *better* than other events, particularly when violent, significant, and repeated over time.

This chapter focuses on a single area of this controversy: the status of empirical tests of the existence and determinants of repressed memories, specifically of child sexual abuse (CSA). Though we mention a related controversy about *false* memories for such traumatic events as sexual abuse, rape, or satanic rituals, we focus on the controversy concerning repression of CSA. We suggest other sources for information about false memories (Davis & Loftus, 2006; De Rivera, 2000; Erdelyi, 2006; Loftus & Davis, 2006; Mazzoni & Lynn, 2007; McNally, 2003b).

We first review crucial differences in perspective between the two sides of the repression controversy that contribute to divergent views of trauma, memory, and repression, and to disagreement about what constitutes adequate evidence for either side's claims: that is, either for the existence of repressed CSA or for implantation of false memories of CSA. Following this summary, we outline scientific criteria for valid demonstrations of the existence and determinants of repression of CSA and review existing research in light of these standards.

REPRESSED MEMORIES?: CORE ISSUES AND CONTROVERSIES

Are Memory Processes Fundamentally Different for Traumatic Events?

The fundamental disagreement concerns the nature of memory processes themselves. Although the memory literature addresses a variety of issues concerning trauma, emotion, and memory, two are especially central to the controversy: "Are traumatic events particularly likely to be 'repressed' versus more likely to be remembered?" and "Are memories of CSA more or less likely to be repressed than those of other kinds of trauma?"

Recovered memory advocates argue that CSA is particularly likely to be repressed, due to the traumatic nature of the event, the unacceptability of behaviors involved, betrayal by significant adults, and dissociative coping mechanisms adopted during the abuse episodes (see McNally, 2003a, for critical review of theories of dissociation and repression). In contrast, critics question the existence of repression as distinct from ordinary forgetting or temporary blocking of retrieval and their application to traumatic memory, arguing that memory for trauma is, if anything, strong and persistent. Schacter (2001) described persistence as one of the "seven sins" of memory, and he and others have presented substantial evidence that although memory for exact details of a traumatic event may fail, memory for the fact it has happened rarely does so.

Common Therapeutic Practices and the Elicitation of True and False Memories

The second basic controversy concerns the potential for clinical procedures to elicit true and false memories, and the related issue of how such procedures operate upon traumatic versus nontraumatic memories. Although the evidence that clinical procedures such as hypnosis, dream interpretation, guided imagery, direct suggestion, "survivor" group participation, and others can elicit false memories is overwhelming (for reviews, see Davis & Loftus, 2007a; Loftus & Davis, 2006), controversy surrounds the *nature* of memories that can be distorted or created. Can memories of truly traumatic events such as CSA be distorted or planted? Whereas therapists tend to believe that such horrific memories as CSA, particularly at the hands of family, or satanic ritual abuse, cannot be simply created from nothing, researchers believe that, given vulnerable individuals, strong social influence, and biasing memory procedures, these and other horrible "memories" (including *committing* horrific crimes; e.g., Kassin, 2007) can be created whole cloth (for reviews, see Davis & Loftus, 2007a; Loftus & Davis, 2006; Mazzoni & Lynn, 2007; McNally, 2003b). The rate at which false memories can be created may be smaller for implausible memories (see Henkel & Coffman, 2004), although plausibility itself is quite malleable.

The Rate of Recovered Accurate Memories versus False Memories of Abuse

The controversy is not just one of the reality of forgetting or of falsely remembering abuse, but also one of the likelihood of each. Although some might deny the existence of any instances of accurate "recovered" memories or of totally fabricated memories, for most, the underlying issue is one of frequency. Though the specific mechanism of repression is disputed, neither the existence of rediscovered memories of abuse nor the ability of therapeutic practices to induce false memories of abuse is truly in question. Both occur at some nonzero rate. Instead, the *base rate* at which each occurs is of primary importance. And, once again, differences in views of these base rates fuel the controversy. If we assume that false as well as true memories of abuse may be elicited via therapeutic practices, the rate of true versus false positives is of considerable importance for patients themselves and for the legal system that must judge their cases. This ratio depends on several unknowns: the base rate of true cases of unremembered abuse among those subjected to the procedures, as well as the base rate with which the procedures elicit both true and false abuse memories. (Note that false memories may be elicited among those who have been abused as well as those never abused, as, e.g., when true victims are led to confabulate nonexistent or exaggerated episodes.) Many practicing clinicians assume large rates of repressed abuse and low-to-zero rates at which false memories of abuse can be planted, and therefore view the likely accuracy of memories elicited in therapy as high. In contrast, many researchers view the base rate of forgetting of abuse (via any mechanism) as low. While they may accept the idea that people can fail to think about upsetting experiences for long periods and then be reminded of them later, they view this as due to ordinary forgetting and remembering. When they see horrific memories that are too extreme to be explained by ordinary forgetting and remembering produced in therapy, they tend to suspect these are false memories.

Therapeutic Goals versus Scientific Methodology

The root of the controversy is perhaps the fundamental differences in training, methods, and modes of hypothesis testing and understanding inherent to scientists (both social/cognitive and clinical) versus many practicing therapists. These differences underlie each side's view of how memory works as well as what constitutes adequate evidence for various hypotheses. Both practitioners and scientists are subject to bias and may have axes to grind. However, scientists have an advantage in one crucial respect: They have the (partial) safeguards of scientific methodology on their side to help prevent them from fooling themselves. The inferential task of the practitioner is typically more subjective and often more subject to error.

Scientists are trained to *objectively* test hypotheses and theories using highly controlled scientific methods, and to scrupulously avoid practices that might bias the responses of research participants. They are trained to use written or oral questions and unbiased valid assessment procedures that are not suggestive or leading, and experiments themselves are carefully structured to avoid "experimenter expectancy effects" or "demand characteristics" that would suggest to participants what responses might be expected of them. Finally, they are trained to avoid suggestion or selective reinforcement of participant responses. Given this core concern with objectivity, it is not surprising that scientists look with horror upon some clinical assessment practices and memory "recovery" procedures and their potential to cause biased reports, memory distortion, and confabulation. In turn, when memories elicited through such practices are litigated in court, where authenticity is paramount, scientists are quite naturally suspicious of their validity. Sometimes many potentially biasing procedures are used repeatedly with a patient, stretching over months or years, raising concerns that her "memory reports" simply cannot be regarded as reliable. As such, it is risky to use them as the sole evidence to sentence defendants to years in prison or to subject individuals to substantial financial damages.

Therapists, in contrast, may or may not be trained scientists. Although some have been trained in scientifically oriented clinical programs, many have not. Until widespread criticism erupted over the potential for therapists to elicit false reports of abuse, therapists were typically neither trained extensively regarding, nor made generally aware of, the biasing influence of many clinical procedures. Instead, training focused on assessing and helping the patient. Given the pervasive influence of Freudian concepts such as repression, clinical understanding of the underpinnings of psychopathology and distress prominently included issues of repressed or unacknowledged material. So, quite naturally, clinical procedures developed to try to unearth the troublesome material. As such, they often included subjective presumptions regarding what these issues might be, subjective assessments of clients and their symptoms, and aggressive, suggestive methods to lead the patient to address the presumed underlying issues.

These subjective interpretive processes brought to bear on individual patients lead some therapists to think in terms of anecdotes and case histories. Furthermore, whereas scientists specify and carefully control experimenter behavior, some practicing therapists do not feel the need to control potentially biasing responses, nor are they particularly aware of them when they occur. Anecdotes may seem compelling to therapists, while causing skepticism for scientists. When cases of recovered memories of abuse are litigated, many clinicians see the truth of the memory in the context of the entire clinical picture and the apparent spontaneity and sincerity of the reports, whereas many scientists see it in terms of myriad sources of potential distortion and human inability to reliably distinguish truthful reports from honest mistakes or deliberate fabrications. Although some scientists believe in repression and recovered memories, and others doubt them, regardless of side, they approach the dispute through scientific research.

The Requirements for Compelling Evidence

A final difference concerns how to assess crucial issues. Constrained by ethics, scientists cannot conduct controlled laboratory studies of memory for trauma comparable in either severity or frequency to that presumed to characterize the experience of CSA. Since recovered memory advocates believe that memory for (especially sexual) trauma works differently than memory for other events and/or that false memories for such traumata cannot be fabricated easily (or at all), they remain unconvinced by laboratory demonstrations of false memories. Given the vivid, compelling experiences of therapists with their patients, laboratory demonstrations planting more pallid false memories are singularly unconvincing. In turn, researchers remain unconvinced by clinical anecdotes and other evidence offered for widespread repression and recovery of memories of CSA. Since most anecdotal data lack sufficient methodological rigor, alternative explanations cannot be ruled out, and hence scientists do not view them as conclusive evidence. Interestingly, many scientists also remain unconvinced by lab research demonstrating various mechanisms of temporary blocking and recovery of mundane material as analogs to "repression" of traumatic material. Ironically, both sides sometimes rely on studies of real-life instances of recovered or false memories and *abductive inference* (an inference to the best explanation).

Commenting on *false* memories, for example, McNally (2003a) notes: "The claim that some people develop false memories of trauma is a warranted *abductive inference* derived from multiple, converging nonexperimental sources of evidence. An abductive inference ... is a form of reasoning whereby one accepts a hypothesis as (likely to be) true because it provides a better explanation for the phenomena of interest than any rival hypothesis" (p. 231). Although McNally refers to the scientific application of such inferences, practicing therapists tend to view their multiple, converging, nonexperimental sources of evidence regarding specific clients as proof of their diagnoses (for a critical review of such therapeutic constructions, see Brenneis, 1999). Both sides must rely on such evidence for interpretation of the real-life experiences they each hope to document—of recovered true memories *and* of false memories and their retraction.

SCIENTIFIC TESTS OF THE REPRESSION
AND FALSE MEMORY HYPOTHESES

In the following sections we review scientific studies attempting to demonstrate the existence and determinants of repression and the many methodological problems inherent to studies of these issues. Since many participants in this controversy are unreceptive to laboratory studies involving memories for relatively mundane events, we restrict our review specifically to the issue of memory for CSA and to studies designed to assess repression in real-life alleged victims.

Repression for CSA been studied in three ways: (1) individual or collections of anecdotes; (2) "subjective forgetting" studies employing either (a) prospective or (b) retrospective designs; and (3) testing memory for abuse among "documented" victims.

Method 1: "Anecdata"

It is not uncommon for therapists writing about repressed memories of CSA to provide anecdotes of such cases. Sometimes they present "composites" that are intended to be close to actual cases (e.g., Herman & Schatzow, 1987), and some researchers published compilations of alleged documented cases of repressed and/or recovered memories (e.g., Schooler, Bendiksen, & Ambadar, 1997) or of false CSA memories developed in therapy (e.g., De Rivera, 2000). But what should we make of anecdata? Granted, a fully verified single instance of a phenomenon provides support for its existence, but verification of original abuse and of repression is exceptionally challenging. Many accounts provide no verification at all, and those offering various forms of verification suffer a variety of problems, as we describe below. The problems with even apparently verified accounts were illustrated in a case thoroughly investigated and analyzed by Loftus and Guyer (2000a, 2000b). Lacking independent and critical evaluation of each anecdote, it is risky to accept them as valid.

Method 2: "Subjective Forgetting"

Attempts to establish failure to remember CSA for some period of time have predominately used the *subjective forgetting* method—sometimes called the *"Do-You-Remember-Whether-You-Forgot?"* strategy (e.g., Pope et al., 2002). For example, respondents in *retrospective studies* are first asked whether they have ever been abused and then queried about any periods of forgetting. Fairly large proportions of alleged (but typically unverified) victims indicate that they experienced periods of forgetting for the events, ranging from 31 to 77% in clinical samples and from 13 to 42% in nonclinical samples (see Ghetti et al., 2006).

One widely cited study (Williams, 1995) employed a *prospective* subjective forgetting design in which children medically assessed for abuse were asked years later whether they had forgotten the abuse for some period of time. Only 16% reported "forgetting" (a number substantially lower than those obtained in other subjective forgetting studies (see Ghetti et al.'s, 2006, reported rate of 15%; for review, see Epstein & Bottoms, 1998; McNally, 2003b; Pope et al., 2002). These findings raise questions regarding the validity of larger numbers reported in designs involving unverified abuse. Moreover, the meaning of having "forgotten" is typically not clear in these studies and may not reflect anything like a repression process.

Method 3: Testing "Documented" Victims

The final method involves identifying a set of "documented" victims and interviewing them years later to determine whether they remember the abuse (e.g., Goodman et al., 2003; Widom & Morris, 1997; Williams, 1994). Although some presumably verified victims fail to report CSA (e.g., 8% by the final phase of the Goodman et al., 2003, study), such studies suffer from the obvious problem of identifying genuine failures of memory versus unwillingness to report.

Unfortunately, these three methods—collections of anecdata and prospective and retrospective forgetting designs—are essentially all that are available to researchers attempting to examine repression of actual CSA. However, as we see in the next sections, these methods are wholly inadequate to test the repression hypothesis.

GAPS IN OUR PRESENT SCIENTIFIC KNOWLEDGE ON REPRESSION: ON THE UNTESTABILITY OF RELEVANT HYPOTHESES

All parties to the recovered memory debate agree that forgetting can occur through a variety of normal mechanisms, and that previously unrecalled material can later be recalled. Disagreement surrounds (1) the likelihood and determinants of forgetting CSA specifically and (2) whether the mechanisms are dissociative—such as "repression," "dissociative amnesia," or "traumatic amnesia" (e.g., Brown et al., 1998)—as opposed to normal mechanisms of forgetting.

The repression hypothesis requires that the material be rendered inaccessible through involuntary, automatic dissociative mechanisms that make it highly resistant or impervious to retrieval through normal mechanisms. Inaccessibility is also crucial to legal claims entailing alleged repressed memories, since such claims would otherwise be precluded by statutes of limitation that would have expired had the abuse been known and remained voluntarily unreported. Unfortunately, the central issue of inaccessibility, or "repression," is hard to test by means of currently available scientific methods. Many difficult, and sometimes impossible, criteria must be achieved to provide a valid assessment of inaccessibility, some or all of which have been lacking in all attempts to test the repression hypothesis with real-life alleged victims of CSA (for more extensive discussion of these issues, see Clancy & McNally, 2005–2006; Davis & Loftus, 2007; Loftus & Davis, 2006; McNally, 2003a, 2003b; Piper et al., 2008; Pope et al., 2002).

Fundamental gaps in our knowledge on this controversy reflect problems with testing the repression hypothesis. Specifically, it is difficult to verify (1) that the specific "traumatic" abuse, fitting theoretical requirements for triggering repression, did occur; (2) that the person experienced a period of forgetting; and (3) that CSA memories were inaccessible via normal mechanisms during the period of forgetting (see Brenneis, 2000; Davis & Loftus, 2007b; Kihlstrom, 1998, 2005; Loftus & Davis, 2006; McNally, 2003b; Pope et al., 2002).

Gap 1: Did "Traumatic" CSA Corresponding to the Reported "Memory" Actually Occur?

Since it is possible to develop false memories of CSA, or to lie, verification of the CSA is necessary to clearly establish instances of repression. However, it is not sufficient to show that some kind of CSA occurred. Theoretically, repression is only triggered under certain conditions, rendering instances of verified CSA not fitting these theoretical requirements irrelevant for tests of the repression hypothesis. Theoretically the CSA must be "traumatic" in order to trigger repression. Since abuse is not consistently "traumatic" at the time it occurs, nor is it always understood as abuse (e.g., Clancy & McNally, 2005–2006; Finkelhor, 1986; Russell, 1986), one must document that the CSA in question was sufficiently "traumatic" that it would not have been forgotten due to lack of sufficient importance, and that it possessed characteristics theoretically sufficient to induce "repression" or other "dissociative" reactions (e.g., McNally, 2003b, 2005). Though theorists differ regarding what constitutes trauma (e.g., life-threatening, terrifying, and overwhelming versus betrayal by a significant attachment figure) (cf. McNally, 2004, 2007; Freyd, 1996, 2001), lacking qualifying trauma, normal mechanisms of forgetting would pose more likely explanations for forgetting (see McNally, 2004, 2007, regarding this issue).

Furthermore, the abuse must have been "traumatic" *at the time it occurred.* "Trauma" may be delayed as, for example, when (or if) the victim is reminded of long past abuse in a culture that tells them that abuse is supposed to be traumatic (for further discussion of the importance of level of subjective trauma at the time of the incident[s], see Clancy & McNally, 2005–2006; McNally, 2004, 2007). If, as reported in several studies, most victims do not find their abuse traumatic at the time it occurred, most fail to meet even the first requirement to demonstrate repression.

Finally, since false memories of abuse may be reported by those who actually did experience some form of abuse, the specific type and episodes of reported abuse must be verified. But, as we elaborate below, problems exist with all levels of necessary verification.

On rare occasions, abuse can be objectively verified, as when photographs or videos are taken. But much CSA leaves no objective evidence, and since semen, injuries, and other evidence are lost over time, many claims cannot be subject to objective proof—rendering problems of conclusive verification essentially insurmountable. Although many studies attempted no verification at all, those that did are inconclusive. Abuse may be reported as "verified" by the patient, the therapist, or others—but with no indication of criteria for "verification." Some report verification by police, therapists, friends or family, or others who presumably know the truth; and some report one person's abuse as validated by others reporting similar abuse (e.g., as offered in support of allegations against some Catholic priests). One study even classified members of incest survivor groups who had never yet remembered any CSA as experiencing periods of amnesia (Herman & Schatzow, 1987).

Some studies use outcomes of legal proceedings as the criteria of verification. These, of course, are subject to a host of confounding influences, including desire to settle even an invalid claim to avoid publicity or risk of conviction. And, particularly for cases involving long-delayed "recovered" memories, jury verdicts can simply reflect lay conclusions regarding the reality of repression (see Read, Connolly, & Welsh, 2006). Even abuse "documented" at or near the time it allegedly occurred cannot always be regarded as proven, since "documentation" can be subject to error (e.g., the outcome of legal proceedings, examinations by medical professionals, recorded reports to authorities, parents, and others). Accurate records are crucial for studies attempting to assess *whether* the person remembers abuse, as well as *accuracy in memory* for details.

Use of unrepresentative samples can exacerbate these problems, as when samples consist of patients in recovered memory or abuse-related therapy or located through a national network of therapists specializing in treatment of abuse survivors (Briere & Conte, 1993). Many such patients have been subjected to procedures with potential to create false memories, and they report recovering memories during such procedures (e.g., under hypnosis; Roe & Schwartz, 1996), only to have their memories "verified" by the very therapist who performed the procedure.

In light of the problems with verification, to assess the rate of "verified" instances of traumatic CSA, data reports must include only, or separately report, instances meeting the necessary criteria for verification. However, it is common to completely fail to assess or report on degree or type of trauma or verification, or to fail to report differentially on those who meet relevant criteria. More seriously, verification may not be reported separately for those with continuous versus discontinuous (the relevant group) memories. And, rarest of all are attempts to verify that the nature of recalled abuse corresponds to details of any verified abuse.

Tests of the mechanism of repression further require comparisons between rates of forgetting for traumatic events such as CSA and otherwise comparable nontraumatic events (see McNally, 2003b). The mere existence of instances of forgetting of CSA do not support an interpretation in terms of repression if the rate at which forgetting occurs for CSA and other traumata are not greater than those for other events. Although some have documented periods of partial or complete amnesia for nontraumatic but compelling childhood events that had actually occurred (e.g., high school graduation or summer camp; Read & Lindsay, 2000), we can locate no studies that compared such rates for traumatic and nontraumatic events. It should also be noted that such comparisons, should they be carried out, are inherently difficult to interpret due to the challenges of equating other aspects of the events likely to affect the likelihood of long-term memory.

Notwithstanding long-noted problems with the "Do you remember whether you forgot?" method of assessing "repression" and with verification, such studies continue to be published. One study purports to report rates of alleged "verified" recovered memories (Geraerts et al., 2007). Apparently supporting the claims of critics of recovered memory therapy, the basic finding was that continuous memories and discontinuous memories recalled outside of therapy were more likely to be corroborated than discontinuous memories recovered in therapy (37% vs. 0%). But the nature of the corroboration is never made very clear. Moreover, there was no apparent attempt to assess the correspondence of detail between the recovered memory and the verified abuse. Even more problematic, in many cases, questionable criteria such as another individual who claimed abuse by the same perpetrator was called verification. To be useful, it is essential that verification be truly independent. A separate issue about these data concerns earlier attempts to corroborate recovered memories by members of the same research group. In a prior study (Geraerts, Merckelbach, Jelicic, Smeets, & van Heerden, 2006), only a single subject could give corroborative evidence, and this group presumably contained many individuals who had recovered memory out of therapy. It is difficult to reconcile the 2006 failure to corroborate with the 2007 report. Thus, even the latest attempts to reported "verified" CSA suffer from the essential problems of all studies in this class, again raising more questions than they answer.[1]

Gap 2: Did the Person Forget CSA for Some Period?

The repression hypothesis requires that we establish two facts: (1) that the person *did not remember* for some period of time, and (2) that the person *could not remember* through normal retrieval processes. Both burdens of proof face overwhelming obstacles in principle. And, in practice, measures of forgetting are often imprecise, without differentiation between those reporting complete amnesia versus forgetting of specific details or specific episodes; and mechanisms of forgetting and retrieval are often poorly assessed and poorly differentiated in measurement and analyses, causing difficulties in interpretation of findings.

Establishing Failure to Remember

Whether prospective or retrospective, most studies have relied on the subjective forgetting method to establish a period of forgetting. Although such studies predominantly lack verification of the CSA, there have essentially been no attempts to verify the alleged periods of forgetting. It may be tempting to assume that participants can accurately report on whether they remembered or not, consistent with the "Do you remember whether you forgot?" label for such experiments (Pope et al., 2002). However, several studies have shown that some who reported periods of forgetting had actually recalled and talked about the CSA in the alleged repression interval—a phenomenon dubbed the "forgot-it-all-along" effect (Geraerts, Raymaekers, & Merckelbach, 2008; Schooler et al., 1997).

In fact, a growing literature on "meta-cognitive" processes has shown that subjective forgetting can be influenced by such factors as beliefs about how memory works, what kinds of things are likely to be forgotten, and how one can tell whether something has been forgotten, among others (e.g., Winkielman, Schwarz, & Belli, 1998). Read and Lindsay (2000), for example, showed that self-reported forgetting can be enhanced by efforts to retrieve details of an event, whereas actual accuracy was enhanced by such efforts, suggesting that needing to "try" to remember leads to the inference that one is not remembering completely or accurately.

A further problem with reports of subjective forgetting involves likely dissociation of measures of subjective and actual forgetting. Insofar as subjective forgetting reflects actual forgetting, *factors that affect subjective forgetting should affect actual forgetting in the same way.* However, the fact that measures of actual forgetting will be affected by willingness to disclose abuse, whereas measures of subjective forgetting must involve individuals who have already disclosed abuse, is illustrative of the many reasons to expect dissociation of the two.

Controversy has also surrounded issues of specific questions used to assess forgetting, participants' interpretation of the specific questions, and the meaning of their responses. If participants agree that there were times when they "forgot" or "didn't remember" CSA, they could be referring to time periods too short to reasonably suggest repression or to normal mechanisms of forgetting (e.g., simple failure to think about it), voluntary avoidance, and possibilities other than an inability to remember. Since one will typically not "try" to remember something of which one has no awareness, answers are unlikely to reflect *inability* to remember. And, in fact, when asked to report on reasons for periods of forgetting, most endorse normal mechanisms such as failure to rehearse, voluntary suppression, passage of time, lack of importance, and so on, suggesting that the material was not truly inaccessible or "repressed" (e.g., Ghetti et al., 2006).

As noted earlier, in some studies "documented" victims of abuse are asked years later about whether they had ever been abused. But failure to report CSA does not equal failure to remember, and several studies have shown that victims who were originally classified as having forgotten later admitted to remembering all along (e.g., Bonnano et al., 2002; Femina, Yeager, & Lewis, 1990; Melchert & Parker, 1997).

Establishing the Mechanism of Failure

Whereas failure to remember CSA is essentially impossible to verify, verification of the *mechanism* of failure is even more difficult. In addition to biological causes such as injury, infantile amnesia, drug use, or other acute impairment during the original incidents and secondary gain motives, normal mechanisms of forgetting must be ruled out. Given that subjective forgetting itself is subject to error and metacognitive influences, how much more subject to error is lay understanding of *why* we forget? But it is precisely such subjective measures of mechanisms of forgetting that have characterized efforts to assess whether memory for CSA was truly inaccessible, and if so, why? Such "subjective mechanism" studies have generally found no support for "repression" as a common mechanism of forgetting. Indeed, participants overwhelmingly endorse normal mechanisms such as voluntary suppression, lack of rehearsal, young age at the time of the incidents, lack of importance, and so on (see Epstein & Bottoms, 2002; Ghetti et al., 2006; Melchert, 1996; Melchert & Parker, 1997).

Several studies have assessed the circumstances under which memories of CSA were reportedly "recovered." Presumably, if retrieval was triggered through such normal mechanisms as everyday reminders, the material was not repressed, whereas repressed memories would be retrieved more slowly and effortfully. Such studies have revealed almost exclusively normal triggers of recall (e.g., Brennies, 2000; Clancy & McNally, 2005–2006; Elliott, 1997; Feldman-Summers & Pope, 1994; Melchert, 1999). Some repression theorists, however, argue that retrieval via normal associative cues is consistent with the theory of repression (e.g., Dalenberg, 2006).

Gap 3: Testing the Determinants of Forgetting

In addition to the very existence of repression, central to the "memory wars" have been the issues of (1) whether greater trauma is associated with enhanced versus impaired memory; and (2) if repression does occur, what kinds of CSA are relatively "traumatic" and more likely to trigger repression. These issues are especially important for litigation involving alleged repression. For example, to make credible the claim that a now 40-year-old woman would have forgotten 10 years of repeated violent abuse by her father until recently, the repressed memory theorist must explain how a person could repeatedly experience violent abuse as an almost daily event and fail to remember it. In this context, the expert will likely present basic theories of trauma and repression and the very counterintuitive predictions of "betrayal trauma theory" (Freyd, 1996), which contends that abuse perpetrated by the closest family members is *less* likely to be remembered, particularly when horrible and repeated. The academic memory expert, in contrast, might present theory suggesting the polar opposite relationship of these variables to memory. Unfortunately, given that the existence of repression is virtually untestable, determinants of repression face yet more formidable obstacles (see Davis & Loftus, 2007b, for a review).

First, because disagreement surrounds the issue of CSA characteristics associated with greater trauma, assessment of trauma is crucial. Most studies have employed "objective" indices of trauma—such as frequency, severity (in terms of sexual acts), violence, or the relationship between perpetrator and victim. However, there are a number of reasons to expect dissociation between objective and subjective indices, with the subjective experience more relevant as a trigger of repression. Indirect evidence of dissociation comes from studies attempting to relate objective characteristics of abuse to emotional reactions and clinical symptoms, which have yielded inconsistent results (e.g., Kendall-Tacket, 2003; Laumann, Gagnon, Michael, & Michaels, 1994; Rind, Tromovitch, & Bauserman, 1998). What some consider the best index of trauma (subjective trauma at the time of the incident; e.g., Clancy & McNally, 2005–2006) is difficult to achieve at all, and impossible in retrospective designs, leaving post-hoc reports as the only alternative, with great potential for distortion through time and both internal and external suggestive influences.

Second, tests of the determinants of "repression" must clearly distinguish between memory for the *occurrence of CSA* versus memory for the *details of CSA*. Whereas repression theorists predict complete amnesia for CSA, memory researchers predict enhanced memory for the fact of CSA (the *gist* of the event), but potentially impaired memory for specific details, specific episodes (among many), timing, and other peripheral aspects of the event(s). However, attempts to test the determinants of repression have often been rendered ambiguous by failure to measure and report on this distinction between gist and detail, and impaired memory for detail or specific incidents has been inappropriately reported as support for repression.

Third, tests of determinants of repression must account for confounds known to influence normal memory processes, such as age at CSA (the event should be beyond the 3- to 4-year period of infantile amnesia), retention interval, factors affecting rehearsal, exposure to biasing rehearsals, exposure to reminders (e.g., legal proceedings and associated interviews and assessments), or clinical status (which predicts degree and direction of memory distortion [e.g., Havery & Bryant, 2000; Schwarz, Kowalski, & McNally, 1993]). Similar factors may confound subjective assessments of trauma, such as psychotherapy, exposure to literature characterizing CSA as traumatic, or multiple interviews about the incident.

Finally, factors theoretically associated with degree of trauma may be confounded with those affecting willingness to disclose. Incest, for example, is, according to some, theoretically more likely to trigger repression, but more shameful and difficult to disclose than CSA by a stranger. This poses serious difficulty for tests of "betrayal trauma theory" (Freyd, 1996, 2001), since the same forces encouraging repression could suppress reporting (e.g., feared effects on family).

While such confounds can render positive findings suspect, they can also obscure real differences as a function of trauma. This would tend to occur when two confounded variables affect memory and reporting in opposite directions. For example, studies of the effects of relationship to the perpetrator have failed to predict either disclosure (Goodman et al., 2003), periods of subjective forgetting (e.g., Ghetti et al., 2006), or memory accuracy (Alexander et al., 2005). This does not necessarily disconfirm the hypothesis, since apparent confirmation or apparent disconfirmation of hypotheses relating trauma and memory cannot be confidently interpreted without attention to factors that could enhance or suppress observed relationships.

WIDESPREAD MYTHS AND MISCONCEPTIONS ABOUT MEMORY AND REPRESSION

Unfortunately, the true scientific status of repression stands in stark contrast to widespread unquestioned acceptance among laypersons and large segments of the therapeutic and legal communities. Witness rampant depictions of repression, dissociative identity disorder, and memory recovery through hypnosis in film and literature, as well as everyday colloquialisms such as "I must have *repressed* it!" This contrast between scientific reality and common cultural "truisms" extends to the entire range of relevant concepts and practices; that is, uncritical acceptance of repression and its relationship to trauma stands in contrast to widespread ignorance of the malleability of memory and the potential for powerful suggestive influences and common techniques such as hypnosis to create false memories.

Overestimating Memory

In addition to acceptance of the idea of repression, the accuracy of memories *one does have* is widely overestimated by the general public. Whereas people readily understand that they can fail to remember things at all, or remember them somewhat inaccurately, the notion that people can be led to remember events that never happened at all, particularly those such as repeated traumatic abuse, is counterintuitive. Confidently reported memories are assumed to be true—as so clearly indicated in the eyewitness literature (e.g., Wells, Memon, & Penrod, 2006).

Failure to Appreciate Subtle Distorting Influences on Memory

Even more troublesome is the necessity to appreciate not only blatant coercive influences on memory, such as clear suggestions that one was abused or active explicit attempts to convince a person that abuse occurred, but also very subtle influences such as selective reinforcement by a therapist, the patient's own need to understand his or her problems, and how imagination can be confused with reality.

The Very Nature of "Memory"

Perhaps most fundamentally we must ask, "What is memory?" How does "memory" differ, if at all, from a "memory report"? Whereas lay notions of memory often involve the idea that it is essentially a recording—albeit sometimes unclear or incomplete—memory scientists view memory as much more complicated, consisting of verbatim images of what occurred, "gist" representations, supportive beliefs about what happened, and criteria for judging what is a memory versus something else (e.g., Brainerd & Reyna, 2005). Thus, memory reports can often reflect beliefs about what happened more than images or mental recordings commonly viewed as memory. And people can be influenced to apply very different criteria to decide what is or is not a memory—as when a patient becomes convinced that body sensations are "memories" of abuse.

These core issues—(1) the scientific status of repression, (2) the very nature of memory and how it works, and (3) blatant and subtle influences that can distort memory—are widely misunderstood in lay and therapeutic communities, and even among some scientists. These areas of ignorance or misunderstanding provide the context in which jurors, judges, attorneys, and their clients attempt to understand an individual claim of repressed and recovered memory.

STANDARDS OF LEGAL ADMISSIBILITY

The preceding discussion has made clear that for real-life traumatic events, including CSA, neither the existence of repression nor the conditions under which it is likely to occur are readily scientifically testable. Despite these significant barriers, there have been a number of published attempts to identify cases of repressed and recovered memories of CSA—all subject to one or more of the previously identified problems (for extensive summaries and critique of existing studies, see McNally, 2003b; Pope et al., 2002). Peer-reviewed publications attempting to establish repression—whether retrospective surveys, prospective studies, or anecdotes—in fact simply do not meet the scientific criteria necessary to establish repression, and therefore do not reflect scientific validity. Furthermore, the hotly contested nature of this issue, as reflected in the commonly applied descriptor "memory wars," reflects widespread disagreement concerning the existence and determinants of repression.

Finally, no sensible error rates can be established. Suppose one believed that memories of CSA can be both repressed and recovered *and* that false memories of CSA can be developed via various clinical procedures or other influences. How could we establish the rate of error for assessment of each alternative? This, too, is an impossible task, since no relevant base rates are known. We don't know the rates of repression of CSA or of recovery of true memories versus development of false memories among those subject to individual procedures or influences, much less among those subject to particular combinations of multiple influences. Therefore, no basis exists for evaluation of the likely validity of any given specific "recovered" memory. It would appear, then, that testimony offered in support of "repression" and theories of causes of repression would fail to meet the standards required in *Daubert, Kumho, Joiner,* or *Frye.*

Sometimes a therapist's testimony, consisting of alleged encounters with patients experiencing repression or apparent recovery of valid previously repressed memories, is considered to reflect experience-based expertise. Indeed, the conflict between rigorous scientific standards of proof and compelling personal experiences with subjectively convincing instances of "repression" is largely the heart of the heated controversy. Therapists who have experienced subjectively convincing instances of "repression" and "recovery" of memories of CSA in patients argue that scientific standards of proof are too rigorous and restrictive in light of such apparently clear real-life instances of repression (e.g., Dalenberg, 2006). In contrast, the more rigorous scientists are wary of biasing procedures and biases in judgment that can lead false memory reports to appear authentic (e.g., Davis & Loftus, 2007b; Faigman, Kaye, Saks, Sanders, & Cheng, 2007; McNally, 2003b, 2007; Pope et al., 2002). Notwithstanding such scientific concerns, experience-based testimony on recovered memories is sometimes admitted in the absence of scientific foundation (see, e.g., *Logerquist v. McVey,* 2000). Indeed, psychological experience-based testimony is sometimes admitted in preference to scientific testimony (see Faigman & Monahan's, Chapter 1, this volume, discussion of this situation; see Piper et al., 2008, for a recent review of legal rulings regarding expert testimony on repressed memories of CSA). We believe that the potential to mislead makes the practice of admitting therapists' intuitions based on "patients they have seen" a risky one.

Though not the focus of this chapter, it should be noted that while testimony on the malleability of memory and the potential for creation of false memories enjoys strong scientific support and easily meets the standards of admissibility regarding science and acceptance, one could argue that it should be excluded under the issue of relevancy. That is, since ethical constraints prohibit research demonstrating implantation of false memories for traumatic events such as CSA, existing memory research can be criticized as lacking demonstrated applicability to real-life traumatic events. Furthermore, case studies of apparently false "recovered" memories of actual CSA can be criticized on issues of verification in the same way as case studies of apparently true "recovered" memories (though case studies of false memories and experiences of "retractors" of recovered memories might be admitted under experienced-based expertise).

In sum, the degree to which a particular area of testimony may be viewed as scientifically supported is context dependent. That is, depending on the standards of admissibility in a specific jurisdiction and/or the particular emphasis of the trial judge on individual criteria, testimony from either side of the repressed memory controversy is sometimes deemed admissible and sometimes not. When emphasizing standards of scientific adequacy, testimony on development of false memories would be judged adequately supported and testimony on repression unsupported. In jurisdictions that emphasize relevance or experience-based expertise, testimony supporting repression would likely be judged adequate and testimony on false memories inadequate—a position with which we, of course, heartily disagree!

COMMUNICATING CONSENSUS AND CONTROVERSIES: TO WHAT CAN WE SENSIBLY TESTIFY IN COURT?

Our preceding discussion has made clear that the hypothesis of repression itself and the nature of conditions under which it is most likely to occur (if at all) lacks credible scientific evidence. Furthermore, though there is overwhelming evidence that memory is malleable and that false memories for a variety of events can be created using common clinical procedures, there are no scientific studies documenting the ability of such procedures to specifically implant memories of CSA (although other traumas have been planted). Finally, given the twin facts that (1) there is little evidence for repression and (2) studies attempting to plant memories of CSA cannot be ethically conducted, it is also impossible to establish the base rates of repression of CSA, or rates of recovery of true and false memories of CSA with or without use of various clinical procedures. How, then, can we inform judgment of a particular claim of recovered memory?

It is our position that the notion of "repression" as distinct from ordinary mechanisms of forgetting has not been established. It is the burden of those presenting criminal or civil claims of repressed, then recovered, memories of abuse to prove them. Hence, the memory expert can present two forms of testimony. The first involves showing that this burden of proof cannot be met by explicating the problems with testing the repression hypothesis, as we have above, and contrasting this with evidence that memory for trauma is particularly strong and persistent. This is most effective when combined with explication of why a person might develop these false beliefs and descriptions of laboratory research documenting development of false memories through clinical procedures such as hypnosis, guided imagery, suggestion, and so on. One might also include evidence that false memories can be experienced with as much detail and emotion as true ones. The bottom line message: Just because a report is confidently offered, just because it is detailed, and just because it is expressed with emotion does not mean the event actually happened.

CONCLUSIONS

Consensus on the issues of whether repression exists and the possibility of planting false memories of traumatic events such as CSA is unlikely to emerge in the foreseeable future. Given strong differences in perspective and views of acceptable evidence between sides, and absent definitive tests of relevant hypotheses, no empirical basis for consensus is immediately possible. Lacking potential for consensus, and given the problems with both scientific tests of repression and the validity of experience-based judgments, the legal system might more profitably focus on the reasoning underlying statutes of limitations for reporting abuse. A number of known factors suppress and delay reporting during childhood. Greater focus on and understanding of these constraints on timely reporting of abuse might suggest longer limits on reporting.

NOTE

1. Fortunately, some courts have addressed the verification requirement more thoroughly than most scientific attempts to test the repression hypothesis. For example, the Supreme Court of South Carolina ruled, in recognition of the "horrific possibility of false accusations," that a plaintiff must present independently verifiable evidence that the abuse did occur: "the element of 'objective verifiability' may be satisfied by corroborating evidence such as (a) an admission by the abuser; (b) a criminal conviction; (c) documented medical history of childhood sexual abuse; (d) contemporaneous records or written statements of the abuser, such as diaries and letters; (e) photographs or recordings of the abuse; (f) an objective eyewitness's account; (g) evidence the abuser had sexually abused others; or (h) proof of a chain facts and circumstances having sufficient probative force to produce a reasonable conclusion that sexual abuse occurred" (*Moriarty v. Garden Sanctuary Church of God*, 341, S. C. 320, 534 S. E.2nd 672 [2000]). Though some of the more subjective categories of evidence are subject to the criticisms noted herein, such requirements of proof are a welcome step toward protection against false recovered memories of abuse.

REFERENCES

Alexander, K. W., Quas, J. A., Goodman, G. S., Ghetti, S., Edelstein, R. S., Redlich, A. D., et al. (2005). Traumatic impact predicts long-term memory for documented child sexual abuse. *Psychological Science, 16*, 33–40.

Bonanno, G. A., Keltner, D., Noll, J. G., Putnam, F. W., Trickett, P., LeJeune, J., et al. (2002). When the face reveals what words do not: Facial expressions of emotion, smiling, and the willingness to disclose childhood sexual abuse. *Journal of Personality and Social Psychology, 83*, 94–110.

Boston Globe Investigative Staff. (2003). *Betrayal: The crisis in the Catholic Church* (rev. ed.). Boston: Little, Brown.

Brainerd, C. J., & Reyna, V. F. (2005). *The science of false memory.* New York: Oxford University Press.

Brenneis, C. B. (1999). The analytic present in psychoanalytic reconstructions of the historical past. *Journal of the American Psychoanalytic Association, 47*, 187–201.

Brenneis, C. B. (2000). Evaluating the evidence: Can we find authenticated recovered memory? *Journal of the American Psychoanalytic Association, 17*, 61–77.

Briere, J., & Conte, J. (1993). Self-reported amnesia for abuse in adults molested as children. *Journal of Traumatic Stress, 6*, 21–31.

Brown, D., Scheflin, A. W., & Hammond, D. C. (1998). *Memory, trauma, treatment, and the law.* New York: Norton.

Clancy, S. A., & McNally, R. J. (2005–2006). Who needs repression?: Normal memory processes can explain "forgetting" of childhood sexual abuse. *Scientific Review of Mental Health Practice, 4*, 1–8.

Dalenberg, C. (2006). Recovered memory and the *Daubert* criteria: Recovered memory as professionally tested, peer reviewed, and accepted in the relevant scientific community. *Trauma, Violence, and Abuse, 7*(4), 274–310.

Davis, D., & Loftus, E. F. (2007a). Internal and external sources of distortion in adult witness memory. In M. P. Toglia, J. D. Read, D. R. Ross, & R. C. L. Lindsay (Eds.), *Handbook of eyewitness memory: Vol. 1. Memory for events* (pp. 195–237). Mahwah, NJ: Erlbaum.

Davis, D., & Loftus, E. F. (2007b). *"Repressed" and "recovered" memories of trauma: On the untestability of relevant hypotheses.* Unpublished manuscript.

De Rivera, J. (2000). Understanding persons who repudiate memories recovered in therapy. *Professional Psychology: Research and Practice, 31*, 378–386.

Elliott, D. (1997). Traumatic events: Prevalence and delayed recall in the general population. *Journal of Consulting and Clinical Psychology, 65*, 811–820.

Epstein, M. A., & Bottoms, B. L. (1998). Memories of childhood sexual abuse: A survey of young adults. *Child Abuse and Neglect, 22*, 1217–1238.

Epstein, M. A., & Bottoms, B. L. (2002). Explaining the forgetting and recovery of abuse and trauma memories: Possible mechanisms. *Child Maltreatment, 7*, 210–225.

Erdelyi, M. H. (2006). The unified theory of repression. *Behavioral and Brain Sciences, 29*, 499–551.

Faigman, D. L., Kaye, D. H., Saks, M. J., Sanders, J., & Cheng, E. K. (2007). *Modern scientific evidence: The law and science of expert testimony* (2nd ed.). Minneapolis, MN: West/Thompson.

Feldman-Summers, S., & Pope, K. S. (1994). The experience of "forgetting" childhood abuse: A national survey of psychologists. *Journal of Consulting and Clinical Psychology, 62*, 636–639.

Femina, D. D., Yeager, C. A., & Lewis, D. O. (1990). Child abuse: Adolescent records vs. adult recall. *Child Abuse and Neglect, 14*, 227–231.

Finkelhor, D. (1986). *A sourcebook on child sexual abuse.* Newbury Park, CA: Sage.

Freyd, J. J. (1996). *Betrayal trauma: The logic of forgetting childhood abuse.* Cambridge, MA: Harvard University Press.

Freyd, J. J. (2001). Memory and dimensions of trauma: Terror may be "all-too-well remembered" and betrayal buried. In J. R. Conte (Ed.), *Critical issues in child sexual abuse: Historical, legal, and psychological perspectives* (pp. 139–173). Thousand Oaks, CA: Sage.

Geraerts, E., Merckelbach, H., Jelicic, M., Smeets, E., & van Heerden, J. (2006). Dissociative symptoms and how they relate to fantasy proneness in women reporting repressed or recovered memories. *Personality and Individual Differences, 40*, 1143–1151.

Geraerts, E., Raymaekers, L., & Merckelbach, H. (2008). Recovered memories of childhood sexual abuse: Current findings and their legal implications. *Legal and Criminological Psychology, 13,* 165–176.

Geraerts, E., Schooler, J. W., Merckelbach, H., Jelicic, M., Hauer, B. J. A., & Ambadar, Z. (2007). The reality of recovered memories: Corroborating continuous and discontinuous memories of childhood sexual abuse. *Psychological Science, 18,* 564–568.

Ghetti, S., Edelstein, R. S., Goodman, G. S., Cordon, I. M., Quas, J. A., Alexander, K. W., et al. (2006). What can subjective forgetting tell us about memory for childhood trauma? *Memory and Cognition, 34,* 1011–1025.

Goodman, G. S., Ghetti, S., Quas, J. A., Edelstein, R. S., Alexander, K. W., Redlich, A. D., et al. (2003). A prospective study of memory for child sexual abuse: New findings relevant to the repressed-memory controversy. *Psychological Science, 14,* 113–118.

Harvey, A. G., & Bryant, R. A. (2000). Memory for acute stress disorder symptoms: A two-year prospective study. *Journal of Nervous and Mental Disease, 188,* 602–607.

Henkel, L. A., & Coffman, K. J. (2004). Memory distortions in coerced false confessions: A source monitoring framework analysis. *Applied Cognitive Psychology, 18*(5), 567–588.

Herman, J. L., & Schatzow, E. (1987). Recovery and verification of memories of childhood sexual trauma. *Psychoanalytic Psychology, 4,* 1–14.

Kassin, S. M. (2007). Internalized false confessions. In M. P. Toglia, J. D. Read, D. F. Ross, & R. C. L. Lindsay (Eds.), *The handbook of eyewitness psychology: Vol. 1. Memory for events* (pp. 175–192). Mahwah, NJ: Erlbaum.

Kendall-Tackett, K. A. (2003). *Treating the lifetime health effects of childhood victimization.* Kingston, NJ: Civic Research Institute.

Kihlstrom, J. F. (1998). Exhumed memory. In S. J. Lynn & K. M. McConkey (Eds.), *Truth in memory* (pp. 3–31). New York: Guilford Press.

Laumann, E., Gagnon, J., Michael, R., & Michaels, S. (1994). *The social organization of sexuality.* Chicago: University of Chicago Press.

Loftus, E. F. (1994). The repressed memory controversy. *American Psychologist, 49*(5), 443–445.

Loftus, E. F., & Davis, D. (2006). Recovered memories. *Annual Review of Clinical Psychology, 2,* 469–498.

Loftus, E. F., & Guyer, M. (2002a). Who abused Jane Doe?: Part I. The hazards of the single case history. *Skeptical Inquirer, 26,* 24–32.

Loftus, E. F., & Guyer, M. J. (2002b). Who abused Jane Doe?: Part II. *Skeptical Inquirer, 26,* 37–40, 44.

Logerquist v. McVey, 1 P.3d 113 (2000).

Mazzoni, G., & Lynn, S. J. (2007). Using hypnosis in eyewitness memory: Past and current issues. In M. P. Toglia, J. D. Read, D. F. Ross, & R. C. L. Lindsay (Eds.), *Hanbook of eyewitness psychology: Vol. 1. Memory for events* (pp. 321–338). Mahwah, NJ: Erlbaum.

McNally, R. J. (2003a). Progress and controversy in the study of posttraumatic stress disorder. *Annual Review of Psychology, 54*, 229–252.

McNally, R. J. (2003b). *Remembering trauma.* Cambridge, MA: Harvard University Press.

McNally, R. J. (2004). Conceptual problems with the DSM-IV criteria for posttraumatic stress disorder. In G. M. Rosen (Ed.), *Posttraumatic stress disorder: Issues and controversies* (pp. 229–252). Chichester, UK: Wiley.

McNally, R. J. (2005). Debunking myths about trauma and memory. *Canadian Journal of Psychiatry, 50*(13), 817–822.

McNally, R. J. (2007). Trauma in childhood [Letters to the editor]. *Archives of General Psychiatry, 64*(12), 1451.

Melchert, T. P. (1996). Childhood memory and a history of different forms of abuse. *Professional Psychology: Research and Practice, 27*, 438–446.

Melchert, T. P. (1999). Relations among childhood memory, a history of abuse, dissociation, and repression. *Journal of Interpersonal Violence, 14*, 1172–1192.

Melchert, T. P., & Parker, R. L. (1997). Different forms of childhood abuse and memory. *Child Abuse and Neglect, 21*, 125–135.

Ofshe, R., & Watters, E. (1994). *Making monsters: False memories, psychotherapy, and sexual hysteria.* New York: Scribner's.

Ost, J. (2003). Seeking the middle ground in the "memory wars." *British Journal of Psychology, 94*, 125–139.

Piper, A., Lillevik, L., & Kritzer, R. (2008). What's wrong with believing in repression?: A review for legal professionals. *Psychology, Public Policy, and Law, 14*, 223–242.

Pope, H. G., Jr., Oliva, P. S., & Hudson, J. I. (2002). Repressed memories. The scientific status of research on repressed memories. In D. L. Faigman, D. H. Kaye, M. J. Saks, & J. Sanders (Eds.), *Science in the law: Social and behavioral science issues* (pp. 487–526). St. Paul, MN: West Group.

Read, J. D., Connolly, D. A., & Welsh, A. (2006). An archival analysis of actual cases of historic child sexual abuse: A comparison of jury and bench trials. *Law and Human Behavior, 30*, 259–285.

Read, J. D., & Lindsay, D. S. (2000). "Amnesia" for summer camps and high school graduation: Memory work increases reports of prior periods of remembering less. *Journal of Traumatic Stress, 13*, 129–147.

Rind, B., Tromovitch, P., & Bauserman, R. (1998). A meta-analytic examination of assumed properties of child sexual abuse using college samples. *Psychological Bulletin, 124*, 22–53.

Roe, C. M., & Schwartz, M. F. (1996). Characteristics of previously forgotten memories of sexual abuse: A descriptive study. *Journal of Psychiatry and the Law, 24*, 189–206.

Rofé, Y. (2008). Does repression exist?: Memory, pathogenic, unconscious and clinical evidence. *Review of General Psychology, 12*(1), 63–85.

Russell, D. H. (1986). *The secret trauma: Incest in the lives of girls and women.* New York: Basic Books.

Schacter, D. L. (2001). *The seven sins of memory: How the mind forgets and remembers.* Boston: Houghton Mifflin.

Schooler, J. W., Bendiksen, M., & Ambadar, Z. (1997). Taking the middle line: Can we accommodate both fabricated and recovered memories of abuse? In M.A. Conway (Ed.), *Recovered memories and false memories* (pp. 251–292). Oxford, UK: Oxford University Press.

Schwarz, E. D., Kowalski, J. M., & McNally, R. J. (1993). Malignant memories: Posttraumatic changes in memory in adults after a school shooting. *Journal of Traumatic Stress, 6,* 95–103.

Wells, G. L., Memon, A., & Penrod, S. D. (2006). Eyewitness evidence: Improving its probative value. *Psychological Science in the Public Interest, 7,* 45–75.

Widom, C. S., & Morris, S. (1997). Accuracy of adult recollections of childhood victimization: Part 2. Childhood sexual abuse. *Psychological Assessment, 9,* 34–46.

Williams, L. M. (1994). Recall of childhood trauma: A prospective study of women's memories of child sexual abuse. *Journal of Consulting and Clinical Psychology, 62,* 1167–1176.

Williams, L. M. (1995). Recovered memories of abuse in women with documented sexual victimization histories. *Journal of Traumatic Stress, 8,* 649–673.

Winkielman, P., Schwarz, N., & Belli, R. F. (1998). The role of ease of retrieval and attribution in memory judgments: Judging your memory as worse despite recalling more events. *Psychological Science, 9,* 124–126.

CHAPTER 4

Forensic Hypnosis

THE STATE OF THE SCIENCE

Steven Jay Lynn, Elza Boycheva, Amanda Deming,
Scott O. Lilienfeld, and Michael N. Hallquist

HYPNOSIS AND MEMORY:
OVERVIEW OF TECHNIQUES AND CONTROVERSIES

From the late 18th century, when Franz Anton Mesmer claimed that his ability to manipulate the alleged healing force of "animal magnetism" could treat all manner of physical illnesses, hypnosis has provoked controversy. In the forensic arena, opinions about hypnosis have swayed from outright rejection of hypnotically elicited testimony in the courtroom, to per se admission of such testimony to the bar. Our review of state laws indicates that as of early 2008, 27 states have ruled that hypnotically elicited recall is per se inadmissible, 13 states examine hypnosis on a case-by-case basis, and 4 states have precedents of per se admissibility (i.e., admissible with no qualifications). As courts have turned an increasingly jaded eye toward hypnosis in the past two decades, professional societies, including divisions and task forces of the American Psychological Association (1995) and the Canadian Psychiatric Association (1996), have recommended against the use of hypnosis for memory retrieval. The American Medical Association (1994) has suggested that hypnosis be used only for investigative purposes in forensic contexts.

Still, there are vociferous defenders of clinical and forensic hypnosis for purposes of memory recovery (e.g., Brown, Scheflin, & Hammond, 1998; Hammond et al., 1995). The American Society of Clinical Hypnosis (ASCH) issued a set of guidelines for the use of hypnosis in clinical and forensic situations, which lends legitimacy to the use of hypnosis in police interrogations (Hammond et al., 1995). Moreover, critiques have been tendered of studies showing that hypnotically enhanced recall is more inaccurate than nonhypnotic recall (Brown et al., 1998).

In this chapter we address the major controversy regarding the forensic use of hypnosis: "Should witnesses' hypnotically elicited memories be admissible in criminal and civil trials?" We also address the following seven subcontroversies and questions nested within the broader controversy regarding the admissibility of such testimony:

1. Does hypnosis compromise witness accuracy with or without leading or misleading questions?
2. Does hypnosis compromise witness confidence in recall?
3. Is hypnotically induced age regression particularly subject to error?
4. Are nonsuggestible witnesses less vulnerable to hypnotically elicited false memories?
5. How does hypnosis compare with other recall techniques?
6. Are research conclusions limited by a lack of ecological validity?
7. Do certain procedures effectively safeguard against hypnotically elicited false memories?

Before proceeding, it is necessary to describe how hypnosis is typically used to recover memories in forensic and therapy situations (Newman & Thompson, 2001; Orne, 1979). When hypnosis is used in investigatory contexts, such as by police or their professional consultants, it often begins with a so-called hypnotic induction that defines the proceedings as hypnosis (e.g., hypnotists inform witnesses that they will experience hypnosis) and contains suggestions for eye closure, relaxation, and enhanced recall. The hypnotist then suggests that it will be possible to mentally relive scenes of interest and to relate the events that occurred in free recall and in response to specific questions. Often suggestions are given to zoom in or otherwise "focus in" on particular details (e.g., a license plate or suspect's face) regarding a crime. The implication throughout is that hypnosis will augment memory and provide police with needed information to solve a crime. Hypnosis proceeds in much the same manner in situations in which therapists attempt to help patients recover purportedly repressed or dissociated memories. The information to be retrieved, in this case, is often hidden memories of childhood abuse or trauma, rather than of a crime scene or suspect.

PSYCHOLOGICAL RESEARCH RELEVANT
TO THESE CONTROVERSIES

The research we review updates and synthesizes summaries of the extant literature on hypnosis and memory that we have presented elsewhere (Lynn, Barnes, & Matthews, in press; Lynn, Neuschatz, & Fite, 2002; Mazzoni & Lynn, 2006). The subcontroversies we examine are relevant to the encompassing issue of the admissibility of hypnotically elicited memories, insofar as the appropriateness of relying on such remembrances turns on their (1) accuracy in various contexts (e.g., leading/nonleading questions, age regression, suggestibility of witnesses), (2) the potential prejudicial effect on the trier of fact (i.e., confidence), and (3) the amenability of hypnotically elicited testimony to procedural safeguards.

Does Hypnosis Compromise Witness Accuracy
with or without Leading or Misleading Questions?

In order to better understand the effects of hypnotic methods on memory, it is necessary to underscore the fact that ordinary memory is replete with errors, ranging from trivial to significant, and vulnerable to a host of suggestive influences (Loftus, 1993). Unfortunately, no memory recovery technique can bypass the inherent limitations of the human memory system. A massive body of research demonstrates that not all events are encoded in the first place, and memories that are encoded decay over time and are influenced by current beliefs, expectations, and evanescent moods (Lynn & McConkey, 1998). Because everyday memories can often be characterized as a patchwork of accurate and inaccurate recollections, any memory recovery procedure must be evaluated against a baseline of memories not augmented by special means. Accordingly, we compare hypnotic and nonhypnotic recall in terms of the amount of information recalled, accurate versus inaccurate information, and the confidence witnesses place in their remembrances (see Lynn, Matthews, & Barnes, 2008).

One thread of evidence consistently runs through the literature on hypnosis and memory: Hypnosis generally produces increases in the sheer amount of information people recall. In 34 studies Erdelyi (1994) reviewed, he found evidence for hypnotically improved recall of high-sense (i.e., meaningful) stimuli such as poetry and pictures. However, no such boost in recall was seen in the case of recognition of high-sense materials and in recall of low-sense stimuli, such as word lists and nonsense syllables. Nevertheless, Erdelyi observed that even when hypnosis produces more memories, there often is a tradeoff in terms of memory accuracy. Moreover, Erdelyi and others (Scoboria, Mazzoni, Kirsch, & Milling, 2002) have suggested that small increases in improved recall can be attributed to the fact that participants' report more ambiguous items or guesses as genuine memories.

When experimenters have controlled for response productivity by means of a forced-choice recall procedure, hypnotic recall does not exceed nonhypnotic recall (Dinges et al., 1992; Whitehouse, Dinges, Orne, & Orne, 1988). In one study (Dinges et al., 1992) that controlled for productivity, hypnosis increased the yield of incorrect information. Relatedly, Dywan and Bowers (1983) determined that a twofold increase in the number of items reported was more than offset by a threefold increase in the number of errors compared with the error rate in nonhypnotic controls.

Although hypnosis has seemingly provided valuable information in a number of criminal investigations (e.g., numbers on license plates), it is unclear whether repeated recall attempts, independent of hypnosis, were responsible for the information garnered (Payne, 1987), or whether other recall techniques would have been equally, if not more, effective. Moreover, cases in which hypnosis yielded valuable information are likely to attract more publicity and attention, compared with cases in which hypnosis yielded no useful information, skewing public and professional perceptions of the value of hypnosis.

Optimistic assessments of hypnotically facilitated recall often are substantially qualified. For example, Steblay and Bothwell's (1994) meta-analysis found evidence for superior recall in hypnosis in response to nonleading questions with a delay of at least 24 hours between event exposure and recall attempt. However, the authors provided three caveats to this conclusion:

1. Even in the delay condition, leading questions that suggest a particular answer, which encompass misleading questions that suggest an erroneous answer, reduced the effect size and eliminated group differences.
2. The confidence intervals for these effect sizes were quite large and encompassed zero, suggesting considerable unaccounted variability.
3. Most significantly, any benefit for hypnosis was limited to delays

of 1–2 days. Even a 1-week delay reverses the effect to favor control subjects.

However, the most serious qualification relevant to triers of fact is that hypnotically assisted recall produces more recall errors, more intrusions of uncued errors, and higher levels of memories for false information relative to nonhypnotic methods (Kebble & Wagstaff, 1997; Orne, Whitehouse, Dinges, & Orne, 1996; Steblay & Bothwell, 1994).

A well-established finding in the memory literature is that leading and misleading questions can produce high rates of recall and recognition errors in adults and children (Krackow & Lynn, 2003; Loftus, 1993). Research that assesses whether hypnosis compounds problems associated with leading and misleading questions has yielded mixed results. Although three studies determined that hypnosis enhanced the effects of leading or misleading questions, five studies did not find this to be the case (see Lynn et al., 2008).

In 1995 the ASCH issued guidelines for the use of hypnosis to improve or recover memories (Hammond et al., 1995). This document suggested that hypnosis could be used with no special risks when the procedures were not accompanied by inappropriately suggestive questions. Two studies respond directly to this contention by independently assessing the effects of hypnosis and misleading questions. Scoboria and his associates (2002) found that hypnosis and misleading questions independently decreased the accuracy of memory reports and decreased "don't know" responses. Interestingly, the effects of misleading questions exceeded the effects of hypnosis, but the two effects were additive. However, in their second study, Scoboria, Mazzoni, and Kirsch (2006) found that hypnosis did not compromise memory: Only misleading questions reduced memory accuracy and "don't know" responses. The reason for the discrepancy may be associated with methodological differences across studies, including the fact that the latter study was conducted in a group rather than an individual test setting, like the initial study (Lynn et al., 2008). Although the evidence regarding the independent effects of hypnosis versus misleading questions is equivocal, research to date does not support the contention that hypnosis enhances recall, relative to waking conditions, or protects against the effects of misinformation.

The weighty effect of misleading questions and methods goes a long way toward explaining why studies find no differences in memories across hypnotic and nonhypnotic procedures. In many of these investigations, misleading questions and procedures are included in both hypnotic and nonhypnotic conditions (see Lynn et al., 2008).

Does Hypnosis Compromise Witness Confidence in Recall?

The confidence that witnesses express in their testimony is the most important factor jurors weigh in assessing the credibility of eyewitness reports (Wells & Bradfield, 1998). If hypnosis inflates witness confidence (an effect termed "memory hardening") independent of memory accuracy, it could have an appreciable prejudicial impact on triers of fact. The available evidence bolsters concerns about admitting hypnotically elicited testimony to the bar. As Lynn and colleagues (2008, in press) report, 23 studies have shown that hypnosis either increases confidence relative to a nonhypnotic group, or participants confidently report inaccurate memories of events they earlier denied occurred when they were not hypnotized (e.g., Laurence & Perry, 1983; Sheehan & Tilden, 1983; Whitehouse, Orne, Orne, & Dinges, 1991).

As a counterpoint, nine studies have failed to detect differences in confidence as a function of hypnosis. However, in five of the studies (Putnam, 1979; Ready, Bothwell, & Brigham, 1997; Sanders & Simmons, 1983; Scoboria et al., 2002; Yuille & McEwan, 1985), hypnosis produced more errors or less accurate information, and in all of the remaining studies (Gregg & Mingay, 1987; Mingay, 1986; Scoboria et al., 2006; Spanos, Gwynn, Comer, Baltruweit, & deGroh, 1989), with one exception (Terrance, Matheson, Allard, & Schnarr, 2000), there were no differences in memory accuracy across hypnotic and nonhypnotic conditions. Accordingly, in the majority of studies reported to date, hypnosis increased confidence in memories. However, when this confidence inflation effect was not present, hypnosis decreased the accuracy of memories, raising serious questions about the use of hypnosis in forensic situations.

It could be argued that the acid test of whether hypnosis should be barred from the courtroom is if it so prejudices eyewitnesses' memories that it renders them resistant to cross-examination. Whereas the effects of hypnosis on confidence are, at times, sizable (see McConkey, 1992; Wagstaff, 1989), this is not invariably the case (Nogrady, McConkey, & Perry, 1985; Sanders & Simmons, 1983; Spanos et al., 1989). Only two studies have examined the effects of cross-examination across hypnotized versus nonhypnotized participants.

Spanos and colleagues (1989) determined that hypnotizable individuals who viewed a videotape of a crime misattributed a substantial number of suggested characteristics to the offender and frequently misidentified a mug shot of the offender. Hypnotic and nonhypnotic interrogations with leading questions produced equivalent effects across the two conditions. During later cross-examination, the hypnotized and nonhypnotized participants were equally likely to "break down" during questioning and disavow their earlier misattributions and misidentifications. The fact that hypnotized participants did not differ from participants who received guided imagery and leading questions is not at all surprising, in that both guided imagery and leading questions have been shown to produce false memories.

Spanos, Quigley, Gwynn, Glatt, and Perlini (1991) reported that hypnosis inflated participant confidence in mug-shot identifications. Moreover, participants who underwent a hypnosis interrogation and were then prepared for cross-examination (i.e., told to tell the truth and to be polite but firm and not let the prosecutor plant doubts in their minds) expressed higher certainty in their mug-shot identifications than participants who were not prepared. In contrast, preparation did not influence nonhypnotized participants' certainty of identifications: Prepared and nonprepared individuals responded equivalently. All participants were cross-examined regarding their earlier testimony. Hypnotized and nonhypnotized individuals were equally likely to break down under cross-examination.

However, it bears mention that the rates of resistance to cross-examination were high across both conditions. More specifically, 37 out of the 78 participants evaluated (47%) did *not* break down in the face of both direct examination and cross-examination. In fact, fully 73% of people who were prepared for cross-examination did not break down under cross-examination. In contrast, 86% of individuals who were not prepared by lawyers to withstand cross-examination did break down and reversed their earlier testimony. Although the combination of hypnosis and routine trial preparation to withstand cross-examination results in a high rate of resistance to retracting earlier testimony, the findings imply that resistance to cross-examination is a problem with respect to both hypnotically and nonhypnotically assisted recall.

Is Hypnotically Induced Age Regression Particularly Subject to Error?

Studies of hypnotic age regression yield conclusions similar to studies of memories of contemporaneous events. Studies of age regression are particularly relevant to legal cases in which therapists use hypnosis to investigate early childhood experiences, including events pertinent to alleged child abuse. In hypnotic age regression, individuals receive suggestions to "go back in time" to reexperience or recall early life events. However, strictly speaking, any time a person is invited to experience an event in the past, however distal, it can be considered "age regression."

In a review of more than 60 years of research on hypnotic age regression, Nash (1987) found that the behaviors and experiences of age-regressed adults were often different from those of actual children. Age-regressed adults do not show the expected patterns on many indices of development. For example, when regressed to childhood, they exhibit the brain waves (electroencephalograph readings; EEG) typical of adults rather than of children. They also tend to perform at adult levels (i.e., formal operations) rather than child levels (e.g., preoperational level) on Piagetian tasks. Nash concluded that despite the fact that suggested experiences during age regression may seem compelling to participants as well as observers, such experiences rarely, if ever, represent literal reinstatements of childhood behaviors and feelings. Instead, studies of age-regressed participants' experiences of events associated with the first few days or years of life (Marmelstein & Lynn, 1999; Spanos, Burgess, Burgess, Samuels, & Blois, 1999; Terrance et al., 2000) and even of alleged past lives (Spanos, Menary, Gabora, DuBreuil, & Dewhirst, 1991) reflect participants' fantasies, beliefs, and assumptions rather than literal reinstatements of childhood experiences, behaviors, and feelings.

Because age regression suggestions are invariably direct and "leading," it is not surprising that many participants (in excess of 60%) "regressed" to very early ages report implausible memories (earlier than 2 years, the traditional cutoff of infantile amnesia) in nonhypnotic as well as hypnotic conditions. However, Bryant and Barnier (1999) demonstrated that none of the individuals in the hypnosis condition retracted their memory reports after being told that research shows that they cannot experience accurate memories of their second birthday. Nevertheless, more than half of the highly suggestible participants who were not hypnotized and reported a memory retracted their memory reports after being provided with the scientific evidence.

Are Nonsuggestible Witnesses Less Vulnerable to Hypnotically Elicited False Memories?

To assert that "hypnosis" per se has much bearing on participants' memories following an hypnotic induction, it is important to show that inaccurate memories and inflated confidence vary with individuals' degree of hypnotic suggestibility. On standardized scales of hypnotic suggestibility, approximately 15–20% of participants score as highly suggestible (pass 9 of 12 suggestions), 15–20% of participants score as low or nonsuggestible (pass 0–3 suggestions), and the remainder score as medium suggestible (4–8 suggestions, 60–70%). High and medium hypnotizable subjects report more inaccurate memories than do low hypnotizable subjects (see Bryant & Barnier, 1999; Lynn et al., 2002); however, in some studies, those in the medium hypnotizable range perform comparably to high scorers (Neuschatz, Lynn, Benoit, & Fite, 2003; Sheehan, Statham, & Jamieson, 1991b; Terrance et al., 2000), whereas in other studies, medium scorers display fewer inaccurate memories than high scorers, but more than low scorers (e.g., Sheehan, Statham, & Jamieson, 1991a). Research also indicates that hypnotizability level plays a role in the degree of confidence expressed, with high suggestible subjects reporting more confidence in recall than low suggestible subjects (Dywan & Bowers, 1983; Sheehan & Tilden, 1983; Spanos et al., 1991).

Even some low suggestible individuals report hypnotically elicited false memories, implying that suggestive elements inherent in recall retrieval procedures jeopardize recall, independent of responsiveness to hypnosis (Orne et al., 1996). Moreover, the fact that highly suggestible individuals are vulnerable to suggested memories in nonhypnotic as well as hypnotic conditions (see Lynn et al., 2008) suggests that false memories are associated with a general suggestibility or compliance factor.

How Does Hypnosis Compare with Other Recall Techniques?

The rationale for the use of hypnosis in forensic situations is weakened by the fact that other recall techniques likely possess greater value and fewer risks. Specifically, the cognitive interview (see Geiselman & Fisher, 1997), which uses a variety of recall strategies (e.g., reinstating the physical and emotional context, recalling information from different perspectives) can produce more accurate information than standard interview techniques (see Milne & Bull, 2003). However, increases in accurate recall may be accompanied by a significant (although smaller) increase in the number of recall errors (Kohnken, Milne, Memon, & Bull, 1999). Studies that have compared hypnotically assisted recall with procedures designed to (1) reinstate the context and (2) motivate individuals to recall pertinent information, have generally favored the latter technique (see Lynn et al., 1997).

Are Conclusions Limited by a Lack of Ecological Validity?

Proponents of the use of hypnosis for memory enhancement (Brown et al., 1998) have argued that the research base is inadequate at best and flawed at worst. This claim rests on the assertion that many extant studies (1) are ecologically invalid because they are based on sterile laboratory research and stimuli far removed from everyday, emotionally laden events; (2) employ relatively short retention intervals, often testing subjects on the same day they are exposed to laboratory stimuli; (3) rely solely on forced-choice recall test procedures that are "predisposed to produce biased, unreliable data" (p. 299); and (4) test for hypnotically created memories during, instead of following, hypnosis (p. 330).

Studies of emotionally valenced stimuli and a recent study (Krackow, Lynn, & Payne, 2005–2006) that responded to these criticisms suggest that the claims made by the proponents of forensic hypnosis are overblown. Krackow and colleagues (2005–2006) selected participants who reported an emotional reaction to the death of Princess Diana and tested their memories for the event 3 days after her death and 11–12 weeks thereafter. One group of nonhypnotized participants received task motivation instructions in which they were instructed to "concentrate and do your best to recall the event ... even if it requires some effort" (p. 207). Another group of individuals was not hypnotized but received instructions to mentally recreate the environment in which they learned of Diana's death and think about the events in different sequences (context reinstatement). The third group of participants received a brief hypnotic induction prior to the recall task. The investigators found that hypnotized individuals' narratives about the event (1) retained less information from their original narratives than task-motivated individuals, (2) contained fewer consistent memories than task-motivated individuals, and (3) omitted more memories than those of participants in the contextual reinstatement condition.

Ethical constraints understandably make researchers chary of testing participants' responses to highly aversive stimuli in the laboratory. Nevertheless, eight studies (see Krackow et al., 2005–2006; Lynn, Lock, Myers, & Payne, 1997) indicate that even when hypnotized participants are exposed to a wide array of emotionally arousing events (e.g., films of shop accidents, depictions of fatal stabbings, a mock assassination, an actual murder video-taped serendipitously), their recall of these events is comparable to that of individuals whose memories are prompted by nonhypnotic methods. Thus, even when the test context is designed to increase the ecological validity of the inferences that could be drawn, there is no evidence for the salutary effects of hypnosis on memory. This conclusion contradicts the authors (Hammond et al., 1995) of the ASCH guidelines, who asserted that "with emotion-laden memories for meaningful material, we believe it likely that hypnosis has the potential to clearly prove helpful with some individuals" (p. 15).

Do Procedural Guidelines Effectively Safeguard against Hypnotically Elicited False Memories?

Courts that admit hypnosis on a case-by-case basis generally do so when a set of procedural guidelines is followed that inform the conduct of the hypnosis session, to some extent, and permit an evaluation of how hypnosis was conducted. The presumption here is that hypnosis is not inherently more biasing than other procedures when certain steps are taken to minimize any tampering with memory (e.g., no leading questions that suggest a particular response), and recall is not corrupted by memory enhancement methods.

In the seminal case of *State v. Hurd* (1981), procedural safeguards against the potentially witness-tainting effects of hypnosis were established as a gatekeeper to the admission of hypnotically elicited testimony in New Jersey. Since *Hurd*, other states that admit testimony case by case either require compliance with the *Hurd* rules or have developed their own set of guidelines. The Federal Bureau of Investigation (FBI) and ASCH have also developed procedural guidelines, which range from making videotapes or other recordings of the procedures to evaluating suggestive influences, writing a report of the session with pertinent observations, to discussing the imperfections of memory "in and out of hypnosis."

Although no set of applied guidelines has been evaluated systematically, it is probably beyond scientific dispute that leading questions should be studiously avoided. Three studies that examined the protective effects of providing individuals with prehypnotic "warnings" about the imperfections of hypnotically elicited recall do not inspire much confidence in their use. Burgess and Kirsch (1999) found that warnings mitigated some of the memory distortions associated with hypnosis but did not improve recall above and beyond a nonhypnotic condition. Green, Lynn, and Malinoski (1998) determined that warnings minimized memory distortions during, but not after, hypnosis. Neuschatz and colleagues (2003) found that repeated warnings that hypnotic and nonhypnotic memories are not necessarily accurate did not improve recall relative to a nonhypnotic condition. In short, the value of procedural guidelines has not been adequately investigated or well established.

Not surprisingly, the use of procedural guidelines is highly controversial. Critics argue that hypnotically elicited testimony is so invalid that no set of procedural measures can outweigh its inherently biasing effects. As stated in *People v. Gonzales* (1981, 1982), the *Hurd* guidelines have the potential to confer an unwarranted "aura of reliability" on hypnotic testimony, thereby raising the specter of a miscarriage of justice. The Supreme Court of New

Jersey found this and other arguments compelling and recently reversed their earlier decision regarding the *Hurd* guidelines. Previous guidelines probably do not go far enough in that they do not recommend assessing participants' confidence in their initial and posthypnotic recall. Without this information, it is impossible to evaluate fully the potentially biasing effect of hypnosis and hypnotic testimony on witnesses (Lynn et al., in press).

GAPS IN SCIENTIFIC KNOWLEDGE

Important gaps exist in our knowledge of hypnotically augmented recall. We identify three areas in need of research attention.

First, research has not examined the extent to which nonhypnotically refreshed memories are tainted by hypnosis, so courts can expect little evidence-based guidance on this issue. This issue is of paramount importance insofar as many courts bar the entire testimony of witnesses who undergo hypnosis.

Second, additional research is necessary to establish the value, if any, of procedural guidelines. However, the few studies conducted to date provide little reason to believe that implementing procedural safeguards will vitiate problems associated with hypnotically augmented recall. What is most pressing are studies that address whether warnings and procedural guidelines are useful in cross-examination situations. Studies that address this issue are imperative to determine whether there are some circumstances in which hypnosis may provide triers of fact with useful and more or less reliable information that is not immune to cross-examination.

Third, little is known about the effects of different types of questions on recall in hypnotic situations. For example, research on the effects of hypnosis on "don't know" responses and on leading versus misleading questions is very limited and is a research priority.

MYTHS AND MISCONCEPTIONS

The central myth concerning hypnosis is that it engenders a trance-like altered state of consciousness that not only increases suggestibility but also enables people to do extraordinary things. Allied with this popular myth is the misconception that hypnosis dramatically improves memory to the point that it serves as a "truth serum" of sorts. Interestingly, this misconception extends beyond the general public to professional circles.

Whitehouse and his colleagues (1991) found that 93% of college-age subjects reported that hypnosis enhances memory retrieval. More than a decade later, Green (2003) reported that, on average, college students tended to agree with the statement "Hypnosis can make subjects remember things that they could not normally remember" (rated 5.42 on a 7-point scale of agreement).

Yapko (1994) surveyed over 850 psychotherapists in independent practice and documented the following rates of endorsement of beliefs concerning hypnosis as a potent memory enhancer: (1) 75%: "Hypnosis enables people to accurately remember things they otherwise could not." (2) 47%: "Therapists can have greater faith in details of a traumatic event when obtained hypnotically than otherwise." (3) 31%: "When someone has a memory of a trauma while in hypnosis, it objectively must actually have occurred." (4) 54%: "Hypnosis can be used to recover memories of actual events as far back as birth." (5) 19%: "Hypnotically obtained memories are more accurate than simply just remembering." As our review indicates, the available evidence supports none of these assertions.

Poole, Lindsay, Memon, and Bull (1995) reported that at least 25% of licensed doctoral-level psychologists surveyed in the United States and Great Britain indicated that they (1) use two or more techniques such as hypnosis and guided imagery to facilitate recall of repressed memories; (2) consider memory recovery an important part of treatment; and (3) can identify patients with repressed or otherwise unavailable memories as early as the first session (see also Polusny & Follette, 1996).

The popular view of hypnosis as akin to a "truth serum" is ironic in the sense that alleged pharmacological truth serums, such as the barbiturate sodium amytal, are far from accurate means of bringing forth accurate memories. Although some early investigators reported dramatic cases of purported recovery of traumatic memories, in many instances, the accuracy of such memories was not ascertained (e.g., Lambert & Rees, 1944). Attempts by the U.S. Central Intelligence Agency to use barbiturates and other substances (e.g., LSD) as "truth drugs" during the Cold War with the Soviet Union proved fruitless, and the quest for such drugs was abandoned (Marks, 1978). Moreover, controlled studies on barbiturate interrogation in which attempts are made to verify memories are entirely lacking (Kihlstrom, 1998; Piper, 1993; Ruedrich, Chu, & Wadle, 1985). In addition, evidence suggests that many subjects can lie under the influence of "truth serum" (Piper, 1993). Clearly, neither hypnosis nor pharmacological methods can be trusted as valid vehicles for enhancing memory in forensic or clinical situations.

CONCLUSIONS

The research base on hypnosis and memory is sufficient to provide guidance to triers of fact regarding the scientifically supported, scientifically unsupported, and still controversial uses of hypnosis for memory retrieval. We therefore proffer the following:

Scientifically Supported Uses

We are unaware of any noncontroversial or unquestionable scientifically supported forensic use of hypnosis, although some workers in the field disagree with us (e.g., Brown et al., 1998; Hammond et al., 1995).

Scientifically Unsupported Uses

We believe that our review provides support for the position that hypnosis does not have scientific evidence as a reliable recall enhancement method. Accordingly, hypnotically elicited testimony should not have a place in the courtroom.

Scientifically Controversial and/or Still Largely Untested Uses

The fact that hypnosis can produce more accurate memories of meaningful material than nonhypnotic methods, and that some research (Scoboria et al., 2006) suggests that hypnosis does not imperil recall in the absence of leading questions, leaves the door open for its use as an investigative tool when other recall methods have been tried and failed. It could be argued that hypnosis can prove beneficial in rare instances in criminal investigations when accurate recall can potentially be corroborated. However, this proposal is controversial in that unwarranted confidence and the tradeoff of inaccurate for accurate memories produced by hypnosis suggests that such testimony should not be admitted to the bar even when procedural guidelines are followed.

Moreover, research on anchoring heuristics and confirmation bias (Garb, 1998; Nickerson, 1998) suggests that even using hypnosis purely as an investigative tool is fraught with dangers, because investigators may be guided too heavily by initial leads generated by hypnosis and selectively seek out evidence consistent with these leads. Hence, it is essential for law enforcement officials who use hypnosis for investigative purposes to look for evidence that not merely confirms, but also contradicts, their initial hunches.

Recent research substantiating the highly prejudicial role of misleading questions has raised concerns about whether hypnosis is being unduly scapegoated in courtrooms across the United States (Scoboria et al., 2006). However, it can also be argued that although a variety of procedures are suggestive (e.g., misleading questions, guided imagery), this fact provides no warrant for the use of hypnosis in criminal investigations or for the admissibility of hypnotically elicited testimony (Lynn et al., in press). Moreover, in contrast to most other suggestive procedures (e.g., leading questions), hypnosis is associated with a widespread perception among the general public (including jurors) of infallibility.

COMMUNICATING CONSENSUS AND CONTROVERSIES

Expert witnesses, including clinicians, should present the scientific evidence regarding hypnosis in clear, accurate terms in testimony and written reports. Accordingly, social framework testimony on the research generally, and expert testimony to rebut the use of hypnosis for memory enhancement, specifically, should encompass the following points. It should be noted that there is considerable consensus regarding the fact that ordinary memory is not necessarily accurate and that it is prone to suggestive influences from a variety of sources, including misleading questions. Moreover, few would contest the claim that hypnosis produces an admixture of accurate and inaccurate memories, and that any increase in memories is typically accompanied by inaccurate memories that equal or surpass the volume of accurate memories. Additionally, the available evidence suggests that hypnosis, relative to waking conditions, can increase confidence in inaccurate as well as accurate memories. The effects of hypnosis on confidence, although typically present and sometimes sizable, are at times negligible or not apparent at all. Moreover, it is important to highlight that many hypnotized and nonhypnotized individuals do not reverse their testimony under cross-examination, especially when they are "prepared" for challenges to their reports. However, the available evidence does not permit definitive conclusions about the stability of hypnotic versus nonhypnotic testimony in the face of cross-examination.

Nor does the available evidence support the use of procedural safeguards as a fail-safe means of protecting testimony from the possible taint of hypnosis. However, it should be made clear to triers of fact that safeguards such as videotaping the hypnosis session are absolutely essential to evaluating the possible pejorative effects of hypnosis on recall.

It is true that not all laboratory findings will necessarily generalize to the panoply of situations that can arise in everyday life. However, studies that expose participants to a variety of emotion-producing stimuli suggest that the effects of hypnosis on recall (1) generalize to a wide variety of situations and (2) are not fully mediated by emotional arousal. Finally, given that little is known about whether hypnosis taints memories that are not explicitly "boosted" or revealed by means of hypnotic methods, experts are not in a position to comment on whether it is unduly restrictive to prohibit a person from testifying even about "nonhypnotic" recollections.

As our review makes plain, there is a wealth of data on the effects of hypnosis on memory, and experts can play an important role in educating triers of fact. Important questions remain that will undoubtedly drive research. However, we believe that the consilience of scientific evidence supports judicial opinions that ban hypnotically elicited testimony from the courtroom.

REFERENCES

American Medical Association. (1994). *Memories of childhood abuse* (Council on Scientific Affairs Report 5-A-94). Washington, DC: Author.

American Psychological Association. (1995, July 25). *Psychotherapy guidelines for working with clients who may have an abuse or trauma history.* Division 17 Committee on Women, Division 4 Trauma and Gender Issues Committee. Washington, DC: Author.

Brown, D., Scheflin, A. W., & Hammond, D. C. (1998). *Memory, trauma treatment, and the law.* New York: Norton.

Bryant, R. A., & Barnier, A. J. (1999). Eliciting autobiographical pseudomemories: The relevance of hypnosis, hypnotizability, and attributions. *International Journal of Clinical and Experimental Hypnosis, 47*(4), 267–283.

Burgess, C., & Kirsch, I. (1999). Expectancy information as a moderator of the effects of hypnosis on memory. *Contemporary Hypnosis, 16*, 22–31.

Canadian Psychiatric Association. (1996, March 25). Position statement: Adult recovered memories of childhood sexual abuse. *Canadian Journal of Psychiatry, 41*, 305–306.

Dinges, D. F., Whitehouse, W. G., Orne, E. C., Powell, J. W., Orne, M. T., & Erdelyi, M. H. (1992). Evaluating hypnotic memory enhancement (hypermnesia and reminiscence) using multi-trial forced recall. *Journal of Experimental Psychology: Learning, Memory, and Cognition, 18*, 1139–1147.

Dywan, J., & Bowers, K. S. (1983). The use of hypnosis to enhance recall. *Science, 222*, 184–185.

Erdelyi, M. (1994). Hypnotic hypermnesia: The empty set of hypermnesia. *International Journal of Clinical and Experimental Hypnosis, 42*, 379–390.

Garb, H. N. (1998). *Studying the clinician: Judgment research and psychological assessment.* Washington, DC: American Psychological Association.

Geiselman, R. E., & Fisher, R. P. (1997). Ten years of cognitive interviewing. In D. G. Payne & F. G. Conrad (Eds.), *Intersections in basic and applied memory research* (pp. 291–310). Mahwah, NJ: Erlbaum.

Green, J. P. (2003). Beliefs about hypnosis: Popular beliefs, misconceptions, and the importance of experience. *International Journal of Clinical and Experimental Hypnosis, 51*, 369–381.

Green, J. P., Lynn, S. J., & Malinoski, P. (1998). Hypnotic pseudomemories, pre-hypnotic warnings, and the malleability of suggested memories. *Applied Cognitive Psychology, 12*, 431–444.

Gregg, V. H., & Mingay, D. J. (1987). Influence of hypnosis on riskiness and discriminability in recognition memory for faces. *British Journal of Experimental and Clinical Hypnosis, 42*(2), 65–75.

Hammond, D. C., Garver, R. B., Mutter, C. B., Crasilneck, H. B., Frischholz, E., Gravitz, M. A., et al. (1995). *Clinical hypnosis and memory: Guidelines for clinicians and for forensic hypnosis.* Des Plaines, IL: American Society of Clinical Hypnosis Press.

Kebble, M. R., & Wagstaff, G. (1997). Hypnotic interviewing: The best way to interview eyewitnesses? *Behavioral Sciences and the Law, 16*, 115–129.

Kihlstrom, J. F. (1998). Exhumed memory. In S. J. Lynn & K. M. McConkey (Eds.), *Truth in memory* (pp. 3–31). New York: Guilford Press.

Kohnken, G., Milne, R., Memon, A., & Bull, R. (1999). The cognitive interview: A meta analysis. *Psychology, Crime, and Law, 5*, 3–27.

Krackow, E., & Lynn, S. J. (2003). Is there touch in the Game of Twister®?: The effects of innocuous touch and suggestive questions on children's eyewitness memory. *Law and Human Behavior, 27*, 589–604.

Krackow, E., Lynn, S. J., & Payne, D. G. (2005–2006). The death of Princess Diana: The effects of memory enhancement procedures on flashbulb memories. *Imagination, Cognition, and Personality, 25*(3), 197–219.

Lambert, C., & Rees, W. L. (1944). Intravenous barbiturates in the treatment of hysteria. *British Medical Journal, 2*, 70–73.

Laurence, J.-R., & Perry, C. (1983). Hypnotically created memory among highly hypnotizable participants. *Science, 222*, 523–524.

Loftus, E. F. (1993). The reality of repressed memories. *American Psychologist, 48*, 518–537.

Lynn, S. J., Barnes, S., & Matthews, A. (in press). Hypnosis and forensic science: Legal decisions and opinions. In C. Edwards (Ed.), *Handbook of forensic science.* New York: Wiley.

Lynn, S. J., Lock, T. G., Myers, B., & Payne, D. G. (1997). Recalling the unrecallable: Should hypnosis be used to recover memories in psychotherapy? *Current Directions in Psychological Science, 6,* 79–83.

Lynn, S. J., Matthews, A., & Barnes, S. (2008). Hypnosis and memory: From Bernheim to the present. In K. D. Markman, W. M. P. Klein, & J. A. Suhr (Eds.), *Handbook of imagination and mental simulation* (pp. 103–119) New York: Psychology Press.

Lynn, S. J., & McConkey, K. M. (Eds.). (1998). *Truth in memory.* New York: Guilford Press.

Lynn, S. J., Myers, B., & Malinoski, P. (1997). Hypnosis, pseudomemories, and clinical guildelines: A sociocognitive perspective. *NATO ASI series: Series A: Life Sciences, 291,* 305–336.

Lynn, S. J., Neuschatz, J., & Fite, R. (2002). Hypnosis and memory: Implications for the courtroom and psychotherapy. In M. L. Eisen, J. A. Quas, & G. S. Goodman (Eds.), *Memory, suggestibility in the forensic interview* (pp. 287–307). Mahwah, NJ: Erlbaum.

Marks, J. (1978). *The search for the Manchurian candidate.* New York: Times Books.

Marmelstein, L., & Lynn, S. J. (1999). Expectancies, group, and hypnotic influences on early autobiographical memory reports. *International Journal of Clinical and Experimental Hypnosis, 47,* 301–319.

Mazzoni, G., & Lynn, S. J. (2006). The use of hypnosis in eyewitness memory: Past and current issues. In M. Toglia (Ed.), *Handbook of eyewitness psychology: Vol. 1. Memory for events* (pp. 321–338). Mahwah, NJ: Erlbaum.

McConkey, K. M. (1992). The effects of hypnotic procedures on remembering: The experimental findings and their implications for forensic hypnosis. In E. Fromm & M. R. Nash (Eds.), *Contemporary hypnosis research* (pp. 405–426). New York: Guilford Press.

Milne, R., & Bull, R. (2003). Does the cognitive interview help children to resist the effects of suggestive questioning? *Legal and Criminological Psychology, 8,* 21–38.

Mingay, D. J. (1986). Hypnosis and memory for incidentally learned scenes. *British Journal of Experimental and Clinical Hypnosis, 3*(3), 173–183.

Nash, M. R. (1987). What, if anything, is age regressed about hypnotic age regression?: A review of the empirical literature. *Psychological Bulletin, 102,* 42–52.

Neuschatz, J., Lynn, S. J., Benoit, G., & Fite, R. (2003). Hypnosis and memory illusions: An investigation using the Deese/Roediger paradigm. *Imagination, Cognition, and Personality, 22,* 3–12.

Newman, A. W., & Thompson, W. (2001). The rise and fall of forensic hypnosis in criminal investigation. *Journal of American Psychiatry and Law, 29,* 75–84.

Nickerson, R. S. (1998). Confirmation bias: A ubiquitous phenomenon in many guises. *Review of General Psychology, 2,* 175–220.

Nogrady, H., McConkey, K. M., & Perry, C. (1985). Enhancing visual memory:

Trying hypnosis, trying imagination, and trying again. *Journal of Abnormal Psychology, 94*, 195–204.

Orne, E. C., Whitehouse, W. G., Dinges, D. F., & Orne, M. T. (1996). Memory liabilities associated with hypnosis: Does low hypnotizability confer immunity? *International Journal of Clinical and Experimental Hypnosis, 44*, 354–369.

Orne, M. T. (1979). The use and misuse of hypnosis in court. *International Journal of Clinical and Experimental Hypnosis, 27*, 311–341.

Payne, D. G. (1987). Hypermnesia and reminiscence in recall: Historical and empirical review. *Psychological Bulletin, 101*, 5–27.

People v. Gonzales, 329 N. W. 2d 743 (Mich. 1982), modified on other grounds, 336 N. W. 2d 751 (Mich. 1983).

Piper, A. (1993). "Truth serum" and "recovered memories" of sexual abuse: A review of the evidence. *Journal of Psychiatry and Law, 21*, 447–471.

Polusny, M. A., & Follette, V. M. (1996). Remembering childhood sexual abuse: A national survey of psychologists' clinical practices, beliefs, and personal experiences. *Professional Psychology: Research and Practice, 27*, 41–52.

Poole, D. A., Lindsay, D. S., Memon, A., & Bull, R. (1995). Psychotherapy and the recovery of memories of childhood sexual abuse: U. S., & British practitioners' opinions, practices, and experiences. *Journal of Consulting and Clinical Psychology, 68*, 426–437.

Putnam, W. H. (1979). Hypnosis and distortions in eyewitness memory. *International Journal of Clinical and Experimental Hypnosis, 28*, 437–488.

Ready, D. J., Bothwell, R. K., & Brigham, J. C. (1997). The effects of hypnosis, context reinstatement, and anxiety on eyewitness memory. *International Journal of Clinical and Experimental Hypnosis, 45*, 55–68.

Ruedrich, S. L., Chu, C. C., & Wadle, C. V. (1985). The amytal interview in the treatment of psychogenic amnesia. *Hospital and Community Psychiatry, 36*, 1045–1046.

Sanders, G. S., & Simmons, W. L. (1983). Use of hypnosis to enhance eyewitness accuracy: Does it work? *Journal of Applied Psychology, 68*(1), 70–77.

Scoboria, A., Mazzoni, G., & Kirsch, I. (2006). Effects of misleading questions and hypnotic memory refreshment on memory reports: A signal detection analysis. *International Journal of Clinical and Experimental Hypnosis, 54*, 340–359.

Scoboria, A., Mazzoni, G., Kirsch, I., & Milling, L. S. (2002). Immediate and persistent effect of misleading questions and hypnosis on memory reports. *Journal of Experimental Psychology: Applied, 8*, 26–32.

Sheehan, P. W., Statham, D., & Jamieson, G. A. (1991a). Pseudomemory effects and their relationship to level of susceptibility to hypnosis and state instruction. *Journal of Personality and Social Psychology, 60*, 130–137.

Sheehan, P. W., Statham, D., & Jamieson, G. A. (1991b). Pseudomemory effects of time in the hypnotic setting. *Journal of Abnormal Psychology, 100*, 39–44.

Sheehan, P. W., & Tilden, J. (1983). Effects of suggestibility and hypnosis on accurate and distorted retrieval from memory. *Journal of Experimental Psychology: Learning, Memory, and Cognition, 9,* 293–293.

Spanos, N. P., Burgess, C. A., Burgess, M. F., Samuels, C., & Blois, W. O. (1999). Creating false memories of infancy with hypnotic and non-hypnotic procedures. *Applied Cognitive Psychology, 13,* 201–218.

Spanos, N. P., Gwynn, M. I., Comer, S. L., Baltruweit, W. J., & deGroh, M. (1989). Are hypnotically induced pseudomemories resistant to cross-examination? *Law and Human Behavior, 13,* 271–289.

Spanos, N. P., Menary, E., Gabora, N. J., DuBreuil, S. C., & Dewhirst, B. (1991). Secondary identity enactments during hypnotic past-life regression: A sociocognitive perspective. *Journal of Personality and Social Psychology, 61,* 308–320.

Spanos, N. P., Quigley, C. A., Gwynn, R. I., Glatt, R. L., & Perlini, A. H. (1991). Hypnotic interrogation, pretrial preparation, and witness testimony during direct and cross-examination. *Law and Human Behavior, 15,* 639–653.

State v. Hurd, 432 A. 2d 86 (N. J. 1981).

Steblay, N. M., & Bothwell, R. K. (1994). Evidence for hypnotically refreshed testimony: The view from the laboratory. *Law and Human Behavior, 18,* 635–651.

Terrance, C. A., Matheson, K., Allard, C., & Schnarr, J. A. (2000). The role of expectation and memory-retrieval techniques in the construction of beliefs about past events. *Applied Cognitive Psychology, 14,* 361–377.

Wagstaff, G. F. (1989). Forensic aspects of hypnosis. In N. P. Spanos & J. F. Chaves (Eds.), *Hypnosis: The cognitive-behavioral perspective* (pp. 340–357). Amherst, NY: Prometheus Books.

Wells, G., & Bradfield, A. L. (1998). "Good, you identified the suspect": Feedback to eyewitnesses distorts their reports of the witnessing experience. *Journal of Applied Psychology, 83,* 360–376.

Whitehouse, W. G., Dinges, D. F., Orne, E. C., & Orne, M. T. (1988). Hypnotic hypermnesia: Enhanced memory accessibility or report bias? *Journal of Abnormal Psychology, 97,* 289–295.

Whitehouse, W. G., Orne, E. C., Orne, M. T., & Dinges, D. F. (1991). Distinguishing the source of memories reported prior waking and hypnotic recall attempts. *Applied Cognitive Psychology, 5,* 51–59.

Yapko, M. D. (1994). Suggestibility and repressed memories of abuse: A survey of psychotherapists' beliefs. *American Journal of Clinical Hypnosis, 36,* 194–208.

Yuille, J. C., & McEwan, N. H. (1985). The use of hypnosis as an aid to eyewitness memory. *Journal of Applied Psychology, 70,* 389–400.

CHAPTER 5

Expert Testimony Regarding Eyewitness Identification

Brian L. Cutler and Gary L. Wells

OVERVIEW OF EXPERT PSYCHOLOGICAL TESTIMONY ON EYEWITNESS IDENTIFICATION

Increasingly, psychologists are giving expert testimony in court on the accuracy of eyewitness identification (Kassin, Tubb, Hosch, & Memon, 2001). Eyewitness experts typically are cognitive or social psychologists who have published research articles on the topic of eyewitness memory. Expert testimony in eyewitness identification is most commonly offered by the defense in criminal cases but is occasionally countered by opposing expert testimony offered by the prosecution. The increasing use of such expert testimony owes largely to the growing recognition that mistaken eyewitness identification is the single most common precursor to the conviction of innocent people (Doyle, 2005). In addition, there is an increasingly strong case that the existing safeguards designed to protect defendants from erroneous conviction resulting from mistaken identification, such as motions to suppress suggestive procedures, cross-examination, and right to counsel at live lineups, are ineffective (Van Wallendael, Devenport, Cutler, & Penrod, 2007).

The decision to admit expert testimony is left to the discretion of the trial judge, and the likelihood of admission varies from state to state and from one federal district to another. States with favorable case law (e.g., California, Georgia, South Carolina) typically admit expert testimony when proffered. States with unfavorable case law (e.g., Florida) rarely admit expert testimony. The most commonly cited reason for not admitting expert testimony is that the testimony is merely a matter of common sense (Schmechel, O'Toole, Easterly, & Lofus, 2006).

Expert testimony is controversial in several respects. One set of controversial issues revolves around the science underlying the expert testimony. In particular, some question the reliability and external validity of the research findings. Reliability in this instance refers to whether the factors about which experts testify (e.g., stress, weapon focus, lineup procedures) demonstrate reliable effects on identification accuracy. This reliability is often determined through the application of statistical procedures within a given experiment (e.g., tests of statistical significance that rule out chance as an explanation) and through procedures that collapse findings across a large set of individual studies (e.g., meta-analyses). External validity, on the other hand, refers to the extent to which eyewitness research conducted in the laboratory generalizes to actual crimes. A second set of controversies pertains to whether expert testimony is needed or helpful to juries. These controversies address such issues as whether the testimony tells jurors something they do not already know and whether the testimony assists them in their deliberation.

RESEARCH RELEVANT TO CONTROVERSIES

The science underlying expert testimony can be divided into two general areas: (1) research on eyewitness identification, which forms the substance of the expert testimony, and (2) research addressing the need for expert testimony and the effects of such testimony on jurors.

Controversy 1: Research on Eyewitness Identification

Experts draw on a large body of literature on human memory in general and eyewitness memory in particular. The research on eyewitness memory has largely developed since the 1970s, though there are studies dating back over 100 years. The research on eyewitness identification uses a common methodology. Research participants, often undergraduate students, are exposed to an enacted crime or event through live staging, videotape, or another similar medium. Following the event, eyewitnesses are asked to attempt to identify the perpetrator from a perpetrator-present lineup or perpetrator-absent lineup. The former lineup represents the situation in which the suspect is guilty, and the latter resembles the situation in which an innocent person is suspected of having committed the crime. Each study has an objective, which is normally to investigate the influence of one or more specific factors on identification accuracy. The factor of interest is systematically manipulated, participants are randomly assigned to conditions, and identification accuracy rates are compared across conditions. For example, Platz and Hosch (1988) investigated the accuracy of same- versus other-race eyewitness identifications in a field study. Black, Hispanic, and white individuals posing as customers visited convenience stores in El Paso, Texas. These customers were served by black, Hispanic, and white clerks. The customers engaged in memorable interactions with the clerks (e.g., paying for a pack of cigarettes with pennies). Following their visits, an investigator asked each clerk to identify the three customers from photographic lineups. Using these procedures, Platz and Hosch were able to compare identification accuracy rates for same-race identifications (e.g., Hispanic clerks' identifications of Hispanic customers) with other-race identifications (e.g., Hispanic clerks' identifications of white and black customers). Platz and Hosch found that cross-race identifications were significantly less likely to be accurate than same-race identifications, a finding that has been replicated numerous times in the research (Meissner & Brigham, 2001).

This common methodology has many positive features. The controlled laboratory setting (or a controlled field setting) permits the investigator to designate the to-be-recognized perpetrator, so, unlike in actual crimes, the accuracy of the witnesses' identifications is known with certainty. The controlled setting permits the investigator to collect multiple observations under the same conditions—an important feature of research, and one that allows for conclusions about the reliability of phenomena. This methodology enables the investigator to hold many important factors constant while systematically manipulating one or more factors of interest and to randomly assign participant-witnesses to these conditions. Systematic manipulation and random assignment are important methods of establishing causal relationships between variables and outcomes. Thus, although it has been criticized as being unrealistic and not representative of actual crimes, the methodology has numerous advantages over investigations of actual crimes. One cannot, for example, control and manipulate conditions, conduct multiple or repeated observations, and know with certainty whether the identifications are correct in studies of actual crimes. The use of college students as participants has also been cited as a limitation, as college students do not represent the range of characteristics found in crime victims. On the other hand, college students are better witnesses than are those who are significantly younger or older (Neuschatz & Cutler, 2008). Accordingly, college students' good visual acuity, general health, memory abilities, and intelligence will, if anything, overestimate the performance of eyewitnesses in general. Aside from these age-related factors, however, there is no reason to believe that the memory processes of college students operate in fundamentally different ways than the memory processes of the public at large.

Research on eyewitness identification can be further divided into two groups of factors: system and estimator variables (Wells, 1978). System variables are under the control of the justice system and can be modified in actual cases to influence the accuracy of identifications. Examples of system variables are the instructions given to an eyewitness prior to a lineup and the manner in which a lineup is presented to an eyewitness. Estimator variables, by contrast, are not under the control of the justice system and can only be used to estimate the accuracy of eyewitness identification. Examples of estimator variables include the stress experienced by the eyewitness and whether the eyewitness and perpetrator are of the same or difference race. The estimator–system variable distinction has been useful as a guiding principle in the research literature by focusing research efforts on factors over which the criminal justice system does or does not exert control. Table 5.1 provides a limited summary of the estimator and system variables that have been examined in the eyewitness identification research.

Controversy 2: Expert Testimony

A second body of research has revolved around the questions of whether expert testimony is needed and whether it is helpful to jurors. This research often becomes the topic of expert testimony when the admissibility of it is challenged. The issues may be debated in briefs to the court, in an admissibility hearing (with or without expert testimony), or both. The most common reason given by judges for not admitting expert testimony is that the testimony is a matter of common sense (Benton, Ross, Bradshaw, Thomas, & Bradshaw, 2006; Schmechel et al., 2006). Considerable research has addressed this issue using a variety of methodologies, such as surveys of lay knowledge of eyewitness memory (e.g., Schmechel et al., 2006), evaluation of peoples' abilities to post-dict (i.e., when persons naive to the results of a study are asked to "guess" the results) the results of eyewitness identification experiments (e.g., Wells, 1984), and examination of mock jurors' decision making in cases involving eyewitness identification (e.g., Cutler, Penrod, & Dexter, 1990). These studies converge on the conclusion that research

TABLE 5.1. Factors Affecting Eyewitness Identification Accuracy

Variable	General conclusion	Study
Weapon focus	Presence of weapon reduces accuracy.	Steblay (1992)
Disguise	Masking cues to hair and hairline reduces accuracy.	Cutler (2006)
Stress	Extreme stress reduces accuracy.	Deffenbacher et al. (2004)
Own-race bias	Accuracy is greater with own-race as compared to other-race IDs.	Meissner & Brigham (2001)
Exposure time	Longer viewing times increase accuracy.	Shapiro & Penrod (1986)
Speed of identification	Decision speed is inversely related to accuracy.	Weber et al. (2004)
Retention interval	Retention interval is inversely related to accuracy.	Shapiro & Penrod (1986)
Confidence accuracy	Relationship is modest under the best of circumstances and for witnesses who make a positive identification.	Sporer et al. (1995)
Distinctiveness	Distinctive perpetrator characteristics improve accuracy.	Shapiro & Penrod (1986)
	System variables	
Instructions	Unbiased instructions improve accuracy.	Steblay (1997)
Filler selection	Match to description strategy increases accuracy over match to suspect strategy.	Wells & Olson (2003)
Blind lineups	Blind procedures increase accuracy.	Russano et al. (2006)
Lineup presentation	Sequential presentation improves accuracy over simultaneous presentation.	Steblay et al. (2001)
Postidentification feedback	Increases witness confidence without increasing accuracy.	Douglass & Steblay (2006)

on eyewitness identification is often at odds with common sense and supports the need for expert testimony. For example, jurors, when left to their own devices, may not be aware of or do not take into consideration certain factors, such as the own-race bias and extreme stress experienced by the witness. Jurors tend to assume that eyewitness identifications are the product of eyewitness memory, and they undervalue the impact of suggestive identification procedures. Furthermore, jurors place more weight on eyewitness confidence—particularly confidence long after an identification is made (e.g., confidence expressed during a trial)—than is warranted. Indeed, the fact that well-accepted lineup procedures that have been used for decades throughout the United States have been found to be inferior to relatively simple modifications devised in the psychological laboratory is itself a form of evidence that eyewitness identification is not merely a matter of common sense (Wells & Hasel, 2008).

Another reason expert testimony is sometimes not admitted is that the judge concludes that the expert opinions are not commonly accepted among research experts. Two published surveys (Kassin, Ellsworth, & Smith, 1989; Kassin et al., 2001) of eyewitness experts have empirically addressed this conclusion. Consensus is evident in these studies, particularly in the more recent survey. For example, the Kassin and colleagues (2001) survey revealed that more than 80% of experts surveyed believed that research findings concerning unconscious transference, exposure time, simultaneous (presenting photos as a set) versus sequential presentation (presenting photos one at a time), the forgetting curve, accuracy–confidence correlation, and weapon focus were reliable enough to warrant expert testimony. Ninety percent or more of experts surveyed believed that research findings concerning the own-race bias, hypnotic susceptibility, alcohol intoxication, child suggestibility, postevent information, mug-shot-induced bias, confidence malleability, lineup instructions, and wording of questions were reliable enough for expert testimony. Comparatively lower percentages agreed about the reliability of other phenomena, for example, stress experienced by the eyewitness (60%), the influence of training for eyewitness testimony (39%), and event violence (37%). Consensus alone is a questionable criterion for admissibility because it is possible for consensus to exist in the absence of sound research. When this happens, invalid techniques or findings may be admitted in court. Likewise valid techniques and findings that are relatively new (and for which consensus has not yet developed) may be ruled inadmissible. The federal courts and many state courts now use consensus as one factor but now consider other factors as well (consistent with U.S. Supreme Court decisions in the *Daubert v. Merrell Dow Pharmaceuticals, Inc.* [1993] and *Kumho Tire Ltd. v, Carmichael* [1999] cases).

Another body of research has examined the impact of expert testimony on mock jurors' decisions, empirically addressing the concern that expert testimony will overwhelm the jury. These studies have revealed mixed findings. Most early research shows that expert testimony makes mock jurors more skeptical about eyewitness identification (Leippe, 1995). Some studies find that expert testimony improves juror sensitivity to eyewitness factors. In these studies, jurors exposed to expert testimony rely more on factors known from the research to influence eyewitness identification and less on factors that are known to not strongly predict identification accuracy, as compared to jurors not exposed to expert testimony (Cutler, Penrod, & Dexter 1989). More recent research, however, also shows that expert testimony may have no effect (Devenport & Cutler, 2004), or its effect may be complex and qualified by other factors in the trial (Leippe, Eisenstadt, Rauch, & Seib, 2004). Hence, research on the effects of testimony by eyewitness experts has not definitively established its positive effects on jury decision making. On the other hand, other areas of expert testimony are routinely accepted without such evidence, and the eyewitness area is somewhat unique in its attempts to test the benefits hypothesis. Furthermore, serious questions can be raised about how well juries are doing *without* the benefit of eyewitness experts in light of the fact that mistaken identification accounts for over 75% of the jury convictions that were later proven wrong based on forensic DNA testing (Innocence Project, 2007). In some ways, it is arbitrary to label expert testimony as the "event" and its absence as the "nonevent" because there can be untoward consequences of the default decision to not provide jurors with expert testimony information.

GAPS IN THE PRESENT SCIENTIFIC KNOWLEDGE

Controversy 1: Research on Eyewitness Identification

The gaps in the research on eyewitness identification prevent the expert from providing the court with the information that it most needs. The issue before the court is whether a given eyewitness identification is correct or incorrect. Information that would be highly diagnostic of a specific eyewitness's accuracy would include base-rate information on the accuracy of eyewitnesses, knowledge about individual differences in identification accuracy (with particular reference about the witness's personal characteristics), and how the specific conditions under which the perpetrator was viewed and identified influenced identification accuracy.

Base-rate information is critical to prediction. In the case of eyewitness identification, a critical base rate for purposes of prediction is the probability that a given lineup actually contains the perpetrator. Because a proper lineup contains only one suspect (the remainder being "fillers" who are known to not be the perpetrator), mistaken identifications of a suspect occur only when the actual perpetrator is not in the lineup (otherwise the identification of the suspect would be accurate). In experiments, the base rate for the suspect being the perpetrator is commonly set at 50%. As this base rate increases, the probability that an identified suspect is the perpetrator also increases (Wells & Lindsay, 1980). This change in the probability of error as a function of the base rate is independent of the accuracy of the eyewitnesses' memories. This happens for precisely the same reasons that a medical test (e.g., prostate test) produces many more false positives in one population (e.g., men under 40) than another population (men over 50) despite the test being equally sensitive: The base rates for the disease are higher in one population than the other. Because we do not know the real-world base rate for perpetrator-present and perpetrator-absent lineups, the science is severely limited in predicting rates of mistaken identification of suspects in the real world. It has been noted, however, that the real-world base rate is not a single figure, but instead is something that varies from one jurisdiction to another as a function of the criteria that a given police department uses to decide whether to place a suspect in a lineup (Wells, 2006; Wells & Olson, 2002).

Furthermore, eyewitness researchers sometimes deliberately calibrate their studies to produce accuracy rates around 50% because this maximum variability in accuracy allows them to detect influence of the variables of interest. Thus, it would be a gross exaggeration to conclude that laboratory research *demonstrates* that eyewitnesses are about 50% accurate. Eyewitness researchers can demonstrate any level of accuracy by manipulating the conditions under which the crime occurred or the identification is made, including mistaken identification rates of nearly 100% (cf. Wells & Bradfield, 1998). The base rate of correct or mistaken identification in actual cases is unknown.

Although it is not possible to know the base rate for the identification of innocent suspects in actual cases, there is a very interesting type of statistic that has been collected from samples of actual police lineups that has some bearing on the issue. Specifically, when a lineup is conducted properly, it is composed of one suspect (who might or might not be the perpetrator) and the remaining lineup members are merely fillers. Fillers are not suspects, and if they are identified by an eyewitness it is immediately clear that the eyewitness has made a mistake. Hence, it can be instructive to find out how often eyewitnesses identify fillers in actual cases. Several studies of this type have now been published that report the rate of filler identifications made by actual eyewitnesses to crimes. Behrman and Davey (2001) found a filler identification rate of 24%; Behrman and Richards (2005) reported a rate of 15%; Slater (1994) reported a rate of 22%; Valentine, Pickering, and Darling (2003) reported a rate of 22%; Wright and McDaid (1996) reported a rate of 20%; and Wright and Skagerberg (2007) reported a rate of 21%. Averaging across these studies yields an estimated filler identification rate of around 21%. In other words, 21% of eyewitnesses to actual crimes picked fillers when shown a lineup. Although we do not know how many of those who picked a suspect were also mistaken, the filler identification rate clearly shows that the chances for an innocent suspect being mistakenly identified are not trivial. In fact, an innocent suspect often stands a higher risk of mistaken identification than does a typical filler because of a variety of biases in the structure of the lineup and cues that the lineup administrator might inadvertently leak to the eyewitness regarding which person is the suspect and which are fillers. For example, if the fillers were chosen based on their resemblance to the suspect, the innocent suspect will inevitably look more like the perpetrator than will the fillers. As another example, if an investigator influences the eyewitness advertently or inadvertently, the influence is more likely to encourage the eyewitness to select the suspect than a filler.

The accuracy of eyewitness identification is also dependent upon individual differences. Put simply, some people are better than others at identifying strangers. Some research has attempted to identify individual characteristics that are associated with identification accuracy, such as self-reported face recognition skill, training in eyewitness identification, demographic characteristics, personality factors, and intelligence. Cutler and Penrod (1995) reviewed this literature and found few witness characteristics that reliably predicted identification accuracy. There are some notable exceptions. Young children (e.g., preschoolers) are more susceptible to mistaken identification than are older children and adults (e.g., Parker & Ryan, 1993), and own-race identifications are more likely to be accurate than other-race identifications (Meissner & Brigham, 2001). Thus, the research literature does not permit us to diagnose identification accuracy from personal characteristics with a high degree of accuracy.

As mentioned above, there is a wealth of research examining how the conditions surrounding the crime and the identification influence identification accuracy. Most of this research examines main effects of specific factors or at most two-way interactions between factors. By main effects we mean the effect of a given factor on identification accuracy while holding all other factors constant or averaging across their effects. The summary statements in Table 5.1 describe main effects of specific factors. Witnessing conditions and identification procedures, by contrast, involve combinations of factors, not main effects. Although some research has examined interactions between factors, we have relatively little knowledge about how these factors work in combination. For example, we know that other-race identifications are more likely to be incorrect than own-race identifications. We also know that the difference between own-race and other-race identifications is exacerbated by brief as compared to longer exposure time to the perpetrator (Meissner & Brigham, 2001). We do not know, however, the extent to which the magnitude of the own-race bias is further qualified by such factors as the amount of stress experienced by the witness, the suggestiveness of the lineup instructions, and the degree of resemblance between the suspect and the other persons in the lineup. Our lack of knowledge about interactions among and between witnessing conditions and lineup procedures limits our ability to assess identification accuracy given a specific set of conditions.

Another factor that would have to be considered in estimating the chances that a given eyewitness is accurate or not in a given case is the "pleading effect," recently described by Charman and Wells (2006) and by Wells, Memon, and Penrod (2006). The pleading effect refers to the fact that approximately 80% of those charged with a serious crime plead guilty and, hence, do not go to trial. Assume that those pleading guilty are almost all guilty, whereas those who are not guilty instead take their case to trial. This means that if only 4% of the suspects identified are innocent (and hence all go to trial), whereas a mere 20% of the 96% who are guilty go to trial (the remaining pleading guilty), then at trial level the rate of mistaken identification is over 17%. Using this same logic, if 10% of the identified suspects are innocent and all go to trial, whereas a mere 20% of the 90% who are guilty go to trial, then the rate of mistaken identification at the trial level leaps to more than 35%.

In summary, the gaps in the research literature on eyewitness identification include lack of knowledge about (1) the base rates of accurate and mistaken eyewitness identification, (2) individual difference factors affecting eyewitness identification, (3) interactions between variables, and (4) the unique characteristics of cases that actually proceed to trial. We turn now to gaps in the research on expert testimony.

Controversy 2: Expert Testimony

In some respects, it is ironic that gaps in the research on expert testimony are used as a basis for denying admissibility. The irony stems from the fact that no other scholarly discipline in which experts testify (i.e., outside of psychology) has empirically addressed the admissibility arguments and their impact on juries. Specifically, psychologists, as noted above, have conducted scientific research on such questions as whether the knowledge gleaned from the research exceeds common sense, whether scholars with relevant expertise agree on the reliability of research conclusions, and the extent to which expert testimony assists or prejudices the jury. Nevertheless, having trained our microscopes on these empirical issues, the scientific methods underlying these studies are fair game for scrutiny. Shortcomings associated with the research have been identified, and the quality of the research has been a basis for cross-examination and argument in admissibility hearings.

Consider the argument that expert testimony should be admitted because lay jurors need to be educated about the factors that influence identification accuracy. The research supporting this assertion relies on general knowledge tests of the public, studies in which participants are asked to estimate the outcomes of scientific experiments on eyewitness identification, and studies of mock juror decisions. Surveys of lay knowledge have been criticized because the act of completing a survey does not resemble the task facing an actual juror. The knowledge tests themselves (i.e., the wording of the questions and the scoring of the answers) have been the subject of critique. Mock juror studies have been criticized because the studies often rely on college students rather than the kinds of people who serve on juries. Furthermore, mock trials by necessity rely on abbreviated trial materials, including written narratives, and have therefore been criticized for not being realistic. The decisions of mock jurors have no real consequences for the defendant. In short, both the surveys of general knowledge and the trial simulation research lack the trappings of an actual court case, and some are unwilling to conclude that the research can be generalized to actual trials. The gap in the literature is research showing that actual jurors judging actual cases lack the requisite knowledge for evaluating the accuracy of eyewitness identification.

In a similar fashion, there are gaps in the research on general acceptance. Indeed, there are only two surveys of experts, both conducted by the same lead investigator (Kassin et al., 1989, 2001). When these studies are reviewed by an expert witness during an admissibility hearing, the methods and conclusions of the research are scrutinized. Cross-examination has focused on such issues as how "experts" are defined in the survey studies. The surveys included only eyewitness experts, but should it have included other cognitive psychologists with expertise on human memory? The sample size (64 in the 2001 study) is small, and therefore the margin of error is substantial. To what extent are the experts' opinions influenced by their vested interest in the admissibility of expert testimony? Were experts whose opinions are known to differ from the consensus included in the survey?

MYTHS AND MISCONCEPTIONS

Several myths and misconceptions about expert testimony are associated with the above-noted gaps in the scientific knowledge and are harbored by the various players within the justice system. First, many defense attorneys would like to believe that citizens make poor eyewitnesses and that eyewitness identifications are usually incorrect. There is no scientific basis for this belief. The research clearly demonstrates that mistaken eyewitness identifications occur and that the likelihood of mistaken identification is systematically influenced by certain factors associated with the crime and identification (see Table 5.1), but the research provides no firm base rate of mistaken identifications. Earlier we noted that laboratory studies yield about a 50% accuracy rate, but this figure should not be mistaken for the base rate in actual cases because laboratory conditions are often *designed to achieve* about a 50% accuracy rate. Prosecuting attorneys occasionally attack expert testimony based on misconceptions, and judges' often deny proffers of expert testimony based on these same misconceptions. These misconceptions include the beliefs that eyewitness research is not generally accepted within the scientific community, the research findings are a matter of common sense, and the research does not apply to actual crimes. Citizens, who serve as jurors, are known to have misconceptions about how certain factors influence identification accuracy. These misconceptions are revealed in surveys of lay knowledge about eyewitness memory and include such mistaken beliefs as extreme stress improves identification accuracy, and eyewitness confidence is strongly related to identification accuracy (Schmechel et al., 2006).

THE STATE OF THE SCIENCE

In discussing the scientifically supported and unsupported use of expert testimony, it is helpful to review the distinction between "social fact" and "social framework" expert testimony as articulated by Monahan and Walker (2002). Social fact testimony refers to testimony about the specific fact in question (e.g., whether the eyewitness identification is accurate). Social framework testimony may be offered when an issue in question is an instance of a scientific finding or theory (e.g., research on the relation between stress experienced by the eyewitness and identification accuracy may be relevant to the ultimate issue of whether the identification is correct). In short, social framework testimony is a scientifically supported use, whereas social fact testimony is a scientifically unsupported use.

Scientifically Supported Uses

Expert testimony has several scientifically supported uses. The main scientifically supported use is to educate jurors and judges about basic processes in human memory and about the factors that are known from the research to predict (and the factors that are known not to predict) the accuracy of eyewitness identifications (i.e., social framework expert testimony). For example, a review of the police reports might reveal the potential for extreme stress and weapon focus to have influenced the accuracy of the identification in the case. If so, it would be reasonable to testify about the research findings concerning the effects of extreme stress and weapon focus.

Another scientifically supported use is to evaluate the quality of identification tests, such as show-ups and lineups. An evaluation can take several forms. A review of the file might reveal that a lineup was given with or without a set of written instructions and that the lineup was not blind (i.e., the investigator who conducted the test knew which photo was of the suspect). One scientifically supported use, therefore, is to testify about the research addressing the effects of instructions and blind administration procedures on identification accuracy. A second method of evaluating identification procedures involves comparing the procedures used in the case with those embodied in scientifically determined best practices (Wells et al., 1998). The procedures used can also be compared against practices recommended by the Department of Justice, American Bar Association, and state- or department-level guidelines. A third method involves empirical assessments of lineups. An empirical assessment may be conducted when there is a concern that the photo of the suspect stands out in such a way that it is obvious which photo in the array is that of the suspect. The photo could stand out because of its similarity to the perpetrator relative to the other photos or because of nature of the photograph itself (e.g., unique background for the photo). There exists a technology for assessing the fairness of lineup composition and metrics for summarizing lineup fairness (Malpass & Lindsay, 1999; Tredoux, 1998; Wells, Leippe, & Ostrom, 1979). Generally, this technology involves providing individuals (non-eyewitnesses) with the eyewitness's description of the perpetrator and asking them to attempt to identify the suspect from the lineup. If the suspect's photo stands out because it is the only one that matches the description of the perpetrator, the "mock witnesses" will be able to identify the perpetrator. This is a sign of a biased lineup. If the suspect's photo does not stand out, the mock witnesses should identify the suspect photo only at chance levels.

Scientifically Unsupported Uses

The main value of expert testimony is to educate the jury about eyewitness memory and the research findings. The state of the science, as summarized above, does not permit an assessment of the accuracy of an individual eyewitness. Accordingly, an opinion that a witness in a specific set of circumstances is unlikely to be accurate (i.e., social fact expert testimony) is not a scientifically supported use of expert testimony. At first glance it may seem as if we have made a straw man argument, for, by law, determination of the accuracy of a witness is the responsibility of the jury, and the judge should not even allow such an expert opinion. Based on this fact, the expert should never be put in the position to give an opinion about the accuracy of an individual eyewitness even if he or she desired to do so. In practice, however, judges vary considerably in their interpretations of what is and what is not allowable. For example, in one case in which the first author testified, the judge expressed surprise and disappointment that the expert was not prepared to give an opinion about the accuracy of the witness. Some judges may allow such an opinion even though it seems at variance with the law. If the judge does not allow it, a clever attorney may find a way to broach the subject, such as with the use of a hypothetical question (e.g., "If a person was robbed by a perpetrator of another race under extremely high stress conditions and was shown a suggestive lineup, is it likely that the victim would make a mistaken identification?"). The judge may permit such a question, thus allowing the expert to given an opinion that may be generalized to the specific witness in the trial. Put bluntly, any statement that allows the jury to infer that the expert believes a specific witness to be inaccurate, whether in response to a direct or hypothetical question, is a scientifically unsupported use of expert testimony. A related scientifically unsupported use of expert testimony is to convey the opinion (directly or indirectly) that an identification procedure is incapable of producing a correct identification. Suggestive identification procedures or procedures that do not meet best practice standards are quite capable of producing correct identifications.

Another category of scientifically unsupported testimony would be testimony that is at odds with the scientific research. As in any field, expert testimony should be limited to conclusions that are based on sound science. General acceptance of the research conclusions is usually a good indictor of the soundness of the underlying science. For a summary of generally accepted findings in the research on eyewitness memory, see Kassin and colleagues (2001).

Scientifically Controversial or Untested Issues

Although the research literature on eyewitness identification is substantial and mature, it is not exhaustive, and it has not examined the effects of all of the factors and combinations of factors that are found in actual crimes. Accordingly, experts may occasionally find themselves in the position to testify about factors that have not been subjected to scientific research or have been studied but with mixed findings. Some, for example, maintain that the research base is not adequate to support testimony that simultaneous presentation yields a greater rate of mistaken identifications than sequential presentation because the potential qualifying conditions have not been sufficiently examined in research (McQuiston-Surrett, Malpass, & Tredoux, 2006). When faced with such situations, the expert might take a conservative approach and offer no testimony about an unstudied phenomenon, or the expert might extrapolate from related research. In the latter case, the expert should, of course, explain the basis for and limits of his or her testimony.

We have discussed scientifically supported uses of expert testimony (explanations of how factors influence accuracy in the research and assessments of identification tests), scientifically unsupported uses of expert testimony (opinions about the accuracy of individual eyewitnesses), and scientifically untested issues (explanations of factors that have not been studied in research or that have mixed findings). Most expert testimony content can be classified into these three categories, and there is little else with respect to the content of testimony that might be labeled controversial. The controversial aspect of this type of expert testimony is whether it should be allowed in the first place, as discussed above.

COMMUNICATING CONSENSUS AND CONTROVERSIES IN EYEWITNESS TESTIMONY

Circumstances in Which Expert Testimony Is Helpful

Having articulated the state of the science underlying expert testimony, we now turn to the manner in which expert testimony is presented. Before providing advice concerning the content of testimony and reports, however, we must consider the more general issue of the conditions under which expert testimony is more or less useful to the jury. This discussion requires that we distinguish between what Wells and Loftus (2003) refer to as "general impairment" and "suspect-bias" factors. General impairment factors roughly correspond to estimator variables; they are the factors that would lead to a general impairment of the eyewitness's ability to encode a perpetrator's characteristics—for example, exposure time, stress experienced by the eyewitness, and cross-race recognition.

Suspect-bias factors are a subset of system variables pertaining to structural features of a photo array or lineup procedure that individuate the suspect among the fillers and increase the likelihood that the suspect will be identified regardless of whether he is the perpetrator. Suspect-bias factors can best be understood in the broader context of the lineup as a forensic test of the hypothesis that the suspect is the perpetrator (see Wells & Luus, 1990, for a similar and more thorough theoretical analysis of lineups). A valid test is one that maximizes the likelihood that the identification is a product of the eyewitness's memory and minimizes the likelihood that the identification is due to other factors. What are those "other" factors that could explain a positive identification of an innocent suspect? We identify five such suspect-bias factors: (1) the suspect has a close physical resemblance to the perpetrator; (2) the eyewitness identified the suspect by guessing; (3) some visual characteristic of the lineup makes the suspect stand out relative to the fillers (e.g., if the suspect is the only one who matches the description of the perpetrator); (4) the suspect is not the perpetrator but is otherwise familiar to the eyewitness (e.g., from having seen the suspect or his or her photo in a prior identification test), and the eyewitness confuses the source of this familiarity; and (5) the eyewitness is influenced by the lineup administrator to select the suspect. Good lineup tests are those that minimize the likelihood that an eyewitness's identification can be explained by one or more of these five suspect-bias factors.

Expert testimony is most helpful when suspect-bias factors are in play. As noted in Table 5.1, experts have a good deal to say about how such factors as lineup instructions, composition, presentation, and investigator bias can increase the likelihood that suspect identifications are due to reasons other than the eyewitness's memory of the perpetrator. In these cases, it is helpful to have the expert address both general impairment and suspect-bias factors. General impairment factors speak to the strength of the eyewitness's memory of the perpetrator, and suspect-bias factors help explain why an eyewitness with a weak memory of the perpetrator might nevertheless identify a suspect and come to believe strongly in the identification. For example, an eyewitness who had minimal opportunity to encode the perpetrator's face due to short exposure time and high stress might identify the suspect from a lineup because the investigator inadvertently conveyed the suspect's identity to the eyewitness during the lineup procedure.

When suspect-bias factors are not in play, however, expert testimony is of limited usefulness, even in the presence of general impairment variables. Consider, for example, a case in which an eyewitness who had only a short time to encode a perpetrator's characteristics identifies the suspect from a lineup conducted by an investigator who is blind to the suspect's identity and uses unbiased lineup instructions and photos of fillers that match the eyewitness's description of the perpetrator presented sequentially to the eyewitness (i.e., a procedure reflecting modern "best practices"). In this case, the expert's explanation of the importance of general impairment factors is not very helpful because it begs the question of why the eyewitness identified the suspect and not one of the fillers. The use of a good lineup procedure minimizes the likelihood that suspect-bias factors explain the eyewitness identification and maximizes the likelihood that the eyewitness identification is explained by the eyewitness's memory of the perpetrator. In this circumstance, therefore, the jury is not helped very much by testimony concerning general impairment factors. In the absence of suspect-bias factors that might explain away a positive identification, the jury would reasonably conclude that the eyewitness's memory, no matter how impaired, was sufficient to produce a positive suspect identification *from memory*. In sum, expert testimony is most helpful in cases in which suspect-bias variables might explain the eyewitness identification and least helpful in cases in which suspect-bias variables are not relevant.

To this point we have focused on cases involving lineup identifications. Some cases, however, involve show-up identifications. Show-ups involve the presentation of a single suspect (or single photo) to the eyewitness. Whereas show-up procedures can vary with respect to the degree to which they are contaminated by suspect-bias factors (e.g., instructions to the eyewitness, influence by the show-up administrator), suspect-bias factors are always present and can explain positive identifications. Because there is only one suspect, the suspect's identity obviously stands out to both the eyewitness and the investigator before any "test" is conducted. In cases that are based on show-ups, therefore, testimony about general impairment factors is helpful. An eyewitness who has a weak memory of the perpetrator can identify the suspect from a show-up by guessing, deduction, or investigator influence, and it is impossible to rule out these explanations even when show-ups are conducted according to best practices.

Content of Reports and Testimony

The requirements and recommended practices for reports and courtroom testimony differ substantially. Written reports usually serve one of two purposes. One purpose is to proffer the expert testimony. The report normally (1) summarizes the proposed content of testimony and the empirically demonstrated need for the proposed expert testimony and (2) describes the witnessing and lineup factors that will comprise the testimony (with scholarly references). The report also summarizes the research showing that the factors in the proposed testimony are based on sound science, generally accepted in the scientific community, and not merely a matter of common sense. In anticipation of concerns by the ruling judge, the report should also clearly indicate that the expert will not offer an opinion about the accuracy of the eyewitness.

A second purpose of a report is to satisfy discovery requirements. In some jurisdictions, the opposing counsel is entitled to a written report summarizing the content of the proffered testimony. The reporting requirements vary by jurisdiction. In some jurisdictions, a brief memo summarizing the factors to be discussed is sufficient; in others, a signed affidavit with more elaborate summary and references may be required. The opposing counsel is entitled to depose the expert in advance of the trial in some jurisdictions.

From the perspective of the court, expert testimony about eyewitness memory is a unique form of *psychological* expert testimony. Often when psychologists testify as experts, the testimony is based on psychological assessment of a specific individual, such as a defendant's competence. The eyewitness expert, however, conducts no assessment of the individual eyewitness, offers no opinion about the individual eyewitness, and instead testifies about general research conclusions (though the expert might offer an opinion about the quality of identification procedures used in the case). Because expert testimony concerns research conclusions, it behooves the expert to take special care in formulating testimony content that will be understood by laypeople. The discourse should be geared toward the level of a college freshman enrolled in and Introductory Psychology course. Scientific concepts that experts use routinely, such as independent variable, manipulated factor, confound, and statistical significance, are terms that may be lost on the jury. The use of concrete examples to illustrate such concepts as manipulated factors and confounding variables is advisable.

A common dilemma for the expert is the level of detail to provide about the research. On one extreme, the expert might offer the conclusions about the research (e.g., eyewitnesses make more mistakes when attempting to identify perpetrators of another race than perpetrators of their own race) without much detail about the research. At the other extreme, the expert might offer much more detail, including sample studies, mean differences between conditions, and effect-size estimates. There are benefits and costs of each approach. The less detailed approach has the advantage of simplicity and efficiency but may leave the jurors wanting more information. The more detailed approach provides the additional information but adds complexity that may be misunderstood and therefore has a greater potential to mislead the jury. For example, a jury might conclude that the magnitude of mean differences between two conditions observed in a laboratory would general-ize to the specific situation in the trial, but this is not an appropriate conclu-sion. The content of the testimony is also dependent upon the preferences of the attorney who is conducting the direct examination, and some attorneys ask for more detail, others ask for less.

In our experience, the attorneys who hire eyewitness experts often do not have previous experience with this form of expert testimony and yet sometimes approach the task with preconceived notions of the content of the testimony. The expert, therefore, must educate the attorney about the scientifically supported and unsupported aspects of expert testimony and work with him or her to develop questions for direct examination that allow the expert to convey the science accurately and in a manner that can be understood by the jury.

CONCLUSIONS

We have divided the territory concerning expert testimony into two sub-topics: controversies about the research and controversies about expert tes-timony. With respect to the former, there is a large body of research on human memory and social influence for experts to draw on to assist the jury in evaluating eyewitness identification (see Table 5.1). Gaps in the literature exist. These gaps include not knowing the base rates of mistaken identifica-tion, individual differences, interactions between variables, and characteris-tics of cases that go to trial.

A large body of research now addresses expert testimony on eyewitness identification itself. Some of this research speaks directly to legal standards of admissibility. The *Frye* test (*Frye v. United States*, 1923), for instance, is concerned with whether the opinion is based on knowledge or techniques that are generally accepted in the expert's field. The survey literature that we described (e.g., Kassin et al., 2001) suggests that eyewitness identification research passes the *Frye* test on most variables. But general acceptance is only one factor in legal admissibility of expert testimony. The more predominant admissibility test today, the *Daubert* (1993) ruling, inquires whether the expert testimony is based on methods and principles that are likely to produce valid opinions. The experimental methods that are used in eyewitness research tend to guarantee internal validity, so the issue is largely one of external validity. We have explained how eyewitness experts can restrict their conclusions (e.g., not claiming that absolute rates of misidentification in experiments are directly applicable to a specific case) and focus instead on descriptions of relations among variables (e.g., cross-race identifications are less reliable than are within-race identifications). A third broad legal consideration for admissibility of expert testimony is relevancy. We have reviewed data indicating that the kind of information eyewitness experts convey appear not to be mere common sense and that expert testimony appears to affect how mock jurors reason about the evidence, suggesting that such expert testimony is relevant to the jury.

We have reviewed scientifically supported and unsupported uses of expert testimony. Scientifically supported uses of expert testimony include educating judges and juries about eyewitness memory and the factors known to influence eyewitness memory, such as those summarized in Table 5.1. Scientifically unsupported uses include offering an opinion about the accuracy of a specific eyewitness. We explained that when suspect-bias factors are not in play, the helpfulness of expert testimony about general impairment factors is limited, and we offered suggestions for how to effectively convey expert knowledge in expert reports and testimony.

We have identified some important factors for eyewitness researchers to consider if they proffer expert testimony, and we have identified some limits to what we think experts can and cannot claim based on the research. At the same time, we have refrained from taking a position as to whether courts are always wrong when they deny admission of expert testimony or are always right when they admit expert testimony. In general, we caution young eyewitness researchers to not be overly eager to proffer expert testimony. The justice system's adversarial structure is a poor fit with the scientist's normal experiences in dealing with other scientists. Some defense attorneys, for instance, are not forthright with information contrary to their client's case. Regardless of which side retains the expert's services, there is pressure to go further than the science itself justifies. And, money from expert fees has the potential to lure the expert to satisfy the retaining attorneys or to win the case instead of educating the jury.

REFERENCES

Behrman, B. W., & Davey, S. L. (2001). Eyewitness identification in actual criminal cases: An archival analysis. *Law and Human Behavior, 25*, 475–491.

Behrman, B. W., & Richards, R. E. (2005). Suspect/foil identification in actual crimes and in the laboratory: A reality monitoring analysis. *Law and Human Behavior, 29*, 279–301.

Benton, T. R., Ross, D. F., Bradshaw, E., Thomas, W. N., & Bradshaw, G. S. (2006). Eyewitness memory is still not common sense: Comparing jurors, judges, and law enforcement to eyewitness experts. *Applied Cognitive Psychology, 20*, 115–129.

Charman, S. D., & Wells, G. L. (2006). Applied lineup theory. In R. C. L. Lindsay, D. F. Ross, J. D. Read, & M. P. Toglia (Eds.), *The handbook of eyewitness psychology: Memory for people* (Vol. II, pp. 219–254). Mahwah, NJ: Erlbaum.

Cutler, B. L. (2006). A sample of witness, crime, and perpetrator characteristics affecting eyewitness identification accuracy. *Cardozo Public Law, Policy, and Ethics Journal, 4*, 327–340.

Cutler, B. L., & Penrod, S. D. (1995). *Mistaken identification: The eyewitness, psychology, and the law.* Cambridge, UK: Cambridge University Press.

Cutler, B. L., Penrod, S. D., & Dexter, H. R. (1989). The eyewitness, the expert psychologist, and the jury. *Law and Human Behavior, 13*, 311–332.

Cutler, B. L., Penrod, S. D., & Dexter, H. R. (1990). Juror sensitivity to eyewitness identification evidence. *Law and Human Behavior, 14*, 185–191.

Daubert v. Merrell Dow Pharmaceuticals, Inc., 113 S. Ct. 2786 (1993).

Deffenbacher, K. A., Bornstein, B. H., Penrod, S. D., & McGorty, E. K. (2004). A meta-analytic review of the effects of high stress on eyewitness memory. *Law and Human Behavior, 28*, 687–706.

Douglass, A. B., & Steblay, N. M. (2006). Memory distortion in eyewitnesses: A meta-analysis of the post-identification feedback effect. *Applied Cognitive Psychology, 20*, 859–869.

Doyle, J. M. (2005). *True witness: Cops, courts, science, and the battle against misidentification.* London: Macmillan.

Frye v. United States, 293 F. 1013 (D.C. Cir. 1923).

Innocence Project. (2007). *The Benjamin N. Cardozo School of Law at Yeshiva University.* Retrieved July 5, 2007, from *www.innocenceproject.org.*

Kassin, S. M., Ellsworth, P. C., & Smith, V. L. (1989). The "general acceptance" of psychological research on eyewitness testimony: A survey of the experts. *American Psychologist, 44*(8), 1089–1098.

Kassin, S. M., Tubb, V. A., Hosch, H. M., & Memon, A. (2001). On the "general acceptance" of eyewitness testimony research: A new survey of experts. *American Psychologist, 56*, 405–416.

Kumho Tire Co. Ltd. v. Carmichael, 526 U.S. 137 (1999).

Leippe, M. R. (1995). The case for expert testimony about eyewitness memory. *Psychology, Public Policy, and Law, 1*(4), 909–959.

Leippe, M. R., Eisenstadt, D., Rauch, S. M., & Seib, J. M. (2004). Timing of eyewitness expert testimony, jurors' need for cognition, and case strength as determinants of trial verdicts. *Journal of Applied Psychology, 89*, 524–541.

Malpass, R. S., & Lindsay, R. C. L. (1999). Measuring lineup fairness. *Applied Cognitive Psychology, 13*, 1–7.

McQuiston-Surrett, D. E., Malpass, R. S., & Tredoux, C. G. (2006). Sequential vs. simultaneous lineups: A review of methods, data, and theory. *Psychology, Public Policy, and Law, 12*, 137–169.

Meissner, C., & Brigham, J. (2001). Thirty years of investigating the own-race bias in memory for faces: A meta-analytic review. *Psychology, Public Policy, and Law, 7*, 3–35.

Monahan, J., & Walker, L. (2002). *Social science in law: Cases and materials* (5th ed.). Westbury, NY: Foundation.

Neuschatz, J. S., & Cutler, B. L. (2008). Eyewitness identification. In H. L. Roediger III (Ed.), *Learning and memory: A comprehensive reference: Vol. 2. Cognitive psychology of memory* (pp. 845–865). Oxford, UK: Elsevier.

Parker, J. F., & Ryan, V. (1993). An attempt to reduce guessing behavior in children's and adults' eyewitness identifications. *Law and Human Behavior, 17*, 11–26.

Platz, S. J., & Hosch, H. M. (1988). Cross-racial/ethnic eyewitness identification: A field study. *Journal of Applied Social Psychology, 18*, 972–984.

Russano, M. B., Dickinson, J. J., Greathouse, S. M., & Kovera, M. B. (2006). "Why don't you take another look at number three?": Investigator knowledge and its effects on eyewitness confidence and identification decisions. *Cardozo Public Law, Policy, and Ethics Journal, 4*, 355–379.

Schmechel, R. S., O'Toole, T. P., Easterly, C., & Loftus, E. F. (2006). Beyond the ken: Testing jurors' understanding of eyewitness reliability evidence. *Jurimetrics Journal, 46*, 177–214.

Shapiro, P., & Penrod, S. D. (1986). Meta analysis of the facial identification literature. *Psychological Bulletin, 100*, 139–156.

Slater, A. (1994). *Identification parades: A scientific evaluation* [Police Research Award Scheme]. London: Police Research Group, Home Office.

Sporer, S. L., Penrod, S., Read, D., & Cutler, B. (1995). Choosing, confidence, and accuracy: A meta-analysis of the confidence–accuracy relation in eyewitness identification studies. *Psychological Bulletin, 118*, 315–327.

Steblay, N. M. (1992). A meta-analytic review of the weapon focus effect. *Law and Human Behavior, 16*, 413–424.

Steblay, N. M. (1997). Social influences in eyewitness recall: A meta-analytic review of lineup instruction effects. *Law and Human Behavior, 21*(3), 283–297.

Steblay, N. M., Dysart, J., Fulero, S., & Lindsay, R. C. L. (2001). Eyewitness accuracy rates in sequential and simultaneous lineup presentations: A meta-analytic comparison. *Law and Human Behavior, 25,* 459–473.

Tredoux, C. G. (1998). Statistical inference on measures of lineup fairness. *Law and Human Behavior, 22,* 217–237.

Valentine, T., Pickering, A., & Darling, S. (2003). Characteristics of eyewitness identification that predict the outcome of real lineups. *Applied Cognitive Psychology, 17,* 969–993.

Van Wallendael, L. R., Devenport, J. L., Cutler, B. L., & Penrod, S. D. (2007). Mistaken identification = erroneous convictions: Assessing and improving legal safe guards. In R. C. L. Lindsay, D. F. Ross, J. D. Read, & M. P. Toglia (Eds.), *Handbook of eyewitness psychology: Memory for people* (Vol. II, pp. 557–572). Mahwah, NJ: Erlbaum.

Weber, N., Brewer, N., Wells, G., Semmler, C., & Keast, A. (2004). Eyewitness identification accuracy and response latency: The unruly 10–12 second rule. *Journal of Experimental Psychology: Applied, 10*(3), 139–147.

Wells, G. L. (1978). Applied eyewitness testimony research: System variables and estimator variables. *Journal of Personality and Social Psychology, 36,* 15461557.

Wells, G. L. (1984). How adequate is human intuition for judging eyewitness testimony? In G. L. Wells & E. F. Loftus (Eds.), *Eyewitness testimony: Psychological perspectives* (pp. 256–272). New York: Cambridge University Press.

Wells, G. L. (2006). *What is wrong with the Manson v. Braithwaite test of eyewitness identification accuracy?* Unpublished manuscript, Iowa State University, Ames.

Wells, G. L., & Bradfield, A. L. (1998). "Good, you identified the suspect": Feedback to eyewitnesses distorts their reports of the witnessing experience. *Journal of Applied Psychology, 83,* 360–376.

Wells, G. L., & Hasel, L. E. (2008). Eyewitness identification: Issues in common knowledge and generalization. In E. Borgida & S. Fiske (Eds.), *Beyond common sense: Psychological science in the courtroom* (pp. 159–176). Malden, MA: Blackwell.

Wells, G. L., Leippe, M. R., & Ostrom, T. M. (1979). Guidelines for empirically assessing the fairness of a lineup. *Law and Human Behavior, 3*(4), 285–293.

Wells, G. L., & Lindsay, R. C. L. (1980). On estimating the diagnosticity of eyewitness nonidentifications. *Psychological Bulletin, 88,* 776–784.

Wells, G. L., & Loftus, E. F. (2003). Eyewitness memory for people and events. In A. Goldstein (Ed.), *Handbook of psychology: Forensic psychology* (Vol. 11, pp. 149–160). New York: Wiley.

Wells, G. L., & Luus, E. (1990). Police lineups as experiments: Social methodology as a framework for properly-conducted lineups. *Personality and Social Psychology Bulletin, 16,* 106–117.

Wells, G. L., Memon, A., & Penrod, S. (2006). Eyewitness evidence: Improving its probative value. *Psychological Science in the Public Interest, 7,* 45–75.

Wells, G. L., & Olson, E. (2002). Eyewitness identification: Information gain from incriminating and exonerating behaviors. *Journal of Experimental Psychology: Applied, 8*, 155–167.

Wells, G. L., & Olson, E. (2003). Eyewitness testimony. *Annual Review of Psychology, 54*, 277–295.

Wright, D. B., & McDaid, A. T. (1996). Comparing system and estimator variables using data from real lineups. *Applied Cognitive Psychology, 10*, 75–84.

Wright, D. B., & Skagerberg, E. M. (2007). Post-identification feedback affects real eyewitnesses. *Psychological Science, 18*, 172–178.

CHAPTER 6

Techniques and Controversies in the Interrogation of Suspects

THE ARTFUL PRACTICE VERSUS THE SCIENTIFIC STUDY

Allison D. Redlich and Christian A. Meissner

Over the past decade the topics of false confessions and police interrogations have received a great deal of deserved attention, both from the scientific community (for reviews, see Gudjonsson, 2003; Kassin, 2005; Kassin & Gudjonsson, 2004) and the popular press (e.g., Grisham, 2006). High-profile cases of proven false confession, such as the Michael Crowe and Joshua Treadway case, provide tragic examples of the cracks—or sometimes gaping holes—in the criminal justice system. Michael Crowe was 14 years old when his sister Stephanie was found murdered in their home. After a total of 9 hours of intense interrogation, which included several false evidence ploys (e.g., claims that Michael had failed the infallible Computer Voice Stress Analyzer test, and that the victim had Michael's hair in her hand), Michael succumbed to the pressure and falsely confessed. Joshua, Michael's friend and believed coperpetrator, was interrogated on tape for a total of 22 hours and eventually falsely confessed as well. Fortunately for Michael and Joshua, their innocence was revealed when Stephanie's blood was discovered on the sweatshirt of a homeless drifter, Richard Tuite, who was subsequently tried and convicted.

Cases such as Crowe's and Treadway's have been instrumental in furthering public awareness regarding the influence of problematic interrogation techniques in leading to false confessions and the inadequacy of current safeguards within the legal system that might otherwise prevent such miscarriages of justice. As a result, psychologists are increasingly asked to provide expert testimony on these topics in the courtroom (see Costanzo & Leo, 2006; Davis & Leo, 2006; Fulero, 2004; Kassin, 2008; Quintieri & Weiss, 2005).

In this chapter we review three defining issues related to the interrogation of suspects by police, addressing the controversies, the techniques employed, and the extant research. We then discuss gaps in our knowledge germane to courtroom testimony and dispel common myths and misconceptions. Throughout this chapter we attempt to make clear the distinction between the science comprising the expert witness's research/testimony and the artful practice of interrogation. In disputed confession cases, triers of fact must weigh the research that supports the experts' testimony against the legitimacy of the interrogation techniques that led to the alleged confession. It is in this context that we frame our discussion.

POLICE INTERROGATION:
OVERVIEW OF TECHNIQUES AND CONTROVERSIES

Contemporary interrogation techniques must be discussed in regard to false confessions, particularly those that emanate from police pressure. There are several exemplary and comprehensive reviews of police interrogation techniques and related research now available (Davis & O'Donohue, 2003; Gudjonsson, 2003; Kassin, 2005; Lassiter, 2004; Leo, 2008). By all accounts, contemporary police interrogators utilize "psychology" in their efforts to obtain confessions (Inbau, Reid, Buckley, & Jayne, 2001; Kassin, 2005; Leo, 1996, 2004). However, it is important not to mistake the process of interrogation for a "science" like psychology. Interrogators are not trained in, nor do they employ, the scientific method, which involves the formulation and testing of hypotheses in support of, or in an attempt to falsify, a general theory. We focus on three controversial aspects that highlight the nonscientific nature of interrogation: (1) the detection of deception, (2) the presumption of guilt, and (3) the techniques employed in real-world interrogations. As will become clear, these aspects are intertwined. The interrogator's perceived ability to detect when suspects are deceitful is the process that leads to perceptions of guilt, and to the interrogation techniques employed thereafter (Meissner & Kassin, 2004). At the point of interrogation, this process of biased hypothesis testing on the part of the interrogator can lead to the use of these other problematic tactics, such as confronting suspects with guilt and disallowing denials, questioning suspects for long periods, presenting false evidence, and minimizing responsibility. Such techniques were developed absent scientific inquiry or verification that might allow for an assessment of their diagnostic value in extracting true confessions of guilt. Below we introduce these concepts and controversies and then describe the psychological research that has sought to address them.

Deception Detection

An important distinction between *interviews* and *interrogations* is often made in manuals of police interrogation (see Inbau et al., 2001, Chapter 1). During the interview period (e.g., the "Behavioral Analysis Interview," or BAI, proposed by Inbau et al., 2001), the investigator is trained to question in a nonaccusatory manner to determine whether the person of interest is indeed "the suspect" and should therefore be formally interrogated. A major part of this determination of guilt is a reliance on nonverbal behavioral cues and analyses of linguistic styles that are believed to indicate deception. For example, Reid and associates offer training in human lie detection that is purported to increase the accuracy with which investigators can distinguish between truth and deceit to 85% (*www.reid.com*). As we discuss below, research has not supported the theory that behaviors or response styles reliably distinguish truth from deception, as opposed to nervousness, stress, or being too hot, for example. Science has also not supported the notion that investigators are adept at detecting deception in interviews, regardless of whether the suspect is guilty or innocent.

PRESUMPTION OF GUILT

By definition, interrogations are guilt-presumptive processes—they are focused on extracting a confession from suspects who are believed to be guilty of the crime (Inbau et al., 2001; Meissner & Kassin, 2002, 2004). As a result, some interrogators claim that they do not interrogate innocent people (see Kassin, 2005). For example, Inbau and colleagues (2001) suggest that interrogation procedures should be applied only against those found to be deceptive in a preinterrogation interview and thereby believed to be guilty of the crime. In presuming guilt, the potential for "confirmation bias" is inherent. Together, the use of questionable deception detection techniques and a strong presumption of guilt on the part of the investigator can be dangerous to innocent suspects, placing them at risk for the pressures of interrogation (Kassin, 2005; Meissner & Kassin, 2004).

Modern Interrogation Techniques

Throughout history, investigators have resorted to a wide variety of techniques intended to break down a suspect's resistance and yield a confession. Interrogation techniques have evolved from overtly coercive, "third-degree" tactics (e.g., beatings, extreme sleep deprivation; see Leo, 2004) to modern-day practices that involve subtler, yet effective, psychologically based techniques. One of the most heralded and widely cited procedures in the United States is known as the Reid Technique of investigative interviewing and interrogation. Other techniques often cited by law enforcement, including the Kinesic Interview (Walters, 2003) and others (Butterfield, 2002; Mac-Donald & Michaud, 1992; Schafer & Navarro, 2004), advocate essentially the same types of procedures for extracting a confession (Narchet, Coffman, Russano, & Meissner, 2004). As Kassin and Gudjonsson (2004) summarize, interrogations can be thought of as involving three general phases: (1) *custody and isolation*, in which the suspect is detained in a small room and left to experience the anxiety, insecurity, and uncertainty associated with police interrogation; (2) *confrontation*, in which the suspect is presumed guilty and told (sometimes falsely) about the evidence against him or her, is warned of the consequences associated with his or her guilt, and is prevented from denying involvement in the crime; and finally, (3) *minimization*, in which a now sympathetic interrogator attempts to gain the suspect's trust, offers the suspect face-saving excuses or justifications for the crime and implies more lenient consequences should the suspect provide a confession.

Reid interrogation techniques, among others, can be effective in eliciting true confessions (e.g., see Leo, 1996; Russano, Meissner, Narchet, & Kassin, 2005) largely as a result of social influence processes that have been shown to produce powerful effects in psychological studies of conformity (Asch, 1956), obedience to authority (Milgram, 1974), and compliance to requests (Cialdini, 2000)—but could such techniques also yield false confessions? Inbau and colleagues (2001) argue that innocent suspects will not be compelled to confess with these methods, primarily due to the belief that such individuals are excluded from interrogation based on a successful preinterview. However, there are no scientific data supporting the effectiveness of interrogation procedures in eliciting *diagnostic information* from a suspect (i.e., a greater likelihood of true vs. false information). In contrast, numerous researchers have expressed concern that some of the techniques regularly employed by law enforcement may, in fact, place innocent suspects, particularly those with identified risk factors, in jeopardy of making false self-incriminating statements (Gudjonsson, 2003; Hartwig, Granhag, Stromwall, & Vrij, 2005; Kassin, 2005; Kassin & Gudjonsson, 2004; Meissner & Russano, 2003; Redlich, 2004).

PSYCHOLOGICAL RESEARCH RELEVANT TO THESE CONTROVERSIES

To be sure, police interrogation techniques can be successful in eliciting admissions of guilt from true perpetrators, and it is unlikely that the use of such techniques produces more false than true confessions (simply given the likely base rates associated with innocent vs. guilty suspects). However, the overarching controversy associated with interrogation methods is that these techniques can, in fact, lead to false confessions when employed on innocent suspects. Although there has been a notable surge in the frequency of false confessions discussed in the media, the actual rate of false confessions is difficult, if not impossible, to determine (cf. Leo & Ofshe, 1998). Drizin and Leo (2004) documented 125 cases of proven false confession in the United States and Davis and Leo (2006) cite more than 300 cases of false confession in the literature. In essence, there are numerous compelling arguments for why the current number of identified false confessions represents just the tip of the iceberg (see Drizin & Leo, 2004; Gross, Jacoby, Matheson, Montgomery, & Patil, 2005). Below we review the psychological research that has assessed the three controversies in police interrogation we outlined above and that are partly responsible for this false confession phenomenon.

Research on Deception Detection Performance

More than three decades of research on deception detection (for reviews, see Bond & DePaulo, 2006; Vrij, 2000) has produced a clear, consistent, and unequivocal pattern of findings: (1) there is *no one behavioral cue* that is definitely indicative of deception, and (2) people (including law enforcement) generally perform *no better than chance* at detecting deception. In regard to the first, DePaulo and colleagues (2003) quantitatively examined 1,338 estimates of 158 cues of deception (e.g., pressed lips, facial pleasantness, self-references) across 120 independent studies, and determined that although there are some cues that associate with deceit, these same cues also associate with anxiety and ambivalence, for example. DePaulo and colleagues concluded that it is not yet possible to distinguish between behavioral cues that are the result of lying, the result of being accused of lying, or simply the result of speaking in public. Furthermore, Vrij, Mann, and Fisher (2006) examined the efficacy of Reid and associates' BAI method (Inbau et al., 2001), specifically in discerning the verbal and nonverbal behaviors of truth tellers from liars. In opposition to what the BAI purports, Vrij and colleagues found that truth tellers were significantly more likely to provide evasive answers, to cross their legs and shift posture, and were less likely to name someone who did not commit the crime than were liars. Thus, not only did Vrij and colleagues demonstrate that truth tellers and liars shared many of the same behaviors, in some instances, truth tellers exhibited behaviors the BAI attributes to liars.

The second consistent finding is that vast majority of studies have found accuracy rates to approximate chance detection performance (Vrij, 2000), despite interrogation training claims of 85% levels of accuracy when evaluating the deception of suspects. A recent meta-analysis of the literature by Bond and DePaulo (2006) evidenced that, across studies, participants averaged 53% accuracy in deception detection tasks. Even professionals who have to make daily decisions of whether people are lying do not demonstrate high rates of accuracy when detecting deception (Meissner & Kassin, 2002; O'Sullivan & Ekman, 2005). Indeed, training on typical interrogation deception detection techniques has been shown to have a deleterious effect on accuracy (Kassin & Fong, 1999; Meissner & Kassin, 2002; see also, Bond & DePaulo, 2006). That is, studies with college students and police officers found that trained participants were less accurate than naïve participants, but were nevertheless significantly more confident in their abilities to detect deception.

In sum, most, if not all, of the available evidence suggests that interrogators who place weight on nonverbal and linguistic cues as indicators of deceit are prone to error. There are numerous examples of proven false confessions in which these supposed clues of deception were misread. For example, police viewed Michael Crowe as "inappropriately bereaved" (Hansen, 1999) upon first impression. This determination of deception led investigators into a process of behavioral confirmation in which multiple psychologically coercive interrogation techniques were used to extract a confession from Crowe—a confession that was eventually deemed to be false with the apprehension and conviction of the true perpetrator.

Research on the Presumption of Guilt

Presumptions during forensic interviews of any kind can lead to obstructions in truth gathering. *Investigator bias* (aka "tunnel vision") is believed to play a significant role in the process leading to the false confession phenomenon (see Meissner & Kassin, 2004) in that it may initiate confirmation bias, the phenomenon in which information that is consistent with one's hypothesis or expectations is given credence, whereas information that is inconsistent is discounted, ignored, or actively reinterpreted to be consistent with the hypothesis (Darley & Fazio, 1980; Nickerson, 1998).

In a series of studies, Kassin, Meissner, and colleagues (Kassin & Fong, 1999; Kassin, Goldstein, & Savitsky, 2003; Kassin, Meissner, & Norwick, 2005; Meissner & Kassin, 2002, 2004) have demonstrated how training in deception detection can lead police officers and others to produce a bias in their perception of *deception* or *guilt* on the part of suspects, and in turn how this bias can trigger a guilt presumptive interrogation process. First, Meissner and Kassin (2002) demonstrated that, in comparison to untrained college students, both students trained in the use of verbal and nonverbal deception cues and police investigators with significant experience in interviewing suspects were more likely to demonstrate a bias toward perceiving *deception* on the part of suspects, regardless of the veracity of their claims. Second, Kassin and colleagues (2005) found that police investigators were also more likely to demonstrate a bias toward perceiving *guilt* in true and false confession statements of actual inmates when compared with student participants. Thus, it appears that (1) police investigators are biased toward viewing suspects as deceptive, and (2) this bias toward deception is unidirectional in that suspects perceived as lying are also perceived to be guilty rather than innocent (see also Meissner & Kassin, 2004). In the end, then, the pivotal decision of whether or not to interrogate a suspect is based on prejudgments of guilt that are confidently made but biased toward guilt and frequently in error.

What impact does an investigative bias have on the process of interrogation? Kassin and colleagues (2003) sought to examine this question by manipulating participant-interrogators' expectations of guilt prior to a forensic interview. Those with expectations of guilt conducted longer interrogations, used more interrogation techniques, and were more likely to ask guilt-presumptive questions and to perceive suspects as guilty (even though half of the suspects were innocent). In turn, suspects who were paired with interrogators in the guilt-expectation condition appeared more defensive to neutral observers, leading these observers to view suspects guilty significantly more often than suspects paired with interrogators in the innocent-expectation condition. This pattern was found regardless of suspects' actual guilt or innocence. Similar patterns of confirmation bias to the exclusion of contradictory evidence are apparent in many false confession cases.

In summary, the extant research on deception detection and presumptions of guilt in interrogation settings suggests that use of this two-pronged approach can lead innocent individuals to be perceived as guilty and thereafter subjected to the pressures of a guilt-presumptive interrogation. Once inside the interrogation room, individuals are faced with psychologically based interrogation techniques that are believed to be reliably effective in yielding "true" confession evidence. If innocent, such a process of investigative bias can place individuals at risk for providing false confessions (see Kassin, 2005).

Research on Police Interrogation Techniques and False Confessions

The range of interrogation techniques and approaches advocated within the criminal justice community (e.g., Inbau et al., 2001; Walters, 2003) is frequently based on authors' many years of experience as police investigators and the conduct of hundreds (if not thousands) of interrogations. It is important to note, however, that these techniques have never been subject to any scientific evaluation by the authors/users. Nevertheless, the increase in identified false confessions within our criminal justice system has spawned a great deal of scientific research evaluating the role of modern-day interrogation practices in this phenomenon.

Two broad methods have been employed to study the impact of interrogation techniques: field/archival research and laboratory research. First, field/archival research has included individual case studies (e.g., Gudjonsson & MacKeith, 1990), archival analyses of actual case documents (e.g., Drizin & Leo, 2004; Leo & Ofshe, 1998), observations of live or taped interrogations (e.g., Moston, Stephenson, & Williamson, 1992; Ofshe & Leo, 1997), and surveys of police investigators (e.g., Kassin et al., 2007). One notable example involves a study by Leo (1996) in which he observed over 300 live and videotaped interrogations and documented the techniques employed by investigators. Leo found that interrogators employed the psychologically oriented techniques found in traditional training manuals, but seldom resorted to tactics courts have deemed coercive, including explicit threats and physical intimidation.

The second research methodology utilized is experimental laboratory research methods. In an effort to extend both internal and external validity,

Russano and colleagues (2005) developed a novel laboratory paradigm to assess the effects of interrogation techniques on the likelihood of both true and false confessions. In this paradigm, participants in the "guilty" condition are enticed by a confederate to share information on a problem they are both solving—an act that violates the experimental rule against sharing information and that is later characterized as "cheating" by the experimenter. Participants in the "innocent" condition perform the same problems with a confederate, but these participants are never enticed to share information. Later, all participants are accused of cheating (with the academic implications thereof), are interrogated by an experimenter who remains blind to the participants' actual guilt or innocence, and are asked to sign a confession statement. Russano and colleagues varied the interrogation techniques used by their experimenters to include the presentation of an explicit offer of leniency (a "deal") and exposure to minimization tactics (i.e., the interrogator expressed sympathy, provided face-saving excuses, and emphasized the importance of cooperation). Results indicated that guilty participants (72%) were significantly more likely to confess than innocent participants (20%); however, the use of interrogation techniques generally increased both true and false confession rates. For example, an explicit offer of leniency increased true confessions by a factor of 1.57 and increased false confessions by a factor of 2.33 when compared with the no-tactic control condition. Similarly, the use of minimization techniques increased true confessions by a factor of 1.76, while also increasing false confessions by a factor of 3.00. When these tactics were combined, true and false confessions increased by factors of 1.89 and 7.17, respectively.

Taken together, it appears that the interrogation techniques advocated by professionals within the field (e.g., Inbau et al., 2001; Walters, 2003) often produce true confessions by guilty suspects, but simultaneously increase the risk of false confessions by innocent individuals who are subjected to these same procedures. Is it true that the use of "preinterrogation interviews" established by the advocates of these procedures will safeguard innocent individuals from being subjected to a guilt-presumptive interrogation? Actually, the contrary may be more likely—namely, that innocent individuals will find themselves assessed as deceptive, and thereby guilty, during the course of a preinterrogation interview, and that this investigative bias will lead investigators to conduct long, aggressive, and guilt-presumptive interrogations in search of the "truth." Furthermore, the available psychological research suggests that the techniques advocated by Inbau and colleagues (2001), among others, are not diagnostic in their extraction of information.

Rather, scientific research has demonstrated these techniques increase the likelihood of *both* true and false confessions.

In addition to the body of scientific research investigating the techniques that generate confessions (either true or false), there is a growing body of research on factors specific to suspects that can lead to statements against oneself. Results from field and laboratory research converge on the identification of several risk factors, most notably young age and mental impairment (Gudjonsson, 2003; Owen-Kostelnik, Reppucci, & Meyer, 2006; Redlich, 2007). Juveniles are overrepresented in proven false confession cases (Drizin & Leo, 2004) and in one laboratory study were found to be significantly more likely than adults to sign false confession statements (Redlich & Goodman, 2003). Mental impairment—both intellectual/developmental deficits (Perske, 1991) and mental illness (Redlich, 2004)—is present in a significant minority of false confession cases and is positively associated with suggestibility and negatively associated with understanding and appreciation of the *Miranda* warning and requirements pertaining to adjudicative competence (Fulero & Everington, 1995; Hoge et al., 1997; Viljoen, Roesch, & Zapf, 2002).

In response to this overrepresentation of juveniles and persons with mental impairment in false confessions, John E. Reid and Associates personnel recently recommended that "every interrogator must exercise extreme caution and care when interviewing or interrogating a juvenile or person who is mentally impaired" (*www.reid.com*). Whether this recommendation is known in the interrogator community or if known, is heeded, has not been examined. However, it is important to note that there is a strong and consistent research base indicating that the majority (e.g., 65% or more) of justice-involved juveniles have mental health problems, most of which involve co-occurring substance use issues (see Redlich, 2007; Redlich & Drizin, 2007). Thus, many of the juveniles who encounter police officers are likely to have the two primary risk factors for false confession; whether the combination of these two factors cumulatively or exponentially increases the risk is worthy of future research.

GAPS IN SCIENTIFIC KNOWLEDGE

Scientific knowledge regarding police interrogations and false confessions has greatly increased over the past decade. Innovative laboratory and field studies have highlighted the potential dangers of using certain interrogation techniques (e.g., Drizin & Leo, 2004; Gudjonsson, 2003; Kassin, 2005; Russano et al., 2005), and using them with certain vulnerable populations (e.g., Owen-Kostelnik et al., 2006; Redlich, 2007). Despite this boon of research, there remain gaps. Below we discuss issues that researchers studying interrogations and confessions may find beneficial to direct future efforts.

Future Research on Deception Detection

As described above, there is ample research indicating that individuals, even experienced investigators, perform at chance levels when making determinations of truthfulness. However, what is less clear is *how often* interrogators rely solely on their perceptions of the suspect, based on a preinterrogation interview, when determining guilt, as opposed to incorporating corroborative evidence of guilt in such assessments. Although these "clues to deception" (MacDonald & Michaud, 1992) are included in interrogation training manuals, the frequency with which behavioral analyses are relied on is unknown. Research examining the "value-added" nature of relying on available evidence for determining veracity in the context of an investigative interview would appear worthwhile, though one must be certain to distinguish between evidence that is highly diagnostic (e.g., a DNA match) and that which is largely circumstantial in nature (e.g., an apparent motive).

A second area of deception detection that would appear worthy of further research regards the development of evidenced-based techniques that could *improve* the ability of investigators to distinguish truth from deception. Current research in the deception literature suggests that verbal cues to deception may prove more diagnostic than nonverbal behavior cues (DePaulo et al., 2003). Techniques such as Statement Validity Analysis (SVA; see Kohnken, 2004; Vrij, 2005) and reality monitoring (see Sporer, 2004) show promise in this regard for evaluating the structural and cognitive components of an individual's verbal statement. In brief, SVA is an analysis utilizing a set of criteria purported to distinguish between credible and noncredible reports. A number of important issues, however, prevent the immediate application of these techniques for use by law enforcement, including the reliability of coding statements, the training of coders, and the establishment of cutoff standards for determining the likely veracity of a given statement.

Future Research on the Presumption of Guilt

Consistent with research directions in the detection of deception, it will be important to gain a better understanding of factors that lead investigators to demonstrate a bias toward perceiving deception or guilt on the part of suspects. Although studies have now suggested that both investigators' experience in law enforcement and their training in methods of deception detection are associated with the observed investigative biases (cf. Kassin et al., 2005; Meissner & Kassin, 2002), and with the use of certain interrogation tactics (Kassin et al., 2007), these associations fail to capture the precise psychological mechanisms leading to such biases in the perception of suspects. For example, it is possible that investigators' "base rates" of interviewing *deceptive* individuals are different from those of the average population, thereby distinguishing the deception biases in investigators from the truth biases shown in normal populations (Vrij, 2000). Furthermore, it would seem important to understand the manner in which investigators might designate an individual to be a "suspect," aside from a finding of deception in a preinterrogation interview. What types of evidence might justify such a designation and lead an investigator to pursue an individual as a suspect, and how might such evidence influence the process of interrogation?

FUTURE RESEARCH ON POLICE INTERROGATION TECHNIQUES AND FALSE CONFESSIONS

Much of the research to date on interrogation tactics has focused on factors that might be associated with a risk of false confessions. The paradigm introduced by Russano and colleagues (2005), however, provides researchers with an opportunity to address a critical issue in the study of interrogations and confessions. Namely, the paradigm permits researchers to estimate the *diagnostic value* of confession evidence that is produced by a given interrogation technique (or set of techniques) by estimating the influence on both true and false confessions. To this end, researchers can pursue the development techniques that might *improve* the diagnostic value of an interrogation, thereby producing evidenced-based techniques that can be advocated to law enforcement. We believe such a direction in research is vitally important if we are to shape the art of interrogation into the science of investigative interviewing.

In a similar vein, much of what has been gleaned from the study of false confessions has concerned police-coerced confessions. The overwhelming majority of false confessions in the Drizin and Leo (2004) sample were of this form, in that the police induced the confessions via coercion and questionable interrogation techniques (e.g., overly long interrogations, presentation of false evidence). Whether what has been learned is applicable to voluntary false confessions—a form that is likely to be more prevalent than coerced (see Gudjonsson, Sigurdsson, & Einarsson, 2004)—has yet to be investigated. Additionally, most (92% in Drizin & Leo, 2004) proven false confessions involved murder and rape—two very serious crimes with low base rates of occurrence. False confessions for property, drug, and minor crimes are less likely to be detected (particularly via DNA exoneration) but may be more prevalent (e.g., Sigurdsson & Gudjonsson, 1996). Thus, knowledge is lacking regarding both voluntary false confessions and those offered for low-severity crimes.

Finally, knowledge concerning the dispositional vulnerability factors associated with false confessions is incomplete. Although scientists have clearly identified risk factors, including young age, mental illness, and low intellect, there are several open questions. For example, mental illness is a catch-all term representing a variety of disorders with distinct symptoms and trajectories. Whether persons with schizophrenia are more or less likely to falsely confess in comparison to persons with major depression, for example, is not yet known. Furthermore, an increased understanding of the effects of multiple risk factors, both situational and dispositional, is needed. More specifically, certain combinations of risk factors may be more predictive of false admissions than others.

MYTHS AND MISCONCEPTIONS

There are numerous erroneously held beliefs about police interrogation practices and false confessions, as well as about the study of these topics. Below, we discuss five misconceptions that commonly arise in the context of expert courtroom testimony.

Myth/Misconception 1: False Confessions Do Not Exist or Are Exceedingly Rare

As discussed previously, numerous cases of false confession have been identified, with a recent report by Davis and Leo (2006) citing more than 300 documented instances. Furthermore, police investigators have themselves reported that false confessions from the innocent occur an estimated 5% of the time (Kassin et al., 2007). It is therefore clearly a myth that false confessions do not exist. In contrast, believing them to be exceedingly rare is more of a misconception. Although scientists are unable to estimate the precise frequency with which true versus false confessions occur in the real world, most experts agree that the number documented to date represents the tip of a much larger iceberg (Drizin & Leo, 2004). As described above, voluntary false confessions and those offered for lower-severity crimes (than murder and rape) have not been well researched or documented, and it may well be the case that false confessions under such situations are even more likely than those for severer crimes. Moreover, whereas DNA evidence has played a significant role in the exonerations of innocent individuals who were *convicted* (another limiting factor), DNA evidence is not available in a much larger pool of cases.

Myth/Misconception 2: Only "Vulnerable" Individuals Falsely Confess

There are many proven false confession cases in which the false confessor had no readily observable dispositional risk factor, such as low intellect or young age (see Drizin & Leo, 2004; Gross et al., 2005). Of course, while it is certainly possible that these proven false confessors had subtler dispositional risk factors that were not identified, often it is the situational factors present, such as investigator tunnel vision, lengthy interrogations, prolonged isolation, and lack of sleep, that make a seemingly "normal" person vulnerable to false confession. Many proven false confessions are the result of the innocent suspect being wrongly targeted and then subjected to coercive interrogation techniques. Christopher Ochoa is one such example. Ochoa, now an attorney, spent more than 12 years in prison for a rape and murder he did not commit. After going to the Pizza Hut where the crime had occurred some weeks before, the police became focused on Ochoa (and his friend, who was also wrongly convicted) and subjected him to two 12-hour interrogations, telling him he would face the death penalty if he did not admit to the crime. Ochoa falsely confessed, signing a statement written by the interrogators. Although we are not aware of a psychological evaluation performed on Ochoa, the abusive circumstances of his interrogation clearly contributed to his false confession and subsequent false conviction. The literature has many examples like Ochoa's. It should also be made clear to judges and juries that an overrepresentation of juveniles, for example, in false confession cases is relative to the number of juveniles in the criminal justice system, not to the number in proven cases. That is, 32% of proven false confessors in the Drizin and Leo (2004) study were younger than 18 years, meaning that the majority (68%) were adults. The overrepresentation of 32% should be compared to the base rates of 10% of juvenile arrests for murder and 15% for rape (Snyder, 2008).

Myth/Misconception 3: The Study of Police Interrogation and False Confessions Is in Its Infancy

Decades of research have been dedicated to understanding the psychological factors leading to true versus false confessions. Gisli Gudjonsson published his first review of the field in 1992, and his most recent update in handbook form was published in 2003. Other reviews of the field and its research efforts have abounded (Kassin & Gudjonsson, 2004), including books by DeClue (2005), Lassiter (2004), Leo (2008), Milne and Bull (1999), White (2003), and Williamson (2005).

Furthermore, the scope of interrogation and confession research is not limited to studies that have directly addressed the topic. As discussed by Kassin (2008), experts have a large body of scientific knowledge to draw from, representing a three-tiered pyramid. At the base of the pyramid are core principles of psychology, such as how people respond to influence tactics (e.g., Cialdini, 2000); how people make decisions under stress, in isolation, or when sleep deprived; the fallibility of human memory and proneness to suggestibility; developmental trajectories; psychiatric symptoms; cognitive functioning, and so on. In the middle of the pyramid are research studies specific to police interrogation, deception detection, and false confessions (e.g., Russano et al., 2005). At the vertex of the pyramid are single and aggregated case studies of proven and probable false confessions (Drizin & Leo, 2004; Leo & Ofshe, 1998) that demonstrate common patterns. In sum, in disputed confession cases, there are more than 100 years of psychological science to draw on, including literature from developmental, cognitive, social, personality, forensic, and abnormal branches of psychology.

Myth/Misconception 4: Jurors Do Not "Need" Expert Testimony

When judges determine the admissibility of expert testimony, they often consider whether the expert's information is necessary for the jury to render a fair and impartial decision. In other words, does the jury "already know" the information that the expert has to offer? Is it a matter of common sense? Can jurors, on their own, recognize coerced and/or false confessions? There is a wealth of research to indicate that juries heavily value confession evidence—even when inappropriate to do so—and are subject to biases of human nature, such as belief in a just world (Lerner, 1980) and the fundamental attribution error (Gilbert & Malone, 1995). There is converging empirical evidence that jurors find it difficult to ignore confessions in decisions of guilt (Kassin & Neumann, 1997; Kassin & Sukel, 1997; Kassin & Wrightsman, 1980). Similar patterns of results have also emerged in studies examining confession evidence from juvenile suspects (Redlich, Ghetti, & Quas, 2008; Redlich, Quas, & Ghetti, 2008).

Furthermore, as discussed above, individuals are poor at distinguishing between true and false confessions (Kassin et al., 2005). Indeed, among proven false confessors who chose to go before a jury (Drizin & Leo, 2004), 81% were convicted (an additional 11% of false confessors pleaded guilty despite their actual innocence). Because it would appear that neither police investigators nor potential jurors are likely to serve as safeguards in recognizing coerced or false confessions (Kassin et al., 2005), the testimony of scientific experts becomes all the more essential.

Myth/Misconception 5: Police Interrogation Is a Science

A point we have tried to make explicit throughout this chapter is that interrogation is more akin to an art than a science (see also Leo, 2004). We believe that this point is important to understand from two perspectives. First, modern-day interrogation techniques were not developed through a process of scientific inquiry; rather, they are the product of interrogative "experience" and the observations of their proponents. As a result, the body of science that has now evaluated these methods has indicated their failures in leading to diagnostic confession evidence and, most importantly, their contributions to cases of wrongful conviction. Second, the process of interrogation, as conducted by investigators, lacks the rigor of a scientific process seeking to test hypotheses and assess the validity of theories regarding human behavior. Rather, the interrogative process, as conducted by investigators, is often fraught with biases and a search for confirmation that excludes, ignores, or reinterprets disconfirming evidence. This point is important because (1) the authority of the expert and his or her information is often informally compared to the authority and experience of the interrogator, and (2) judgments, such as the suppression of a confession statement by a judge or a finding of guilt versus innocence by a jury, derive from this comparison. We provide two examples to illustrate the point that if interrogations were more akin to a scientific endeavor, false confessions could potentially be reduced.

The first example relates to falsification. An underlying aim of science is to form theories and then attempt to *disprove* them (Popper, 1972). In contrast, arguably the aim of law enforcement is to form theories (about who, how, and why crimes were committed) and then attempt to *prove* them. The potential for confirmation bias, for example, might be reduced if interrogators worked from a model in which they identified suspects but then had to gather evidence that refuted their suspicions. The process of gathering evidence would remain the same, but the mindset of the investigator would be different in that the goal would now be to disprove suspicions. Furthermore, because other evidentiary collectors and examiners (e.g., fingerprint, hair, and DNA testers; see Saks, Risinger, Rosenthal, & Thompson, 2003) are also prone to confirmatory biases or "context effects," reducing the bias among police interrogators may serve to prevent a chain of further errors in judgment.

The second example relates to the peer-review process. The purpose of peer review is to provide an independent, objective assessment of the methods and results on which conclusions are based, thereby helping to ensure that the scientific literature is comprised of reliable research. Peer review also serves as an objective measure of the expert's qualifications (if an expert had no peer-reviewed publications on the topic at hand, he or she would likely not qualify). Of importance, peer review is conducted prior to publication. Imagine if the standard were, in essence, reversed: Scientists could publish articles without prior review, and review came only after the article was in circulation for months or years *and* only then was called into question. The fact that the article had been in circulation (and likely cited by others) would alone be seen as negating the credibility of its problematic nature. This is what occurs with alleged false confessions: The confession is accepted as an indication of guilt by police and others (e.g., victims and their families, attorneys, trial judge), sometimes for years, and when questioned at a later date, the fact that the confession was accepted as such is used to bolster its credibility.

If interrogations and statements of admission from proven false confession cases had undergone a process similar to peer review soon after they were conducted and obtained, these miscarriages of justice may have been identified earlier. Postconfession analyses by independent assessors could (1) determine if objective corroboration existed for the statements; (2) independently verify the source of the knowledge indicating guilt (e.g., did it come directly from the suspect, or was it provided by police during the interrogation, or from media reports read by the suspect prior to interrogation?); and (3) examine the level of consistency between crime scene evidence and statements provided by the suspect (see Davis & Leo, 2006). Peer review is an objective standard for expert testimony to be considered admissible; a similar set of standards could be instituted when evaluating the admissibility of confession statements to be used against defendants in our courts.

CONCLUSIONS

We believe that much is known regarding factors that can lead to false confessions, and that current police interrogation methods and practice represent little more than an art, much less a science. In regard to legal admissibility standards and contemporary interrogation techniques, we posit the following:

Scientifically Supported Techniques

In our opinion, there is no one interrogation technique that is diagnostic of guilt, or one that we feel confident defining as "scientifically supported." The interrogation techniques advocated by the variety of training manuals available to law enforcement have generally been developed experientially by their proponents, but they possess no scientific basis on which they might be seen as reliable and diagnostic in approach. Instead, the available scientific research suggests that these methods are just as likely to produce true and false confessions from suspects, particularly those suspects with vulnerabilities. Well-grounded theories concerning obedience to authority, social validation, and compliance gaining provide some scientific support that the psychologically oriented police interrogation techniques used today "work" (i.e., they produce true confessions) when employed on *guilty suspects*. However, these same techniques also "work" (i.e., they produce false confessions) when employed on innocent suspects.

Scientifically Unsupported Techniques

The ability to detect when suspects are lying versus telling the truth (or guilty vs. innocent) is unreliable. Just as evidence collected via lie detectors (polygraph machines) is now inadmissible in court, we believe it is time for the courts to consider the validity and reliability of evidence collected by human lie detectors. Confessions from suspects who were subjected to interrogation on the basis of nonverbal/behavioral deception detection techniques should be examined comprehensively before being presented to jurors, who as noted, are generally unable to distinguish between true and false confessions.

Scientifically Controversial and/or Largely Untested Techniques

While the current research literature has done well to evaluate the perils associated with interrogative procedures, we believe it could benefit from a shift in direction: that is, focusing rather on the development of evidence-based techniques that could lead to the conduct of more diagnostic interrogations and the extraction of "guilty knowledge." Numerous specific interrogation techniques are amenable to scientific study in the laboratory and the field that have yet to be examined. For example, and as discussed below, alternatives to adversarial interrogation, such as models that emphasize open-ended questions and "fact-finding" (as opposed to confession seeking) have shown preliminary effectiveness overseas.

In Great Britain, high-profile wrongful conviction cases and subsequent research have led to the development of new interrogation standards that prohibit the use of psychologically manipulative techniques, mandate the recording of custodial interrogations and the uniform training of interviewers, and institute special precautions for vulnerable suspects. Of utmost importance, investigators are also prohibited from deceiving suspects (Milne & Bull, 1999; Mortimer & Shepherd, 1999). Evaluation research conducted by Clarke and Milne (2001) suggests that these methods have been effective in changing the culture of police interviewing without significantly reducing the likelihood of obtaining confessions in practice, and that these methods appear to reduce the number of unwarranted claims of false confession. Such inquisitorial approaches are deserving of further research and evaluation both in the laboratory and in the field.

COMMUNICATING CONSENSUS AND CONTROVERSIES

To address these admissibility standards, the electronic preservation of interviews and interrogations from start to finish is essential. This is a reform that is relatively simple to implement and can serve to protect both law enforcement and suspects, eliminating the contradictory he-said/she-said accounts. Electronic accounts of interrogations do not eliminate the need for experts, however. It is important that experts who conduct research on interrogations and confessions be permitted to inform the court regarding the 100-plus years of psychological science informing the process and mechanisms of interrogation and confessions, as well as to dispel commonly held myths. As echoed in other chapters in this volume, experts who consult and/or testify in court have an obligation to present information fairly, accurately, and in its entirety. Because interrogation is best viewed as an art and because the validity of the techniques currently employed is partly dependent upon whom they are employed (guilty vs. innocent), experts in disputed confession cases must be sure to present the science objectively. Among scientists who serve in this capacity as expert witnesses there is much consensus on the techniques that are likely to produce false confessions when the situational and dispositional circumstances are taken into account. Of course, there are those who are in disagreement who fail to appreciate the contributions of the research. In written communications and in the courtroom, it is important that experts communicate this consensus, attend to any perceived controversies, and address the unknowns. In this manner, the totality of knowledge can be imparted, thereby allowing judges and jurors to make informed decisions.

REFERENCES

Asch, S. E. (1956). Studies of independence and conformity: A minority of one against a unanimous majority. *Psychological Monographs, 70*, 416.

Bond, C. F., & DePaulo, B. M. (2006). Accuracy of deception judgments. *Personality and Social Psychology Review, 10*, 214–234.

Butterfield, R. (2002). *The official guide to interrogation: A complete manual for extracting the truth.* Philadelphia: Xlibris Corporation.

Cialdini, R. B. (2000). *Influence: Science and practice.* Des Moines, IA: Allyn & Bacon.

Clarke, C., & Milne, R. (2001). *National evaluation of the PEACE investigative interviewing course.* Police Research Award Scheme. London: Home Office.

Costanzo, M., & Leo, R. A. (2006). Research and expert testimony on interrogations and confessions. In M. Costanzo, D. Krauss, & K. Pezdek (Eds.), *Expert psychological testimony for the courts* (pp. 69–98). Mahwah, NJ: Erlbaum.

Darley, J. M., & Fazio, R. H. (1980). Expectancy confirmation processes arising in the social interaction sequence. *American Psychologist, 35*, 867–881.

Davis, D., & Leo, R. (2006). Strategies for preventing false confessions and their consequences. In M. R. Kebbell & G. M. Davies (Eds.), *Practical psychology for forensic investigations and prosecutions* (pp. 121–149). Chichester, UK: Wiley.

Davis, D., & O'Donohue, W. (2003). The road to perdition: "Extreme influence" tactics in the interrogation room. In W. O'Donohue, P. Laws, & C. Hollin (Eds.), *Handbook of forensic psychology* (pp. 897–996). New York: Basic Books.

DeClue, G. (2005). *Interrogations and disputed confessions: A manual for forensic psychological practice.* Sarasota, FL: Professional Resource Press.

DePaulo, B. M., Lindsay, J. J., Malone, B. E., Muhlenbruck, L., Charlton, K., & Cooper, H. (2003). Cues to deception. *Psychological Bulletin, 129,* 74–118.

Drizin, S. A., & Leo, R. A. (2004). The problem of false confessions in the post-DNA world. *North Carolina Law Review, 82,* 891–1008.

Fulero, S. M. (2004). Expert psychological testimony on the psychology of interrogations and confessions. In G. D. Lassiter (Ed.), *Interrogations, confessions, and entrapment* (pp. 247–263). New York: Kluwer Academic.

Fulero, S. M., & Everington, C. (1995). Assessing competency to waive *Miranda* rights in defendants with mental retardation. *Law and Human Behavior, 19,* 533–543.

Gilbert, D. T., & Malone, P. S. (1995). The correspondence bias. *Psychological Bulletin, 117,* 21–38.

Grisham, J. (2006). *The innocent man: Murder and injustice in a small town.* New York: Doubleday.

Gross, S. R., Jacoby, K., Matheson, D. J., Montgomery, N., & Patil, S. (2005). Exonerations in the United States: 1989 through 2003. *Journal of Criminal Law and Criminology, 95,* 523–560.

Gudjonsson, G. H. (2003). *The psychology of interrogations and confessions.* Chichester, UK: Wiley.

Gudjonsson, G. H., & MacKeith, J. A. C. (1990). A proven case of false confession: Psychological aspects of the coerced-compliant type. *Medicine, Science, and the Law, 30,* 329–335.

Gudjonsson, G. H., Sigurdsson, J. F., & Einarsson, E. (2004). The role of personality in relation to confessions and denials. *Psychology, Crime, and Law, 10,* 125–135.

Hansen, M. (1999, July). Untrue confessions. *American Bar Association Journal,* pp. 50–53.

Hartwig, M., Granhag, P. A., Stromwall, L. A., & Vrij, A. (2005). Detecting deception via strategic disclosure of evidence. *Law and Human Behavior, 29,* 469–484.

Hoge, S. K., Poythress, N. G., Bonnie, R. J., Monahan, J., Eisenberg, M., & Feucht-Haviar, T. (1997). The MacArthur adjudicative competence study: Diagnosis, psychopathology, and competence-related abilities. *Behavioral Sciences and the Law, 15,* 329–345.

Inbau, F. E., Reid, J. E., Buckley, J. P., & Jayne, B.C. (2001). *Criminal interrogation and confessions* (4th ed.). Gaithersburg, MD: Aspen.

Kassin, S. M. (2005). On the psychology of confessions: Does innocence put innocents at risk? *American Psychologist, 60,* 215–228.

Kassin, S. M. (2008). Expert testimony on the psychology of confessions: A pyramidal framework of the relevant science. In E. Borgida & S. T. Fiske (Eds.), *Beyond common sense: Psychological science in the courtroom* (pp. 195–218). Oxford, UK: Blackwell.

Kassin, S. M., & Fong, C. T. (1999). "I'm innocent!": Effects of training on judgments of truth and deception in the interrogation room. *Law and Human Behavior, 23,* 499–516.

Kassin, S. M., Goldstein, C. C., & Savitsky, K. (2003). Behavioral confirmation in the interrogation room: On the dangers of presuming guilt. *Law and Human Behavior, 27,* 187–203.

Kassin, S. M., & Gudjonsson, G. H. (2004). The psychology of confessions: A review of the literature and issues. *Psychological Science in the Public Interest, 5,* 33–67.

Kassin, S. M., Leo, R. A., Meissner, C. A., Richman, K. D., Colwell, L. H., Leach, A. M., et al. (2007). Police interviewing and interrogation: A self-report survey of police practices and beliefs. *Law and Human Behavior, 31,* 381–400.

Kassin, S. M., Meissner, C. A., & Norwick, R. J. (2005). "I'd know a false confession if I saw one": A comparative study of college students and police investigators. *Law and Human Behavior, 29,* 211–227.

Kassin, S. M., & Neumann, K. (1997). On the power of confession evidence: An experimental test of the "fundamental difference" hypothesis. *Law and Human Behavior, 21,* 469–484.

Kassin, S. M., & Sukel, H. (1997). Coerced confessions and the jury: An experimental test of the "harmless error" rule. *Law and Human Behavior, 21,* 27–46.

Kassin, S. M., & Wrightsman, L. S. (1980). Prior confessions and mock juror verdicts. *Journal of Applied Social Psychology, 10,* 133–146.

Kohnken, G. (2004). Statement validity analysis and the "detection of the truth." In P. A. Granhag & L. A. Stromwall (Eds.), *The detection of deception in forensic contexts* (pp. 41–63). Cambridge, UK: Cambridge University Press.

Lassiter, G. D. (Ed.). (2004). *Perspectives in law and psychology: Interrogations, confessions, and entrapment.* New York: Kluwer Academic.

Lerner, M. J. (1980). *The belief in a just world: A fundamental delusion.* New York: Springer.

Leo, R. A. (1996). Inside the interrogation room. *Journal of Criminal Law and Criminology, 86,* 266–303.

Leo, R. A. (2004). The third degree and the origins of psychological interrogation in the United States. In G. D. Lassiter (Ed.), *Perspectives in law and psychology: Interrogations, confessions, and entrapment* (pp. 37–84). New York: Kluwer Academic.

Leo, R. A. (2008). *Police interrogation and American justice.* Cambridge, MA: Harvard University Press.

Leo, R. A., & Ofshe, R. J. (1998). The consequences of false confessions: Deprivations of liberty and miscarriages of justice in the age of psychological interrogation. *Journal of Criminal Law and Criminology, 88,* 429–496.

MacDonald, J. M., & Michaud, D. L. (1992). *Criminal interrogation*. Denver, CO: Apache Press.

Meissner, C. A., & Kassin, S. M. (2002). "He's guilty!": Investigator bias in judgments of truth and deception. *Law and Human Behavior, 26,* 469–480.

Meissner, C. A., & Kassin, S. M. (2004). "You're guilty, so just confess!": Cognitive and behavioral confirmation biases in the interrogation room. In G. D. Lassiter (Ed.), *Perspectives in law and psychology: Interrogations, confessions, and entrapment* (pp. 85–106). New York: Kluwer Academic/Plenum Press.

Meissner, C. A., & Russano, M. B. (2003). The psychology of interrogations and false confessions: Research and recommendations. *Canadian Journal of Police and Security Services, 1,* 53–64.

Milgram, S. (1974). *Obedience to authority: An experimental view*. New York: Harper & Row.

Milne, R., & Bull, R. (1999). *Investigative interviewing: Psychology and practice*. Chichester, UK: Wiley.

Miranda v. Arizona, 384 U.S. 436 (1966).

Mortimer, A., & Shepherd, E. (1999). Frames of mind: Schemata guiding cognition and conduct in the interviewing of suspected offenders. In A. Memon & R. Bull (Eds.), *Handbook of the psychology of interviewing* (pp. 293–315). Chichester, UK: Wiley.

Moston, S., Stephenson, G. M., & Williamson, T. M. (1992). The incidence, antecedents and consequences of the use of the right to silence during police questioning. *Criminal Behavior and Mental Health, 3,* 30–47.

Narchet, F. M., Coffman, K. A., Russano, M. B., & Meissner, C. A. (2004, November). *A qualitative analysis of classic and modern-day police interrogation manuals*. Paper presented at the American Society of Criminology conference, Nashville, TN.

Nickerson, R. S. (1998). Confirmation bias: A ubiquitous phenomenon in many guises. *Review of General Psychology, 2,* 175–220.

Ofshe, R. J., & Leo, R. A. (1997). The social psychology of police interrogation: The theory and classification of true and false confessions. *Studies in Law, Politics, and Society, 16,* 189–251.

O'Sullivan, M., & Ekman, P. (2005). The wizards of detection deception. In P. A. Granhag & L. A. Stromwall (Eds.), *The detection of deception in forensic contexts* (pp. 269–286). Cambridge, UK: Cambridge University Press.

Owen-Kostelnik, J., Reppucci, N. D., & Meyer, J. R. (2006). Testimony and interrogation of minors: Assumptions about maturity and morality. *American Psychologist, 61,* 286–304.

Perske, R. (1991). *Unequal justice: What can happen when people with retardation or other developmental disabilities encounter the criminal justice system*. Nashville, TN: Abingdon Press.

Popper, K. R. (1972). *Objective knowledge: An evolutionary approach*. New York: Oxford University Press.

Quintieri, P., & Weiss, K. J. (2005). Admissibility of false-confession testimony: Know thy standard. *Journal of the American Academy of Psychiatry and the Law, 33,* 535–538.

Redlich, A. D. (2004). Mental illness, police interrogations, and the potential for false confession. *Psychiatric Services, 55,* 19–21.

Redlich, A. D. (2007). Double jeopardy in the interrogation room: Young age and mental illness. *American Psychologist, 62,* 609–611.

Redlich, A. D., & Drizin, S. (2007). Police interrogation of youth. In C. L. Kessler & L. Kraus (Eds.), *The mental health needs of young offenders: Forging paths through reintegration and rehabilitation* (pp. 61–78). Cambridge, UK: Cambridge University Press.

Redlich, A. D., Ghetti, S., & Quas, J. A. (2008). Perceptions of children during a police interview: A comparison of alleged victims and suspects. *Journal of Applied Social Psychology, 38,* 705–735.

Redlich, A. D., & Goodman, G. S. (2003). Taking responsibility for an act not committed: The influence of age and suggestibility. *Law and Human Behavior, 27,* 141–156.

Redlich, A. D., Quas, J. A., & Ghetti, S. (2008). Perceptions of children during a police interrogation: Guilt, confessions, and interview fairness. *Psychology, Crime, and Law, 14,* 201–223.

Russano, M. B., Meissner, C. A., Narchet, F. M., & Kassin, S. M. (2005). Investigating true and false confessions within a novel experimental paradigm. *Psychological Science, 16,* 481–486.

Saks, M. J., Risinger, D. M., Rosenthal, R. C., & Thompson, W. C. (2003). Context effects in forensic science: A review and application of the science of science to crime laboratory practice in the United States. *Science and Justice, 43,* 77–90.

Schafer, J. R., & Navarro, J. (2004). *Advanced interviewing techniques: Proven strategies for law enforcement, military, and security personnel.* Springfield, IL: Charles C Thomas.

Sigurdsson, J. F., & Gudjonsson, G. H. (1996). The psychological characteristics of false confessors: A study among Icelandic prison inmates and juvenile offenders. *Personality and Individual Differences, 20,* 321–329.

Snyder, H. (2008, November). *Juvenile arrests 2006.* Washington, DC: Office of Juvenile Justice and Delinquency Prevention.

Sporer, S. (2004). Reality monitoring and detection of deception. In P. A. Granhag & L. A. Stromwall (Eds.), *The detection of deception in forensic contexts* (pp. 64–102). Cambridge, UK: Cambridge University Press.

Viljoen, J. L., Roesch, R., & Zapf, P. A. (2002). An examination of the relationship between competency to stand trial, competency to waive interrogation rights, and psychopathology. *Law and Human Behavior, 26,* 481–506.

Vrij, A. (2000). *Detecting lies and deceit: The psychology of lying and its implications for professional practice.* Chichester, UK: Wiley.

Vrij, A. (2005). Criteria-based content analysis: A qualitative review of the first 37 studies. *Psychology, Public Policy, and Law, 11*, 3–41.

Vrij, A., Mann, S., & Fisher, R. P. (2006). An empirical test of the behavior analysis interview. *Law and Human Behavior, 30*, 329–345.

Walters, S. B. (2003). *The principles of kinesic interview and interrogation* (2nd ed.). Boca Raton, FL: CRC Press.

White, W. (2003). Miranda's *waning protections: Police interrogation practices after Dickerson*. Ann Arbor: University of Michigan Press.

Williamson, T. (Ed.). (2005). *Investigative interviewing: Rights, research, regulation*. Portland, OR: Willan.

CHAPTER 7

Reliability of Child Witnesses' Reports

Maggie Bruck and Stephen J. Ceci

When children report being a victim of, or a witness to, a crime, two primary sets of issues arise in evaluating their testimony. The first set of issues concerns the memories of children who have been actual witnesses to, or victims of, a trauma. Topics related to this set of issues include the cognitive, motivational, and emotional factors that influence the accuracy of the child's report of the traumatic event in question. The research in this area is based on the assumption that the child has actually experienced the traumatic event.

The second set of issues, and the focus of the present chapter, concerns whether it is possible to elicit false reports from a child about nonexperienced traumatic events; that is, events that would be traumatic had the child been a witness to, or victim of, them. The major topics in this area of research include the conditions that precipitate false reports (e.g., suggestive interviews), the psychological status of false reports (false beliefs vs. lies), and developmental trends in both. In this chapter we focus on forensic techniques that may elicit false reports.

CORE ISSUES AND CONTROVERSIES

Distinguishing Suggestive and Neutral Interviews: Misleading and Open-Ended Questions

The Nature of the Controversy

As a result of more than a decade of intensive study on the factors that affect the reliability of children's testimony, it is fairly well agreed by all professionals that suggestive techniques can compromise the accuracy of children's reports. For most professionals (and laypersons), suggestive techniques are synonymous with the use of misleading questions, whereas nonsuggestive techniques are equated with open-ended questions to obtain information from the child.

The controversy concerns whether the absence of misleading questions and the sole use of open-ended questions constitute "a safe interview." We have argued (see Bruck, Ceci, & Principe, 2006; Ceci & Bruck, 1995) that the number of leading versus open-ended questions is not a good index of the suggestiveness of an interview; rather, the best interviews are characterized by the absence of (1) what we have termed "interviewer bias" and (2) a number of specific suggestive techniques.

Science Relevant to the Controversy: Characteristics of a Suggestive Interview

According to Bruck and Ceci's model (Bruck et al., 2006), interviewer bias is the central characteristic that drives the structure of suggestive interviews. Interviewer bias characterizes interviewers who hold *a priori* beliefs about the occurrence of certain events and, as a result, conduct their interviews so as to obtain confirmatory evidence for these beliefs without considering plausible alternative hypotheses. When children provide such interviewers with inconsistent or bizarre evidence, it is either ignored or interpreted within the framework of the biased interviewer's initial hypothesis.

According to our model, interviewer bias influences the entire architecture of an interview and is revealed through a variety of suggestive interviewing techniques. One of the main dimensions of such interviews is the absence of open-ended questions ("Tell me about it; then what happened?"); thus, one does not hear the child's narrative but rather the child's monosyllabic responses to specific questions (e.g., "Did he ever touch you here?"; "Did he do it upstairs?"; "Was it upstairs or downstairs?"). The repetition of these questions (or themes of these questions) within and between interviews is quite suggestive; the repetition provides the child clues about the interviewer's beliefs.

Other suggestive techniques include repeated interviews (especially when the child does not provide satisfactory statements in the first interview), implicit or explicit threats, bribes, and rewards for the desired answer, stereotype induction (e.g., telling children the suspected perpetrator "does bad things"), the use of peer pressure (telling the child that other children have told the truth and now it is his or her turn), and guided imagery (asking children to create a mental picture of a specific event and to think about its details; see Bruck et al., 2006; Ceci & Bruck, 1995, for details). The use of nonverbal props, including anatomically detailed dolls, can also be suggestive, especially with preschool-age children (e.g., Bruck, Ceci, & Francoeur, 2000). Although each suggestive technique is associated with error, the risk for false statements is greatly augmented when interviews contain a combination of suggestive techniques that increases the salience of the interviewer's bias.

Below we provide two examples of scientific studies of the influence of interviewer bias on children's report accuracy, followed by a summary of some of the research on the effects of suggestive techniques on children's reports.

CHESTER THE JANITOR

Thompson, Clarke-Stewart, and Lepore (1997) conducted a study in which children ages 5–6 viewed a staged event that could be construed as either a misdeed or an innocent act. Some children interacted with a confederate named "Chester" as he cleaned some dolls and other toys in a playroom. Other children interacted with Chester as he handled the dolls roughly and in a mildly abusive manner. The children were then questioned about this event. The interviewer was either (1) "accusatory" (suggesting that the janitor had been inappropriately playing with the toys instead of working), (2) "exculpatory" (suggesting that the janitor was just cleaning the toys and not playing), or (3) "neutral" and nonsuggestive. Following the first interview, all children were asked to tell in their own words what they had witnessed and then they were asked questions about the event. Immediately after the interview and 2 weeks later, parents asked their children to recount what the janitor had done.

When questioned by a neutral interviewer or by an interviewer whose interpretation was consistent with the activity viewed by the child, children's accounts were both factually correct and consistent with the janitor's script.

However, when the interviewer was biased in a direction that contradicted the activity viewed by the children, those children's stories conformed to the suggestions or beliefs of the interviewer. In addition, children's answers to interpretive questions (e.g., "Was he doing his job or just being bad?") were in agreement with the interviewer's point of view, as opposed to what actually happened. When asked neutral questions by their parents, the children's answers remained consistent with the interviewers' biases.

SURPRISE PARTY

Bruck, Ceci, Melnyk, and Finkelberg (1999) showed how interviewer bias can quickly develop in natural interviewing situations, and how it not only taints the responses of child interviewees but also the reports of the adult interviewers. In their study, a special event was staged for 90 preschool children in their school. In groups of three children, and with the guidance of research assistant A, the children surprised research assistant B with a birthday party, played games, ate food, and watched magic tricks. Another 30 children did not attend the birthday party but in groups of two, they simply colored a picture with research assistants A and B. These children were told that it was assistant A's birthday and saw one of the magic tricks.

Interviewers (who were recruited from graduate degree programs in social work or counseling and who had training and experience in interviewing children) were asked to question four children individually about what had happened when special visitors came to the school. The interviewers were not told about the events but were simply told to find out from each child what had happened. The first three children that each interviewer questioned attended the birthday party and the fourth child attended the coloring event.

Bruck and colleagues (2006) found that the fourth child (who attended the coloring event and was interviewed last) produced twice as many errors as the children who attended the birthday party. For example, 60% of the children who only colored made false claims that involved attending a birthday party. This result suggests that the interviewers had built up a bias that all the children had attended a birthday party as a result of interviewing three consecutive children who actually had done so. By the time they interviewed the fourth child, they structured their interviews to elicit claims consistent with this hypothesis. Thus, if interviewers have the belief that all the children had experienced a certain event, then it is probable that many of the children will come to make such claims even though they were nonparticipants (or nonvictims). Another important finding from this study was that even when the fourth child denied attending a birthday party, 84% of their interviewers later reported that all four of the children they interviewed had reported to them that they attended a birthday party. These data suggest that regardless of what children actually say, biased interviewers inaccurately report children's claims, rendering them consistent with their own hypotheses. Biased interviewers often do not have a conscious desire or goal to manipulate the testimony of their interviewee; they are unaware of the strategies they use.

These two studies and others like them (Bruck et al., 2006) provide evidence that interviewers' beliefs about an event can influence their judgments as well as their style of questioning. These beliefs, in turn, can affect the accuracy of children's testimony. Finally, interviewers' beliefs can affect their own ability to accurately recollect what children actually told them during the interview. These findings highlight the dangers of having only one hypothesis about the event in question, especially when this hypothesis is incorrect.

A review of actual forensic interviews with children reveals a number of interviewing techniques that may allow the child to infer the beliefs of the interviewer. Using a variety of techniques in the laboratory, children are interviewed about events they have and have not experienced. The accuracy of their reports is examined as a function of the types of techniques used in the interview. Briefly, when children are questioned about events they did not experience (e.g., seeing a thief steal food from the day care center; Bruck, Ceci, & Hembrooke, 2002) or about non-occurring details within experienced events (e.g., "The man put something yucky in your mouth"; Poole & Lindsay, 2001), their reports are more error-prone if suggestive techniques are used than if the questioning takes place in a neutral, nonsuggestive manner (see Bruck et al., 2006, for details).

Some studies show that interviews can be completely devoid of leading questions and still be quite suggestive because of the presence of interviewer bias. Conversely, sometimes leading questions may not pose a risk to the reliability of children's reports in the absence of interviewer bias. For example, a study by Garven, Wood, and Malpass (2000) illustrates both of these points. They asked kindergarten children to recall details when a visitor named Paco came to their classroom and read a story, gave out treats, and wore a funny hat. The children were asked misleading questions about plausible events (e.g., "Did Paco break a toy?") and about bizarre events (e.g., "Did Paco take you in a helicopter to a farm?"). Some of the children were given selective feedback after their answers to the misleading questions.

"No" responses were met with negative appraisals by the interviewer, as in the following exchange:

INTERVIEWER: Did Paco take you somewhere in a helicopter?

CHILD: No.

INTERVIEWER: You're not doing good.

"Yes" responses were positively evaluated, as the following example illustrates:

INTERVIEWER: Did Paco break a toy?

CHILD: Yes.

INTERVIEWER: Great; you're doing excellent now.

Children who were asked leading questions with selective reinforcement provided the desired but false answer to 35% of the plausible questions and to 52% of the bizarre questions. In contrast, a second group of children who did not receive this selective feedback falsely agreed with 13% of the plausible and 5% of the bizarre questions. Two weeks later, when the children were asked nonleading questions with no selective feedback, the same level of between-group differences was obtained. Thus, interviewer bias in a prior interview in the form of selective feedback had long-lasting negative effects on accuracy in a later unbiased interview.

There are two important points to bear in mind when analyzing transcripts of an interview: First, just because that particular interview may be neutral, prior interviews may have been suggestive, seeding false claims made in the second, neutral, interview. Second, the number of leading or suggestive questions deployed in an interview is not a good index of suggestiveness.

The Use of Suggestive Interviewing under Special Circumstances

The Nature of the Controversy: Child Sexual Abuse Accommodation Syndrome

There is a common belief among professionals who assess and treat children suspected of sexual abuse that it is necessary to engage in suggestive interviews because sexually abused children do not readily or spontaneously disclose abuse. The most popular embodiment of this idea is Summit's (1983) "child sexual abuse accommodation syndrome" (CSAAS). Roland Summit proposed that because of the traumatic characteristics of abuse, shame, and guilt, sexually abused children often delay or fail to disclose during childhood and deny abuse even when asked. Furthermore, it is thought that when children do disclose, it is a slow process whereby they provide a few details and then recant these earlier claims.

Because of these circumstances, it is argued, it is necessary to use as many techniques as possible to extract disclosures in order to protect these otherwise silent children. Young children present the most concerns because, under most circumstances, they do not provide much information in response to open-ended questions; therefore, it is necessary to use a variety of strategies to elicit relevant information from this age group.

In contrast, some experts and professionals state that there is no scientific evidence to support the strong version of CSAAS, which is the foundation of the rationale for suggestive interviews, especially with young children. According to this position, it is important to develop structured nonsuggestive interviews that are feasible and effective for children of all ages.

Science Relevant to the Controversy: Empirical Support for the CSAAS Model

Because the CSAAS model was based on clinical intuitions rather than on data, we have reviewed the literature to determine its empirical support (London, Bruck, Ceci, & Shuman, 2005; London, Bruck, Wright, & Ceci, 2008). We identified studies in which adults with histories of childhood abuse were asked to recall their disclosures in childhood. Across studies, an average of only 33% of the adults remembered disclosing the abuse in a timely fashion. These data support the CSAAS model insofar that sexually abused children are silent about their victimization and delay disclosure for long periods of time, sometimes even decades.

Although these studies are informative on the issue of delay of reporting, they are not informative on the issue of denial of abuse when asked. This is because the adult participants were never asked, "As a child, did anyone ever ask you or question you about abuse?" Thus, the data are silent on the phenomena of denial and recantation.

To address this aspect of the CSAAS model, we located another set of studies that provide some data relevant to this point. In the most recent article (London et al., 2008), we identified 18 studies conducted since 1990 that examined rates of denial and recantation by sexually abused children who had been asked directly about abuse when they were assessed or treated at clinics for sexually abused children. The rates of denial during these assessment interviews were highly variable (4–76%), as were the rates of recantation (4–27%). We found that the methodological adequacy of each study was directly related to the denial and recantation rates observed: The weakest studies—those that included children who had made false allegations of abuse—produced the highest rates of denial, an average value of 61%. For example, the Sorenson and Snow (1991) study had the highest citation rate of all 18 studies, although it is the most methodologically compromised. Studies that included unrepresentative samples of abused children (e.g., those who had previously denied abuse) produced an average rate of denial of 51%. The set of studies that did not differentiate unfounded from founded cases produced a lower rate of denial, 31%. Finally, for the six methodologically superior studies, the average rate of denial was only 14%. The rate of recantation was also low for this last set of studies, 7%. These six studies provided denial and recantation data on children whose abuse status was considered "highly probable" (i.e., valid) and who were not selected because of special characteristics (e.g., sexually transmitted diseases [STDs]; peer abuse; single-parent families). These latter studies of sexually abused children's response patterns indicate that if they are directly asked, they do not deny their abuse, but disclose it. These findings lend no support to the notion that children who deny having been abused must be pursued with relentless suggestive questioning because otherwise they will not disclose the details of their abuse.

Although this analysis and conclusions about the empirical status of CSAAS have been generally accepted in the scientific community, they are not without detractors. Specifically, Lyon (2007) has claimed that the methods used to ensure valid cases of sexual abuse result in biased samples that exclude actual cases of abuse. To remedy the problem of valid diagnoses, Lyon reviewed the literature of the disclosure patterns of children with STDs. The average rate of denial across 21 studies was 57%. However, the generalizability of these findings are highly limited because only a small minority (2–3%) of sexually abused children have STDs and those who do have STDs are demographically very different from those who do not (see London et al., 2008). Also, most of the studies that Lyon cited in his survey were conducted before 1990 (when many of the current issues were not taken into account and thus resulted in less sophisticated studies), and most were not designed to examine disclosure patterns but rather the characteristics of children with STDs. Consequently, it is difficult to estimate disclosure rates from such data.

Lyon and colleagues (Malloy, Lyon, & Quas, 2007) also argued that recantation rates are much higher than calculated by London and colleagues (2005). To reach this conclusion they examined children (mainly Hispanic) facing dependency court hearings (i.e., removal from the home) as a consequence of their disclosures of abuse; 23% of these children recanted. Although this is one of the higher estimates of recantation, in actuality one might have predicted even higher rates given the dilemma of this special sample of children who were facing removal from the home and possible deportation or other punishment of a parent, unless they recanted. In addition, such children are often pressured by the nonoffending parent to withdraw their accusations. Thus even when there are a number of pressures to retract true allegations, only a minority of sexual abused children will do so. When these pressures are absent, recantation is rare.

Although most children will disclose abuse when directly asked, the question then becomes how to "directly ask" children. Because young children will provide more detailed answers to specific or cued questions than to open-ended questions, and because children's free recall is often sparse (Goodman & Reed, 1986; Peterson & Bell, 1996), a common view is that it is necessary to ask younger children specific and sometimes leading questions to elicit important information. With the acquisition of cognitive structures that organize events into coherent narratives, the need for specific questions declines with age (Kulkofsky, Wang, & Ceci, 2008). In addition, in the context of disclosures of sexual abuse, there is the belief that the child must be helped (through a variety of techniques) to overcome motivational and emotional barriers.

In fact, Bruck and colleagues (2002) found that highly suggestive interviews increased the chances that children would report otherwise embarrassing incidences of being punished. In this study, children were asked to tell an interviewer about a specific punishment they had recently experienced. The classroom teacher provided details of a punishment for each child (e.g., being placed in "time out" for calling other children bad names). When first asked in a neutral manner if the punishment had ever happened to them, 37% of the children answered negatively. A week later when suggestively interviewed (this interview involved the use of peer pressure, leading questions, repeated questions, positive feedback), 44% children still denied the punishment. But in the next interview, a week later, only 25% of the children denied, and by the next suggestive interview all children told about the embarrassing event. Thus, suggestive interviews promote children's reports about true events. However, these same techniques had the same effect on the elicitation of children's reports about never-experienced events. For example, in this same study after two highly suggestive interviews, children not only assented to, but gave highly elaborate false reports about, helping a lady find her monkey in the park (only 6% of the children denied) and about witnessing a thief steal food from the day care (only 12% denied). Thus there are benefits but also very high risks to using suggestive interviewing techniques when one does not know what the child experienced; using such techniques, the interviewer will be successful in eliciting disclosures, but will not know whether these are accurate or inaccurate. Thus, the scientific literature indicates that under all circumstances (unless the truth is known, in which case there is no need to interview), unbiased, nonsuggestive interviews should be conducted.

We should note that, although a significant proportion of children denied a true event in this study, this figure should not be generalized to the proportion of sexually abused children who might deny abuse when first asked. This is because the motives to deny an actual punishment are quite different from denying sexual abuse. The former involve protecting oneself from revealing an embarrassing wrongdoing.

Research by Michael Lamb, Kathleen Sternberg, and colleagues has shown that the use of specific/leading questions is not necessary to elicit informative reports from children who are questioned about abuse (e.g., Lamb, Sternberg, & Esplin, 2000; Lamb et al., 2003; Sternberg et al., 1996). This team created a structured interview protocol and then trained interviewers of suspected child abuse victims in its use. The major feature of the protocol is to encourage the child to provide detailed life-event narratives through the guidance of open-ended questions (e.g., "Tell me what happened"; "And then what happened next?"; "And you said it happened at the store—tell me about the store"). The use of specific questions is allowed only after exhaustive free-recall prompting. Suggestive questions are highly discouraged. In one study, Lamb and colleagues (2003) examined the interviews of 16 trained police officers with 130 children (4–8 years old), all of whom had made allegations of sexual abuse. They found that 78% of preschoolers' allegations and disclosures were elicited through free-recall questions, and 66% of all children identified the suspect through open-ended questions (60% for preschoolers). These data dispel the belief that young children need to be bombarded with specific (suggestive) questions to elicit details of their traumatic events; in fact, children can provide detailed information through open-ended prompts, and, if a child denies abuse when asked directly, there is no scientifically compelling evidence that the child is "in denial." Abused children usually disclose when directly asked.

MYTHS AND MISCONCEPTIONS

Multiple Suggestive Interviews Are Needed to Taint a Report

To justify a suggestive interview, some experts have claimed that one suggestive interview is insufficient to taint a child's report and that taint only occurs when multiple suggestive techniques are used in repeated interviews (e.g., Ceci & Bruck, 1995).

This belief is not supported by the scientific literature, which shows that children can incorporate suggestions about salient events after a single interview (e.g., Bruck, London, Landa, & Goodman, 2007; Garven et al., 2000; Thompson et al., 1997). In the Paco study by Garven and colleagues (2000), for example, children's reports were significantly tainted after a single short suggestive interview. Other studies have directly compared the effects of multiple versus one suggestive interview on children's suggestibility. Evidence suggests that under a number of circumstances, one suggestive interview produces the same amount of taint as two or more suggestive interviews. The impact of a second interview depends on the spacing of the interviews from the initial events and from the final interview, and also on the strength of the original memory trace (Marche, 1999; Melnyk & Bruck, 2004; Powell & Thompson, 1997).

It is also true that children's reports can be tainted in the absence of highly suggestive, coercive techniques. Poole and Lindsay (2001) had parents read their children short narratives that outlined the children's previous encounters with a character known as Mr. Science at the researchers' laboratory. Unbeknownst to the parents, some of the details in the stories were inaccurate and thus were not experienced by the children when they met Mr. Science. Nonetheless, even under these mildly suggestive conditions, significant numbers of children (4- to 8-year-olds) later told an interviewer that they had experienced the suggested events (e.g., "The man put something yucky in my mouth").

Suggestibility Is Primarily a Problem for Preschoolers

Although much of the literature pays lip service to the concept that suggestibility exists at all ages, including in adults, the common view is that preschool children are disproportionately suggestible, and that there should be less concern about the tainting effects of suggestive interviews with older school-age children. This belief is reflected in the following expert testimony:

Well, in virtually all these studies, two- and three-year-olds do not do well in suggestibility, and the four- and five-year-olds do pretty well. It's true that the sorts of questioning that were asked of the children [in the case at hand] are not supported by basic research into suggestibility, but these children [in the case at hand] were all over the age of 6, the cut-off for suggestibility proneness in scientific studies. (expert testimony by a prosecution witness *In the matter of Riley Blanchard, Shelby Blanchard, and Austin Blanchard*, CA 2001; Tr. p. 1,441)

Yet although a number of findings show that elementary school-age children are less susceptible to suggestion than preschool children (e.g., Bright-Paul, Jarrold, & Wright, 2005; Ceci & Bruck, 1993; Ceci, Ross, & Toglia, 1987; Chae & Ceci, 2005; Holliday, 2003; Poole & Lindsay, 2001; Strange, Sutherland, & Garry, 2006), in most studies it is a matter of degree. That is, elementary school-age children show significant suggestibility effects even when preschoolers exhibit more suggestibility. Second, the results of a number of other studies show that not only is susceptibility to suggestion common in middle childhood, but that under some conditions there are small to no developmental differences in suggestibility. For example, Finnila and colleagues staged an event (a version of the Paco visit we described earlier) for 4- to 5-year-olds and 7- to 8-year-olds. One week later, half the children were given a low-pressure interview that contained some misleading questions with abuse themes (e.g., "He took your clothes off, didn't he?"). The other children received a high-pressure interview; they were told that their friends had answered the leading questions affirmatively, they were praised for assenting to the misleading questions, and when they did not assent, the question was repeated. In both conditions, there were no significant age differences in the percentage of misleading questions answered affirmatively, although a significant number (68%) were assented to in the high-pressure condition (Finnila, Mahlberga, Santtilaa, Sandnabbaa, & Niemib, 2003; see also Bruck et al., 2007).

Finally, under some conditions, older children are actually more suggestible than younger children (e.g., Ceci, Papierno, & Kulkofsky, 2007; Connolly & Price, 2006; Finnila et al., 2003; Schreiber & Parker, 2004). These reverse trends often reflect age differences in children's knowledge or what has been called "gist processing" (Reyna & Brainerd, 1998), such that higher levels of knowledge are sometimes associated with larger suggestibility effects. Sometimes, these reverse age trends are associated with social factors involving older children's greater sensitivity to the intent of some suggestive devices (e.g., a repeated question is a signal that the original answer was incorrect or that the interviewer did not like the first answer). Brainerd, Reyna, and Ceci (2008) extensively reviewed the evidence for reverse developmental effects in which older children's greater knowledge renders them more vulnerable to suggestions than younger children. The bottom line is that, all age groups are vulnerable to misleading suggestions, even if preschoolers are sometimes disproportionately more vulnerable.

Children's Spontaneous Reports Are Always Accurate

A commonly held belief is that although children's prompted statements may be suspect, their spontaneous statements are generally accurate, and errors only occur in suggestive interviews. This belief has led some expert witnesses to opine that a child's statement must be correct because it was produced in response to a free-recall probe ("Tell me what happened"), rather than in response to direct suggestions, forced-choice questions, or limited-option questions.

It is true that children tend to be more accurate when asked open-ended questions that allow them to freely recall, compared to when they are asked more directed questions; this fact has been recognized since the earliest studies on children's suggestibility (Ceci & Bruck, 1995). However, it is not the case that children's spontaneous statements are always accurate. When children have been questioned suggestively, the suggestions can taint not only the statements made during that interaction but also the reports in later suggestion-free interactions, as seen in the Chester the Janitor study, described earlier. For example, the children in Poole and Lindsey's (2001) "Mr. Science" study, discussed earlier, were simply asked to describe everything they remembered from interacting with Mr. Science after they had been exposed to a misleading narrative by their parents about the event. A full 21% of the children's spontaneous statements had not been experienced, but had been suggested by their parents at a prior time. Furthermore, some of these events included bodily touch, such as Mr. Science putting something yucky in the child's mouth. In a different study, Poole and White (1993) interviewed children about an event that had occurred 2 years previously. Following the first event the children had been exposed to repeated questions, some of which were misleading. Two years later 39% of 6-year-olds' (who were 4 years old at the time of the original event) statements in response to the open-ended request, "Tell me what happened," were incorrect. Older children did not fare that much better, with 23% of 8-year-olds' and 25% of 10-year-olds' statements being incorrect.

Furthermore, even if children have not been exposed to misleading suggestions, their open-ended recall is not guaranteed to be accurate. This is especially true if the child is interviewed about a confusing or ambiguous event. For example, Ornstein and colleagues (1998) engaged children in a mock medical exam in which some common features (e.g., listening to the child's heart) were omitted and atypical features (e.g., wiping the child's belly button with alcohol) were added. When children were interviewed about the event 12 weeks later, 42% of 4-year-olds and 74% of 6-year-olds spontaneously reported at least one of the nonexperienced common features. In another study, Goodman and her colleagues (1994) interviewed children about a painful genital catheterization procedure. Among the children who were 3–4 years old, 23% of their free-recall statements were incorrect. Finally, Greenhoot (2000) examined 5- and 6-year-olds' recall of ambiguous stories, where the protagonist may have been considered acting either prosocially or antisocially. Error rates on open-ended recall ranged between 20 and 30%.

Taken together, these studies (and others reviewed by Kulkofsky et al., 2008) show that although children's free recall and spontaneous statements are generally more accurate than their responses to directed questions, free recall is by no means error free. Errors can result from suggestive techniques, but they can also reflect other factors that distort memory (e.g., forgetting, use of schemas to reconstruct theme-consistent but inaccurate details, misunderstanding). These distortions can turn into quite detailed false reports if the child is interviewed by a biased interviewer who conducts the interview to confirm the child's initial inaccurate statement. In contrast, an unbiased interviewer may be able to question the child in such a way as to test various hypotheses about the origin of the child's statements.

False Reports Produced by Suggestive Interviews Are Distinguishable from Accurate Reports

Expert witnesses often state that it is easy to detect false reports that are the product of false suggestions because such children (1) merely "parrot" the words of their interrogators, (2) sound rehearsed, and (3) provide unemotional narratives that have no sensory information (e.g., "It hurt"). These beliefs at times reflect confusion about reports that emerge as a result of suggestions, coaching, or lying. Coaching differs from suggestibility in that it implies a deliberate attempt on the part of the interviewer to put words into the child's mouth and to have the child actively rehearse these statements. In contrast, there is no deception involved when children provide false reports in suggestive interviews. Children's inaccurate responses to the suggestions initially may reflect social pressure; they provide a response to please the interviewer. However, with time children come to believe that the falsely suggested event had actually happened. In other words, they develop a false belief about a statement they initially realized was false. In addition, deliberate attempts to coach the child are rare. In most cases, the interviewer is not consciously trying to put words into the child's mouth, and there are rarely deliberate attempts to rehearse the child's false testimony.

Thus, one cannot use the same criteria for detecting lies as for detecting false beliefs that result from suggestions. Yi and Ceci (2007) found that adult judges assess these coached children's reports as less credible than those of children who produced false reports as a result of suggestion or of children whose reports were accurate. In their study, nine preschool children reported either accurate or inaccurate information as a result of being coached to lie or being exposed to misinformation. College students rated the credibility of each child's statements. Children who were inaccurate due to having been exposed to misinformation appeared every bit as credible as children who were accurate, and both appeared more credible than children who had been coached to lie. We should note that other research, which has not included a suggestibility condition, indicates that adult judges cannot easily discriminate lies from truths in children who have been coached (Leach, Talwar, Lee, Bala, & Lindsay, 2004; Talwar, Lee, Bala, & Lindsay, 2006).

There are other consistent findings. Children who make false reports after being suggestively interviewed appear highly credible to trained professionals in the fields of child development, mental health, and forensics (e.g., Ceci, Crotteau-Huffman, Smith, & Loftus, 1994; Ceci, Loftus, Leichtman, & Bruck, 1994; Leichtman & Ceci, 1995). As was the case with Yi and Ceci's college raters, these professionals cannot reliably discriminate children whose reports are accurate from those whose reports are inaccurate as a result of suggestive interviewing techniques. The children who provided the false reports spoke sincerely and provided accounts laden with emotion and perceptual details. Part of the difficulty in discerning true from false reports in children is that when children are suggestively interviewed, their subsequent narratives may include false reports that go beyond what was suggested to them but that are consistent with the suggestions (e.g., Bruck et al., 1995, 2002). For example, Leichtman and Ceci (1995) found that when children were given false suggestions that a person was "clumsy," they later generalized this information to make false claims that this individual spilled, ripped, soiled, or broke things during his visit to their classroom, even though these behaviors had not been part of the interviewer's suggestions.

Another set of studies has searched for objective characteristics that might differentiate suggested true from suggested false narratives. The frequency of linguistic markers, such as the amount of elaboration or temporal connectivity, do not consistently differentiate true from false narratives that emerge as a result of repeated suggestive interviews (Bruck et al., 2002; Powell, Jones, & Campbell, 2003; Scullin, Kanaya, & Ceci, 2002). In the Bruck and colleagues (2002) study described earlier, analyses showed that narratives of false events actually contained more embellishments (including descriptions and emotional terms) and details than their narratives of true events. The false narratives also had more spontaneous statements than the true narratives and included more temporal connectors. The robustness of false narratives may emerge because when children are suggestively interviewed they often learn that the truth value of their statements is not important; rather, the amount of detail about events that are of interest to the interviewer is what counts. This sometimes results in children providing very elaborate and sometimes bizarre reports about nonexperienced events.

These findings show that reliability and credibility are orthogonal dimensions. Children may appear highly credible (or their interviews may have the characteristics of credible narratives) and yet their reports may be unreliable. Children can also be very reliable and yet not appear credible in the eyes of judges and jurors. Accordingly, one cannot use perceived credibility to judge reliability. However, in the forensic arena, it is crucial for those who make judgments about credibility (i.e., the court) to make such judgments based on the reliability of the report. In other words, the judgment must take into account the degree to which suggestive interviewing specifically, and interviewer bias more generally, were used to elicit the child's statements. The role of the expert is to educate the court about the risks of various techniques that can taint children's testimony. With this knowledge, it is up to the court to decide if the facts of the case reveal the presence of such tainting mechanisms and the degree to which they are important for assessing the child's credibility.

GAPS IN RELEVANT SCIENTIFIC KNOWLEDGE

Since the late 1980s, there has been tremendous interest and progress in the field of children's suggestibility. Nevertheless, there are still many large gaps in our knowledge; here, we provide our list of the most crucial ones. First, there is almost no work on suggestibility and the factors that distort the testimony of adolescents. Given the great changes in the emotional, social, neurobiological, and cognitive development of adolescents, it does not seem appropriate to treat them as big children or even as little adults. Compared with younger children and college students, adolescents may display very different mechanisms and motives for false allegations. One possibility is that they may be more sensitive to peer-group influences that would sway the accuracy of their testimony.

Second, although there are a number of good protocols for interviewing children who are victims of, or participants in, crimes, the training of interviewers does not specifically focus on the concept of "interviewer bias." Rather, existing guidelines mainly incorporate strategies that may decrease the number of suggestive techniques in an interview. Consequently, one could conduct a suggestion-free interview but end up with statements that, when put together, do not make sense or present a coherent narrative. This incoherence occurs because interviewers focus so much on the elements of the protocol and on the elicitation of single details that they never step back and ask, "Does this make sense?" or "What is this child trying to tell me?" This line of problem solving involves constructing a set of alternative hypotheses "online"—indeed a difficult task, but one that must be deconstructed and taught to obtain the best information from children.

Third, although there is now a substantial body of research dealing with individual differences among children that make some prone to suggestions and others highly resistant (e.g., Bruck & Melnyk, 2004; Chae & Ceci, 2005; Roebers & Schneider, 2001), there are virtually no data on individual differences that might render one better able to conduct a developmentally appropriate interview while avoiding interviewer bias. Although it would not be surprising if there were large differences among prospective trainees in the ability to multitask (e.g., keep track of the child's utterances, bearing in mind the case details, posit new hypotheses online), the more interesting and next question to address is the degree to which training can minimize such differences.

CONCLUSIONS

Scientifically Supported Uses of Interviewing

Children must be questioned by unbiased interviewers whose major task is to collect "untainted" evidence. If the child makes abuse-consistent statements, the interviewer must test alternative hypotheses about why the child is making that statement. Children's statements need to be elicited through open-ended questions or nonsuggestive techniques.

Scientifically Unsupported and Controversial Uses of Interviewing

We reviewed a number of suggestive techniques at the beginning of this chapter. When these techniques are used—especially by biased interviewers—the child may make abuse-consistent statements. The problem is that one cannot establish with any certainty whether the child's statement is accurate or false as a consequence of the suggestive techniques. In other words, the child's statements may have been tainted. Furthermore, there is no valid "Pinocchio test" that allows one to decide with any certainty whether a child's statements are accurate or false. Although suggestive interviewing techniques may still be controversial in some quarters, they are not supported by scientific evidence. Nevertheless, as we noted earlier, interviewer bias can distort the results of childhood interviews even in the absence of suggestive techniques, such as leading questions.

COMMUNICATING RELEVANT SCIENCE IN THE COURTROOM AND IN WRITTEN REPORTS

In our experience in the courtroom, the content of the material described in this chapter has been admissible under the *Daubert* standards. The studies have been published, the findings have been replicated, and there is general agreement in the field about most of these principles. Furthermore, based on surveys of potential jurors, this information is unfamiliar to laypersons.

It is always important to make sure that the court understands that this type of testimony speaks to the reliability (i.e., the trustworthiness) of the evidence, not to the honesty or credibility of a witness. Statements or reports can be unreliable due to normal processes of forgetting, distortion, and reconstruction. Statements can also be rendered unreliable if they are elicited in certain suggestive contexts. Thus, this type of testimony focuses on factors that enhance or degrade the quality of children's and adults' reports. Although this testimony does not assess the credibility (believability) of the child's allegations of abuse, information concerning the reliability of the child's report is crucial (for the court and nonexperts) to draw conclusions about the credibility of the children's allegations.

We have written a number of documents for the court that have presented the relevant scientific evidence and used it to provide possible explanations for the statements of the children in a particular case (e.g., see *Fuster-Escalona v. Singletary*; *www.oranous.com/innocence/FrankFuster/MaggieBruck.htm*;

New Jersey v. Michaels, www.falseallegations.com/amicus.htm). There are some common themes in our written and oral testimonies. First, we only agree to educate the triers of fact in cases in which it is very clear that there was suggestive interviewing. We do not accept cases where there is little evidence or where we are asked to present a "theory" of why a child *might* make false statements. Consequently, on many occasions we have declined to participate because we found no evidence of taint in the case materials. In fact, in a few cases we worked with, and testified for, the prosecution regarding the clear absence of taint.

Second, our analysis ultimately examines the degree to which interviewer bias may have tainted the evidence in the case. This aspect involves more than examining the suggestive techniques during interviews, but extends to the whole conduct of the investigation; so this type of testimony is not always child-specific. For example, interviewer bias can be observed in a specific interview or by how an interviewer assesses the content or the impact of specific interviews. At a higher level, interviewer (or investigator) bias is revealed by the types of evidence that are pursued or ignored at the investigational level. For example, in many cases important leads are not followed up (because the primary and only hypothesis is that the prime suspect was the perpetrator).

Finally, although experts in this field cannot provide expert opinions as to the guilt of the alleged perpetrator or to the accuracy of the child's statements, they can provide an expert opinion concerning the amount of suggestion and taint present in the case. They can then conclude that, based on the scientific literature, this amount of taint or suggestion renders the child's statements unreliable.

REFERENCES

Brainerd, C. J., & Reyna, V. F., & Ceci, S. J. (2008). Developmental reversals in false memory: A review of data and theory. *Psychological Bulletin, 134,* 343–382.

Bright-Paul, A., Jarrold, C., & Wright, D. (2005). Age-appropriate cues facilitate source-monitoring and reduce suggestibility in 3- to 7-year-olds. *Cognitive Development, 20,* 1–18.

Bruck, M., Ceci, S. J., & Francoeur, E. (2000). A comparison of three and four year old children's use of anatomically detailed dolls to report genital touching in examination. *Journal of Experimental Psychology: Applied, 6,* 74–83.

Bruck, M., Ceci, S. J., Francoeur, E., & Barr, R. J. (1995). "I hardly cried when I got my shot!": Influencing children's reports about a visit to their pediatrician. *Child Development, 66,* 193–208.

Bruck, M., Ceci, S. J., & Hembrooke, H. (2002). Nature of true and false narratives. *Developmental Review, 22,* 520–554.

Bruck, M., Ceci, S. J., Melnyk, L., & Finkelberg, D. (1999, April). *Does interview bias create tainted reports?* Paper presented at the biannual meeting of the Society for Research in Child Development, Albuquerque, NM.

Bruck, M., Ceci, S. J., & Principe, G. (2006). The child and the law. In W. Damon & R. Lerner (Gen. Eds.), and K. A. Renninger & I. E. Sigel (Vol. Eds.), *Handbook of child psychology: Vol. 5. Child psychology in practice* (6th ed., pp. 776–816). New York: Wiley.

Bruck, M., London, K., Landa, R., & Goodman, J. (2007). Autobiographical memory and suggestibility. *Development and Psychopathology, 19,* 73–95.

Bruck, M., & Melnyk, L. (2004). Individual differences in children's suggestibility: A review and synthesis. *Applied Cognitive Psychology, 18,* 947–996.

Ceci, S. J., & Bruck, M. (1993). The suggestibility of the child witness: A historical review and synthesis. *Psychological Bulletin, 113,* 403–439.

Ceci, S. J., & Bruck, M. (1995). *Jeopardy in the courtroom: A scientific analysis of children's testimony.* Washington, DC: American Psychological Association.

Ceci, S. J., Crotteau-Huffman, M., Smith, E., & Loftus, E. W. (1994). Repeatedly thinking about nonevents. *Consciousness and Cognition, 3,* 388–407.

Ceci, S. J., Loftus, E. W., Leichtman, M., & Bruck, M. (1994). The role of source misattributions in the creation of false beliefs among preschoolers. *International Journal of Clinical and Experimental Hypnosis, 62,* 304–320.

Ceci, S. J., Papierno, P. B., & Kulkofsky, S. (2007). Representational constraints on children's suggestibility. *Psychological Science, 18*(6), 503–509.

Ceci, S. J., Ross, D., & Toglia, M. (1987). Suggestibility of children's memory: Psycholegal implications. *Journal of Experimental Psychology: General, 116,* 38–49.

Chae, Y., & Ceci, S. J. (2005). Individual differences in children's recall and suggestibility: The effect of intelligence, temperament, and self-perceptions. *Applied Cognitive Psychology, 19,* 383–407.

Connolly, D., & Price, H. (2006). Children's suggestibility for an instance of a repeated event versus a unique event: The effect of degree of association between variable details. *Journal of Experimental Child Psychology, 93*(3), 207–223.

Finnila, K., Mahlberga, N., Santtilaa, P., Sandnabbaa, K., & Niemib, P. (2003). Validity of a test of children's suggestibility for predicting responses to two interview situations differing in their degree of suggestiveness. *Journal of Experimental Child Psychology, 85,* 32–49.

Garven, S., Wood, J. M., & Malpass, R. S. (2000). Allegations of wrongdoing: The effects of reinforcement on children's mundane and fantastic claims. *Journal of Applied Psychology, 1,* 38–49.

Goodman, G. S., Quas, J. A., Batterman-Faunce, J. M., Riddlesberger, M., &

Kuhn, J. (1994). Predictors of accurate and inaccurate memories of traumatic events experienced in childhood. *Consciousness and Cognition, 3,* 269–294.

Goodman, G. S., & Reed, R. S. (1986). Age differences in eyewitness testimony. *Law and Human Behavior, 10,* 317–332.

Greenhoot, A. F. (2000). Remembering and understanding: The effects of changes in underlying knowledge on children's recollections. *Child Development, 71,* 1309–1328.

Holliday, R. (2003). The effect of a prior cognitive interview on children's acceptance of misinformation. *Applied Cognitive Psychology, 17,* 443–457.

Horner, T. M., Guyer, M. J., & Kalter, N. M. (1993a). The biases of child sexual abuse experts: Believing is seeing. *Bulletin of the American Academy of Psychiatry and Law, 21,* 281–292.

Horner, T. M., Guyer, M. J., & Kalter, N. M. (1993b). Clinical expertise and the assessment of child sexual abuse. *Journal of the American Academy of Child and Adolescent Psychiatry, 32,* 925–931.

Kulkofsky, S. C., Wang, Q., & Ceci, S. J. (2008). Do better stories make better memories?: Narrative quality and memory accuracy in preschool children. *Applied Cognitive Psychology, 21,* 21–38.

Lamb, M. E., Sternberg, K. J., & Esplin, P. W. (2000). Effects of age and delay on the amount of information provided by alleged sex abuse victims in investigative interviews. *Child Development, 71,* 1586–1596.

Lamb, M. E., Sternberg, K. J., Orbach, Y., Esplin, P. W., Stewart, H., & Mitchell, S. (2003). Age differences in young children's responses to open-ended invitations in the course of forensic interviews. *Journal of Consulting and Clinical Psychology, 71*(5), 926–934.

Leach, A., Talwar, V., Lee, K., Bala, N., & Lindsay, R. (2004). "Intuitive" lie detection of children's deception by law enforcement officials and university students. *Law and Human Behavior, 28*(6), 661–685.

Leichtman, M. D., & Ceci, S. J. (1995). The effects of stereotypes and suggestions on preschoolers' reports. *Developmental Psychology, 31*(4), 568–578.

London, K., Bruck, M., Ceci, S. J., & Shuman, D. (2005). Disclosure of child sexual abuse: What does the research tell us about the ways that children tell? *Psychology, Public Policy and Law, 11,* 194–226.

London, K., Bruck, M., Wright, D., & Ceci, S. J. (2008). Review of the contemporary literature on how children report sexual abuse to others: Findings, methodological issues, and implications for forensic interviewers. *Memory, 1,* 29–47.

Lyon, T. D. (2007). False denials: Overcoming methodological biases in abuse disclosure research. In M. E. Pipe, M. E. Lamb, Y. Orbach, & A. C. Cederborg (Eds.), *Disclosing abuse: Delays, denials, retractions, and incomplete accounts* (pp. 41–62). Mahwah, NJ: Erlbaum.

Malloy, L. C., Lyon, T. D., & Quas, J. A. (2007). Filial dependency and recantation of child sexual abuse allegations. *Journal of the American Academy of Child and Adolescent Psychiatry, 46*(2), 162–170.

Marche, T. A. (1999). Memory strength affects reporting misinformation. *Journal of Experimental Child Psychology, 73,* 45–71.

Melnyk, L., & Bruck, M. (2004). Timing moderates the effect of repeated suggestive interviewing on children's suggestibility. *Applied Cognitive Psychology, 18,* 613–631.

Ornstein, P. A., Merritt, K. A., Baker-Ward, K., Furtado, E., Gordon, B. N., & Principe, G. (1998). Children's knowledge, expectation, and long-term retention. *Applied Cognitive Psychology, 12,* 387–405.

Peterson, C., & Bell, M. (1996). Children's memory for traumatic injury. *Child Development, 67,* 3045–3070.

Poole, D. A., & Lindsay, D. S. (2001). Children's eyewitness reports after exposure to misinformation from parents. *Journal of Experimental Psychology: Applied, 7,* 27–50.

Poole, D. A., & White, L. T. (1993). Two years later: Effects of question repetition and retention interval on the eyewitness testimony of children and adults. *Developmental Psychology, 29,* 844–853.

Powell, M. B., Jones, C. H., & Campbell, C. (2003). A comparison of preschooler's recall of experienced versus non-experienced events across multiple interviewers. *Applied Cognitive Psychology, 17,* 935–952.

Powell, M. B., & Thomson, D. M. (1997). The effect of an intervening interview on children's ability to remember an occurrence of a repeated event. *Legal and Criminological Psychology, 2,* 247–262.

Reyna, V. F., & Brainerd, C. J. (1998). Fuzzy-trace theory and false memory: New frontiers. *Journal of Experimental Child Psychology, 71,* 194–209.

Roebers, C. M., & Schneider, W. (2001). Individual differences in children's eyewitness recall: The influence of intelligence and shyness. *Applied Developmental Science, 5,* 9–20.

Schreiber, N., & Parker, J. (2004). Inviting witnesses to speculate: Effects of age and interaction on children's recall. *Journal of Experimental Child Psychology, 89,* 31–52.

Scullin, M., Kanaya, T., & Ceci, S. J. (2002). Measurement of individual differences in children's suggestibility across situations. *Journal of Experimental Psychology: Applied, 8,* 233–246.

Sorenson, T., & Snow, B. (1991). How children tell: The process of disclosure in child sexual abuse. *Child Welfare, 70,* 3–15.

Sternberg, K. J., Lamb, M. E., Hershkowitz, I., Sternberg, K. J., Lamb, M. E., Hershkowitz, I., et al. (1996). The relation between investigative utterance types and the informativeness of the child witness. *Journal of Applied Developmental Psychology, 17,* 439–451.

Strange, D., Sutherland, R., & Garry, M. (2006). Event plausibility does not determine children's false memories. *Memory, 14*(8), 937–951.

Summit, R. (1983). The child sexual abuse accommodation syndrome. *Child Abuse and Neglect, 7,* 177–193.

Talwar, V., Lee, K., Bala, N., & Lindsay, R. C. L. (2006) Adults' judgments of child witness credibility and veracity. *Law and Human Behavior, 30,* 561–570.

Thompson, W. C., Clarke-Stewart, K. A., & Lepore, S. J. (1997). What did the janitor do?: Suggestive interviewing and the accuracy of children's accounts. *Law and Human Behavior, 21,* 405–426.

Yi, S., & Ceci, S. J. (2007, May). *Misinformation and deception detection among preschool children.* Paper presented at the annual meeting of the Association for Psychological Science, Washington, DC.

PART III

SPECIFIC TESTS AND TECHNIQUES

CHAPTER 8

The Psychopathy Checklist in the Courtroom

CONSENSUS AND CONTROVERSIES

John F. Edens, Jennifer L. Skeem,
and Patrick J. Kennealy

Psychopathic personality disorder, or more simply, *psychopathy*, is a term that has had an array of meanings throughout history, in both professional discourse and the public eye. In the mental health field, early uses of the term referenced general *psychopathology*. In the legal arena, psychopathy similarly reflected a broader concept than contemporary conceptualizations, as evidenced by Chicago's "Juvenile Psychopathic Institute," which was founded in the early 1900s to provide treatment for a wide spectrum of mental health problems. Remnants of these conceptualizations—with a sensationalistic twist—are apparent among laypeople today, as it is common to see such descriptors as psychopathic, psychosis, psychotic, and "psycho" used interchangeably and indiscriminately in the public media to describe persons who display wide-ranging types of criminal, aberrant, socially deviant, or simply peculiar or puzzling symptoms, traits, behaviors, or actions (Wahl, 2003).

Despite this ambiguity, the term "psychopathic" has taken on a relatively precise meaning in professional discourse over the last 50–60 years. In the mental health field, the term has become fairly closely aligned with

Hervey Cleckley's (1941/1976) seminal description derived from case studies of individuals who manifested significant emotional detachment. In the psycholegal field, however, the term has become shorthand for describing an individual—typically one with an extensive criminal background—who obtains a high score on one particular instrument, the Psychopathy Checklist—Revised (PCL-R; Hare, 1991, 2003). Over the years, the PCL-R has been described as an unparalleled predictor of violence (Salekin, Rogers, & Sewell, 1996), as an essential component of ethical risk assessments (Hart, 1998), and as operationalizing the most important clinical construct in the criminal justice system (Hare, 1996b). As such, in this chapter we focus on issues specifically relevant to the PCL measures because they have (1) gained tremendous traction in the applied psycholegal field, (2) been applied often in relevant research, and (3) spawned controversies about the use of psychopathy in legal contexts. Alternative measures of psychopathy are available (see, e.g., Lilienfeld & Fowler, 2006), but thus far have had less psycholegal impact than the PCL measures.

The PCL-R is described in the most recent manual (Hare, 2003) as a "20-item scale for the assessment of psychopathy in research, clinical, and forensic settings [using] a semistructured interview, file, and collateral information to measure inferred personality traits and behaviors" (p. 1). The PCL-R items are summed to yield a total score that ranges from 0 to 40 points, with scores of 30 or greater traditionally being used to identify a "psychopath." Highly similar instruments—in terms of content, structure, and correlations with their parent measure—have been developed for juveniles, the Psychopathy Checklist: Youth Version (PCL:YV; Forth, Kosson, & Hare, 2003), and for adults in mostly noncorrectional settings, the Psychopathy Checklist: Screening Version (PCL:SV: Hart, Cox, & Hare, 1995). For the sake of simplicity, these measures are referred to as the "PCL" throughout this chapter unless specific reference is being made to a specific version.

In many ways, the PCL items are similar to criteria for diagnosing antisocial personality disorder (APD) in the text revision of the fourth edition of the *Diagnostic and Statistical Manual of Mental Disorders* (DSM-IV-TR; American Psychiatric Association, 2000). The two overlap heavily in their focus on criminal history and antisocial conduct. Unlike the APD criteria, however, the PCL includes several additional items that tap affective (e.g., remorselessness, shallow affect) and interpersonal (e.g., grandiosity, deceptiveness) features that overlap with Cleckley's (1941/1976) seminal description of psychopathy. Moreover, when the focus is on offenders, the PCL-R identifies a more circumscribed group than APD, in that most high scorers on the PCL-R are diagnosable as having APD, yet many offenders who meet diagnostic criteria for APD would *not* be classified as psychopathic (scores ≥30) on the PCL-R (Hare, 2003).

OVERVIEW OF CONTROVERSIES

There is no shortage of controversies about PCL psychopathy. Given space constraints, we focus on four controversies with direct implications for using the PCL as evidence bearing on a legal issue. First, we address the extent to which the PCL is *reliable* when applied in "real-world" adversarial settings, outside the lab. Second, we highlight a debate about the extent to which *criminal conduct is an essential component* of psychopathy, as assumed in the PCL measures. This debate relates to the third controversy, which revolves around the *predictive utility* of the PCL for violence and other crime. Fourth, we address the extent to which PCL psychopathy can have a *prejudicial* effect on such legal decisions (see Slobogin, 2006). Several recent studies have begun to examine the implications of PCL-based descriptors in relation to attributions made about adult and juvenile offenders. In the next section we summarize research relevant to each of these controversies.

RESEARCH RELEVANT TO THE CONTROVERSIES

How Reliable Is the PCL in Adversarial Settings?

When administered and scored by appropriately trained examiners as part of research projects, the PCL typically yields scores that meet minimally acceptable standards (e.g., Heilbrun, 1992) of interrater reliability suggested for the use of psychological tests in forensic practice (for summaries, see Campbell, Pulos, Hogan, & Murry, 2005; Hare, 2003). This appears to be true whether interviews are included in the scoring process or scores are based solely on file reviews. However, these findings only suggest that the PCL *can be* scored reliably across examiners; they do not indicate whether it *has been* scored reliably in any given case (e.g., Edens, 2006; Edens & Petrila, 2006; Hare, 2004, as cited in Weaver, Meyer, Van Nort, & Tristan, 2006), and anecdotal accounts of rather large discrepancies across expert witnesses have been reported in the literature (e.g., Edens, 2006; Edens & Petrila, 2006; Edens & Vincent, 2008), bolstering concerns that research-based estimates of reliability are overly optimistic for real-world contexts.

Murrie and colleagues (Murrie, Boccaccini, Johnson, & Janke, 2008) recently summarized available data on the interrater reliability of the

PCL-R in clinical practice, rather than research settings. In the few studies published, reliability statistics generally were on par with results reported in research samples (although, see Tyrer et al., 2005). However, none of these studies examined the reliability of the PCL in such adversarial contexts as criminal trials or civil commitment proceedings. To address this important limitation, Murrie and colleagues retrospectively examined the concordance between PCL-R scores provided by experts called by opposing sides (termed "petitioners" and "respondents") in 43 Texas "sexually violent predator" (SVP) cases. In these cases, state-hired doctoral-level psychologists routinely assess PCL-R psychopathy to inform civil commitment decisions. In just over half of these cases ($n = 23$), an expert retained by the respondent also administered the PCL-R. For this subset of cases, the authors found a pronounced and statistically significant disparity in average PCL-R total ratings, with mean state expert ratings of 26 ($SD = 8.48$) and mean respondent expert ratings of 18 ($SD = 6.62$). Given that the range of PCL scores is between 0 and 40 in theory, and between 6 and 38 in practice with male criminal offenders (Hare, 2003, p. 25), an *average* difference of 8 points is both remarkable and troubling.

Although no other published accounts have surfaced to replicate or counter the findings of Murrie and colleagues (2008), similar results have been demonstrated in an unpublished case law review of 98 Canadian criminal trials. Clark and Forth (2005) reported significant differences in PCL-R scores provided by experts called by the prosecution versus those called by the defense, with prosecution experts reporting higher average scores. Notably, defense expert scores did not differ significantly from court-appointed expert scores.

These data on the applied reliability of PCL assessments across examiners in adversarial legal cases are limited. Moreover, the examiner bias conveyed by these data may well generalize from the PCL to other semistructured interviews and rating scales applied in adversarial settings—particularly those that rely heavily on examiners' subjective judgments. Nonetheless, these data raise serious concerns that (1) reliability statistics from published research studies on the PCL may not generalize outside the lab, and (2) PCL scores presented in court may be biased toward the side that called the examiner to testify. Although this discrepancy is arguably less problematic in cases in which opposing examiners give conflicting results—as they are likely to cancel each other out, to some extent—it is of even greater concern in the relatively high percentage of cases in which apparently only one PCL-R score is provided (Murrie et al., 2008).

Is Criminal Behavior Essential to Psychopathy, as Assumed in the PCL?

In expert testimony and elsewhere, it is common to see the PCL globally described as a "valid" instrument (DeMatteo & Edens, 2006; Edens & Petrila, 2006). However, the construct validity of the tool is hotly debated (Cooke, Michie, & Skeem, 2007; Skeem & Cooke, in press; cf. Hare, 2003). This debate focuses on the assumption that criminal behavior is a central component of psychopathic personality disorder. Classic conceptualizations of psychopathy (Karpman, 1948; McCord & McCord, 1964), including the conceptualization on which the PCL ostensibly is based (Cleckley, 1941/1976), focus heavily on interpersonal and affective traits that we referred to earlier as "emotional detachment" (following Patrick, Bradley, & Lang, 1993). These traits include callousness, remorselessness, low trait anxiety, deceitfulness, egocentricity, superficial charm, and a failure to form close emotional bonds (Lilienfeld, 1998). However, the PCL weighs criminal behavior as strongly as—if not more strongly than—traits of emotional detachment in assessing "psychopathy." In part, this is because the PCL expressly was developed with and for correctional inmates (see Hare, 1980) who, by definition, have histories of criminal conduct. Without a history of violent or other unlawful behavior (best represented in PCL "Factor 2"), even an individual with pronounced interpersonal and affective traits of psychopathy (best represented in PCL "Factor 1") is unlikely to surpass the PCL's diagnostic cut score to be considered "psychopathic."

On one side of the debate, personality-focused researchers argue that emotional detachment is essential to psychopathy, whereas criminal behavior is an epiphenomenon that is neither diagnostic of psychopathy nor specific to personality deviation (e.g., Cooke et al., 2007). For example, Skeem and Cooke (in press) contend that, as the field has grown to conflate the PCL with the theoretical construct of psychopathy, it has embraced the assumption that basic psychopathic tendencies chiefly are expressed as criminal behavior. In doing so, the field has established this as a literature on *unsuccessful* psychopathy, ignoring the possibility that psychopathic tendencies may be manifested in one individual's criminality, in another individual's heroism, and in still another's worldly success (see Cleckley, 1941/1976; Harkness & Lilienfeld, 1997; Lykken, 1995). On the other side, scholars who favor the PCL argue that criminal behavior is an integral and central component of psychopathy (Hare & Neumann, 2005). This debate is not merely an academic one: The special influence that "psychopathy" has on moral and legal judgments about an individual (see the section "To What Extent Is the 'Psychopathic' Label Prejudicial?") underscores the importance of clearly measuring the intended construct. Here we highlight two points in this debate—one conceptual, one practical—and both relevant to the psycholegal assessment of psychopathy.

First, seminal conceptualizations of psychopathy, including the one on which the PCL is based, posit that the disorder is an affective deficit that is largely inherited (Cleckley, 1941/1976; Karpman, 1948). When available evidence is evaluated in light of such conceptualizations, there is greater support for emotional detachment as an indicator of psychopathy than deviant and antisocial behavior (Skeem & Cooke, in press). For example, PCL scores are associated with a diminished startle response to negative or aversive emotional cues (Patrick et al., 1993), less autonomic arousal during fear and distress imagery (Blair, Jones, Clark, & Smith, 1997; Patrick, 1994), and greater recall for the peripheral details of aversive images (Christianson et al., 1996). Although more research on this topic is needed, when PCL scale scores are examined, these deficits tend to be more strongly associated with the old Factor 1 than with Factor 2 (Harpur, Hare, & Hakstian, 1989; Patrick, Zempolich, & Levenston, 1997). In short, we would argue that emotional detachment—not criminal behavior—identifies those who are "less able to process or use the deep semantic meanings of language and to appreciate the emotional significance of events or experiences" (Hare, 1996a, p. 1).

Second, the majority of the PCL's predictive utility for violence and recidivism stems from its assessment of past criminal behavior (Factor 2)—not the emotional detachment of psychopathy per se (Factor 1; e.g., Camp, 2007; Salekin et al., 1996; Skeem & Mulvey, 2001; Walters, 2003a). Widespread use of the PCL (see Tolman & Mullendore, 2003) arguably is founded on the assumption that the link between the PCL and violence risk means that emotionally detached psychopaths callously use violence to achieve control over and exploit others. Available research does not support this assumption (Camp, 2007; Salekin et al., 1996; Skeem & Mulvey, 2001; Walters, 2003a). Instead, the link could often mean that violence is likely among people who have a long history of aggressive behavior and antagonistic personality traits (arrogant, irritable, hot-tempered, argumentative, and hostile; Skeem, Miller, Mulvey, Monahan, & Tiemann, 2005)—even if they lack many traits that Cleckley and others viewed as central to psychopathy.

These points underscore the importance of separating the pursuit of understanding psychopathy as a personality construct (which seeks validity) from the enterprise of predicting violence (which seeks utility). Substantial professional energy has been expended on the exercise of using the PCL to infer traits from criminal behavior and then using those traits to explain criminal behavior. A trait cannot both embody the observed tendency and then also explain it (people commit crime because of their psychopathy, which includes criminal behavior). Ellard (1998) makes the point starkly: "Why has this man done these terrible things? Because he is a psychopath. And how do you know that he is a psychopath? Because he has done these terrible things" (p. 387).

To What Extent Does the PCL Possess Predictive Validity for Violence?

Setting aside debates about the extent to which the PCL adequately assesses the construct of psychopathy, we now turn to a pragmatic question about the measure's predictive validity. In legal contexts, the PCL primarily is used to bolster predictions about the future behavior of an examinee, including his or her likelihood of engaging in criminal conduct or responding to intervention. PCL scores have been used to make such predictions to inform legal decisions about whether an offender should be executed (Edens, Petrila, & Buffington-Vallum, 2001), civilly committed as a sexual predator (Petrila & Otto, 2001), denied parole (Hemphill & Hart, 2003), or subjected to an indeterminant sentence (Zinger & Forth, 1998) or commitment (Cooke et al., 2007). Given legal concerns regarding relevancy and probative value (Slobogin, 2006), the courts should ask pragmatic questions about predictive utility, such as "Is the PCL a valid means of informing violence risk assessments for convicted sex offenders who will be released from prison or committed as a sexually violent predator?" and "Are PCL scores predictive of violent behavior among individuals convicted of capital murder who receive life sentences rather than capital punishment?" (e.g., DeMatteo & Edens, 2006; Edens, 2006; Edens & Petrila, 2006).

Given this backdrop, what then do the data tell us about the utility of the PCL in predicting violence, recidivism, and other sanctioned behavior? The answer to this question, as is true with almost any psychological issue—and much to the chagrin of lawyers and judges—is, "It depends." And it depends on many different things, such as the context (e.g., laboratory assessments of aggression, responses to self-report scales, criminal offenses in the community, violence within institutions) and severity of the criterion of interest (e.g., "hostile" verbal interactions between patients and staff on a psychiatric ward, prison assaults, child abuse, murder in the community), to name only two. Given the voluminous and ever-expanding literature on the relationship between psychopathy, criminality, and violence, it is not possible to review original research in any detail here. Thankfully, there have been several recent meta-analyses (Edens & Campbell, 2007; Edens, Campbell, & Weir, 2007; Gendreau, Goggin, & Smith, 2002; Guy, Edens, Anthony, & Douglas, 2005; Walters, 2003a, 2003b) and other extensive reviews (Douglas, Vincent, & Edens, 2006; Forth et al., 2003; Hare, 2003) of the literature most directly relevant to the types of violent and criminal behavior of interest to the legal system. The most salient findings are briefly summarized below.

Gendreau and colleagues (2002) obtained a weighted effect size for the PCL-R of Φ = .23 (95% confidence interval [CI] = .17–.28) for general recidivism (κ = 33 studies) and .21 (95% CI = .17–.25) for violent recidivism (κ = 26 studies). Considerable heterogeneity was observed among these effects (Gendreau et al., 2002). The following year Walters (2003a) reported a weighted point biserial correlation of .26 (95% CI = .24–.29) for the prediction of general recidivism across 33 studies, with a follow-up report (Walters, 2003b) indicating that PCL Factor 1 showed significantly weaker predictive relations with general (r = .15) and violent (r = .18) recidivism than Factor 2 (r = .32 and .26, respectively). The criterion of institutional misconduct also has been the focus of recent meta-analyses and literature reviews. Guy and colleagues (2005) reported weighted effect sizes between .17 and .29 for various types of institutional infractions for the PCL-R total score. PCL Total and Factor 1 and 2 scores consistently produced the smallest mean effect sizes for violent misconduct, however (r_w = .17, .14, and .15, respectively).

Meta-analyses also have been conducted of studies that focus on juveniles. Edens and colleagues (2007) recently obtained weighted mean effect sizes (biserial correlations) of .24, .25, and .07 between PCL:YV scores and general, violent, and sexual community recidivism, respectively. Similarly, Edens and Campbell (2007) reported weighted correlations of .24, .25, and .28 between PCL:YV scores and measures of general, aggressive (broadly defined), and physically violent institutional misconduct, respectively. Similar to the adult meta-analyses, these effect sizes are informative in the aggregate and suggest that, *in general*, there is a statistically significant association between the PCL:YV and these outcome measures, although the effect sizes tend to be in the small-to-medium range.

These meta-analyses also point to several limitations of the extant literature, however, as well as several unresolved questions based on the available data. First, the total number of studies (and aggregated sample sizes) that have examined these outcomes is not particularly large by meta-analytic standards, particularly those examining the PCL:YV. Second, the heterogeneity evident in these meta-analyses raises some concerns about the aggregation of very diverse effect sizes across available studies, and suggests that there may be some (as yet, unidentified) factors that significantly moderate the association between the PCL and recidivism. For example, racial/ethnic diversity has been shown to moderate this relationship in some of the meta-analyses conducted to date. Third, almost all of the research in this area has used relatively short follow-up periods (e.g., M follow-up = 32 months; Edens et al., 2007). Although two 10-year follow-up studies of the PCL:YV's utility in predicting long-term recidivism have been conducted, they have yielded conflicting results (Edens & Cahill, 2007; Gretton, Hare, & Catchpole, 2004). These limitations call for cautious interpretation of the modest-to-moderate empirical relationship between the PCL and indices of recidivism.

To What Extent Is the "Psychopathic" Label Prejudicial?

Recall two points. First, the inclusion of criminal behavior (particularly Factor 2) raises questions about the extent to which the PCL excessively focuses on antisocial conduct in operationalizing psychopathy. Second, meta-analytic and other studies suggest that much of the PCL's predictive utility is based on its assessment of criminal behavior (Factor 2) rather than the emotional detachment of psychopathy per se (Factor 1). These points bring us to our fourth and final controversy. If we are using the PCL in legal contexts chiefly to assess risk, does it matter whether we attribute that risk to "psychopathy" or to "impulsive, angry, criminal behavior"? If not, we can use the PCL as a risk assessment tool in courtroom contexts, disregarding concerns about the construct(s) it assesses. If it does matter, we should be concerned about the construct validity of the PCL, and in particular the application of the term "psychopath" in legal contexts.

Until recently, little research addressed the effects of labeling individuals as psychopaths or attributing prototypically psychopathic traits to them. Two studies of college undergraduates (primarily students in introductory psychology courses; $N = 238, N = 203$) focused on the context of capital punishment (Edens, Colwell, Desforges, & Fernandez, 2005; Edens, Desforges, Fernandez, & Palac, 2004). Here, the authors tested the effects of expert testimony regarding the presence/absence of a mental disorder (psychopathy, psychosis, or no disorder) and violence risk (low or high) on mock jurors' sentencing decisions in a capital murder trial. As predicted, a defendant who was described as psychopathic by a mental health expert was rated as more likely to commit future acts of violence than one whose evaluation results indicated no diagnosis. However, the same pattern was true when the defendant was assessed as being psychotic. Nevertheless, only in the psychopath condition did respondents strongly support executing the defendant (Edens et al., 2005); 60% of these participants voted for death, in contrast to only 30% in the psychosis condition, and 38% in the non-mentally-disordered condition.

Experiments have also tested the effect of psychopathy on decision making in SVP cases. Guy and Edens (2003) examined the effects of testimony based on three types of risk assessment instruments or methodologies: clinical opinion, actuarial assessment, and ratings of psychopathy. A sample of 172 undergraduates reviewed a case summary that included prosecution and defense expert testimony related to violence risk. Women who were exposed to testimony regarding psychopathy were significantly more likely to vote for commitment than women who reviewed testimony based on actuarial risk assessment data or clinical opinion, but no such effect was noted for men. Notably, a much higher percentage of women who were exposed to testimony regarding psychopathy were in favor of civil commitment at the prosecution phase of the trial than men who were presented with this same testimony (92.5% vs. 63.2%, respectively). A subsequent study (Guy & Edens, 2006), employing the same basic methodology but with a larger sample of mock jurors (*n* = 599), replicated the main finding in terms of gender differences in support for commitment (86.5% of women vs. 62.5% of men).

In addition to these studies of adult capital and SVP cases, researchers have begun to examine the impact of psychopathy labels and traits among youths involved in the juvenile justice system. Edens, Guy, and Fernandez (2003) examined the effects of ascribing psychopathic traits to a juvenile defendant tried for capital murder. Undergraduates (*N* = 360) read a newspaper account of the trial and testimony provided by various witnesses that manipulated the presence/absence of prototypic traits (lack of guilt and remorse, grandiosity, pathological lying) used to describe the defendant, who was accused of homicide. A significantly higher percentage of those in the psychopathic traits condition endorsed the death penalty (36%) compared to those in the nonpsychopath condition (21%). Participants in the psychopathic traits condition also generally were more punitive in their attitudes toward the defendant.

Using a more elaborate vignette methodology, Murrie, Cornell, and McCoy (2005) examined the impact of diagnostic labels (including psychopathy), antisocial history, and the presence/absence of psychopathic traits

on the attitudes and hypothetical decision making of 260 juvenile probation officers. Of particular note, the ascription of psychopathic traits alone
(regardless of antisocial history) increased probation officers' ratings of the
likelihood that the youth would reoffend and would be a criminal as an
adult. However, it did not have an effect on the sanctions they would recommend.

Using the same basic approach, Murrie and colleagues published two
more recent studies examining the perceptions and attitudes of 326 juvenile
court judges (Murrie, Boccaccini, McCoy, & Cornell, 2007) and 109 clinicians who work in the juvenile justice system (Rockett, Murrie, & Boccaccini, 2007). Murrie and colleagues reported that the personality attributes
of psychopathy had significant effects on judges' perceptions that defendants
would be violent in the future, and that they were less likely to recommend deferred adjudication in these cases. They also rated the youth as
disproportionately more likely to be a criminal as an adult than a defendant
with conduct disorder, with this effect being particularly pronounced when
paired with a description of having a minimal (rather than extensive) history
of antisocial conduct.

Rockett and colleagues (2007) reported that clinicians rated a youth
who was described with a minimal antisocial history *but* also labeled as
meeting criteria for psychopathy as being a greater risk than when the
minimal antisocial history was paired with a diagnosis of conduct disorder. When antisocial history was more extensive, however, the groups were
rated comparably. Clinicians also rated youths with psychopathic traits as at
higher risk than those without.

Of some import, Boccaccini, Murrie, Clark, and Cornell (2008) recently
examined the impact of the type of psychopathy descriptor provided in these
simulation studies in a large sample (N = 891) of jury pool members. In
their previous research, described above, the psychopathy condition involved
a statement to the effect that the juvenile "meets criteria for psychopathy."
However, when this phraseology was modified to "is a psychopath," jurors
were more likely to perceive the juvenile as dangerous and recommend more
harsh punishments. This suggests that the effects reported in their earlier
studies likely would have been even more pronounced had they used the
descriptor "is a psychopath" to label the juvenile rather than the more eso-
teric "meets criteria" terminology.

That descriptor, along with interpersonal and affective traits of psychopathy, was applied in a recent experiment by Vidal and Skeem (2007).
The authors performed a vignette study assessing juvenile probation officers'
(N = 204) expectancies, recommendations, and supervision strategies in

relation to experimental manipulations of an offender's level of psychopathy, abuse history, and ethnicity. They found that officers' decision-making and supervision approaches were affected by an offender's psychopathic traits and history of child abuse, but not ethnicity. Both abused and psychopathic youth were perceived as violence-prone, challenging cases on a path toward adult criminality. Nonetheless, officers expressed greater hope and sympathy for abused youths than psychopathic youths. Officers would "go the extra mile" for an abused youth, but were "extra strict" with a psychopathic youth and expected poorer treatment outcomes. Here, the basis for the violence risk (abuse vs. psychopathy) mattered.

The results of this study are somewhat consistent with those found in a vignette study of 83 judges. In that study, Chauhan, Reppucci, and Burnette (2007) found that judges perceived juvenile offenders with psychopathic traits as more dangerous than offenders without such traits. Although judges recommended longer sentences for offenders with these psychopathic traits, they perceived them as no less amenable to treatment and no more appropriate for transfer to adult court than those without such traits.

The results of these experiments are supported by more naturalistic studies suggesting that prototypically psychopathic traits are highly influential in the decision making of various players in the legal system. For example, capital jurors have reported posttrial that defendant characteristics such as lack of remorse, grandiosity, callousness, and manipulation are critical to determining whether death sentences are meted out (Sundby, 1998; see also Costanzo & Peterson, 1994). This finding is consistent with experimental evidence presented earlier that persons who construe a defendant as psychopathic are much more likely to support capital punishment than those who do not make such construals. In short, describing someone as "psychopathic" matters; it carries considerable weight within the courtroom and with forensic/correctional personnel.

GAPS IN KNOWLEDGE

Although substantial research has been conducted on psychopathy over the past two decades, there are a number of gaps in knowledge. We cover only three here. Given that the PCL largely has been developed and tested with adult European American offenders, the extent to which the measure validly can be extended downward to adolescents (e.g., Edens, Skeem, Cruise, & Cauffman, 2001; Frick, 2002; Hart, Watt, & Vincent, 2002; Lynam, 2002) and laterally to women (e.g., Nicholls & Petrila, 2005; Verona & Vitale,

2006) and African American men (Skeem, Edens, Camp, & Colwell, 2004; Sullivan & Kosson, 2006) is unclear.

As suggested by the availability of such measures as the PCL:YV, the PCL model has been extended to adolescents, under the assumption that psychopathy is manifested in much the same manner whether one is 13 or 33 years old. This assumption is subject to considerable debate, given that many features that may be indicative of psychopathy during adulthood (e.g., impulsivity, parasitic lifestyle, lack of long-term goals) may be viewed as normative or temporary features of adolescence (e.g., Edens, Skeem, et al., 2001; Hart et al., 2002; Skeem & Cauffman, 2003). Adolescence is something one grows out of; psychopathy is not. Presently, there is no compelling longitudinal evidence that individuals who score high on measures of psychopathy during adolescence transition into psychopathic adults. The four studies that have addressed this issue have yielded low-to-moderate stability estimates across follow-ups of 2 years (intraclass correlation [ICC] = .34; Cauffman, Skeem, & Dmietrieva, 2008), of 6–7 years (ICC = .47–.60; Blonigen, Hicks, Krueger, Patrick, & Iacono, 2006; ICC = .40–.41; Loney, Taylor, Butler, & Iacono, 2007), and 10 years (ICC = .27; Lynam, Caspi, Moffitt, Loeber, & Stouthamer-Loeber, 2007). In the latter study, almost three-quarters (71%) of adolescents who obtained extremely high scores on a measure of psychopathy at age 13 (i.e., top 5%) were not classified as psychopathic at age 24. Moreover, adolescents' scores on the PCL have been shown to decrease over time significantly more than those of adults (Cauffman et al., 2008). Although *some* adolescents manifest stable psychopathic traits over time—perhaps those with affective deficiencies (see Vincent, 2006)—we do not know how to identify them at present. Given this fundamental gap in knowledge about whether "juvenile psychopathy" is a valid concept, the application of PCL measures to youths in the juvenile justice system seems ill-advised at this time—particularly given that other risk measures appear to work at least as well as the PCL:YV in predicting violence (Edens, Campbell, & Weir, 2007). Although there appears to be enough group-level stability on psychopathy scales to warrant further research, the available research offers little support for claims that those with scores in the "psychopathic range" will continue to demonstrate such extreme scores over several years of follow-up. And, it should be stressed, it is the "extreme score" subgroup in which the legal system is most interested.

The assessment of psychopathy also has been relatively understudied in women. This issue is important, given the increasing prevalence of women in offender populations (Harrison & Beck, 2006), in which PCL measures often are used. The PCL's level of reliability (in nonadversarial settings) seems to generalize across gender (Kennealy, Hicks, & Patrick, 2007; Vitale & Newman, 2001; Vitale, Smith, Brinkley, & Newman, 2002), and men and women's PCL scores relate in a similar pattern to such variables as criminality, substance use, and constellations of personality traits (Kennealy et al., 2007). However, gender-related divergences in factor structure have been reported (Salekin et al., 1997), and women's PCL scores are positively associated with measures of anxiety and negative affect, and inversely associated with intelligence in a manner that runs counter to predictions based on Cleckleyan psychopathy (Vitale et al., 2002). Moreover, deficits in affective processing previously identified in psychopathic male samples have not generalized to psychopathic female samples. Specifically, auditory startle response to unpleasant pictures was not significantly inhibited in comparison to neutral pictures (Sutton, Vitale, & Newman, 2002), and perseverative responding during a card-playing task, which was thought to demonstrate disinhibition (Vitale & Newman, 2001), has not been replicated in psychopathic female samples. Women also tend to obtain lower PCL scores than men (Hare, 2003; Salekin et al., 1997; Skeem, Douglas, Edens, Poythress, & Lilienfeld, 2005). Moreover, item response theory (IRT) analyses indicate that the PCL item indexing lack of empathy may be less discriminating in women than men (Cooke, Michie, Hart, & Hare, 1999), and PCL items indexing social deviance and criminal behavior are less informative about psychopathy in women (Bolt, Hare, Vitale, & Newman, 2004). Although these differences may average out at the total score or test level, they raise questions about whether there is bias present in application of the PCL to women (Grann, 2000) or whether there are true, sex-linked biological and socialization differences in psychopathy (Cale & Lilienfeld, 2002). Future work is needed to determine whether male-based measures and conceptions of psychopathy generalize neatly to women (Verona & Vitale, 2006).

Also relatively understudied is the generalization of PCL psychopathy to African American men, who are disproportionately represented in U.S. correctional populations. In contrast with controversial evolutionary theories (Lynn, 2002), African Americans do not obtain systematically higher scores on the PCL than do European Americans (McCoy & Edens, 2006; Skeem et al., 2004). However, IRT analyses indicate ethnic differences in item functioning, with five items associated with the Behavioral factor, evincing statistically significant, although small, differential item functioning in threshold parameters (Cooke, Kosson, & Michie, 2001). Perhaps most troubling is the finding that African Americans with high scores on the PCL may not manifest the same deficits in inhibiting behavior that lead to punishment as do European Americans with high scores on the measure. Specifically, African Americans demonstrated less extreme levels of passive-avoidance learning deficits as a function of psychopathy in comparison to European Americans (Newman & Schmitt, 1998; Thornquist & Zuckerman, 1995; cf. Kosson, Smith, & Newman, 1990). Thus, African Americans could be obtaining comparable PCL scores to European Americans without featuring the same level of behavioral deficits. Further research is needed to determine whether these differences are the result of scoring biases, ethnic differences in the manifestations of psychopathy, or ethnic differences in etiological processes that underpin the disorder (Skeem et al., 2004; Sullivan & Kosson, 2006). Finally, noted earlier, meta-analyses of the PCL's predictive validity have suggested that ethnic status may impact the strength of the relationship between these instruments and criminal outcomes, with more ethnically diverse samples demonstrating weaker outcomes than predominantly European American samples (Edens et al., 2006; see also Guy et al., 2005).

MYTHS AND MISCONCEPTIONS

Myth 1: Psychopathic Individuals Are Uniformly Dangerous "Superpredators"

Hare (1996a) defined psychopaths as "remorseless predators who use charm, intimidation and, if necessary, impulsive and cold-blooded violence to attain their ends" (p. 1). Similarly, the general public's prototype of a psychopath (e.g., Theodore Bundy, Jeffrey Dahmer, Charles Manson) is someone who has committed such horrific violent crimes as serial murder, cannibalism and necrophilia, and mass murder. As explained earlier, one need not be violent, or even criminal, to manifest features of emotional detachment that many view as central to psychopathy. Psychopathic individuals may be found in all walks of life, among businesspeople, lawyers, academics, and those in the military (Babiak & Hare, 2006; Lykken, 1995). Indeed, Cleckley (1941/1976) viewed tendencies toward violence and major crime as something "independent, to a considerable degree, of the other manifestations which we regard as fundamental" to psychopathy (p. 262).

Myth 2: Psychopathy Is Reducible to a PCL Score

People in the mental health field often equate the PCL measure with the construct of psychopathy—a mistake called pseudo-operationalism. All too frequently, the phrase "gold standard" is used in reference to the PCL (e.g., Fulero, 1995; Vitacco, Neumann, & Jackson, 2005). Because this phrase implies a strict criterion for an abstract construct, its use would be problematic in virtually any mental health context (see Faraone & Tsuang, 1994). A PCL score is no more one's degree of psychopathy than a Wechsler Adult Intelligence Scale–III (WAIS-III) score is one's degree of intelligence. Like other measures, we would argue that the PCL underrepresents psychopathy by omitting some key features of the disorder (e.g., lack of anxiety) and introduces construct-irrelevant variance by including other features that are not specific to the disorder (e.g., criminal history). The PCL is "one way," not "*the* way," to assess psychopathy.

Myth 3: Treatment Has No Effect on Psychopaths...or Makes Them "Worse"

Few assumptions in the psycholegal field are more fervently held—and less often tested—than the one that "the behavioral sciences have nothing to offer for treating those with psychopathy" (Gacono, Nieberding, Owen, Rubel, & Bodholdt, 2001, p. 111). As shown in Chapter 16 of this volume, the related assumption that "treatment makes psychopaths worse" chiefly rests on one retrospective, quasi-experimental study of a radical treatment program (Rice, Harris, & Cormier, 1992). Recent prospective and quasi-experimental studies suggest that psychopathy does *not* moderate the effect of treatment in reducing (1) adult psychiatric patients' violence (Skeem, Monahan, & Mulvey, 2003), (2) serious adolescent offenders' violent recidivism (Caldwell, Skeem, Salekin, & Van Ryobeck, 2006), or (3) adult offenders' general recidivism (Skeem, Douglas, et al., 2005). Although individuals with psychopathic traits can be difficult to manage in treatment, their future behavior may improve as much as that of others, provided they receive sufficient doses of treatment (see Salekin, 2002).

Myth 4: There Is "One" PCL Psychopath

One might assume that individuals who surpass traditional PCL threshold scores for diagnosing psychopathy would be fairly similar to one another: a homogeneous group of psychopaths. An increasing body of research suggests this is not the case: PCL "psychopaths" can be disaggregated into variants that appear consistent with historical conceptions of primary psychopathy and secondary psychopathy (for reviews, see Poythress & Skeem, 2006;

Skeem, Poythress, Edens, Lilienfeld, & Cale, 2003). Relative to primary or "Cleckleyan" psychopaths, secondary psychopaths appear more emotionally unstable, anxious, withdrawn, irritable, aggressive, and prone to violence (e.g., Hicks, Markon, Patrick, Krueger, & Newman, 2004; Kimonis, Skeem, & Cauffman, 2008; Poythress et al., 2008; Skeem, Johansson, Andershed, Kerr, & Eno Louden, 2007). Secondary psychopaths also endorse greater exposure to child abuse experiences (Kimonis et al., 2008; Poythress et al., 2008), providing at least some evidence for Karpman's (1941, 1948) notion that secondary psychopathy is the product of such environmental factors as abuse, which create hostility that disturbs the functioning of an otherwise well-developed conscience, whereas primary psychopathy largely is the product of constitutional factors. Whether these particularly high-risk secondary individuals are "psychopaths" per se is a question open to debate (see Poythress & Skeem, 2006).

CONCLUSIONS

The PCL is a psychological test that *can* be reliably scored and *can* have some relevance to estimating risk for future crime and violence. However, there are important questions about its construct validity that relate directly to the prediction task. At present, the link between the PCL and future misbehavior appears to reflect the tool's ability to capture past behavior and antagonistic traits more so than its ability to assess emotional detachment. Practitioners who use the measure *may* be aware of, and clearly communicate these facts to, legal decision-makers. Some practitioners *may* avoid treating the PCL score as an individual's quantum of psychopathy and equating a high score with inalterable dangerousness. When these "cans" and "mays" apply in a given case, use of the PCL in the courtroom may not have prejudicial effects. However, holding all else constant (including violence risk), when a defendant is deemed "psychopathic," he or she *can* be perceived and treated more harshly by stakeholders in the justice and correctional systems.

Each of the conditions above is important to consider in determining whether a particular psycholegal use of the PCL is scientifically supported, controversial, or unsupported. As noted below, inappropriate application of the PCL could transform any scientifically supported or controversial use mentioned below into an unsupported one. Here, we focus on general legal uses for which the PCL measures appear to evidence some degree of predictive validity, given data generated for groups of people in research contexts.

Scientifically Supported Uses

There is support for legal issues that involve assessing risk of violence or other criminal behavior in the community (e.g., short-term, general sentencing or placement decisions), particularly for adult, white, male offenders.

Scientifically Unsupported Uses

Scientifically unsupported uses include any legal issue listed above where the PCL is used inappropriately (e.g., biased scoring; reification of the PCL; promotion of myths or misconceptions about the inalterably dangerous PCL "superpredator"; potentially prejudicial effects of the psychopathy label on legal decisions).

Scientifically Controversial or Still Largely Untested Uses

Legal issues that involve assessing risk of violence in prison, identifying offenders who cannot be rehabilitated (e.g., capital punishment, juvenile transfer), assumptions that psychopathy will remain stable during the transition from adolescence to adulthood (e.g., juvenile transfer), or assumptions that the PCL and relevant research generalize to understudied populations (e.g., women, ethnic minorities) still warrant further investigation.

COMMUNICATING CONSENSUS AND CONTROVERSIES

When the PCL is used to inform decisions about a legal issue, a few additional points about communicating findings—beyond those addressed above—should be borne in mind. First, examiners should convey that the PCL is a useful risk assessment tool chiefly because it distills variables and traits associated with a history of criminal and violent behavior. Reviews of legal cases suggest that at least some examiners called by the prosecution focus heavily on Factor 1 traits when writing reports on, or testifying about, psychopathy and violence risk (DeMatteo & Edens, 2006; Edens, Petrila, et al., 2001). Perhaps this emphasis is motivated by the belief that such traits (remorselessness, superficial charm) are likely to be more influential to juror decision making than those Factor 2 traits (e.g., impulsivity, irresponsibility) that are more strongly predictive of violence (see Costanzo & Peterson, 1994; Sundby, 1998).

Second, examiners should use the categorical term "psychopath" and the traditional threshold score for diagnosing psychopathy with caution—if at all. Taxometric research shows that PCL-psychopathic individuals differ from nonpsychopathic offenders more in degree than in kind (e.g., Edens et al., 2006; Walters, Duncan, & Mitchell-Perez, 2007; Walters et al., 2007; cf. Harris, Rice, & Quinsey, 1994), and there is little to be gained by making categorical statements about the results of an instrument that measures a dimensional construct. Of note, some examiners provide percentile ranks to indicate where a score falls in relation to other prison inmates or forensic patients, which helps provide some context for interpreting an examinee's results in relation to this continuum.

Finally, elsewhere (Edens & Petrila, 2006) we have argued that examiners should consider reporting 95% confidence intervals based on standard errors of measurement along with "raw" PCL scores so that the inherent level of error in these assessments is made clear to the consumers of these evaluations. Given the troubling findings reported by Murrie and colleagues (2008) concerning the extremely poor "field reliability" of the PCL, however, one wonders whether such estimates are overly optimistic in terms of the true degree of reliability of this instrument in courtroom settings. Although we continue to believe that confidence intervals should be reported for these scores, we would argue that examiners should be clear that these confidence intervals are based on PCLs completed in research contexts—and that intervals for PCLs completed in adversarial contexts may be considerably wider.

Having provided these recommendations, we suggest that examiners consider alternatives to using the PCL in legal cases. We do so because (1) the PCL chiefly is used as a violence risk assessment (not diagnostic) tool; (2) most of the PCL's predictive utility is not attributable to its assessment of emotional detachment; and (3) the PCL generally lacks incremental predictive utility over such specifically designed risk assessment tools as the Level of Service Inventory—Revised (e.g., see Gendreau et al., 2002)—and these tools ostensibly would have less potential for stigmatization than the *Psychopathy* Checklist (Edens et al., 2003). Violence risk can be assessed well and communicated quite clearly if the PCL and psychopathy are not invoked.

REFERENCES

American Psychiatric Association. (2000). *Diagnostic and statistical manual of mental disorders* (4th ed., text rev.). Washington, DC: Author.

Babiak, P., & Hare, R. (2006). *Snakes in suits: When psychopaths go to work.* New York: Regan Books.

Blair, R. J. R., Jones, L., Clark, F., & Smith, M. (1997). The psychopathic individual: A lack of responsiveness to distress cues. *Psychophysiology, 34,* 192–198.

Blonigen, D. M., Hicks, B. M., Krueger, R. F., Patrick, C. J., & Iacono, W. G. (2006). Continuity and change in psychopathic traits as measured via normal-range personality: A longitudinal-biometric study. *Journal of Abnormal Psychology, 115,* 85–95.

Boccaccini, M., Murrie, D., Clark, J., & Cornell, D. (2008). *Describing, diagnosing, and naming psychopathy: How do youth psychopathy labels influence jurors?* Manuscript submitted for publication.

Bolt, D. M, Hare, R. D., Vitale, J. E., & Newman, J. P. (2004). A multigroup item response theory analysis of the Psychopathy Checklist—Revised. *Psychological Assessment, 16,* 155–168.

Caldwell, M., Skeem, J., Salekin, R., & Van Ryoboek, G. (2006). Treatment response of adolescent offenders with psychopathy features: A two-year follow-up. *Criminal Justice and Behavior, 33,* 571–596.

Cale, E. M., & Lilienfeld, S. O. (2002). Sex differences in psychopathy and antisocial personality: A review and integration. *Clinical Psychology Review, 22,* 1179–1207.

Camp, J. P. (2007). *Understanding psychopathy and violence: The role of motivation.* Unpublished master's thesis, University of Nevada, Las Vegas.

Campbell, J. S., Pulos, S., Hogan, M., & Murry, F. (2005). Reliability generalization of the Psychopathy Checklist applied in youthful samples. *Educational and Psychological Measurement, 65,* 639–656.

Cauffman, E., Skeem, J., & Dmietrieva, J. (2008). *Are we capturing the "fledgling psychopath"?* Manuscript submitted for publication.

Chauhan, P., Reppucci, N. D., & Burnette, M. L. (2007). Application and impact of the psychopathy label to juveniles. *International Journal of Forensic Mental Health, 6*(1), 3–14.

Christianson, S. A., Forth, A. E., Hare, R. D., Strachan, C., Lidberg, L., & Thorell, L. H. (1996). Remembering details of emotional events: A comparison between psychopathic and nonpsychopathic offenders. *Personality and Individual Differences, 20,* 437–443.

Clark, H., & Forth, A. (2005, July). *Psychopathy in the courts: Fantasy, fiction, and reality.* Poster presented at the biennial meeting of the Society for the Scientific Study of Psychopathy, Vancouver, British Columbia.

Cleckley, H. (1976). *The mask of sanity* (5th ed.). St. Louis, MO: Mosby. (Original work published 1941)

Cooke, D. J., Kosson, D. S., & Michie, C. (2001). Psychopathy and ethnicity: Structural, item, and test generalizability of the Psychopathy Checklist—Revised (PCL-R) in Caucasian and African American participants. *Psychological Assessment, 13,* 531–542.

Cooke, D. J., Michie, C., Hart, S. D., & Hare, R. D. (1999). Evaluating the screening version of the Hare Psychopathy Checklist—Revised (PCL:SV): An item response theory analysis. *Psychological Assessment, 11*, 3–13.

Cooke, D. J., Michie, C., & Skeem, J. (2007). Understanding the structure of the Psychopathy Checklist—Revised: An exploration of methodological confusion. *British Journal of Psychiatry, 190*(Suppl. 49), 539–550.

Costanzo, M., & Peterson, J. (1994). Attorney persuasion in the capital penalty phase: A content analysis of closing arguments. *Journal of Social Issues, 50*, 125–147.

DeMatteo, D., & Edens, J. F. (2006). The role and relevance of the Psychopathy Checklist-Revised in court: A case law survey of U.S. courts (1991–2004). *Psychology, Public Policy, and Law, 12*, 214–241.

Douglas, K. S., Vincent, G. M., & Edens, J. F. (2006). Risk for criminal recidivism: The role of psychopathy. In C. J. Patrick (Ed.), *Handbook of psychopathy* (pp. 533–554). New York: Guilford Press.

Edens, J. F. (2006). Unresolved controversies concerning psychopathy: Implications for clinical and forensic decision-making. *Professional Psychology: Research and Practice, 37*, 59–65.

Edens, J. F., & Cahill, M. A. (2007). Psychopathy in adolescence and criminal recidivism in young adulthood: Longitudinal results from a multiethnic sample of youthful offenders. *Assessment, 14*, 57–64.

Edens, J. F., & Campbell, J. S. (2007). Identifying youths at risk for institutional misconduct: A meta-analytic investigation of the psychopathy checklist measures. *Psychological Services, 4*, 13–27.

Edens, J. F., Campbell, J. S., & Weir, J. M. (2007). Youth psychopathy and criminal recidivism: A meta-analysis of the Psychopathy Checklist measures. *Law and Human Behavior, 31*, 53–75.

Edens, J. F., Colwell, L. H., Desforges, D. M., & Fernandez, K. (2005). The impact of mental health evidence on support for capital punishment: Are defendants labeled psychopathic considered more deserving of death? *Behavioral Sciences and the Law, 23*, 603–625.

Edens, J. F., Desforges, D. M., Fernandez, K., & Palac, C. A. (2004). Effects of psychopathy and violence risk testimony on mock juror perceptions of dangerousness in a capital murder trial. *Psychology, Crime, and Law, 10*, 393–412.

Edens, J. F., Guy, L. S., & Fernandez, K. (2003). Psychopathic traits predict attitudes toward a juvenile capital murderer. *Behavioral Sciences and the Law, 21*, 807–828.

Edens, J. F., Marcus, D. K., Lilienfeld, S. O., & Poythress, N. G. (2006). Psychopathic, not psychopath: Taxometric evidence for the dimensional structure of psychopathy. *Journal of Abnormal Psychology, 115*, 131–144.

Edens, J. F., & Petrila, J. (2006). Legal and ethical issues in the assessment and treatment of psychopathy. In C. J. Patrick (Ed.), *Handbook of psychopathy* (pp. 573–588). New York: Guilford Press.

Edens, J. F., Petrila, J., & Buffington-Vollum, J. K. (2001). Psychopathy and the death penalty: Can the Psychopathy Checklist—Revised identify offenders who represent "a continuing threat to society"? *Journal of Psychiatry and Law, 29,* 433–481.

Edens, J. F., Skeem, J. L., Cruise, K. R., & Cauffman, E. (2001). Assessment of "juvenile psychopathy" and its association with violence: A critical review. *Behavioral Sciences and the Law, 19,* 53–80.

Edens, J. F., & Vincent, G. M. (2008). Juvenile psychopathy: A clinical construct in need of restraint? *Journal of Forensic Psychology Practice, 8,* 186–197.

Ellard, J. (1988). The history and present status of moral insanity. *Australian and New Zealand Journal of Psychiatry, 22,* 383–389.

Faraone, S. V., & Tsuang, M. T. (1994). Measuring diagnostic accuracy in the absence of a "gold standard." *American Journal of Psychiatry, 151,* 650–657.

Forth, A. E., Kosson, D., & Hare, R. D. (2003). *Psychopathy Checklist: Youth Version manual.* Toronto: Multi-Health Systems.

Frick, P. J. (2002). Juvenile psychopathy from a developmental perspective: Implications for construct development and use in forensic assessments. *Law and Human Behavior, 26,* 247–253.

Fulero, S. (1995). Review of the Hare Psychopathy Checklist—Revised. In J. C. Conoley, J. C. Impara, & L. L. Murphy (Eds.), *Twelfth mental measurements yearbook* (pp. 453–454). Lincoln, NE: Buros Institute.

Gacono, C., Nieberding, R., Owen, A., Rubel, J., & Bodholdt, R. (2001). Treating conduct disorder, antisocial, and psychopathic personalities. In J. Ashford & B. Sales (Eds.), *Treating adult and juvenile offenders with special needs* (pp. 99–129). Washington, DC: American Psychological Association.

Gendreau, P., Goggin, C., & Smith, P. (2002). Is the PCL-R really the "unparalleled" measure of offender risk?: A lesson in knowledge cumulation. *Criminal Justice and Behavior, 29,* 397–426.

Grann, M. (2000). The PCL-R and gender. *European Journal of Psychological Assessment, 16,* 147–149.

Gretton, H. M., Hare, R. D., & Catchpole, R. E. H. (2004). Psychopathy and offending from adolescence to adulthood: A 10-year follow-up. *Journal of Consulting and Clinical Psychology, 72,* 636–645.

Guy, L. S., & Edens, J. F. (2003). Juror decision-making in a mock sexually violent predator trial: Gender differences in the impact of divergent types of expert testimony. *Behavioral Sciences and the Law, 21,* 215–237.

Guy, L. S., & Edens, J. F. (2006). Gender differences in attitudes toward psychopathic sexual offenders. *Behavioral Sciences and the Law, 24,* 65–85.

Guy, L. S., Edens, J. F., Anthony, C., & Douglas, K. S. (2005). Does psychopathy predict institutional misconduct among adults?: A meta-analytic investigation. *Journal of Consulting and Clinical Psychology, 73,* 1056–1064.

Hare, R. D. (1980). A research scale for the assessment of psychopathy in criminal populations. *Personality and Individual Differences, 1,* 111–119.

Hare, R. D. (1991). *Hare Psychopathy Checklist—Revised manual.* Toronto: Multi-Health Systems

Hare, R. D. (1996a). Psychopathy and antisocial personality disorder: A case of diagnostic confusion. *Psychiatric Times, 13,* 39–40.

Hare, R. D. (1996b). Psychopathy: A clinical construct whose time has come. *Criminal Justice and Behavior, 23,* 25–54.

Hare, R. D. (2003). *Hare Psychopathy Checklist—Revised manual* (2nd ed.). Toronto: Multi-Health Systems.

Hare, R. D., & Neumann, C. S. (2005). Structural models of psychopathy. *Current Psychiatry Reports, 7,* 57–64.

Harkness, A. R., & Lilienfeld, S. O. (1997). Individual differences science for treatment planning: Personality traits. *Psychological Assessment, 9,* 349–360.

Harpur, T. J., Hare, R. D., & Hakstian, A. R. (1989). Two-factor conceptualization of psychopathy: Construct validity and assessment implications. *Psychological Assessment, 1,* 6–17.

Harris, G., Rice, M., & Quinsey, V. (1994). Psychopathy as a taxon: Evidence that psychopaths are a discrete class. *Journal of Consulting and Clinical Psychology, 62,* 387–397.

Harrison, P. M., & Beck, A. J. (2006). Prisoners in 2005. *Bureau of Justice Statistics Bulletin,* pp. 1–13. Washington, DC: U.S. Department of Justice.

Hart, S. D. (1998). Psychopathy and risk for violence. In D. J. Cooke, A. E. Forth, & R. D. Hare (Eds.), *Psychopathy: Theory, research, and implications for society* (pp. 355–373). Dordrecht, The Netherlands: Kluwer.

Hart, S. D., Cox, D., & Hare, R. (1995). *The Hare Psychopathy Checklist: Screening Version.* Toronto: Multi-Health Systems.

Hart, S. D., Watt, K. A., & Vincent, G. M. (2002). Commentary on Seagrave and Grisso: Impressions of the state of the art. *Law and Human Behavior, 26,* 241–245.

Heilbrun, K. (1992). The role of psychological testing in forensic assessment. *Law and Human Behavior, 16,* 257–272.

Hemphill, J. F., & Hart, S. D. (2003). Forensic and clinical issues in the assessment of psychopathy. In I. B. Weiner (Series Ed.) & A. Goldstein (Vol. Ed.), *Handbook of psychology: Vol. 11. Forensic psychology* (pp. 87–107). New York: Wiley.

Hicks, B., Markon, K., Patrick, C., Krueger, R., & Newman, J. (2004). Identifying psychopathy subtypes on the basis of personality structure. *Psychological Assessment, 16,* 276–288.

Karpman, B. (1941). On the need for separating psychopathy into two distinct clinical types: Symptomatic and idiopathic. *Journal of Criminology and Psychopathology, 3,* 112–137.

Karpman, B. (1948). Conscience in the psychopath: Another version. *American Journal of Orthopsychiatry, 18,* 455–491.

Kennealy, P. J., Hicks, B. M., & Patrick, C. J. (2007). Validity of factors of the Psychopathy Checklist—Revised in female prisoners: Discriminant relations with antisocial behavior, substance abuse, and personality. *Assessment, 14*, 323–340.

Kimonis, E., Skeem, J., & Cauffman, E. (2008). *Examining psychopathy variants in youth: Are secondary variants less stable and more violent than primary variants?* Manuscript submitted for publication.

Kosson, D. S., Smith, S. S., & Newman, J. P. (1990). Evaluating the construct validity of psychopathy in African American and European American male inmates: Three preliminary studies. *Journal of Abnormal Psychology, 99*, 250–259.

Lilienfeld, S. O. (1998). Methodological advances and developments in the assessment of psychopathy. *Behaviour Research and Therapy, 36*, 99–125.

Lilienfeld, S. O., & Fowler, K. A. (2006). The self-report assessment of psychopathy: Problems, pitfalls, and promises. In C. J. Patrick (Ed.), *Handbook of psychopathy* (pp. 107–132). New York: Guilford Press.

Loney, B. R., Taylor, J., Butler, M. A., & Iacono, W. G. (2007). Adolescent psychopathy features: 6-year temporal stability and the prediction of externalizing symptoms during the transition to adulthood. *Aggressive Behavior, 33*, 242–252.

Lykken, D. T. (1995). *The antisocial personalities*. Hillsdale, NJ: Erlbaum.

Lynam, D. R. (2002). Fledgling psychopathy: A view from personality theory. *Law and Human Behavior, 26*, 255–259.

Lynam, D. R., Caspi, A., Moffitt, T. E., Loeber, R., & Stouthamer-Loeber, M. (2007). Longitudinal evidence that psychopathy scores in early adolescence predict adult psychopathy. *Journal of Abnormal Psychology, 116*, 155–165.

Lynn, R. (2002). Race differences in psychopathic personality. *Personality and Individual Differences, 32*, 273–316.

McCord, W., & McCord, J. (1964). *The psychopath: An essay on the criminal mind*. Princeton, NJ: Van Nostrand.

McCoy, W., & Edens, J. F. (2006). Do black and white youths differ in levels of psychopathic traits?: A meta-analysis of the Psychopathy Checklist measures. *Journal of Consulting and Clinical Psychology, 74*, 386–392.

Murrie, D. C., Boccaccini, M. T., Johnson, J., & Janke, C. (2008). Does interrater (dis)agreement on Psychopathy Checklist scores in sexually violent predator trials suggest partisan allegiance in forensic evaluations? *Law and Human Behavior, 32*, 352–362.

Murrie, D. C., Boccaccini, M. T., McCoy, W., & Cornell, D. (2007). Diagnostic labeling in juvenile court: How do descriptions of psychopathy and conduct disorder influence judges? *Journal of Clinical Child and Adolescent Psychology, 36*, 228–241.

Murrie, D. C., Cornell, D., & McCoy, W. (2005). Psychopathy, conduct disorder, and stigma: Does diagnostic labeling influence juvenile probation officer recommendations? *Law and Human Behavior, 29*, 323–342.

Newman, J. P., & Schmitt, W. A. (1998). Passive avoidance in psychopathic offenders: A replication and extension. *Journal of Abnormal Psychology, 107,* 527–532.

Nicholls, T. L., & Petrila, J. (2005). Gender and psychopathy: An overview of important issues and introduction to the special issue. *Behavioral Sciences and the Law, 23,* 729–741.

Patrick, C. J. (1994). Emotion and psychopathy: Startling new insights. *Psychophysiology, 31,* 319–330.

Patrick, C. J., Bradley, M. M., & Lang, P. J. (1993). Emotion in the criminal psychopath: Startle reflex modification. *Journal of Abnormal Psychology, 102,* 82–92.

Patrick, C. J., Zempolich, K. A., & Levenston, G. K. (1997). Emotionality and violent behavior in psychopaths: A biosocial analysis. In A. Raine, P. A. Brennan, D. P. Farrington, & S. A. Mednick (Eds.), *Biosocial bases of violence* (pp. 145–161). New York: Plenum Press.

Petrila, J., & Otto, R. K. (2001). Admissibility of expert testimony in sexually violent predator proceedings. In A. Schlank (Ed.), *The sexual predator* (Vol. 2, pp. 3-1–3-25). Kingston, NJ: Civic Research institute.

Poythress, N. G., Edens, J. F., Skeem, J. L., Lilienfeld, S. O., Douglas, K. D., Wang, T., et al. (2008). *Parsing antisocial personality disorder: An investigation of Lykken's (1995) theory of antisocial subtypes.* Manuscript in preparation.

Poythress, N. G., & Skeem, J. L. (2006). Disaggregating psychopathy: Where and how to look for subtypes. In C. J. Patrick (Ed.), *Handbook of psychopathy* (pp. 172–192). New York: Guilford Press.

Rice, M. E., Harris, G. T., & Cormier, C. A. (1992). An evaluation of a maximum security therapeutic community for psychopaths and other mentally disordered offenders. *Law and Human Behavior, 16,* 399–412.

Rockett, J. L., Murrie, D. C., & Boccaccini, M. T. (2007). Diagnostic labeling in juvenile justice settings: Do psychopathy and conduct disorder findings influence clinicians? *Psychological Services, 4,* 107–122.

Salekin, R. T. (2002). Psychopathy and therapeutic pessimism: Clinical lore or clinical reality? *Clinical Psychology Review, 22,* 79–112.

Salekin, R. T., Rogers, R., & Sewell, K. W. (1996). A review and meta-analysis of the Psychopathy Checklist and Psychopathy Checklist—Revised: Predictive validity of dangerousness. *Clinical Psychology: Science and Practice, 3,* 203–215.

Salekin, R. T., Rogers, R., & Sewell, K. W. (1997). Construct validity of psychopathy in a female offender sample: A multitrait–multimethod evaluation. *Journal of Abnormal Psychology, 106,* 576–585.

Skeem, J. L., & Cauffman, E. (2003). Views of the downward extension: Comparing the Youth Version of the Psychopathy Checklist with the Youth Psychopathic Traits Inventory. *Behavioral Sciences and the Law, 21,* 737–770.

Skeem, J. L., & Cooke, D. (in press). Is antisocial behavior essential to psychopathy?: Conceptual directions for resolving the debate. *Psychological Assessment.*

Skeem, J. L., Douglas, K., Edens, J., Poythress, N., & Lilienfeld, S. (2005, March).

Whether and how antisocial and psychopathic traits moderate the effect of substance abuse treatment. In N. Poythress (Chair), *Research in antisocial personality and psychopathy.* Symposium conducted at the American Psychology Law Society conference, San Diego, CA.

Skeem, J. L., Edens, J. F., Camp, J., & Colwell, L. H. (2004). Are there ethnic differences in levels of psychopathy? A meta-analysis. *Law and Human Behavior, 28,* 505–527.

Skeem, J. L., Johansson, P., Andershed, H., Kerr, M., & Eno Louden, J. (2007). Two subtypes of psychopathic violent offenders that parallel primary and secondary variants. *Journal of Abnormal Psychology, 116,* 395–409.

Skeem, J. L., Miller, J., Mulvey, E., Monahan, J., & Tiemann, J. (2005). Using a five-factor lens to explore the relation between personality traits and violence in psychiatric patients. *Journal of Consulting and Clinical Psychology, 73,* 454–465.

Skeem, J. L., Monahan, J., & Mulvey, E. (2003). Psychopathy, treatment involvement, and subsequent violence among civil psychiatric patients. *Law and Human Behavior, 26,* 577–603.

Skeem, J. L., & Mulvey, E. (2001). Psychopathy and community violence among civil psychiatric patients: Results from the MacArthur Violence Risk Assessment Study. *Journal of Consulting and Clinical Psychology, 69,* 358–374.

Skeem, J. L., Poythress, N. G., Edens, J. F., Lilienfeld, S. O., & Cale, E. (2003). Psychopathic personality or personalities?: Exploring potential variants of psychopathy and their implications for risk assessment. *Aggression and Violent Behavior, 8,* 513–546.

Slobogin, C. (2006). Dangerousness and expertise redux. *Emory Law Journal, 56,* 275–325.

Sullivan, E. A., & Kosson, D. S. (2006). Ethnic and cultural variations in psychopathy. In C. J. Patrick (Ed.), *Handbook of psychopathy* (pp. 437–458). New York: Guilford Press.

Sundby, S. E. (1998). The capital jury and absolution: The intersection of trial strategy, remorse, and the death penalty. *Cornell Law Review, 83,* 1557–1598.

Sutton, S. K., Vitale, J. E., & Newman, J. P. (2002). Emotion among women with psychopathy during picture perception. *Journal of Abnormal Psychology, 111,* 610–619.

Thornquist, M. H., & Zuckerman, M. (1995). Psychopathy, passive-avoidance learning, and basic dimensions of personality. *Personality and Individual Differences, 19,* 525–534.

Tyrer, P., Cooper, S., Seivewright, H., Duggan, C., Rao, B., & Hogue, T. (2005). Temporal reliability of psychological assessments for patients in a special hospital with severe personality disorder: A preliminary note. *Criminal Behaviour and Mental Health, 15,* 87–92.

Verona, E., & Vitale, J. (2006). Psychopathy in women: Assessment, manifestations, and etiology. In C. J. Patrick (Ed.), *Handbook of psychopathy* (pp. 415–436). New York: Guilford Press.

Vidal, S., & Skeem, J. L. (2007). Effect of psychopathy, abuse, and ethnicity on juvenile probation officers' decision-making and supervision. *Law and Human Behavior, 31*, 479–498.

Vincent, G. M. (2006). Psychopathy and violence risk assessment in youth. *Child and Adolescent Psychiatric Clinics of North America, 15*, 407–428.

Vitacco, M. J., Neumann, C. S., & Jackson, R. L. (2005). Testing a four-factor model of psychopathy and its association with ethnicity, gender, intelligence, and violence. *Journal of Consulting and Clinical Psychology, 73*, 466–476.

Vitale, J. E., & Newman, J. P. (2001). Response perseveration in psychopathic women. *Journal of Abnormal Psychology, 110*, 644–647.

Vitale, J. E., Smith, S. S., Brinkley, C. A., & Newman, J. P. (2002). The reliability and validity of the Psychopathy Checklist—Revised in a sample of female offenders. *Criminal Justice and Behavior, 29*, 202–231.

Wahl, O. (2003). *Media madness: Public images of mental illness.* New Brunswick, NJ: Rutgers University Press.

Walters, G. D. (2003a). Predicting criminal justice outcomes with the Psychopathy Checklist and Lifestyle Criminality Screening Form: A meta-analytic comparison. *Behavioral Sciences and the Law, 21*, 89–102.

Walters, G. D. (2003b). Predicting institutional adjustment and recidivism with the Psychopathy Checklist factor scores: A meta-analysis. *Law and Human Behavior, 27*, 541–558.

Walters, G. D., Duncan, S., & Mitchell-Perez, K. (2007). The latent structure of psychopathy: A taxometric investigation of the Psychopathy Checklist—Revised in a heterogeneous sample of male prison inmates. *Assessment, 14*, 270–278.

Walters, G. D., Gray, N., Jackson, R., Sewell, K., Rogers, R., Taylor, J., et al. (2007). A taxometric analysis of the Psychopathy Checklist: Screening Version (PCL:SV): Further evidence of dimensionality. *Psychological Assessment, 19*, 330–339.

Weaver, C. M., Meyer, R. G., Van Nort, J., & Tristan, L. (2006). Two-, three-, and four-factor PCL-R models in applied sex offender risk assessments. *Assessment, 13*, 208–216.

Zinger, I., & Forth, A. E. (1998). Psychopathy and Canadian criminal proceedings: The potential for human rights abuses. *Canadian Journal of Criminology, 40*, 237–276.

CHAPTER 9

Projective Techniques in the Courtroom

James M. Wood, M. Teresa Nezworski,
Scott O. Lilienfeld, and Howard N. Garb

OVERVIEW OF PROJECTIVE TECHNIQUES

No projective technique is more widely used or controversial than the Rorschach Inkblot Test (Hunsley & Bailey, 1999). A psychologist begins administration of the test by showing the respondent a series of 10 inkblots on cardboard cards and asking: "What might that be?" People typically report about two images per blot, or 20 images in all. For instance, one blot tends to be seen as a bat, whereas another is often perceived as an underwater scene with blue crabs and green seahorses. These images, recorded in a written record called a "protocol," are said to provide an in-depth view of the respondent's personality. For example, if the respondent reports seeing several inanimate objects in motion ("a flag flapping in the wind"), this is taken to indicate that he or she is under significant stress. Similarly a reflected image ("a woman looking in a mirror") is interpreted as a sign of self-centeredness or narcissism (Exner, 2003).

Projective tests such as the Rorschach have a distinctive format that sets them apart from self-report inventories, which are the type of test most commonly used to measure personality traits. A respondent taking a self-report inventory reads a series of statements or questions (e.g., "I often feel like crying") and then rates them on a scale with a few limited options (yes/

no). In contrast, a respondent taking a projective test such as the Rorschach is presented with a deliberately ambiguous stimulus or task and asked to give an open-ended response.

Proponents argue that the loosely structured format of projective tests constitutes their greatest strength (Bornstein, 2001). According to this line of reasoning, a respondent answering a self-report inventory can easily discern its purpose and consciously decide whether to give accurate information. Thus, an inventory can reveal only "explicit" personality—the traits of which the respondent is aware and willing to admit. In contrast, the ambiguity of projective tests prevents respondents from guessing how to manipulate their responses. For this reason, projective tests are supposedly superior at uncovering "implicit" personality—the traits that the respondent fails to recognize or wants to hide.

If projective tests could truly provide a window into an individual's hidden or "implicit" personality, they would be of enormous value in forensic settings. One can imagine how the Rorschach might function as a sort of psychological PET scan in a custody case, exposing the parents' flaws despite their strenuous efforts to present themselves in a flattering light. However, critics have long warned that this scenario is more science fiction than fact. With a few exceptions, it is argued, the Rorschach and other projective tests do a poor job of measuring either implicit or explicit personality (Anastasi & Urbina, 1997; Kaplan & Saccuzzo, 2005; Lilienfeld, Wood, & Garb, 2000, 2001).

Since the mid-1950s, projective tests have been exposed to a torrent of withering scientific criticism. Only a handful are still in widespread use today, and only three are likely to be encountered in forensic settings: the Rorschach, the Thematic Apperception Test (TAT), and projective drawings, each of which we briefly describe before continuing.

The format of the Rorschach has already been summarized. There are several different methods or "systems" for using the test, but one method, John Exner's (2003) Comprehensive System for the Rorschach, has become overwhelmingly popular during the past 25 years. Because other Rorschach systems are rarely encountered in forensic settings anymore, we focus exclusively on the Comprehensive System and use the term "Rorschach" to refer only to this system.

The second projective test discussed here, the TAT (Murray, 1943), presents the respondent with a series of cards, most of which depict evocative but deliberately ambiguous tableaus. For instance, one drawing depicts a bare-shouldered woman in bed with her eyes closed; nearby stands a man in anguish. For each drawing, the respondent is asked to tell an impromptu story, which is later interpreted thematically. For example, if the respondent were to say that the man in the drawing was in anguish because he had strangled the woman in the bed, this story might be interpreted as indicating a negative or even violent attitude toward women. Tests similar to the TAT have been developed for use with children, including the Children's Apperception Test (CAT; Bellak & Abrams, 1997) and Roberts Apperception Test (RAT; McArthur & Roberts, 1990). However, because they are used much less frequently than the TAT and have a considerably smaller scientific literature, these variants of apperception tests are not discussed further in this chapter.

Projective drawings, the third technique discussed here, are more commonly used with children than adults. Asking a child to make a drawing and talk about it can be an attractive way to build rapport and gather information. Several tests are based on projective drawings, including the Draw-a-Person (DAP) test, Kinetic Family Drawing (KFD) test, and the House–Tree–Person (HTP) test (Anastasi & Urbina, 1997). The interpretation of projective drawings tends to follow a simple "this-means-that" formula. For instance, the author of a still-influential book on the topic advised that buttons in a drawing should be interpreted as evidence that the respondent is "dependent, infantile, and inadequate," whereas pockets are suggestive of "psychopathic adjustment" (Machover, 1949, pp. 67 and 79).

Despite their controversial scientific status, the Rorschach, and to a lesser degree the TAT and projective drawings, play a role in a substantial number of legal cases. For example, the recently published *Handbook of Forensic Rorschach Assessment* (Gacono & Evans, 2008) includes chapters that discuss how the test can be used in child custody cases, tort and employment litigation, immigration evaluations, dangerousness risk assessments, and death penalty cases. In two relatively recent national surveys, approximately 45% of psychologists conducting custody evaluations reported that they used the Rorschach to evaluate the parents, and the same percentage reported that they used projective drawings to evaluate the children (Hagen & Castagna, 2001; Quinnell & Bow, 2001). Another study found that approximately 50% of psychologists who assessed defendants' competency to stand trial used projective tests (Skeem, Golding, Cohn, & Berge, 1998). The Rorschach is used by approximately one-third of forensic psychologists (Archer, Buffington-Vollum, Stredny, & Handel, 2006), including 35% of psychologists who evaluate children for abuse or neglect (Pinkerman, Haynes, & Keiser, 1993) and 16% who conduct dangerousness risk assessments (Tolman & Mullendore, 2003).

According to some critics, projective tests exhibit a marked tendency to "overpathologize"; that is, to portray individuals as seriously disturbed when in fact they are not (Wood, Nezworski, Lilienfeld, & Garb, 2003). This criticism, if correct, explains why these tests are usually introduced into legal proceedings as evidence that a litigant or defendant is supposedly psychologically "sick" or dangerous. Three uses of the Rorschach in civil proceedings illustrate this point. First, the Rorschach is commonly introduced into custody cases as evidence that one of the parents is emotionally unstable, impulsive, self-centered, or gravely distorted in his or her thinking. Second, the Rorschach is sometimes introduced into tort or employment suits by defendants to demonstrate that the plaintiff is psychologically disturbed. For instance, elsewhere we have reported the case of an African American policeman who was removed from his job after accusing his superiors of racial discrimination (Wood et al., 2003, p. 301). During a wrongful termination hearing, the policeman's department presented his Rorschach to show that he was paranoid and his accusations were delusional (a contention eventually rejected by the judge). Third, the Rorschach is sometimes introduced into personal injury cases to help prove that the plaintiff has developed posttraumatic stress disorder (PTSD) after suffering wrongful harm.

Projective tests sometimes even play a similar role in murder cases. In California in 2002, defense attorneys introduced the Rorschach to support an insanity plea by Cary Stayner, who was accused of murdering and mutilating three women in Yosemite National Park. Unconvinced by the inkblot evidence, the jury convicted Stayner and sentenced him to death (Finz, 2002). As a second example, in a 1999 Colorado case that also involved murder and mutilation, psychologist J. Reid Meloy, a leading proponent of projective tests, appeared as an expert witness for the prosecution. He testified that drawings by defendant Tim Masters revealed personality characteristics typical of men who commit homicide for sexual purposes. Meloy's testimony played a key role in Masters's subsequent conviction. However, Masters was released 9 years later when evidence emerged that another man had committed the murder (Campbell, 2008).

CONTROVERSIES

Because the scientific controversies regarding projective tests have been raging for more than half a century, they cannot be described here in complete detail. Interested readers are referred to critiques by Anastasi and Urbina (1997), Kaplan and Saccuzzo (2005), and Lilienfeld and colleagues (2000, 2001). We have also published a book-length critique of the Rorschach (Wood et al., 2003) and a shorter summary of relevant points (Wood, Nezworski, Garb, & Lilienfeld, 2006). Defenses of the Rorschach have been published by Meyer and Archer (2001), Hilsenroth and Stricker (2004), Weiner and Greene (2007), and Gacono and Evans (2008).

The next section focuses on six controversial questions that are especially relevant to the forensic use of projective tests:

1. Does the Rorschach tend to overpathologize individuals, falsely identifying nonexistent psychiatric problems?
2. Is the Rorschach useful for diagnosing psychiatric disorders and symptoms?
3. Are Rorschach scores related to violence, criminal recidivism, psychopathy, or other personality traits associated with criminality?
4. Should the Rorschach be used in custody evaluations?
5. Should the test be used with children and adolescents?
6. Turning to projective tests other than the Rorschach, do the TAT and projective drawings provide valid information that is relevant to forensic issues?

RESEARCH RELEVANT TO CONTROVERSIES

Does the Rorschach Overpathologize?

The concept of *norms* lies at the heart of several important controversies surrounding the Rorschach. Norms can be defined as the average test scores of a relevant comparison group. Because they provide an essential basis for interpreting test scores, norms are critically important when a test is used in clinical and forensic settings. In the case of Exner's (2003) Comprehensive System, however, there is fierce disagreement regarding the accuracy of its norms and, by extension, the interpretations based on them.

As an example, consider *Distorted Form* (also known as $X - \%$), a score of major importance in the Comprehensive System. Distorted Form is a measure of "poor fit" in responses to the blots. For example, consider the Rorschach blot mentioned earlier that's shaped like a bat. If a patient reports that it looks like a cat (which it definitely does not), this response is said to have "poor fit" or "poor form quality," because the response does not correspond to or "fit" the shape of the blot. The Distorted Form score is calculated as the percentage of the patient's Rorschach responses that exhibit poor form quality. This percentage can have major diagnostic significance, because research has shown that an abnormally high Distorted Form score can indicate schizophrenia or other forms of pathologically distorted thinking.

When, then, should a Distorted Form score be considered "abnormally high"? Of course, this question can be answered only by comparison with norms. The results from 35 studies involving thousands of nonpatient adults in both the United States and other countries have shown that the average Distorted Form score of nonpatient adults in the community is about 19% (Meyer, Erdberg, & Shaffer, 2007; Wood, Nezworski, Garb, & Lilienfeld, 2001). In other words, if an average person without serious psychological problems gives 20 responses to the blots, about 4 can be expected to exhibit poor form quality. But—and this is the crucial point—according to Exner's (2003) norms, the average Distorted Form score among nonpatient adults is only 10%, and a score of 19% is unusually high.

Now consider an American adult whose Distorted Form score is 21%. According to the 35 studies just mentioned, a score of 21% is "just about average." But according to Exner's norms (2003, pp. 373–374) and the interpretive rules based on them, the score of 21% is so abnormally high that it indicates "a pervasive tendency to distort reality." In fact, if Exner's norms and interpretive rules were applied to participants in the 35 studies just mentioned, more than 40% of nonpatient adults in the United States and elsewhere would be classified as exhibiting a level of thought disturbance suggestive of schizophrenia. The African American policeman mentioned earlier is a case in point. His Distorted Form score was well within the normal range. However, when compared with the Exner norms, he appeared to be suffering from thought disorder and thus was given a diagnosis of paranoia that was almost certainly incorrect.

In an article published in 2001 (Wood, Nezworski, et al., 2001) that pooled data from dozens of studies in the United States, we reached two conclusions: First, the norms for many scores in Exner's Comprehensive System are seriously inaccurate; second, in almost all cases the inaccuracies tend to "overpathologize" respondents. That is, when the Exner norms are used, the large majority of American adults and children appear seriously disturbed.

In the years since our critique of the Exner norms was published, at least 20 additional relevant studies have been conducted in the United States and other countries (Meyer et al., 2007). The results strongly confirm our conclusion that the Exner norms are in error and seriously overpathologize. Despite this overwhelming evidence, considerable controversy still exists. Leading Rorschach proponents (Erard, 2007; Exner, 2001; Meyer, 2001; Weiner & Greene, 2007) have repeatedly denied that there is a problem with the Exner norms. However, some Rorschach proponents now recommend that psychologists who use the Comprehensive System should also use a new set of "international norms" that is substantially different from the Exner norms (Meyer et al., 2007). Thus the Comprehensive System is presently in the strange position of having two sets of norms—those published by Exner and the new "international norms." It's unclear which norms psychologists should use when making test interpretations. As one wag commented, the situation is reminiscent of the era during the Middle Ages when the Catholic church had two popes.

Is the Rorschach Useful for Diagnosing Psychiatric Disorders and Symptoms?

Psychologists who work in forensic settings frequently use tests to help them diagnose possible psychopathology—that is, psychological disorders or symptoms—in the individuals they evaluate. Such diagnoses can be forensically important to the degree that the psychopathology is functionally linked with impairment in the abilities that are relevant to the legal questions at issue (e.g., parental fitness; ability to assist counsel; dangerousness).

To be useful for such purposes, tests must be diagnostically valid. In the terminology of psychologists, a test score is said to be *valid* if it is related to the phenomenon it's intended to measure. For example, if a test is intended to measure depression and is actually related to depression, then it is said to be a valid measure of that disorder.

It's often asked whether *any* Rorschach scores are valid measures of psychiatric diagnoses and symptoms. Both critics and proponents of the test agree that the answer is "yes" (Dawes, 1994; Garb, Wood, Lilienfeld, & Nezworski, 2002). Most notably, several Rorschach scores are related to psychotic disorders, such as schizophrenia and bipolar disorder, and to personality disorders that involve thought disorder, such as schizotypal personality disorder and borderline personality disorder. These Rorschach scores include those related to "poor fit" (e.g., Distorted Form) and those that measure oddities in speech and thinking (e.g., *WSum6* and the *Perceptual-Thinking Index* or *PTI*). Besides the Rorschach scores related to psychosis, several scores bear a modest but valid relationship to intelligence and to psychological disorders that involve impaired intelligence (e.g., mental retardation).

Despite the consensus that some Rorschach scores are related to psychosis, thought disorder, and intelligence, there is profound controversy concerning three other aspects of the Rorschach as a diagnostic test. First, critics of the test argue that the scores of the Exner system bear no demonstrated relationship to psychiatric diagnoses or symptoms other than those just noted. Specifically, critics deny that research has shown any consistent relationship of Comprehensive System scores with diagnoses or symptoms of posttraumatic stress disorder or other anxiety disorders, depression, antisocial or narcissistic personality disorders, or conduct disorder (Hunsley &

Bailey, 1999; Wood, Lilienfeld, Garb, & Nezworski, 2000). The response of Rorschach proponents to these criticisms has been mixed. For example, Irving Weiner (1999, pp. 336–337), a leading Rorschach proponent, has acknowledged the Rorschach's weakness as a diagnostic instrument: "The Rorschach Inkblot Method is not a diagnostic test, it was not designed as a diagnostic test, it is not intended to be a diagnostic test, and it does not in fact work very well as a diagnostic test." However, elsewhere Weiner has advanced a different and seemingly contradictory argument that Rorschach scores are useful for "differential diagnosis" and can help to diagnose post-traumatic stress disorder, depression, paranoid symptoms, and obsessive–compulsive personality disorder (Weiner & Greene, 2007, pp. 396–399).

In a second area of controversy, Rorschach proponents have sometimes suggested that the Rorschach might perform better as a diagnostic tool when it is used *in combination* with other tests, rather than when it is used *in isolation* by itself (Meyer et al., 2001). However, this idea has been vigorously rejected by critics of the test, who cite studies showing that the Rorschach may even slightly *decrease* the accuracy of diagnoses when it is used in combination with other tests (Garb, Wood, Lilienfeld, & Nezworski, 2005).

A third area of controversy surrounds the use of the Rorschach scores related to psychotic disorders. Critics agree that these scores bear a valid relationship to psychosis and thought disorder—that is, patients with thought disorder are more likely than other individuals to show "poor fit" and distorted thinking on the Rorschach. Nevertheless, the critics contend, due to inaccuracies in the Exner norms, these scores tend to misdiagnose a large number of relatively normal individuals as disturbed. For example, critics acknowledge the relationship between Distorted Form and thought disorder, but point out that when the Exner norms for Distorted Form are used, more than 40% of adults in the general population will be identified as having seriously disordered thinking. Proponents of the Rorschach have responded to such criticisms mainly by denying that there are problems with the Exner norms (Meyer, 2001; Weiner & Greene, 2007; but see Meyer et al., 2007).

Can the Rorschach Predict Violence, Criminal Recidivism, or Criminal Personality Traits?

Based on their research in the late 1980s and early 1990s, Carl Gacono and J. Reid Meloy in 1994 published a book that claimed to have identified several Rorschach scores relevant to violence, psychopathy, and other personality characteristics associated with criminality. Heated controversy has come to surround these claims, however, as critics have questioned the methodology of Gacono and Meloy's original research. Furthermore, the critics have pointed out that studies by later researchers have seriously undermined Gacono and Meloy's claims (Wood, Lilienfeld, Nezworski, & Garb, 2001; Wood et al., 2003, pp. 251–252).

For instance, Gacono and Meloy (1994) devoted a chapter of their book to Rorschach "reflection responses," which, as previously noted, involve imagery of mirrors or reflections, such as "a woman looking in a mirror." Rorschach tradition claims that reflection responses indicate the presence of narcissism (which is moderately to highly associated with psychopathy), and according to Gacono and Meloy, such responses are frequently given by psychopathic prisoners who are administered the Rorschach. However, critics have forcefully disputed this claim. Nezworski and Wood (1995) pointed out that the connection between reflection responses and narcissism has never been demonstrated by careful research. Furthermore, Wood and his colleagues (2003, pp. 251–252) identified 10 studies that tested Gacono and Meloy's ideas. Nine of the 10 studies found no significant relationship between reflection responses and psychopathy.

Critics have also disputed claims by Gacono and Meloy (1994) that the Rorschach bears a demonstrated relationship with violence, recidivism, antisocial personality disorder, conduct disorder, psychopathy, and any other personality characteristic associated with criminality (Wood, Lilienfeld, et al., 2001; Wood et al., 2003). For instance, the critics argue that despite extensive research on the topic, there is no solid scientific evidence that the Rorschach scores of criminals or juvenile delinquents differ from the scores obtained for the general population, or that any Rorschach score indicates a heightened risk for impulsiveness or violence. As the controversy has expanded, Gacono and Meloy have vigorously disputed the critics' conclusions and accused them of "commercialism," "deceptive tactics," and "bias against the Rorschach" (Gacono, Evans, & Viglione, 2002, pp. 33–35; Meloy, 2005, p. 346).

Should the Rorschach Be Used in Custody Evaluations?

Leading advocates of the Rorschach began to promote its use in custody cases in the early 1980s (Exner & Weiner, 1982), so that, as already noted, the test is presently used by more than 40% of psychologists who conduct custody evaluations (Quinnell & Bow, 2001). However, critics (Dawes, 1994; Erickson, Lilienfeld, & Vitacco, 2007a, 2007b) contend that use of the Rorschach in custody evaluations is unjustified and potentially harmful for several reasons. First, the critics argue that the scoring of many Rorschach tests is unreliable and potentially subjective. Second, they say that a clinician using the Rorschach is likely to overestimate a parent's level of psychopathology. Third, critics assert that the test lacks demonstrated validity for most of the purposes for which it is used. Fourth, and perhaps most importantly, the critics point out that there is a lack of solid scientific evidence that Rorschach scores bear a relationship to parental fitness. Thus Erickson and colleagues (2007a, pp. 165–166) concluded: "With the possible exception of detecting severe thought disorder in parents, there appears to be scant support for the use of the Rorschach test in family court evaluations.... The continued pervasive use of the Rorschach test in family court evaluations is unwise at best and unethical at worst." Dawes (1994) put the case even more strongly, warning not only about the use of the Rorschach but also other projective tests:

> If a professional psychologist is "evaluating" you in a situation in which you are at risk and asks you for responses to inkblots ... walk out of that psychologist's office. Going through with such an examination creates the danger of having a serious decision made about you on totally invalid grounds. (pp. 152–153)

The critics' conclusions have been disputed by Rorschach proponents (e.g., Erard, 2007; Weiner & Greene, 2007) and so must be regarded as controversial. However, the very fact that the Rorschach is controversial may be a reason for caution. In a recent major review article on custody evaluations, three psychologists otherwise uninvolved in the Rorschach controversy offered the following observation:

> There is a considerable difference of opinion and ongoing, active debate regarding the general utility of projective measures such as the Rorschach Inkblot Technique.... The very existence of this debate, in combination with some of the specific criticisms and potential dangers in the custody context, lead us to suggest that such measures not be used in child custody evaluation contexts, or any other evaluation contexts for that matter. (Emery, Otto, & O'Donohue, 2005, p. 9)

Should the Rorschach Be Used with Children and Adolescents?

As the preceding discussion has made clear, considerable disagreement surrounds the use of the Rorschach in clinical and forensic settings. However, controversy is especially intense regarding use of the test with children. We have strongly recommended that, given its tendency to overpathologize, the Rorschach should not generally be used with children (Wood et al., 2003, pp. 271–273). Specifically, children who are wrongly identified as seriously disturbed based on their Rorschach scores may be stigmatized by peers and teachers or, in a worst-case scenario, be administered psychotropic medications or other inappropriate treatments. Serious consequences can also arise when the test is used in forensic settings. For example, numerous misclassifications and faulty decisions are bound to ensue if the test is used to assess delinquents for dangerousness, to evaluate children for possible physical or sexual abuse, or as part of custody evaluations.

Some prominent Rorschach proponents have ignored or dismissed critics' contention that the Comprehensive System represents a danger to children. For example, Irving Weiner recently recommended that the Rorschach "can be used to good effect in evaluating children and early adolescents" (Weiner & Greene, 2007, p. 416). However, in a surprising recent development, three prominent Rorschach proponents have apparently adopted a view similar to the critics and concluded that the Exner norms for children and adolescents are "dated and atypical" and that their continuing use "would incorrectly result in some very unhealthy inferences and attributions of psychopathology" (Meyer et al., 2007, p. S214). These three Rorschach proponents advise that it is usually inappropriate to use the Exner norms to evaluate children. Thus, there is now support on "both sides of the aisle"— that is, from Rorschach critics as well as some Rorschach proponents—to discontinue use of the Comprehensive System with children and adolescents, at least until the problems with the norms are resolved.

Do the TAT and Projective Drawings Provide Valid Information That Is Relevant to Forensic Settings?

The preceding discussion has focused on the Rorschach, the projective test most likely to be encountered in court. However, because the TAT and projective drawings are also sometimes used in forensic settings, a brief discussion is appropriate regarding the most important controversies surrounding them.

The TAT has been frequently and severely criticized on the grounds that, as typically used in clinical practice, it is a free-form and highly subjective technique that lacks important features of a psychological test (Anastasi & Urbina, 1997; Lilienfeld et al., 2000, 2001; Vane, 1981). For instance, a good test requires *standardized administration and scoring* (Anastasi & Urbina, 1997). That is, it must always be administered and scored in precisely the same manner. Otherwise, if these procedures are allowed to vary, respondents' scores can be distorted in unpredictable ways.

As originally developed, the TAT included procedures for administering 20 of the test's 31 cards during two sessions (Murray, 1943). However, even these loosely standardized procedures soon dropped by the wayside. Instead, psychologists have adopted the more convenient practice of selecting a subset of 5–12 cards and administering them in a single session (Vane, 1981). The decision of which cards to include is left to the discretion of the individual clinician, who can "mix and match" cards in any way desired. The scoring of the patient's TAT responses is similarly unstructured, allowing the clinician to identify "themes" and interpret their psychological significance in an intuitive and often highly subjective manner.

Critics argue that the TAT's amorphous nature is further accentuated by its lack of norms (Anastasi & Urbina, 1997; Lilienfeld et al., 2000). Without norms as a standard of comparison, interpretations are inevitably impressionistic, and the danger of overpathologizing becomes significant. One classic study found that clinicians using the TAT often misidentified medical patients with no known psychological problems as seriously disturbed (Little & Shneidman, 1959).

In summary, critics argue that the TAT, as commonly used in clinical practice, does not really merit the appellation of "test," but is an idiosyncratic procedure that invites subjectivity and lacks demonstrated validity. Critics acknowledge that there is some research supporting the validity of the TAT when it is used with highly structured scoring rules and for certain narrowly defined purposes (e.g., measurement of achievement motivation or of object relations, that is, interpersonal perceptions of others; see Lilienfeld et al., 2000). However, the critics contend that this research is almost entirely irrelevant to the free-form TAT as it is used in forensic practice.

Interestingly, proponents of the TAT have tended to agree with critics that the procedure lacks the standardization and norms expected of a psychological test (e.g., Weiner & Greene, 2007). However, the proponents argue that the TAT is best viewed as an unstructured but useful clinical interaction that can yield valuable hypotheses about the inner functioning of the respondent.

Turning next to projective drawings, it is important to distinguish between two broad approaches to scoring drawings: the "sign" approach and the "global maladjustment" approach. The sign approach has much in common with the dream interpretation books sold in supermarket checkout lines. Details in the projective drawing tend to be interpreted in a formulaic way as "signs" of some underlying psychological predisposition (e.g., Machover, 1949). For example, if eyes are overemphasized in the drawing, they may be interpreted as a sign of paranoia. Broad shoulders may be taken as an indication that the respondent is carrying a heavy emotional burden. The sign approach has been severely criticized on the grounds that research has shown it to have little if any validity (see reviews by Kahill, 1984; Lilienfeld et al., 2000; Motta, Little, & Tobin, 1993; Thomas & Jolley, 1998). Even proponents of projective techniques acknowledge the legitimacy of these scientific criticisms, but argue that the sign approach can be helpful if clinicians approach the drawings with "caution, artistry, and skill" (Weiner & Greene, 2007, pp. 505–508).

The global maladjustment approach to projective drawings is far less controversial than the sign approach (Naglieri, McNeish, & Bardos, 1991). In the global maladjustment approach, a drawing is scored for the presence or absence of several supposed "indicators" of possible maladjustment. The total number of indicators is then calculated to yield a "global maladjustment" score. Although research findings have been mixed, they suggest that the number of such indicators is greater in the drawings of emotionally disturbed children than in those of normal children (Naglieri & Pfeiffer, 1992; see also review by Lilienfeld et al., 2000). Thus, by calculating the global maladjustment score, a psychologist might be able to form an impression about whether a child is psychologically disturbed. A very approximate estimate of a child's intelligence can also sometimes be gained from projective drawings (Kamphaus & Pleiss, 1991). In summary, there is broad agreement that projective drawings can provide a rough "global" estimate of a child's adjustment level and perhaps intelligence, but all other uses of projective drawings are highly controversial.

GAPS IN KNOWLEDGE

Although the Rorschach and other projective techniques have been studied for more than 80 years, the gaps in knowledge are large and numerous. Only a few of the most important issues can be discussed here.

First, even though the Rorschach has been in use since the 1920s, the test still lacks adequate norms for children or adolescents and thus lacks an adequate basis for interpreting children's Rorschachs. Second, the test presently lacks clear-cut norms for adults. Instead, as already indicated, there are two Rorschach "popes"—the Exner norms and the new "international norms"—which differ markedly from each other. Third, assuming that the international norms eventually replace the Exner norms in general usage, there will be a need to completely revamp the interpretive decision rules developed by Exner that still guide psychologists who use the Comprehensive System.

Fourth, there is an enormous gap between the purposes for which the Rorschach is routinely used—for instance, identifying posttraumatic stress disorder or psychopathy—and the scientific evidence that the test is valid for these purposes. Fifth, there is an even larger gap in knowledge concerning the Rorschach's relevance to legal issues. For example, there is no adequate scientific basis for claims that the Rorschach is related to (1) adequacy of parenting (e.g., in custody disputes), (2) criminal recidivism, or (3) violence or aggression (Erickson et al., 2007a, 2007b; Garb, Lilienfeld, & Wood, 2003).

Finally, regarding the TAT and projective drawings, the gaps in knowledge are not so great as with the Rorschach, at least in our opinion. There is ample scientific evidence that the "free-form" approach to the TAT and the sign approach to projective drawings lack validity for the purposes for which they are commonly used. Research on these issues need not be a major priority among personality assessment investigators. Rather, what is needed is a greater willingness by some psychologists to change their practices in response to the knowledge that already exists.

MYTHS AND MISCONCEPTIONS

Several false notions regarding projective tests are widespread. Most important is the myth, first promulgated by Rorschach proponents in the 1940s, that the test is like a psychological x-ray with stunning power to penetrate behind surface appearances. This misconception was recently revived, albeit in a more contemporary guise, in a White Paper published by the Society for Personality Assessment (an organization long known for promoting the Rorschach), which suggests that the test is as valid as mammography, MRIs, and PET scans (Board of Trustees of the Society for Personality Assessment, 2005; but see Wood et al., 2006).

Comparisons between the Rorschach and medical imaging techniques are misleading for three reasons. First, unlike magnetic resonance imaging (MRIs) and positron emission tomography (PET) scans, the Rorschach is not on the cutting edge of science. Rather, it is nearly 90 years old and has been vigorously criticized by scientists during most of that time. Second, whereas medical imaging techniques can yield a detailed and precise picture of brain structure, the Rorschach provides a comparatively crude measure of a few characteristics, most notably thought disorder and intelligence. Third, unlike imaging techniques, the Rorschach has no demonstrated power to penetrate appearances and reveal deeply hidden truths. Rather, the characteristics measured by the Rorschach—disordered thinking and intelligence—can also be assessed through direct observation. For example, on the basis of a few minutes of conversation, well-trained diagnosticians can often tell whether a patient is psychotic or mentally impaired.

A second related myth about the Rorschach is especially relevant in forensic settings: that the test is difficult or impossible to fake. In fact, research has demonstrated just the opposite (see reviews by Elhai, Kinder, & Frueh, 2003; Schretlen, 1997). For example, after only a few minutes of coaching, normal individuals can learn to give responses to the blots that are "schizophrenia-like." Alternatively, the test can be faked by copying the Rorschach responses of a patient from a textbook and memorizing them—a memory feat that is surprisingly easy. Unlike the Minnesota Multiphasic Personality Inventory–II (MMPI-2; Butcher, Dahlstrom, Graham, Tellegen, & Kaemmer, 1989), which is the most widely used self-report measure of psychopathology, the Rorschach does not include any well-validated scales to detect faking. Thus, individuals who fake the Rorschach are probably more likely to escape detection than those who fake the MMPI-2.

CONCLUSIONS: STATE OF THE SCIENCE

The present section discusses scientifically supported uses of projective tests, scientifically unsupported uses, and finally controversial uses. Here we focus on uses relevant to the courtroom.

Scientifically Supported Uses

The Rorschach—that is, the Comprehensive System for the Rorschach—currently lacks any well-supported uses in the courtroom. However, if the new international norms for the Rorschach proposed by Meyer and colleagues (2007) become generally accepted, and if these norms are used to develop new appropriate decision rules, then some of the Rorschach scores discussed earlier in this chapter could legitimately be used to help determine whether an adult has thought disorder, a symptom that appears in several different types of psychological disorders.

There is also scientific support for the use of global maladjustment scores on projective drawing tests to help identify general emotional disturbance in children. However, it should be noted that Rorschach and projective drawing scores, by themselves, constitute relatively weak and often ambiguous evidence of serious psychological disturbance. Thus, when these tests are used for the purposes described here, their findings should not be accepted unless they are also confirmed by high-quality behavioral and observational data.

Scientifically Unsupported Uses

The use of the unstructured TAT, without standardized administration procedures and norms, has been repeatedly rejected as invalid by the scientific community. Likewise, the sign approach to projective drawings has been similarly rejected. Thus, neither of these uses meets the "general acceptance" criterion that is widely used in judging legal admissibility.

Scientifically Controversial Uses

Virtually all aspects of the Rorschach fall into the "scientifically controversial" category. The reason is that scientific critics have mounted broad and vigorous attacks on the test for more than 50 years, whereas proponents of the test have responded with equally vigorous defenses. Wood and colleagues (2003) provide a history of the scholarly controversy, which began in the 1950s and has become particularly fierce in the years since 1995.

As might be expected given the magnitude of the debate, several published articles have questioned the Rorschach's legal admissibility under the *Frye* and *Daubert–Kumho–Joiner* standards (Erickson et al., 2007a, 2007b; Grove & Barden, 1999; Grove, Barden, Garb, & Lilienfeld, 2002; but see Erard, 2007; Hilsenroth & Stricker, 2004; Ritzler, Erard, & Pettigrew, 2002a, 2002b). The present chapter cannot review all the relevant issues, but instead focuses on a single key question that is directly relevant to the admissibility criteria articulated by the U.S. Supreme Court in the *Daubert* decision (*Daubert v. Merrell Dow Pharmaceuticals, Inc.*, 1993): What is the Rorschach's error rate?

As already discussed, critics argue that the large majority of Rorschach scores lack any demonstrated validity—that is, the scores are largely or entirely unrelated to the phenomena that they are supposed to measure (Erickson et al., 2007a; Wood et al., 2003). According to the critics, therefore, the error rate of these scores is not appreciably better than chance. For this reason, critics reject use of the Rorschach for the following purposes in forensic settings: evaluation of mood or anxiety disorders (including posttraumatic stress disorder); evaluation of recidivism risk, violence risk, or psychopathy; evaluation of parental suitability; evaluation of impulsivity, self-centeredness, or other antisocial personality traits. The critics' conclusions are not accepted by many Rorschach proponents, however, (e.g., Gacono & Evans, 2008; Weiner & Greene, 2007) and so must be regarded as controversial.

According to Rorschach critics and even some Rorschach proponents, another serious source of error arises from the inaccurate norms of Exner's Comprehensive System. As already indicated, the problems with the norms for children and adolescents are now widely recognized, and there is a broad, though not universal, consensus that use of these norms is inappropriate and potentially harmful (Erickson et al., 2007a; Meyer et al., 2007; Wood et al., 2003; but see Erard, 2007; Weiner & Greene, 2007). Use of the Exner norms for adults is highly controversial. It remains to be seen whether the new international norms for the test will achieve broader acceptance.

COMMUNICATING CONSENSUS AND CONTROVERSIES

Three topics merit special attention when the Rorschach and other projective tests are presented in court. First, it is always important to inform the court regarding the intense and long-lasting scientific controversy regarding projective tests and especially the Rorschach. Even if a projective test is ruled admissible in the courtroom under current legal rules, the credibility of expert witnesses can be undermined if they are shown to have relied on a controversial method in forming their opinions. Forensic experts who use projective techniques sometimes minimize the controversial nature of the tests or suggest that criticisms emanate from fringe groups within the profession. However, such suggestions can easily be shown to contradict the historical facts (Wood et al., 2003).

The second issue that deserves special attention in any presentation of projective tests—particularly the Rorschach—is their tendency to overpathologize. It will be highly educational to compare a respondent's Rorschach results with the new international norms proposed by Meyer and colleagues (2007). An individual who appears "sick" when compared with the Exner norms may well appear "just average" when compared with the more broadly based international norms.

The third issue worthy of attention concerns validity. It is often helpful for experts to focus on the validity of the *specific scores* that are most important in the case at hand. That is, instead of focusing on the general lack of validity of Rorschach scores, it is often productive to focus more narrowly. For example, in one case the most relevant question might concern the Rorschach's validity for predicting future dangerousness. In another case, the most relevant question might concern the test's validity for diagnosing posttraumatic stress disorder, or for identifying deficiencies in parenting. In almost all cases, the test will be found to lack demonstrated validity for the purpose for which it is used, although a review of the relevant scientific literature may be necessary to shed light on a particular issue.

In closing, we offer the observation, based on personal experience, that projective tests are often vulnerable to devastating attack in legal cases. When confronted by well-prepared attorneys, experts who have based their testimony on the Rorschach or other projective techniques frequently retreat or are discredited. If their testimony is vigorously opposed in depositions or pretrial hearings, it may well be withdrawn without being introduced at trial.

REFERENCES

Anastasi, A., & Urbina, S. (1997). *Psychological testing* (7th ed). Upper Saddle River, NJ: Prentice Hall.

Archer, R. P., Buffington-Vollum, J. K., Stredny, R. V., & Handel, R. W. (2006). A survey of psychological test use patterns among forensic psychologists. *Journal of Personality Assessment, 87,* 84–95.

Bellak, L., & Abrams, D. M. (1997). *The Thematic Apperception Technique, the Children's Apperception Test, and the Senior Apperception Test in clinical use* (6th ed.). Boston: Allyn & Bacon.

Board of Trustees of the Society for Personality Assessment. (2005). The status of the Rorschach in clinical and forensic practice: An official statement by the Board of Trustees of the Society for Personality Assessment. *Journal of Personality Assessment, 85,* 219–237.

Bornstein, R. F. (2001). Clinical utility of the Rorschach Inkblot Method: Reframing the debate. *Journal of Personality Assessment, 77,* 39–47.

Butcher, J. N., Dahlstrom, W. G., Graham, J. R., Tellegen, A., & Kaemmer, B. (1989). *MMPI-2: Manual for administration and scoring.* Minneapolis: University of Minnesota Press.

Campbell, G. (2008). *The Tim Masters case: Chasing Reid Meloy.* Retrieved April 10, 2008, from *www.fortcollinsnow.com/article/20080201/NEWS/297958975.*

Daubert v. Merrell Dow Pharmaceuticals, Inc., 509 U.S. 579, 583 (1993).

Dawes, R. M. (1994). *House of cards: Psychology and psychotherapy built on myth.* New York: Free Press.

Elhai, J. D., Kinder, B. N., & Frueh, B. C. (2003). Projective assessment of malingering. In M. Hilsenroth & D. Segal (Eds.), *Personality assessment* (pp. 553–561). Hoboken, NJ: Wiley.

Emery, R. E., Otto, R. K., & O'Donohue, W. T. (2005). A critical assessment of child custody evaluations: Limited science and a flawed system. *Psychological Science in the Public Interest, 6,* 1–29.

Erard, R. E. (2007). Picking cherries with blinders on: A comment on Erickson et al. (2007) regarding the use of tests in family court. *Family Court Review, 45,* 175–184.

Erickson, S. K., Lilienfeld, S. O., & Vitacco, M. J. (2007a). A critical examination of suitability and limitation of psychological tests in family court. *Family Court Review, 45,* 157–174.

Erickson, S. K., Lilienfeld, S. O., & Vitacco, M. J. (2007b). Failing the burden of proof: The science and ethics of projective tests in custody evaluations. *Family Court Review, 45,* 185–192.

Exner, J. E. (2001). A comment on "The misperception of psychopathology: Problems with the norms of the Comprehensive System for the Rorschach." *Clinical Psychology: Science and Practice, 8,* 386–388.

Exner, J. E. (2003). *The Rorschach: A Comprehensive System: Vol. 1. Basic foundations and principles of interpretation* (4th ed.). Hoboken, NJ: Wiley.

Exner, J. E., & Weiner, I. B. (1982). *The Rorschach: A comprehensive system: Vol. 3. Assessment of children and adolescents.* New York: Wiley.

Finz, S. (2002, August 23). Jury begins deliberation in Stayner trial. *San Francisco Chronicle,* p. A-23. Retrieved June 25, 2007, from *sfgate.com/cgi-bin/article. cgi?f=/c/a/2002/08/23/BA129058.DTL.*

Gacono, C. B., & Evans, F. B. (2008). *The handbook of forensic Rorschach assessment.* New York: Routledge.

Gacono, C. B., Evans, F. B., & Viglione, D. J. (2002). The Rorschach in forensic practice. *Journal of Forensic Psychology Practice, 2*(3), 33–53.

Gacono, C. B., & Meloy, J. R. (1994). *The Rorschach assessment of aggressive and psychopathic personalities.* Hillsdale, NJ: Erlbaum.

Garb, H. N., Lilienfeld, S. O., & Wood, J. M. (2003). The scientific status of research on projective techniques. In D. L. Faigman, D. H. Kaye, M. J. Saks, & J. Sanders (Eds.), *Modern scientific evidence: The law and science of expert testimony* (2nd ed., Vol. 4, Suppl., pp. 75–104). St. Paul, MN: West/Thompson.

Garb, H. N., Wood, J. M., Lilienfeld, S. O., & Nezworski, M. T. (2002). Effective use of projective techniques in clinical practice: Let the data help with selection and interpretation. *Professional Psychology: Research and Practice, 33,* 454–463.

Garb, H. N., Wood, J. M., Lilienfeld, S. O., & Nezworski, M. T. (2005). Roots of the Rorschach controversy. *Clinical Psychology Review, 25,* 97–118.

Grove, W. M., & Barden, R. C. (1999). Protecting the integrity of the legal system: The admissibility of testimony from mental health experts under *Daubert/Kumho* analyses. *Psychology, Public Policy, and Law, 5,* 224–242.

Grove, W. M., Barden, R. C., Garb, H. N., & Lilienfeld, S. O. (2002). Failure of Rorschach Comprehensive System-based testimony to be admissible under the Daubert–Joiner–Kumho standard. *Psychology, Public Policy, and Law, 8,* 216–234.

Hagen, M. A., & Castagna, N. (2001). The real numbers: Psychological testing in custody evaluations. *Professional Psychology: Research and Practice, 32,* 269–271.

Hilsenroth, M. J., & Stricker, G. (2004). A consideration of challenges to psychological assessment instruments used in forensic settings: Rorschach as exemplar. *Journal of Personality Assessment, 83,* 141–152.

Hunsley, J., & Bailey, J. M. (1999). The clinical utility of the Rorschach: Unfulfilled promises and an uncertain future. *Psychological Assessment, 11,* 266–277.

Kahill, S. (1984). Human figure drawing in adults: An update of the empirical evidence, 1967–1982. *Canadian Psychology, 25,* 269–292.

Kamphaus, R. W., & Pleiss, K. L. (1991). Draw-a-Person techniques: Tests in search of a construct. *Journal of School Psychology, 29,* 395–401.

Kaplan, R. M., & Saccuzzo, D. P. (2005). *Psychological testing: Principles, applications, and issues* (6th ed.). Belmont, CA: Thomson & Wadsworth.

Lilienfeld, S. O., Wood, J. M., & Garb, H. N. (2000). The scientific status of projective techniques. *Psychological Science in the Public Interest, 1,* 27–66. Available at *www.psychologicalscience.org/newsresearch/publications/journals/pspi1_2.html*

Lilienfeld, S. O., Wood, J. M., & Garb, H. N. (2001). What's wrong with this picture? *Scientific American, 284*(5), 80–87.

Little, K. B., & Shneidman, E. S. (1959). Congruencies among interpretations of psychological test and anamnestic data. *Psychological Monographs, 73*(6, Whole No. 476).

Machover, K. (1949). *Personality projection in the drawing of the human figure.* Springfield, IL: Thomas.

McArthur, D. S., & Roberts, G. E. (1990). *Roberts Apperception Test for Children manual.* Los Angeles: Western Psychological Services.

Meloy, J. R. (2005). Some reflections on *What's Wrong with the Rorschach? Journal of Personality Assessment, 85,* 344–346.

Meyer, G. J. (2001). Evidence to correct misperceptions about Rorschach norms. *Clinical Psychology: Science and Practice, 8,* 389–396.

Meyer, G. J., & Archer, R. P. (2001). The hard science of Rorschach research: What do we know and where do we go? *Psychological Assessment, 13,* 486–502.

Meyer, G. J., Erdberg, P., & Shaffer, T. W. (2007). Toward international normative reference data for the Comprehensive System. *Journal of Personality Assessment, 89,* S201–S216.

Meyer, G. J., Finn, S. E., Eyde, L. D., Kay, G. G., Moreland, K. L., Dies, R. R., et al. (2001). Psychological testing and psychological assessment: A review of evidence and issues. *American Psychologist, 56,* 128–165.

Motta, R. W., Little, S. G., & Tobin, M. I. (1993). The use and abuse of human figure drawings. *School Psychology Quarterly, 8,* 162–169.

Murray, H. A. (1943). *Thematic Apperception Test.* Cambridge, MA: Harvard University Press.

Naglieri, J. A., McNeish, T. J., & Bardos, A. N. (1991). *Draw-A-Person: Screening Procedure for Emotional Disturbance.* Austin, TX: PRO-ED.

Naglieri, J. A., & Pfeiffer, S. I. (1992). Performance of disruptive behavior-disordered and normal samples on the Draw-A-Person: Screening procedure for emotional disturbance. *Psychological Assessment, 4*, 156–159.

Nezworski, M. T., & Wood, J. M. (1995). Narcissism in the Comprehensive System for the Rorschach. *Clinical Psychology: Science and Practice, 2*, 179–199.

Pinkerman, J. E., Haynes, J. P., & Keiser, T. (1993). Characteristics of psychological practice in juvenile court clinics. *American Journal of Forensic Psychology, 11*(2), 3–12.

Quinnell, F. A., & Bow, J. N. (2001). Psychological tests used in child custody evaluations. *Behavioral Sciences and the Law, 19*, 491–501.

Ritzler, B., Erard, R., & Pettigrew, G. (2002a). A final reply to Grove and Barden: The relevance of the Rorschach Comprehensive System for expert testimony. *Psychology, Public Policy, and Law, 8*, 235–246.

Ritzler, B., Erard, R., & Pettigrew, G. (2002b). Protecting the integrity of Rorschach expert witnesses: A reply to Grove and Barden (1999) Re: The admissibility of testimony under *Daubert/Kumho* analyses. *Psychology, Public Policy, and Law, 8*, 201–215.

Schretlen, D. J. (1997). Dissimulation on the Rorschach and other projective measures. In R. Rogers (Ed.), *Clinical assessment of malingering and deception* (2nd ed., pp. 208–222). New York: Guilford Press.

Skeem, J. L., Golding, S. L., Cohn, N. B., & Berge, G. (1998). Logic and reliability of evaluations of competence to stand trial. *Law and Human Behavior, 22*, 519–547.

Thomas, G. V., & Jolley, R. P. (1998). Drawing conclusions: A re-examination of empirical and conceptual bases for psychological evaluations of children from their drawings. *British Journal of Clinical Psychology, 37*, 127–139.

Tolman, A. O., & Mullendore, K. B. (2003). Risk evaluations for the courts: Is service quality a function of specialization? *Professional Psychology: Research and Practice, 34*, 225–232.

Vane, J. R. (1981). The Thematic Apperception Test: A review. *Clinical Psychology Review, 1*, 319–336.

Weiner, I. B. (1999). What the Rorschach can do for you: Incremental validity in clinical applications. *Assessment, 6*, 327–339.

Weiner, I. B., & Greene, R. L. (2007). *Handbook of personality assessment.* Hoboken, NJ: Wiley.

Wood, J. M., Lilienfeld, S. O., Garb, H. N., & Nezworski, M. T. (2000). The Rorschach test in clinical diagnosis: A critical review, with a backward look at Garfield (1947). *Journal of Clinical Psychology, 56*, 395–430.

Wood, J. M., Lilienfeld, S. O., Nezworski, M. T., & Garb, H. N. (2001). Coming to grips with negative evidence for the Comprehensive System for the Rorschach: A comment on Gacono, Loving, & Bodholdt; Ganellen; and Bornstein. *Journal of Personality Assessment, 77,* 48–70.

Wood, J. M., Nezworski, M. T., Garb, H. N., & Lilienfeld, S. O. (2001). The misperception of psychopathology: Problems with the norms of the Comprehensive System for the Rorschach. *Clinical Psychology: Science and Practice, 8,* 350–373.

Wood, J. M., Nezworski, M. T., Garb, H. N., & Lilienfeld, S. O. (2006). The controversy over Exner's comprehensive system for the Rorschach: The critics speak. *Independent Practitioner, 26*(2). Available at *www.division42.org/MembersArea/IPfiles/Spring06/practitioner/rorschach.php.*

Wood, J. M., Nezworski, M. T., Lilienfeld, S. O., & Garb, H. N. (2003). *What's wrong with the Rorschach?: Science confronts the controversial inkblot test.* San Francisco: Jossey-Bass.

CHAPTER 10

Psychophysiological Detection of Deception and Guilty Knowledge

William G. Iacono

Probably no form of psychological assessment is more likely to change the lives of those who submit to the procedure than the polygraph test. Whatever good comes from polygraph testing needs to be weighed against outcomes that can lead to mistaken prosecution, unjustified imprisonment, freedom for criminals, blackened reputations, loss of livelihood, family discord, and the lengthening of a sentence. The profound consequences that follow from polygraph verdicts, coupled with their lack of scientific foundation, also ranks polygraphy among the most controversial of applied psychological procedures. In this chapter I provide insights regarding how polygraph tests have attained such standing, focusing on their forensic applications in the United States. Because different types of polygraph tests are used for personnel screening, and these tests virtually never find their way into court, I have not covered these procedures (for recent reviews, see Iacono & Lykken, 2006; Iacono & Patrick, 2006).

OVERVIEW OF TECHNIQUES AND CONTROVERSIES

After almost a century of research, no one has discovered a physiological reaction associated exclusively with lying. Hence, the outcome of polygraph tests depends on the magnitude of physiological reactions to different types of questions. Three types of physiological reactions are recorded on the typical field polygraph. A partially inflated blood pressure cuff around the arm is used to monitor the relative changes in blood pressure that occur as the heart pumps blood under the cuff. Pneumatic tubes placed around the upper chest and abdomen monitor respiration. Electrodes placed on the fingertips measure changes in palmar sweating. These signals can be recorded with a conventional polygraph as tracings on moving chart paper, but now they are more commonly digitized by a computer that displays the reactions on a monitor as they would normally appear on a polygraph chart. Computerized polygraphs yield objectively scored test results and a probability statement signifying the degree to which deception is likely. However, most examiners hand-score their charts, assigning numbers to the reactions evident in each physiological channel to quantify the magnitude of the response to one question relative to that of another.

The application of these techniques has spawned significant controversy focusing on the validity of forensic applications. The polygraph profession argues that their methods produce few errors, those errors that do arise are due to examiner mistakes rather than problems with the techniques, and that decades of experience administering tests has shown that they are effective at detecting liars. Critics of polygraph testing have concluded that the claims of the polygraph profession are unfounded because credible validity evidence is lacking, as is a plausible theory for how these methods work. In addition, they are vulnerable to easily learned countermeasures that can be used by liars to manipulate their physiological reactions to simulate truthfulness.

Control (or Comparison) Question Test

Virtually all polygraph tests that come before courts are a variant of what has come to be known as the control question test (CQT). All CQTs have certain basic elements in common. As its name implies, the CQT includes "control" questions along with the "Did you do it?" or relevant questions that are expected in polygraph tests. Relevant questions deal with the issue at hand. In a case of child sexual abuse, they might take the form "Did you place your mouth on Kara's genitals?" and "Did you perform oral sex on Kara?" The physiological reactions to this item are then compared to those elicited by a "probable lie control" question with which it is paired, e.g., "Have you ever lied to get out of trouble?" Control questions are answered "No." Because they cover possible past transgressions that are presumed to be a part of everyone's life, they are presumed to index a lie response. A typical test is likely to have three pairs of relevant and control questions, all of which are asked during the run of one "chart." Most tests consist of three charts, each involving the same questions presented in a different order. All the questions are reviewed with the examinee during the "pretest" phase of a polygraph session, where it is stressed that the examinee needs to be able to answer all the questions honestly. Many examinees will admit to misdeeds associated with the control questions, in which case these questions are reworded to exclude them; e.g., "Other than what you told me about, have you ever lied to get out of trouble?"

CQT theory assumes that the truthful person will not be bothered as much by honest denial to the relevant question as he or she will be by the probable lie to the control question. The liar is expected to respond more strongly to the relevant question because it deals with a more serious matter. To the extent that neither control nor relevant questions yield a consistently stronger reaction across charts and question repetitions, an inconclusive outcome may result. These outcomes occur about 10% of the time and typically lead to a readministration of the test on another occasion.

The primary weakness of the CQT concerns the degree to which the control questions work as required for truthful individuals. A true scientific control would require the control question to match the relevant question in all respects except one: whether lying is involved. This might occur if a person were charged with two equally serious crimes, one of which was known not to involve the suspect because it was a fiction created by the police (e.g., "In the course of investigating the sexual assault of Kara, we have learned that her neighborhood friend, Kristi, was also abused. On this test we will be including additional questions that cover your possible involvement with Kristi"). An innocent person would have no reason to respond more to one of these allegations than the other, and the questions concerning Kristi would index the reaction to an emotionally charged question that was honestly denied. The guilty person, lying only in response to allegations about Kara, might reasonably be expected to respond more strongly to them.

With the CQT, the relevant question is just as relevant for the innocent as it is for the guilty. To the extent that the innocent person understands that the test outcome depends on the relevant question, the control question is inconsequential. The fact that it may not even elicit a lie or be psychologically disturbing further undermines its legitimacy. Unable to refute these criticisms, the CQT was renamed the "comparison question test" by the American Polygraph Association in 1999.

A variant comparison question method has been promoted as a means of circumventing some of the problems with the probable lie question. With this variant, one or more of the probable lie questions is replaced with a "directed lie" (Horowitz, Kircher, Honts, & Raskin, 1997). As the name implies, the examiner asks the subject to lie deliberately and formulates a question that both agree will tap a lie (e.g., "Have you ever made even one mistake?"). The examinee is told to think of a specific instance of the mistake when responding to the question. In this way, the issue of whether the probable lie control question is, in fact, eliciting a lie is eliminated. However, the directed lie question still does not match the relevant question in psychological significance, thus leaving the directed lie vulnerable to the same criticism leveled against probable lie controls.

Guilty Knowledge Test

In forensic settings virtually all polygraph tests are CQTs. However, an alternative procedure, called the guilty knowledge test (GKT; sometimes referred to as the concealed information test) is occasionally used in the United States. Rather than detect lying, the GKT assesses recognition memory, in particular, whether an individual has specific memories associated with the commission of a crime that would be discoverable by the police but otherwise hidden from the public. As originally conceived by its inventor (Lykken, 1959, 1960), the GKT consists of a series of multiple-choice questions, each containing a relevant alternative that a guilty suspect might be expected to recognize. For instance, continuing with our child sex abuse example, questions might take the form: "If you assaulted Kara, then you'll know which part of her body you contacted inappropriately. Was it her mouth ... breasts ... buttocks ... thighs ... genitals? And you'll know where this occurred. Was it in her bedroom ... the playroom ... the living room ... the bathroom ... the den?" Given enough multiple-choice questions, it is highly unlikely that an innocent person would consistently react physiologically to the relevant alternatives simply by chance. Hence, false-positive outcomes are not likely with this procedure, especially with well-designed GKTs (Ben-Shakar & Elaad, 2003). False negatives are much more likely and occur in inverse proportion to how well the questions tap details of the crime that a perpetrator is likely to recall (Ben-Shakar & Elaad, 2003; Iacono, 1985; Iacono, Boisvenu, & Fleming, 1984).

A variant of the GKT that has been commercially marketed as "brain fingerprinting" (*brainwavescience.com*) relies on the P3 component of the brain event-related potential (ERP) to index recognition memory rather than autonomic nervous system responses. The P3 wave is elicited by an infrequently occurring stimulus of special significance, such as the relevant alternatives in a GKT. For this test the multiple-choice items can be flashed repeatedly every second or so on a computer monitor and the electroencephalogram (EEG) to each alternative recorded. In order to obtain a P3 wave, EEGs that are time-locked to the presentation of each stimulus are averaged over many stimulus presentations, resulting in waveforms with well-defined P3 components.

To ensure that stimuli are attended to, the GKT format can be modified to require a manual response. With this requirement, the ERP–GKT is composed of three types of stimuli: relevants (guilty knowledge alternatives), irrelevants (foils to these alternatives), and targets (alternatives that require a response). Targets consist of items that the examiner is certain the examinee knows, perhaps aspects of the crime that are public knowledge. Examinees are instructed: "You will see a series of words and phrases flash on the computer monitor every second or so. When you see a phrase that is associated with the crime, press the red button. For everything else, press the green button." In the ERP–GKT, irrelevants are common (e.g., 70% of trials), associated with frequent green button presses, and thus elicit only a weak P3. Targets are both infrequently presented (e.g., 15% of trials) and associated with less common red button presses, thus eliciting a strong P3.

Critical to the outcome of the ERP–GKT is whether the brain response to the relevants resembles more that of the targets or the irrelevants. Innocent individuals possess no knowledge that enables them to distinguish among the irrelevants and the relevants. Hence, their P3 to the relevants should resemble their response to the irrelevants. For the guilty, the relevants stand out, and their response to these items should resemble their response to the targets. The degree to which the P3 to the relevants resembles either that of the targets or the irrelevants can be easily determined and used to indicate the likelihood that an individual possesses guilty knowledge. Note that relevants are supposed to be accompanied by green button presses. Because the innocent has no basis to differentiate relevants from irrelevants, pressing the green button is straightforward. However, for the guilty, the relevants reflect information that is associated with the crime, setting up a response conflict where the tendency to press the red button must be inhibited in favor of manipulating the green button. This conflict has the potential to both produce errors (inadvertently pressing the red button) and delayed response times to the green button press. These performance measures may also provide useful guilty knowledge information.

From a law enforcement perspective, the GKT has two important limitations. One is the belief that it is not appropriate for most crimes, either because guilty knowledge information cannot be developed from the case facts or because all the relevant case facts are publicly known. The other is that it is difficult to know for sure that an item captures a salient crime feature unlikely to be forgotten by the perpetrator. This limitation means that we cannot know whether a passed GKT is to be trusted, thereby severely undermining its perceived value to law enforcement, which places a premium on catching and successfully prosecuting criminals. This dismissal is unfortunate because there is a wealth of research supporting the potential utility of the GKT (Ben-Shakhar & Elaad, 2003), including the variant based on the P3 brain potential (Iacono, 2007).

RESEARCH RELEVANT TO CONTROVERSIES

Because the use of the GKT in forensic practice is so slight as to be negligible, there are no meaningful controversies surrounding its use. The CQT, by contrast, has been under fire throughout its 60-year history. What makes the controversy especially sharp is the degree to which practitioners and scientists disagree regarding CQT accuracy. Practitioners generally assert that scientists' armchair criticism of CQT theory and their speculation that it is error prone simply do not square with the facts evident through its application. Almost all practicing polygraph examiners assert that the CQT is nearly infallible. Many will say they are unaware of ever having made an error. Although they acknowledge the potential for errors, these are believed to come at the hands of incompetent polygraphers. They further believe that the scientific literature supports these conclusions. They use as their source authority the American Polygraph Association whose webpage (*polygraph.org*) advertises as evidence of CQT validity a review of 12 field studies involving 2,174 forensic examinations that proclaim an overall accuracy of 98% (Forensic Research Incorporated, 1997). The handful of scientists who practice polygraphy tend to reach similar conclusions. For instance, Raskin and Honts (2002) argue that field studies support an accuracy of 97.5% for CQTs likely to be introduced as evidence in court.

Scientists at arms' length from the polygraph profession, critically reviewing the same studies on which proponents rely, have consistently and repeatedly found these studies methodologically inadequate and thus inadequate to substantiate such claims (Ben-Shakar, 2002; Fiedler, Schmod, & Stahl, 2002; Furedy, 1996; Iacono, 2008; Iacono & Lykken, 2005; Lykken, 1998; National Research Council, 2003; Oksol & O'Donohue, 2003). In addition, surveys of scientific opinion regarding the CQT and its forensic applications have been highly negative (Iacono & Lykken, 1997).

The most likely explanation for this disparity of opinion derives from the fact that in their practice, polygraphers often learn when their decisions are correct but virtually never learn of errors. Under these circumstances, it is easy to dismiss the methodological criticisms scientists level at validity studies because the very high accuracy rates they claim are consistent with examiner field experience. These field practices not only lead examiners to have unfaltering faith in their techniques, as I show next, they also give rise to the major confound that undermines validity studies of the CQT.

Following a failed CQT, examiners are trained to interrogate examinees to obtain confessions. When an individual confesses, the examiner learns that the CQT outcome was correct. However, when an innocent person fails a test and resists a false confession, the examiner is unlikely to ever learn of this error. Likewise, when a guilty person passes, no confession is sought, and again this error is unlikely to be uncovered. Although a confession is not the only criterion applicable to determine "ground truth," it is the generally accepted standard in the polygraph profession. The accuracy of trial outcomes is unlikely to be better than 98%, so examiners attribute disagreement between their assessment and a courtroom verdict as due to imperfections in legal proceedings (e.g., suspects must be proven guilty beyond reasonable doubt, legal technicalities lead to criminals going free, juries make errors). Hence, because their mistakes are hidden from them while their correct decisions are often reinforced, examiners have no reason to doubt their accuracy.

Unfortunately, examiner-obtained confessions serve as the criterion for ground truth in field investigations of CQT validity, creating a methodological confound that leads these studies to overestimate accuracy. In the standard field study design, confessions serve to identify the guilty while establishing as innocent cosuspects in the same case. Hence, the only cases selected for study inclusion become those where a deceptive polygraph test was corroborated by a posttest confession obtained by the polygrapher. All the cases chosen in field studies based on confessions can thus be expected to come from original examiners who were correct almost all the time, and this is in fact what the literature shows (Raskin & Honts, 2002). That is, every instance where the original examiner judged a guilty person to be nondeceptive or an innocent person deceptive will be excluded from the field study because, absent a confession, these undetected errors will never generate the criterion required for case inclusion.

In the best field studies, the original examiner's polygraph charts are rescored by experts who are blinded to the case facts, questions asked, and details regarding test administration. The results of this blind chart analysis are then compared to ground truth, and this becomes the accuracy estimate. Because polygraph chart scoring is highly reliable (Patrick & Iacono, 1991), showing how often the blind evaluator matched the criterion does not provide an unbiased estimate of accuracy. As I have noted elsewhere, under these circumstances, the CQT could appear in such studies to have perfect accuracy while in fact performing no better than chance (Iacono, 1991), a conclusion that was recently echoed in a comprehensive review of polygraph testing by the National Research Council of the National Academy of Sciences (2003).

Only one field study has attempted to circumvent this criterion contamination problem (Patrick & Iacono, 1991). This study, which was conducted with the Royal Canadian Mounted Police, examined every case (over 400 total) in which a CQT was administered during a specified period of time. However, rather than relying on examiner-obtained confessions, Patrick and Iacono (1991) examined all police records obtained subsequent to the administration of the CQT for evidence of ground truth. The study sample thus consisted of cases where postpolygraph detective work indicated that individuals being investigated confessed or it was later determined that no crime was committed (e.g., lost possessions believed to be stolen were later found to be misplaced). When the charts associated with these independently confirmed cases were blindly rescored, they yielded a hit rate of 57% for verified innocent individuals. However, a corresponding rate for guilty suspects could not be determined because all but one of the confessions obtained in these local police files were from people whose confession cleared as innocent the person who took the CQT.

Two important conclusions follow from this study. First, the CQT performs little better than chance with innocent people, confirming that probable lie control questions are not having their intended effect. Second, it is not possible to estimate the accuracy of the CQT with guilty persons. All field studies, including this one, have failed to eliminate the effect of the confession bias problem on estimates of CQT accuracy for guilty individuals.

The polygraph profession ignores this confession bias problem, and, reinforced by field practices that lead them to erroneously conclude that few errors are made, are comfortable relying on studies reporting near perfect (97–98%) accuracy. Scientists with no ties to the profession find these studies methodologically inadequate. This inadequacy, coupled with the obvious theoretical shortcomings of the CQT, leads them to dismiss the high accuracy claims of polygraph proponents.

GAPS IN KNOWLEDGE

The only important psychometric property firmly established for the CQT is its interscorer reliability, which is uniformly high, often reported as around

.90. Because polygraph tests are sometimes administered twice by independent parties (e.g., defense counsel and the police), test–retest reliability is of considerable interest, but it has not been systematically investigated. Every examiner's CQT is unique. No two tests of the same person are likely to use the same questions paired, ordered, and repeated the same way, yet research to date has not addressed the degree to which these procedural variations might affect outcomes.

The single most important psychometric feature of the CQT concerns its validity. At present, its validity is indeterminate. Because of this, also unknown is how the CQT's validity may be affected by a host of potentially moderating factors, such as culture, personality, psychopathology, intelligence, fuzzy memory of the crime, being under the influence of a drug during the commission of a crime or during the administration of a CQT, the passage of time since the crime was committed, and so on.

The reliability and validity of the GKT, as it might be employed in forensic contexts, are also unknown. Most importantly, there is a dearth of research regarding how to construct a GKT so that it captures perpetrator memories. A number of hypotheses follow logically from the theory underlying the GKT. Not all crimes and criminals are likely to make good candidates for GKTs. Premeditated, carefully planned crimes are both more likely to yield good GKT items and recognition memory than impulsively committed crimes. Sex crimes are well suited for the development of GKTs because victims are likely to be able to provide detailed information about the crime that can be developed into test items. The degree to which perpetrators maintain specific crime-related memories with the passage of time is unknown. Criminals who commit multiple similar crimes may make poor candidates for the GKT because they may be unable to remember details that are specific to each instance of the crime they committed. Laboratory studies have begun to address some of these issues, but quality field research will be required to guide the development of the GKT for forensic applications.

MYTHS AND MISCONCEPTIONS

The CQT Is a Psychological Test

The CQT does not satisfy criteria psychologists have established for a psychological test (American Educational Research Association, 1999). It is not standardized; it is a collection of procedures that have in common only the inclusion of control and relevant questions. The number of these questions and their wording, order, and juxtaposition vary with the many CQT formats. Even examiners who are trained to use the same format are not capable of reproducing each other's CQT procedures. The CQT is best characterized as an interview that is assisted by psychophysiological recording. As such, it is not objective and has no norms. Because the computer software used to score CQTs is proprietary, the nature of the scoring algorithms has not been made available for review. The fact that these programs assign probabilities indicating the likelihood of deception is indefensible. Numerical scoring of CQT charts is based on arbitrary criteria that have not been systematically evaluated, and there is no generally accepted requirement that CQTs be formally scored using numerical or computerized systems.

The Polygraph Profession Is an Authoritative Source Regarding the Scientific Basis of the CQT

The training of polygraph examiners typically consists of less than one semester of coursework and practical experience completed at one of the 20 or so polygraph schools accredited by the American Polygraph Association. Training at nonaccredited schools is also possible, and only about half the states license examiners. Probably the most important qualification that most examiners possess is law enforcement experience; very few are trained as scientists. The American Polygraph Association is a trade organization that promotes and defends the use of polygraph tests. Because polygraphers are not scientists, *they are not qualified to critique the relevant science*. This is an important point because psychologists often defer to the expertise of other scientist professionals (e.g., physicians) regarding the basis of a test or its interpretation. Psychologists have a responsibility *not* to follow this practice as it pertains to the expertise of polygraph examiners and their test interpretations.

Because Government Law Enforcement Agencies Use Polygraphs, They Must Be Accurate

About two dozen federal government agencies administer tens of thousands of polygraph tests annually, and countless other tests are administered by state and local police departments. Why is this the case if polygraph tests have uncertain validity? The answer lies in the fact that few question the *utility* of these tests, especially as a tool to extract information from examinees. Examiners are skilled interrogators adept at using physiological data to convince suspects that it is to their advantage to explain away any doubts the examiner may have about the suspect's truthfulness. There is overwhelmingly anecdotal evidence that many suspects confess under the pressure of these interrogations (National Research Council, 2003). Police CQTs are typically administered in situations where case facts are ambiguous, the outcome perhaps turning on the credibility of a suspect, witness, or victim. If an examinee confesses under these circumstances, a case that might otherwise never have been prosecuted successfully is solved, leading to a conviction and the conservation of law enforcement resources that might be profitably applied in other cases.

Polygraphers Can Detect Countermeasures

Examiners routinely assert that the guilty cannot manipulate the outcome of a CQT. This assertion is based partly on experience they have with individuals who use clumsy methods to foil test outcomes, such as holding their breath or tensing muscles in an arm to which sensors are attached. Because examiners can easily spot these manipulations, they assume that countermeasures are ineffective. Of course, if a suspect successfully adopted countermeasures, their use would go undetected. Although no one knows how often this occurs, laboratory research has clearly shown that if "guilty" individuals augment their responses to control questions, most can produce truthful charts accepted as bona fide even by skilled examiners (Honts, Hodes, & Raskin, 1985; Honts, Raskin, & Kircher, 1994). Because effective countermeasures include mental exercises and light tongue biting when answering control questions, as research on countermeasures has illustrated (Honts et al., 1985, 1994), there is no practical way to detect them. Instructions regarding how to use these techniques can readily be accessed from the journal articles themselves, popular texts (Lykken, 1998), and the Internet (*antipolygraph.org*, *polygraph.com*). Truthful CQT verdicts can thus never be wholly trusted.

Laboratory Studies Provide a Legitimate Means of Estimating CQT Accuracy in Real-Life Applications

A great many laboratory studies have examined CQT outcomes for individuals (often university students) who are assigned to guilty or innocent conditions centered on whether they are asked to participate in a simulated crime. The advantage of laboratory studies is that ground truth can be firmly established. The disadvantage, recognized by many (National Research Council, 2003), is that subjects have little at stake, and the ethical constraints guiding research with human subjects make it unlikely that a laboratory study could ever duplicate the consequences surrounding failure of a real-life test (e.g., public humiliation or criminal incarceration). There is no reason to fear detection; the conflict and shame associated with lying or getting caught that are present in real life are absent in the lab. Guilty participants have little incentive (and no time) to learn about countermeasures, and innocent subjects are likely to be more aroused by privacy-invading control questions than relevant questions that involve something so inconsequential as an experimenter-directed phony crime. Laboratory investigations provide useful opportunities to explore many issues related to CQT applications (e.g., how easy it is for subjects to learn countermeasures), but they likely overestimate hit rates in real-life cases (National Research Council, 2003).

The GKT Is Not Suitable for Most Crimes

Although the GKT will never be applicable for all crimes, the same applies to other types of evidence such as fingerprints and DNA. A review of Federal Bureau of Investigation (FBI) case files concluded that the information they contained would not lend itself to the development of GKT items (Podlesny, Nimmich, & Budowle, 1995). A review of FBI files 100 years ago would yield the same information about DNA. However, once the evidentiary value of DNA was established, crime scene data were collected so as to ensure that available DNA evidence was preserved. There is no reason why crime scene investigators could not be trained to collect and preserve information suitable for developing GKT items as appropriate.

The Application of New Methodologies Will Lead to Breakthroughs in Applied Lie Detection

Although technological breakthroughs leading to new discoveries are always possible, it seems unlikely that a valid human lie detector will become available any time soon. Nevertheless, applications derived from new technologies are continually being introduced, fueled in part by the heightened importance national security has received since the 9/11 terrorist attacks. Technologies employed for this purpose include voice stress analysis (see the National Institute of Truth Verification webpage at *www.cvsa1.com*), thermal imaging (Pavlidis, Eberhardt, & Levine, 2002), transcranial magnetic stimulation (Lo, Fook-Chong, & Tan, 2003), and functional magnetic resonance imaging (fMRI) (Kozel et al., 2005; Langleben et al., 2002). The cited fMRI work has been used to launch two competing companies working to market this technology to detect lying (*www.cephoscorp.com*, *www.noliemri.com/index. htm*). However, none of the research evaluating these techniques has been able to overcome the methodological problems that have plagued nearly a century of lie detector research.

These problems derive from the fact that since there is no unique physiological signature associated with lying, these procedures are based on interrogation formats that approximate the CQT or GKT. As such, they essentially are replacing the autonomic nervous system measures used in polygraph tests with different sensors for recording human physiological responses. Some of these new methods may offer advantages over the conventional technology. For instance, thermal imaging can be used to measure blood flow to the face from a remote location without the target individual's knowledge. This technology could be used with passengers answering screening questions during their flight check-in at an airport. However, there would still be no way of knowing when observed change in blood flow was indexing a lie or merely emotional arousal triggered by the question for some other reason. Thus far, this work has been based on laboratory simulations, leaving unanswered how these methods would perform in the emotionally charged atmosphere accompanying real-life investigations. In addition, they have not examined the effectiveness of countermeasures. For many of these investigations, the simplest countermeasure would involve simply not following experimenter instructions because few of these studies include manipulation checks to determine if subjects remain true to procedural requirements.

CONCLUSIONS

Scientifically Supported Uses

There are as yet no scientifically supported uses of polygraph tests. As has been noted in detail elsewhere (Ben-Shakhar, Bar-Hillel, & Kremnitzer, 2002; Iacono & Lykken, 2006), the CQT does not meet *Daubert* or other standards for what constitutes admissible scientific evidence. In particular, there is no consensus in the scientific community that the CQT is accurate or based on sound scientific principles (the consensus is, in fact, the opposite; see Iacono & Lykken, 1997), the error rate is indeterminate, and there are no controlling standards for test administration or interpretation. Because the GKT has a firm scientific footing, a case can be made that it has evidentiary value when associated with a guilty verdict. Suppose a 10-question GKT was administered to a suspect who failed 8 of the 10 items, indicating guilty knowledge. Assuming that the questions were well constructed and the suspect could not explain the result (e.g., "OK, yes, I witnessed the crime, but I didn't commit it"), wouldn't this result provide compelling evidence of guilt? In fact, a survey of scientists who belong to the Society for Psychophysiological Research included a question like this and found that 72% agreed that it would be reasonable to conclude that the suspect possessed knowledge of the crime (Iacono & Lykken, 1997).

Scientifically Controversial Uses

No studies have been carried out to examine the efficacy of polygraph tests as investigative aids. As noted, anecdotal evidence indicates that skilled examiners have frequently resolved potentially unsolvable cases as a direct consequence of a confession obtained during the posttest phase of the examination. In the absence of corroborating evidence, there is no way to know for certain whether a polygraph-prompted confession is veridical, and there are occasional accounts of confessions that are likely to be false (Barthel, 1976). In addition, polygraph testing may help reduce the number of case suspects in a manner that could increase investigative efficiency, for instance, by not focusing resources on individuals who pass a CQT. However, as we found in our field study of police practices, investigators do not recognize the fallibility of polygraph tests; they generally accept failed polygraphs as pointing to the guilty party (Patrick & Iacono, 1991). Although potentially helpful to law enforcement, in the absence of scientific evidence supporting their effectiveness, these uses must be balanced against the civil liberties of those undergoing these procedures.

Polygraph testing is perhaps most controversial when it is used as the ultimate arbiter of truthfulness. This occurs any time an individual's disposition is decided largely by the results of a polygraph test. Stipulated CQTs fall into this category. Typically, stipulated tests are offered to defendants in cases where the evidence against them is questionable. If the test is passed, charges are likely to be dropped. If failed, the defendant agrees, in advance of the test results becoming known, to proceed to trial with the knowledge that the jury will learn of the outcome. Under the circumstances, the failed polygraph is likely to weigh heavily in a jury's verdict.

A more common controversial use arises in sex offender treatment. Many states are making polygraph testing a condition for treatment. CQTs are administered to ensure that sex offenders have honestly completed offense history questionnaires, complied with rules regarding their sexual behavior during treatment, and have not reoffended during parole or probation. The CQT is seen as a therapeutic tool because under the pressure of polygraph testing, many offenders admit to previously unknown sexual deviations, fantasies, and victims (Grubin, Madsen, Parsons, Sosnowski, & Warberg, 2004). However, problems arise when in order to progress in treatment or to be released from a correctional facility, the offender must pass a polygraph test. This problem is compounded by the widely held belief that sex offenders are almost always hiding some of their sexual misdeeds, a view that is likely to be pervasive among polygraph examiners. In Abrams's *The Complete Polygraph Handbook* (1989), a textbook for the training of examiners, the author warns: "In no case should the subject be allowed to leave [an examination] believing that he has beaten the test" (p. 177). Ironically, this admonition derives from the fact that in order to pass a CQT, the offender is believed to be lying to control questions that typically tap sex themes (e.g., Have you ever committed a sex act you were ashamed of?"). The problem, Abrams notes, is that if the offender "passes the test, it also implies to him that he has been truthful on the control questions, which he has almost definitely responded to deceptively" (p. 176).

COMMUNICATING CONSENSUS AND CONTROVERSIES

The polygraph field is highly polarized. On one side are the many thousands of polygraph operators (the American Polygraph Association lists 3,200 members) gainfully employed in a profession that is undergoing considerable growth. On the other side is a handful of scientists who have carefully reviewed the extant literature and concluded that polygraph testing has no scientific basis. Other than the fact that both of these groups concur that polygraph testing has utility, there is little else on which they agree. This lack of consensus is perhaps most clearly evident in a series of chapters authored by scientists on both sides of this issue: There is a complete lack of consensus, including no agreement on what studies are appropriate to evaluate or how to interpret their findings (Honts, Raskin, & Kircher, 2002; Iacono & Lykken, 2002). That said, it is nevertheless clear that scientists outside of the polygraph profession have consistently and repeatedly reviewed the extant literature and found no basis for the claims of practitioners. Conveying this message to the public has been difficult because few psychologists are familiar with this literature. In addition, there are many proponents of polygraph testing, including the American Polygraph Association and the Department of Defense Academy for Credibility Assessment (until recently, known as the Department of Defense Polygraph Institute), representing thousands of practitioners who vigorously defend polygraph applications. For psychological scientists to better inform the legal community and policy decision makers about the limitations of polygraph testing, they need to become more knowledgeable about the subject matter. This process would be greatly assisted if major psychological societies, such as the Association for Psychological Science or the American Psychological Association, adopted positions on the scientific basis of polygraph testing and provided relevant information to their members through their publications and conferences.

REFERENCES

Abrams, S. (1989). *The complete polygraph handbook*. Lexington, MA: Lexington Books.

American Educational Research Association. (1999). *Standards for educational and psychological testing*. Washington, DC: American Educational Research Association.

Barthel, J. (1976). *A death in Canaan*. New York: Dutton.

Ben-Shakhar, G. (2002). A critical review of the control questions test (CQT). In M. Kleiner (Ed.), *Handbook of polygraph testing* (pp. 103–126). San Diego, CA: Academic Press.

Ben-Shakhar, G., Bar-Hillel, M., & Kremnitzer, M. (2002). Trial by polygraph: Reconsidering the use of the guilty knowledge technique in court. *Law and Human Behavior, 26*, 527–541.

Ben-Shakhar, G., & Elaad, E. (2003). The validity of psychophysiological detection of information with the guilty knowledge test: A meta-analytic review. *Journal of Applied Psychology, 88*, 131–151.

Fiedler, K., Schmod, J., & Stahl, T. (2002). What is the current truth about polygraph lie detection? *Basic and Applied Social Psychology, 24*, 313–324.

Forensic Research Incorporated. (1997). The validity and reliability of polygraph testing. *Polygraph, 26*, 215–239.

Furedy, J. J. (1996). The North American polygraph and psychophysiology: Disinterested, uninterested, and interested perspectives. *International Journal of Psychophysiology, 21*, 97–105.

Grubin, D., Madsen, L., Parsons, S., Sosnowski, D., & Warberg, B. (2004). A prospective study of the impact of polygraphy on high-risk behaviors in adult sex offenders. *Sex Abuse, 16*, 209–222.

Honts, C. R., Hodes, R. L., & Raskin, D. C. (1985). Effects of physical countermeasures on the physiological detection of deception. *Journal of Applied Psychology, 70*, 177–187.

Honts, C. R., Raskin, D., & Kircher, J. (1994). Mental and physical countermeasures reduce the accuracy of polygraph tests. *Journal of Applied Psychology, 79,* 252–259.

Honts, C. R., Raskin, D., & Kircher, J. (2002). The scientific status of research on polygraph techniques: The case for polygraph tests. In D. L. Faigman, D. H. Kaye, M. J. Saks, & J. Sanders (Eds.), *Modern scientific evidence: The law and science of expert testimony* (Vol. 2, pp. 446–483). St. Paul, MN: West.

Horowitz, S. W., Kircher, J. C., Honts, C. R., & Raskin, D. C. (1997). The role of comparison questions in physiological detection of deception. *Psychophysiology, 34,* 108–115.

Iacono, W. G. (1985). Guilty knowledge. *Society, 22,* 52–54.

Iacono, W. G. (1991). Can we determine the accuracy of polygraph tests? In J. R. Jennings, P. K. Ackles, & M. G. H. Coles (Eds.), *Advances in psychophysiology* (pp. 201–207). London: Jessica Kingsley.

Iacono, W. G. (2007). Detection of deception. In J. Cacioppo, L. Tassinary, & G. Berntson (Eds.), *Handbook of psychophysiology* (3rd ed., pp. 688–703). New York: Cambridge University Press.

Iacono, W. G. (2008). Effective policing: Understanding how polygraph tests work and are used. *Criminal Justice and Behavior, 35,* 1295–1308.

Iacono, W. G., Boisvenu, G. A., & Fleming, J. A. (1984). The effects of diazepam and methylphenidate on the electrodermal detection of guilty knowledge. *Journal of Applied Psychology, 69,* 289–299.

Iacono, W. G., & Lykken, D. T. (1997). The validity of the lie detector: Two surveys of scientific opinion. *Journal of Applied Psychology, 82,* 426–433.

Iacono, W. G., & Lykken, D. T. (2002). The scientific status of research on polygraph techniques: The case against polygraph tests. In D. L. Faigman, D. H. Kaye, M. J. Saks, & J. Sanders (Eds.), *Modern scientific evidence: The law and science of expert testimony* (Vol. 2, pp. 483–538). St. Paul, MN: West.

Iacono, W. G., & Lykken, D. T. (2005). The case against polygraph tests. In D. L. Faigman, D. H. Kaye, M. J. Saks, & J. Sanders (Eds.), *Modern scientific evidence: The law and science of expert testimony: Vol. 4. Forensics* (pp. 605–655). Eagan, MN: West.

Iacono, W. G., & Lykken, D. T. (2006). The case against polygraph tests. In D. L. Faigman, D. H. Kaye, M. J. Saks, J. Sanders, & E. K. Cheng (Eds.), *Modern scientific evidence: The law and science of expert testimony: Vol. 4. Forensics* (pp. 831–895). Eagan, MN: Thomson West.

Iacono, W. G., & Patrick, C. J. (2006). Polygraph ("lie detector") testing: Current status and emerging trends. In I. B. Weiner & A. K. Hess (Eds.), *The handbook of forensic psychology* (pp. 552–588). Hoboken, NJ: Wiley.

Kozel, F. A., Johnson, K. A., Mu, Q., Grenesko, E. L., Laken, S. J., & George, M. S. (2005). Detecting deception using functional magnetic resonance imaging. *Biological Psychiatry, 58,* 605–613.

Langleben, D. D., Schroeder, L., Maldjian, J. A., Gur, R. C., McDonald, S., Ragland, J. D., et al. (2002). Brain activity during simulated deception: An event-related functional magnetic resonance study. *NeuroImage, 15*, 727–732.

Lo, Y. L., Fook-Chong, S., & Tan, E. K. (2003). Increased cortical excitability in human deception. *Neuroreport, 14*, 1021–1024.

Lykken, D. T. (1959). The GSR in the detection of guilt. *Journal of Applied Psychology, 43*, 385–388.

Lykken, D. T. (1960). The validity of the guilty knowledge technique: The effects of faking. *Journal of Applied Psychology, 44*, 258–262.

Lykken, D. T. (1998). *A tremor in the blood: Uses and abuses of the lie detector* (2nd ed.). New York: Plenum Press.

National Research Council. (2003). *The polygraph and lie detection.* Washington, DC: National Academies Press.

Oksol, E. M., & O'Donohue, W. T. (2003). A critical analysis of the polygraph. In W. T. O'Donohue & E. R. Levensky (Eds.), *Handbook of forensic psychology: Resource for mental health and legal professionals* (pp. 602–631). San Diego, CA: Academic Press.

Patrick, C. J., & Iacono, W. G. (1991). Validity of the control question polygraph test: The problem of sampling bias. *Journal of Applied Psychology, 76*, 229–238.

Pavlidis, I., Eberhardt, N. L., & Levine, J. A. (2002). Seeing through the face of deception: Thermal imaging offers a promising hands-off approach to mass security screening. *Nature, 415*, 35.

Podlesny, J. A., Nimmich, K. W., & Budowle, B. (1995). *A lack of case facts restricts applicability of the guilty knowledge deception detection method in FBI criminal investigations.* Quantico, VA: FBI Forensic Research and Training Center.

Raskin, D. C., & Honts, C. R. (2002). The comparison question test. In M. Kleiner (Ed.), *Handbook of polygraph testing* (pp. 1–47). San Diego, CA: Academic Press.

PART IV

FORENSIC EVALUATION OF PSYCHOLEGAL ISSUES

Criminal Profiling

FACTS, FICTIONS, AND COURTROOM ADMISSIBILITY

Richard N. Kocsis

CRIMINAL PROFILING: DEFINING THE CONTROVERSY

Criminal profiling is a forensic behavioral technique that has traditionally been used to assist police investigations. At its most basic level, it represents "a process whereby behaviors and/or actions exhibited in a crime are assessed and interpreted to form predictions concerning the characteristics of the probable perpetrator(s) of the crime" (Kocsis, 2006, p. 2). The amalgamation of the various predicted characteristics is commonly referred to as a criminal profile and can be used as a guiding mechanism for investigative inquiries (Douglas & Burgess, 1986; Holmes & Holmes, 1996). Various derivations of this original concept also exist, such as the behavioral assessment of different crimes to determine whether they were committed by the same perpetrator(s) (e.g., Woodhams, Bull, & Hollin, 2007), and the evaluation of offense spatial locations (e.g., Rossmo, 2000). Much like the various schools of thought within the discipline of psychology that endeavor to explain human personality (e.g., Monte, 1995), there now exists a range of rivaling methodological approaches or schools of thought concerning the construction of criminal profiles (see Palermo & Kocsis, 2005).

It is important to recognize and differentiate the technique of criminal profiling in the context of the present chapter from a number of other techniques that share conceptually similar nomenclature. Criminal profiling should not be confused with the similarly titled concept of "actuarial profiling" (aka racial profiling) that develops aggregated templates of "typical" offenders (see Harcourt, 2007). Similarly, although emanating from a disciplinary base in forensic psychology, concepts such as "psychological profiles" or "threat assessment"—gauging the severity and likely manifestation of threats—are also distinctly different techniques that are not encompassed by the term "criminal profiling" or the source of discussion of this chapter.

Despite an apparent growth in the use of criminal profiling by law enforcement agencies over approximately the past three decades, the technique remains encumbered with one overarching controversy as to its fundamental validity (Kocsis, 2007). That is, can suitable expert "profilers" accurately predict the characteristics of an unknown offender based on behavior patterns exhibited in a crime? The following discussion examines the currently available evidence relevant to the validity (typically construed as the "accuracy") (Anastasi, 1976) of criminal profiling and then considers its admissibility as evidence in legal proceedings.

SCIENCE RELEVANT TO THE CONTROVERSY

Claims, Testimonials, and Consumer Satisfaction

Possibly the earliest known document concerning the accuracy of criminal profiling is an internal report assessing the profiling services of the Federal Bureau of Investigation's (FBI) Behavioral Science Unit (Institutional Research and Development Unit, 1981). Although not currently available to the public, the report appears to be the source of a claim that profiles composed by members of the FBI Behavioral Science Unit contain an approximate 80% degree of accuracy (Pinizzotto, 1984; Rossmo, 2000; State v. Stevens, 2001). Unfortunately, the rigor of this statistic does not appear to be the subject of independent scrutiny. Consequently, while appealing, this statistic should be regarded as a currently unverifiable claim.

Besides this report, arguably the most prolific source of evidence attesting to the accuracy of criminal profiles comes in the form of "anecdotal testimonials": Profiles have been provided and then subsequently described as accurate when considered in reference to an apprehended offender. A large proportion of these testimonials are found in semiautobiographical works published in the true crime genre (e.g., Britton, 1997; Canter, 1994; Douglas & Olshaker, 1995; Hazelwood & Michaud, 2001; McCrary & Ramsland, 2003; Ressler & Shachtman, 1992; Vorpagel & Harrington, 1998). Although these accounts certainly provide qualitatively rich illustrations of profiling, their merits in the context of scientifically robust evidence for establishing the validity of profiling must be treated with caution. Given that such accounts are often authored by either current or retired profilers, their objectivity requires judicious evaluation.

Another pertinent body of material that has examined criminal profiles is what can loosely be described as "consumer satisfaction surveys." These are typically studies that have endeavored to gauge the use and/or perceived satisfaction derived from criminal profiles (e.g., Copson, 1995; Jackson, van Koppen, & Herbrink, 1993; Pinizzotto, 1984; Trager & Brewster, 2001). The general consensus among such studies is that policing agencies are often receptive and seem to derive some sense of benefit from the use of criminal profiles. Beyond this favorable, albeit nebulous, conception of criminal profiles, however, ascertaining precisely how they are beneficial is a less conclusive matter. For example, in a survey of police agencies that had utilized profiles provided by the FBI Behavioral Science Unit, Pinnizzotto (1984) found that 77% of respondents reported a profile as useful in helping to focus the investigation in some capacity. Only 17%, however, regarded the profile as actually assisting with the identification of the offender. In another survey of police agencies, Trager and Brewster (2001) found that 63% of respondents had used criminal profiles to assist with their investigations, but only 38% reported that they assisted with the identification of a suspect, and 25% indicated that the profile had hindered their investigation in some capacity.

It should be apparent that these surveys serve to describe the perceived satisfaction and thus perhaps utility of profiles. This circumstance most likely accounts for the continued use of profiles among policing agencies as an investigative tool. However, a state of affairs appears to have developed whereby evidence regarding satisfaction and the use of profiles is juxtaposed to suggest accuracy and ergo validity (e.g., Jeffers, 1992; *State v. Stevens*, 2001; U.S. House of Representatives, 1990).

The Illusions of Accuracy

While the aforementioned consumer satisfaction surveys serve to illustrate that policing agencies hold a generally favorable view toward the use of criminal profiles, it is crucial not to confuse this positive response with the validity (i.e., accuracy) of the profile itself. That is, satisfaction with a technique does not necessarily equate with proof of its accuracy (Kocsis &

Palermo, 2007). This point is particularly relevant, first, in light of attempts to argue such connections, and second, in light of a series of studies highlighting the unreliability of anecdotal perceptions of criminal profiles.

For example, Alison, Smith, Eastman, and Rainbow (2003) examined the predictions contained in a sample of criminal profiles and found that 24% of the statements were ambiguous and open to subjective interpretation, with 55% of the predictions difficult to ever ascertain objectively. Another study by Alison, Smith, and Morgan (2003) provided two groups with criminal profiles, which they were asked to evaluate in terms of perceived accuracy. One profile was genuine while the other was nongenuine but designed to appear plausible. Despite distinct variations between the genuine and nongenuine profile, they were both rated as exhibiting approximately equal degrees of accuracy.

Even more troubling have been the findings of three recent studies exploring potential bias and belief factors that may influence an individual's perception of the accuracy of a profile. As previously mentioned, some argument has been advanced to suggest that the continued use of profiles can be inferred to be evidence of their validity (e.g., Jeffers, 1992; *State v. Stevens*, 2001; U.S. House of Representatives, 1990). This proposition has been described previously as the "operational utilitarian" argument (Kocsis, 2006). The logic underpinning this argument is that if profiles were not accurate and thus of no use, then investigators would not continue to use them. The fact that requests for profiles continue is construed as evidence (albeit indirect) in support of the accuracy and thus validity of profiles. In effect, therefore, the operational utilitarian argument is a manifestation of the old adage, "The proof is in the pudding."

Although intuitively appealing, the premise of the operational utilitarian argument is dependent upon one pivotal assumption: namely, that perceptions of criminal profiles, which sponsor their continued use, are indeed reliable and thus not subject to bias and/or extraneous influences. To test this issue, Kocsis and Hayes (2004) examined whether variations on the labeled author of a criminal profile had any influence on the perceptions of its accuracy. This study found that profiles were perceived to be more accurate when simply labeled as being written by a "professional profiler" as opposed to when the same material was presented under an anonymous author label. In two subsequent studies, Kocsis and Heller (2004) and Kocsis and Middledorp (2004) examined whether individuals' beliefs in criminal profiling had any impact on their perceptions of a criminal profile. These studies found an incremental relationship between belief in profiling and perceptions of the accuracy of a criminal profile. Simply put, the more an individual believes (or is induced to believe) in the merits of profiling, the more accurate the predictions within a criminal profile are likely to appear.

These studies suggest some troubling issues. First, they highlight the ambiguous nature of criminal profiles, and more importantly, the dubious nature of anecdotal perceptions regarding the accuracy of criminal profiles. These studies also challenge the validity of the operational utilitarian argument and raise the possibility of the practice and use of criminal profiling being trapped in an illusionary cycle. That is, favorable public media representations of profiling may have elevated levels of belief in the technique, which raise expectations and perceptions concerning profiling accuracy. These elevated perceptions, in turn, sponsor the continued use of profiles and serve to promote and further elevate beliefs in profiles—and thus the cycle continues. These studies collectively highlight the need for the validity of criminal profiling to be grounded in scientifically based research incorporating direct empirical measures.

Direct Tests of Profiler Accuracy

What is arguably the first piece of publicly available empirical research to impartially and directly test the abilities of profilers in relation to the accuracy of profiles constructed by them occurred in a subcomponent of a larger study conducted by Pinizzotto and Finkel (1990). This study collected small samples (4–6 participants) of various skill-based participants, including police detectives, psychologists, students and, of course, trained profilers. Each of these groups was then presented with a case file involving a murder and a rape. The participants were asked to predict (i.e., profile) the characteristics of the probable offender of each of these crimes via a multiple-choice questionnaire that itemized and thus quantified predictable characteristics. Both of the cases used in this experiment had been previously solved, with the respective offender apprehended and convicted. Accordingly, the identity of the offender was known (i.e., model answers), and thus the responses from the various participants could be objectively scored for accuracy. Accuracy was measured in terms of participants' overall score in providing correct responses (i.e., predicting the correct attribute) on the various items of the multiple-choice questionnaire.

The findings of this experiment were somewhat mixed. The profilers demonstrated some comparative superiority in accurately profiling the offender characteristics in the rape case, with the detectives being the second-most proficient group, followed by the psychologists, and lastly the students. However, this superiority in accurately profiling offender characteristics was not similarly observed in the murder case. Rather, the profilers demonstrated the lowest mean score, with the detectives achieving the highest level of accuracy, followed by the psychologists and then the students (Pinizzotto & Finkel, 1990).

Subsequent to Pinizzotto and Finkel (1990), a series of studies by Kocsis (2004, 2007; Kocsis, Hayes, & Irwin, 2002; Kocsis, Irwin, Hayes, & Nunn, 2000; Kocsis, Middledorp, & Karpin, 2008) used a similar quasi-experimental design to test the capabilities of profilers via the use of cases that also required predicting offender characteristics on a multiple-choice questionnaire. Once again, as the cases used in these experiments had been previously solved and the characteristics of the offender(s) known, the responses to the questionnaire by the various participants could be objectively scored for accuracy and compared. Akin to the study by Pinizzotto and Finkel, accuracy was tabulated as participants' correct responses to the various items on the multiple-choice questionnaire.

Beyond simply gauging the general accuracy of the profiles, however, these studies also included a number of additional methodological features. First, specific examination of the inherent skills that may account for proficient (i.e., accurate) profiling was undertaken. Previously, authors such as Hazelwood, Ressler, Depue, and Douglas (1995) had nominated a number of attributes that, although not empirically tested, were believed to be integral to effective profiling. Some of these included intuition, an understanding of human behavior, and a capacity for logical/objective reasoning. The quintessential attribute nominated by Hazelwood and colleagues, however, was experience in the investigation of crime. In the context of the aforementioned studies, these attributes were tested by assembling groups of participants (alongside profilers) who possessed each of these respective skills. To assess the input of investigative experience, groups of police officers with varying degrees of investigative experience were tested. Similarly, to garner some impression of the value in possessing an understanding of human behavior and psychological knowledge, trained psychologists were tested. Finally, as a simple measure of what might be accomplished through logical and objective reasoning, samples of science students were similarly tested.

A second key methodological feature to the studies by Kocsis and colleagues was to incorporate control mechanisms that would measure and thus account for what could be predicted simply through chance and/or guessing at the attributes of the possible offender. This was accomplished by the inclusion of various "control" participants in the experiments, who were presented with only the multiple-choice questionnaire without any of the case information and then asked to respond to the questionnaire by simply guessing at what they believed were the attributes of the typical offender.

A number of interesting findings emerged from these studies. Foremost among them was empirically based evidence of the sampled expert profilers' abilities to surpass the other tested groups (including the control condition) in terms of their overall accuracy scores in predicting the characteristics of the unknown offenders (Kocsis, 2006). Although this finding may seem to simply reinforce previously held views concerning the value of profiling, it is important to appreciate, especially in light of the material previously discussed, that such views had not been sufficiently demonstrated in scientifically vetted research.

Unfortunately, while providing some tentative support for the validity of criminal profiling, a number of caveats need also be noted. First, although the profilers demonstrated a comparatively superior degree of proficiency in accurately predicting offender characteristics, they also demonstrated the highest degree of statistical variance. This finding suggests that not all individuals who identify themselves as a "profiler" are likely to demonstrate a comparatively similar degree of proficiency. Second, despite the research conducted by Kocsis and colleagues spanning close to a decade, these studies have thus far only managed to test a modest number of profilers. Consequently, further replication and testing of profilers is clearly warranted in the future.

Perhaps the most surprising finding to emerge from these studies, however, concerns the constituent attributes that may be aligned to proficient profiling. In contrast to the view of Hazelwood and colleagues (1995), little evidence could be found to support the notion that experience in the investigation of crimes plays an integral role in the construction of an accurate profile. Instead, the two skill bases that were found to be most closely aligned with proficient profiling was an understanding of human behavior and, most notably, an ability to critically evaluate case material in a logical and objective manner (Kocsis, 2006).

In conclusion, some tentative empirical evidence has emerged to lend support to the concept that expert profilers can demonstrate a comparatively superior degree of accuracy in predicting the characteristics of an unknown offender, based on the behaviors exhibited in a crime. It is important to note however, that this evidence in support of the validity of criminal profiling does not quantify the degree of accuracy profilers are typically capable of demonstrating. Thus, this evidence should be interpreted only as indicating that some suitably skilled individuals tend to be more accurate in comparison to various other groups that have thus far been tested.

GAPS IN OUR KNOWLEDGE

Despite the promising evidence that has begun to emerge about the capabilities of expert profilers in accurately predicting characteristics of an unknown offender, there nonetheless exists a number of frustrating gaps in the scientific knowledge about the technique. Possibly the most pronounced is the absence of clear data on error rates concerning the predictions of criminal profiles. It is important to recognize that the aforementioned studies have thus far utilized quasi-experimental designs that have assessed accuracy only in the context of comparative tests of performance between various groups. However, reliable empirical research to measure the accuracy of expert profilers in terms of quantifiable error rates has yet to emerge. This circumstance is not evidently due to a lack of desire. Rather, the development of such error rates appears to be hampered by a number of problems pertaining to a range of methodological issues, such as precisely what can be uniformly conceived as a criminal profile and what constitutes accuracy beyond the structured confines of quasi-experimental studies (see Kocsis et al., 2008).

Similarly, although there appear to be several different ideological schools of thought influencing the task of constructing criminal profiles, robust scientific evidence testing the comparative merits of these differing approaches has yet to be undertaken (Kocsis et al., 2008). Unfortunately, an answer to this gap in our understanding is unlikely to eventuate any time in the near future, as clear dissension has evolved between proponents of rivaling approaches (e.g., see Kocsis & Palermo, 2007). The basis for these differences among proponents is, in many respects, analogous to the long-standing debate in psychological discourse concerning the reliability of clinical versus statistical/actuarial prediction (e.g., Garb, 1998; Meehl, 1954).

Surprising gaps in current knowledge can be found even in seemingly elementary issues concerning an individual's expertise and/or training to engage in profiling. Although clearly a derivative of the disciplinary knowledge base of forensic psychology (Kocsis, 2006), the practice of profiling is not subject to any regulation concerning who is professionally equipped or formally approved to engage in the technique. Accordingly, the qualifications and skills of "profilers" often vary dramatically. As a consequence, empirically grounded answers to seemingly simple questions regarding whether more experienced profilers do indeed perform better than less experienced profilers are frustratingly confounded and thus remain unknown. Intuitive reasoning would suggest that experience in seemingly similar tasks would result in a greater degree of proficiency and thus some comparative relationship with more experience in profiling. However, as previously canvassed in empirical tests of profilers' capabilities, a number of antithetical findings have emerged; profilers demonstrate high degrees of statistical variance in their abilities, and vocationally skill-based groups who are nominated as integral to proficient profiling such as police detectives demonstrate surprisingly poor proficiency in profiling crimes (Kocsis, 2006).

MYTHS AND MISCONCEPTIONS

As it should be apparent from the discussion, a number of myths and misconceptions surround the topic of criminal profiling—many of which seem to be either sponsored and/or perpetuated by fictional media depictions of the technique. What is possibly the greatest misconception surrounding criminal profiling is not a fundamental absence, but rather an overestimation, of the scientific basis that has been reliably developed thus far in support of criminal profiling. There exists a growing corpus of scientific literature examining the coherent patterns offenders demonstrate during the commission of violent crimes and how these patterns are reflective of common offender characteristics (Palermo & Kocsis, 2005).

As previously discussed, some modest findings are emerging to empirically demonstrate the superior predictive capabilities of suitable experts in comparison to those of other individuals. Prior to these findings something of a veritable folklore had developed around criminal profiles as being 80% accurate (Kocsis, 2006). As already mentioned while certainly tantalizing, the origin of this statistic comes from an internal report that thus far does not appear available for independent scrutiny.

Another commonly held belief concerning criminal profiling and what the scientific evidence has thus far revealed relates to the inherent skills for profiling. The concept of criminal profiling is popularly viewed as a form of specialized investigative knowledge enhanced by extensive experience in criminal investigation. Once again, the empirical evidence thus far appears to suggest that the attributes inherently aligned to the proficient (i.e., accurate) construction of a criminal profile are most likely based in a fundamental appreciation of human behavior and a capacity for logical and objective reasoning to critically evaluate the crime.

Finally, within the context of operational criminal investigations there is a perception that profiling is a virtual panacea for the investigation of all manner of crimes when in practice it is a specialized technique better suited to the investigation of more perplexing crimes where standard investigative procedures have stalled (Kocsis, 2006). Moreover, there still does not exist clear evidence that the use of criminal profiling does indeed effectively assist in the resolution of crimes (Farrington, 2007). That is, various consumer satisfaction surveys of police personnel typically report a generally favorable attitude toward the value of criminal profiles in criminal investigations. Similarly, numerous anecdotal case examples exist where, in retrospect, some remarkable congruities appear evident between the predictions contained in a given criminal profile and the apparent characteristics of offenders following their arrest. However, what has thus far remained largely absent has been any compelling evidence demonstrating that the input of criminal profiles directly and tangibly leads investigators to identify and apprehend the criminal perpetrator (Kocsis, 2007).

THE LEGAL ADMISSIBILITY OF CRIMINAL PROFILING

One issue that has also gained momentum in the profiling arena is the admissibility of criminal profiles and/or the testimony of profilers in some capacity as expert evidence witnesses in court proceedings. Before critiquing the legal merits of this notion, it is perhaps worthwhile to consider why this circumstance has arisen. The original concept of criminal profiling was to aid investigators of crimes that were typically of an aberrant, violent nature and resistant to resolution via conventional investigative methods (Fisher, 1993; Kocsis, 2006; Rossi, 1982; Vorpagel, 1982). In such a context, and as Ormerod and Sturman (2005) have observed, there are typically "no rigid legal rules" on what resources investigators may employ, with the exception that they "comply with statutory and common-law rules relating to processes of search, arrest and interviewing etc., and the rules relating to the collection and disclosure of material gathered" (p. 171). Accordingly, in the investigative sphere, the use of criminal profiles/profilers is certainly justifiable if investigators view them as being of some assistance and provided that their use does not contravene the aforementioned legal confines. However, as has been poignantly noted, "The use of psychological [criminal] profiling as an aid to police investigations is one thing, but its use as a means of proof in court is another" (R. v. Guilfoyle, 2001, p. 68).

In light of the original purpose of profiling, it is therefore something of a mystery as to how and why the technique and testimony of profilers have gradually found their way into the courtroom and proffered as evidence, given the inherently probabilistic nature of profiling and its modest scientific foundation (Kocsis, 2006). What is prompting attempts to use profiles and/or profilers in legal proceedings is unclear and open to speculation. Unquestionably, the topic of criminal profiling is one that enjoys considerable popularity in the public media (Herndon, 2007). This popularity may encourage interested individuals to pursue careers in this field. Attempts to introduce profiling into trial proceedings may be a result of market forces: namely, a surplus of profilers and a deficit of investigative contexts in which such services can be applied. Coupled with these market forces could also be an element of excessive confidence in the capabilities of the technique. Indeed, one member of the Australian judiciary has ruefully noted, in regard to evidence of an expert nature generally, that

> [the] courts must exercise constant vigilance to ensure that they are not unwittingly misled. Amongst the many factors which may lead an expert witness into error is a malady which, if encountered in a new car salesperson, might be described as gross product enthusiasm. Some witnesses seem to become so fervid about the potential of their chosen discipline that they lose sight of its limitations and are borne by their enthusiasm into making claims that could not be supported by more sober and objective assessment of the available evidence. (*R. v. Hillier*, 2003, p. 10)

Irrespective of the factors spawning the use of criminal profiles in legal proceedings, the response of the judiciary to such evidence has thus far been one that can be described euphemistically as disinclination (Freckelton & Selby, 2005). Cases where such evidence has been presented have, akin to some foreign jurisdictions such as the United Kingdom and Australia, been disallowed from the outset (e.g., *R. v. Guilfoyle*, 2001; *R. v. Hillier*, 2003; *R. v. Stagg*, 1994; *State v. Stevens*, 2001). Conversely, something of a checkered pattern has emerged in the United States whereby evidence has been accepted at first instance by lower courts but then subsequently disallowed on appeal (*R. v. Guilfoyle*, 2001). Perhaps in light of this generally unfavorable reception by the bench, a shift in approach appears to have transpired whereby techniques that are arguably derivations or variations are instead being submitted. Examples of these techniques include the comparative analysis of, and the linking of behavioral patterns in, different crimes (referred to as linkage analysis), or the limited assessment and interpretation of crime patterns and/or their authenticity (respectively referred to as crime scene analysis and staging; Douglas, Burgess, Burgess, & Ressler, 2006). Efforts to admit these techniques, which endeavor to avoid making inferences about the probable offender associated with the behavioral analysis, appear to have received a mixed reception by differing U.S. courts (e.g., *Commonwealth v. DiStefano*, 2001; *State v. Fortin*, 2000, 2004; *State v. Stevens*, 2001).

In light of the standards governing the legal admissibility of evidence (e.g., *Daubert v. Merrell Dow Pharmaceuticals, Inc.,* 1993; Federal Rules of Evidence, 2004; *Frye v. United States*, 1923; *General Electric Co. v. Joiner*, 1997; *Kumho Tire Ltd. v. Carmichael*, 1999), there are numerous hurdles confronting criminal profiling. These hurdles are not lessened when the technique is solely considered in the original context of the *"general acceptance"* paradigm established by *Frye* in 1923. For example, while profiling appears to enjoy a generally favorable reputation within the law enforcement community, its reception among mental health practitioners (arguably more analogous to the conceptualized "scientific" community) is not as encouraging. In a survey of police psychologists, Bartol (1996, p. 79) found that 70% of respondents "seriously questioned its [criminal profiling] validity and usefulness. This skepticism was especially pronounced for the in-house psychologist (78%)." This trepidation with profiling appears to be undiminished in a subsequent survey of forensic mental health professionals undertaken by Torres, Boccaccini, and Miller (2006), who similarly found that fewer than 25% of respondents believed that profiling was scientifically valid. Another interesting finding that emerged from this study was that a simple title change from "profiling" to "criminal investigative analysis" increased the perceived validity of the technique, thereby suggesting that "profiling is likely to be viewed more favorably if it is referred to by another name" (Torres et al., p. 56). This is a particularly illuminating discovery, given that attempts to present derivations of profiling in court proceedings (e.g., linkage/crime scene analysis) have attracted criticism to the effect that such techniques are analogous to "a different suit on the same animal" or "a distinction without a difference" (Grezlak, 1999, p. 2).

Beyond even the concept of general acceptance, the principles espoused in *Daubert* (1993) have also raised questions about the evidentiary value of criminal profiling. An increasing amount of theoretical literature on profiling is emerging, which has been subjected to the peer-review process. Similarly, a growing body of testable theory is also emerging with the potential development of quantifiable error rates (e.g., Woodhams et al., 2007). Whether these error rates are, or will be, determined to be sufficiently acceptable for the domain of legal evidence remains to be seen. In some instances, where derivative techniques such as crime scene and linkage analysis have been used, there seems to be tentative acceptance among a number of foreign jurisdictions (e.g., Labuschangne, 2006; *R. v. Clark*, 2004; *R. v. Ranger*, 2003).

However, what is most likely the greatest hurdle, if not an insurmountable barrier, is the probabilistic nature of profiling; courts must decide whether the probative value of profiling testimony is outweighed by its prejudicial impact (Davis & Follette, 2002; Kirkpatrick, 1998). The determinations of criminal courts predominantly operate on the evaluation of relevant factual evidence pertinent to the specific matter under consideration. The dilemma for the testimony of criminal profilers is that they are not capable of being sufficiently specific in attesting that their predictions relate to a particular individual under suspicion for a crime. Momentarily setting aside all issues concerning accuracy/validity, criminal profiles can only attest to an accused party's possession of characteristics that may be matched to the *probable* perpetrator of the crime. They cannot unequivocally attest that because the accused possesses matching characteristics with their profile that he or she is indeed the guilty party. Accordingly, profiles have been viewed as "evidence intended to address guilt by likening a defendant to a profile or stereotype of those likely to commit the crime in question," and as some commentators have observed, this practice "has great potential for introducing bias and error" (Davis & Follette, 2002, p. 152). For this reason the U.S. judiciary has, thus far, disallowed such evidence as it is "mindful that an opinion couched in terms of probabilities and/or possibilities is to be excluded as lacking the requisite certainty to be admissible" (Grezlak, 1999, p. 2). Furthermore, the use of such evidence to suggest the guilt of an accused has the potential to encourage juries to "decide the facts based on typical, and not the actual facts" (*State v. Thomas*, 1981, p. 521).

As a final note, a recent study by Paclebar, Myers, and Brineman (2007) explored the influence criminal profilers had on mock juror decision making. This study involved the presentation of a fictional murder trial to participants (i.e., mock jurors), who were asked to evaluate various aspects of evidence, including an accurate and deliberately inaccurate profile. The study found that the testimony from an accurate profiler was equally as influential as the testimony from an inaccurate profiler. This finding suggests that profile evidence is likely to be confusing and may therefore have a prejudicial impact upon juror decision making, as the jurors appeared to be unable to give such evidence an appropriate degree of probative weight (Paclebar et al., 2007). However, even more revealing was that the participants' overall decisions concerning their determinations of guilt in respect of the accused, the possible linkage of two crimes, and the potential danger the accused may pose to the community were not significantly influenced by the input of a criminal profiler's testimony. In light of this finding that profiles had no significant input upon the mock jurors' decision making, it needs to be queried what benefit(s) may be derived from the use of profiling in the context of the courtroom.

CONCLUSIONS

It should be apparent from the foregoing material that something of a disparity exists between the reputation of criminal profiling and the scientifically grounded evidence in support of its capabilities and value in the courtroom. In this modern age of forensic sciences, the prospect of coherently assessing the behaviors exhibited in a crime to assist with the identification of an offender is one that is likely to have enormous appeal. However, whereas the concept of profiling holds considerable attraction, its operationalization into scientifically grounded principles that are reliable and accurate remains elusive. Although modest, scientific evidence is beginning to emerge to support the basic concept that suitably skilled experts can demonstrate a comparatively superior degree of insight when seeking to accurately predict the likely characteristics of a perpetrator to a crime, based on an assessment of the exhibited crime behaviors. This modicum of evidence, however, is a far cry from supporting some of the more popular beliefs and perceptions of criminal profiling. As a consequence, and at this stage in the scientific development of criminal profiling and its derivative techniques, it seems prudent to avoid the use of profiling in the courtroom and to instead confine its application to its more traditional investigative context. If, on the other hand, the courts see fit to use profiling in some capacity in the courtroom in the pursuit of justice, those courts ought, as commentators have observed, exercise "the shortest and most carefully constructed judicial leash" (Risinger & Loop, 2002, p. 285) in allowing it as evidence. Arguably, the reach of this leash should be determined by a thorough consideration of the probative value over the prejudicial impact of such evidence, combined with the rigorous scrutiny of the technique itself.

REFERENCES

Alison, L., Smith, M., Eastman, O., & Rainbow, L. (2003). Toulmin's philosophy of argument and its relevance to offender profiling. *Psychology, Crime, and Law, 9,* 173–183.

Alison, L., Smith, M., & Morgan, K. (2003). Interpreting the accuracy of offender profilers. *Psychology, Crime, and Law, 9,* 185–195.

Anastasi, A. (1976). *Psychological testing* (4th ed.). New York: Macmillan.

Bartol, C. (1996). Police psychology: Then, now, and beyond. *Criminal Justice and Behavior, 23,* 70–89.

Britton, P. (1997). *The jigsaw man.* London: Bantam Press.

Canter, D. (1994). *Criminal shadows.* London: HarperCollins.

Commonwealth of Pennsylvania v. DiStefano, 72A. 2d 574, 582 (PA. Super. 2001).

Copson, G. (1995). *Coals to Newcastle? Part 1: A study of offender profiling* (paper 7). London: Police Research Group Special Interest Series, Home Office.

Daubert v. Merrell Dow Pharmaceuticals, Inc., 509 U. S. 579 (1993).

Davis, D., & Follette, W. C. (2002). Rethinking the probative value of evidence: Base rates, intuitive profiling, and the *"post*diction" of behavior. *Law and Human Behavior, 26,* 133–158.

Douglas, J. E., & Burgess, A. W. (1986). Criminal profiling: A viable investigative tool against violent crime. *FBI Law Enforcement Bulletin, 55*(12), 9–13.

Douglas, J. E., Burgess, A. W., Burgess, A. G., & Ressler, R. K. (Eds.). (2006). *Crime classification manual* (2nd ed.). San Francisco: Jossey-Bass.

Douglas, J. E., & Olshaker, M. (1995). *Mindhunter.* New York: Scribner.

Farrington, D. P. (2007). Review of criminal profiling: Principles and practice. *International Journal of Offender Therapy and Comparative Criminology, 4*(51), 486–487.

Federal Rules of Evidence. (2004). Washington, DC: U.S. Government Printing Office.

Fisher, A. J. (1993). *Techniques of crime scene investigation* (5th ed.). New York: Elsevier.

Freckelton, I., & Selby, H. (2005). *Expert evidence: Law, practice, procedure and advocacy* (3rd ed.). Sydney, Australia: Lawbook Co.

Frye v. United States, 293 F. 1013 (D. C. Cir. 1923).

Garb, H. E. (1998). *Studying the clinician: Judgment research and psychological testing.* Washington, DC: American Psychological Association.

General Electric v. Joiner, 522 U. S. 136 (1997).

Grezlak, H. (1999, April 12). Profiling testimony inadmissible in murder trial: Too speculative, prejudicial judge says. *Pennsylvania Law Weekly,* pp. 1–2.

Harcourt, B. E. (2007). *Against prediction: Profiling, policing, and punishing in an actuarial age.* Chicago: University of Chicago Press.

Hazelwood, R., Dietz, P. E., & Burgess, A. W. (1982). Sexual fatalities: Behavioral reconstruction in equivocal cases. *Journal of Forensic Sciences, 27,* 763–773.

Hazelwood, R., & Michaud, S. G. (2001). *Dark dreams.* New York: St. Martin's Press.

Hazelwood, R., Ressler, R. K., Depue, R. L., & Douglas, J. C. (1995). Criminal investigative analysis: An overview. In R. R. Hazelwood & A. W. Burgess (Eds.), *Practical aspects of rape investigation: A multidisciplinary approach* (2nd ed., pp. 115–126). Boca Raton, FL: CRC Press.

Herndon, J. S. (2007). The image of profiling: Media treatment and general impressions. In R. N. Kocsis (Ed.), *Criminal profiling: International theory, practice, and research* (pp. 290–303). Tottowa, NJ: Humana Press.

Holmes, R. M., & Holmes, S. T. (1996). *Profiling violent crimes: An investigative tool* (2nd ed.). Thousand Oaks, CA: Sage.

Institutional Research and Development Unit. (1981). *FBI academy: Evaluation of the psychological profiling program.* Unpublished manuscript.

Jackson, J. L., van Koppen, P. J., & Herbrink C. M. (1993). *Does the service meet the needs? An evaluation of consumer satisfaction with the specific profile analysis and investigative advice as offered by the scientific research advisory unit of the National Criminal Intelligence Division (CRI)* (NISCALE Report NSCR 93–05). Leiden, The Netherlands: The Netherlands Institute for the Study of Criminality and Law Enforcement.

Jeffers, H. P. (1992). *Profiles in evil.* London: Warner Brothers.

Kirkpatrick, L. C. (1998). Profile and syndrome evidence: Its use and admissibility in criminal prosecutions. *Security Journal, 11,* 255–257.

Kocsis, R. N. (2004). Psychological profiling in serial arson offenses: An assessment of skills and accuracy. *Criminal Justice and Behavior, 31,* 341–361.

Kocsis, R. N. (2006). *Criminal profiling: Principles and practice.* Tottowa, NJ: Humana Press.

Kocsis, R. N. (2007). Skills and accuracy to criminal profiling. In R. N. Kocsis (Ed.), *Criminal profiling: International theory, practice, and research* (pp. 335–358). Tottowa, NJ: Humana Press.

Kocsis, R. N., & Hayes, A. F. (2004). Believing is seeing?: Investigating the perceived accuracy of criminal psychological profiles. *International Journal of Offender Therapy and Comparative Criminology, 48,* 149–160.

Kocsis, R. N., Hayes, A. F., & Irwin, H. J. (2002). Investigative experience and accuracy in psychological profiling of a violent crime. *Journal of Interpersonal Violence, 17*(8), 811–823.

Kocsis, R. N., & Heller, G. Z. (2004). Believing is seeing: II. Beliefs and perceptions of criminal psychological profiles. *International Journal of Offender Therapy and Comparative Criminology, 48,* 313–329.

Kocsis, R. N., Irwin, H. J., Hayes, A. F., & Nunn, R. (2000). Expertise in psychological profiling: A comparative assessment. *Journal of Interpersonal Violence, 15,* 311–331.

Kocsis, R. N., & Middledorp, J. T. (2004). Believing is seeing: III. Perceptions of content in criminal psychological profiles. *International Journal of Offender Therapy and Comparative Criminology, 48,* 477–494.

Kocsis, R. N., Middledorp, J., & Karpin, A. (2008). Taking stock of accuracy in criminal profiling: The theoretical quandary for investigative psychology. *Journal of Forensic Psychology Practice, 8*(3), 244–261.

Kocsis, R. N., & Palermo, G. B. (2007). Contemporary problems with criminal profiling. In R. N. Kocsis (Ed.), *Criminal profiling: International theory, practice, and research* (pp. 335–358). Tottowa, NJ: Humana Press.

Kumho Tire Ltd. v. Carmichael, 526 U. S. 137 (1999).

Labuschangne, G. N. (2006). The use of a linkage analysis as evidence in the conviction of the Newcastle serial murderer, South Africa. *Journal of Investigative Psychology and Offender Profiling, 3,* 183–191.

McCrary, G. O., & Ramsland, K. (2003). *The unknown darkness: Profiling the predators among us.* New York: HarperCollins.

Meehl, P. E. (1954). *Clinical versus statistical prediction: A theoretical analysis and a review of the evidence.* Minneapolis: University of Minnesota Press.

Monte, C. (1995). *Beneath the mask: An introduction to personality* (5th ed.). New York: Harcourt Brace.

Ormerod, D., & Sturman, J. (2005). Working with the courts: Advice for expert witnesses. In L. J. Alison (Ed.), *The forensic psychologist's casebook* (pp. 170–193). London: Willan.

Paclebar, A. M. R., Myers, B., & Brineman, J. (2007). Criminal profiling: Impact on mock juror decision making and implications for admissibility. In R. N. Kocsis (Ed.), *Criminal profiling: International theory, practice, and research* (pp. 249–262). Tottowa, NJ: Humana Press.

Palermo, G. B., & Kocsis, R. N. (2005). *Offender profiling: An introduction to the sociopsychological analysis of violent crime.* Springfield, IL: Thomas.

Pinizzotto, A. J. (1984). Forensic psychology: Criminal personality profiling. *Journal of Police Science and Administration, 12,* 32–40.

Pinizzotto, A. J., & Finkel, N. J. (1990). Criminal personality profiling: An outcome process study. *Law and Human Behavior, 14,* 215–233.

R. v. Clark, 13 C. C. C (3d) 117 (Canada, 2004).

R. v. Guilfoyle, 2 Cr. App. Rep. 57 (United Kingdom, 2001).

R. v. Hillier, ACTSC 50, 25 (Australia, 2003).

R. v. Ranger, 178 C. C. C. (3d) 375 (Ontario, Canada, 2003).

R. v. Stagg, 7 MVP (2d) 283 (United Kingdom, 1994).

Ressler, R. K., & Shachtman, T. (1992). *Whoever fights monsters.* London: Simon & Schuster.

Risinger, D. M., & Loop, J. L. (2002). Three card Monte, Monte Hall, modus operandi, and "offender profiling": Some lessons of modern cognitive science for the law of evidence. *Cardozo Law Review, 24,* 193–285.

Rossi, D. (1982). Crime scene behavioral analysis: Another tool for the law enforcement investigator. *Police Chief, 18,* 152–155.

Rossmo, K. (2000). *Geographic profiling.* Boca Raton: FL: CRC Press.

State v. Fortin, 162 NJ 517, 745 A. 2d 509 (2000).

State v. Fortin, 178 NJ 540 (2004).

State v. Stevens, 78 SW 3d 817, 852 (Tenn. 2001).

State v. Thomas, 423 NE2d 137 (Ohio 1981).

Torres, A. N., Boccaccini, M. T., & Miller, H. (2006). Perceptions of the validity and utility of criminal profiling among forensic psychologists and psychiatrists. *Professional Psychology: Research and Practice, 37,* 51–58.

Trager, J., & Brewster, J. (2001). The effectiveness of psychological profiles. *Journal of Police and Criminal Psychology, 16,* 20–28.

U.S. House of Representatives. (1990). USS Iowa *tragedy: An investigative failure.* Report of the investigation's subcommittee and the defense policy panel of the Committee on Armed Services. Washington, DC: Author.

Vorpagel, R. E. (1982). Painting psychological profiles: Charlatanism, coincidence, charisma, or new science. *Police Chief, 3,* 156–159.

Vorpagel, R. E., & Harrington, J. (1998). *Profiles in murder.* New York: Plenum Press.

Woodhams, J., Bull, R., & Hollin, C. R. (2007). Case linkage: Identifying crimes committed by the same offender. In R. N. Kocsis (Ed.), *Criminal profiling: International theory, practice, and research* (pp. 117–133). Tottowa, NJ: Humana Press.

CHAPTER 12

The Science and Pseudoscience of Assessing Psychological Injuries

William J. Koch, Rami Nader, and Michelle Haring

OVERVIEW OF TECHNIQUES AND CONTROVERSIES

The assessment of psychological injuries and associated disability in a forensic context is a complex process, made more so by the lack of fit between what the law needs to know and decide, and what psychological science and practice are best suited to address. Legal decision makers must primarily decide whether (1) a person's postevent condition is sufficiently worse than his or her pre-event condition; (2) if so, whether the alleged wrongdoing caused the worsened condition; and (3) whether the alleged wrongdoing will continue to cause dysfunction and impairment in the future. Optimally, the assessment process would address these areas, as follows: (1) determining the presence of one or more substantial mental health problems or diagnoses; (2) estimating contributions to these problems by different precipitating or maintaining variables (e.g., the subject trauma at the center of litigation, vs. a preexisting condition, vs. secondary gain leading to feigned distress); (3) estimating the contribution of such mental health problems to work or personal disability; (4) estimating the prognoses of such problems; and (5) recommending rehabilitation strategies.

Given the number and complexity of these issues, we have chosen to limit our discussion to two major controversial areas within the forensic assessment of psychological injuries: (1) the understanding of psychological injuries themselves—in particular, whether posttraumatic stress disorder (PTSD) is a valid diagnosis; and (2) the (in)ability of psychological science and practice to directly inform the key legal questions at play—namely, the causal nexus between an alleged wrongdoing (e.g., a tortuous act, a work-related accident) and the purported psychological consequences, and the causal nexus between those psychological consequences and functional (e.g., vocational) disability. A thorough review of assessment methods and techniques is available elsewhere (Koch, Douglas, Nicholls, & O'Neill, 2006; Koch, O'Neill, & Douglas, 2005; Melton, Petrila, Poythress, & Slobogin, 1997).

Is Psychological PTSD a Valid Construct?

Defining the Controversy

Approximately 150 years ago, Lord Wensleydale of the House of Lords stated in *Lynch v. Knight* (1861), "mental pain and anxiety the law cannot value, and does not pretend to redress" (p. 859). This quote is an apt summary of the reticence with which the law has greeted claims of psychological injury until relatively recently. Legal skeptics remain, such as Eden (2001), who wrote "I am having a flashback ... all the way to the bank" (p. 180). Of course, the fact that people have successfully sued others for seemingly innocuous affronts to mental tranquility has cast doubt on the validity of psychological reactions to traumatic events in the eyes of the law.

And yet, "psychological injury" is now quite well established as a remediable harm under tort, workers' compensation, and civil rights laws. In fact, the emergence of PTSD as a formal diagnostic entity in the *Diagnostic and Statistical Manual of Mental Disorders* (DSM) system in 1987 greatly facilitated the already emerging tolerance of such claims in the legal systems (Koch et al., 2006). The beauty of PTSD from a legal perspective is that it is caused, by definition, by the same traumatic events that often form the basis for claims of negligence. Now, as Andreasen (1995) quipped, "It is rare to find a psychiatric disorder that anyone likes to have, but PTSD seems to be one of them" (p. 164).

Throughout medicolegal history, "psychological injury" has faced an uphill battle in terms of its status as a legally recognized and compensable harm. Until recently, and even today in some jurisdictions, legal limits have been placed on such claims, such as requiring either physical contact as part of the alleged wrongful act or requiring physical manifestation of injury alongside psychological distress (see Douglas, Huss, Murdoch, Washington,

& Koch, 1999; Koch et al., 2006). Furthermore, some psychological commentators have challenged the basis of PTSD as a discrete, valid diagnostic entity (Bowman, 1999), and have instead argued that it is better conceptualized as an amalgam of preexisting personality dispositions that interact with a more nebulous anxiety-related psychiatric construct. Herein lies our first controversy: Is the "discrete" diagnosis that opened the doors—some would say the floodgates—to psychological injury litigation and forms the basis of many successful claims of emotional distress *actually* a valid psychiatric diagnosis?

Research Relevant to the Controversy

There is little doubt that the PTSD diagnostic criteria can be assessed reasonably reliably using semistructured interviews (see Koch et al., 2006, for a review). Similarly, a large body of empirical evidence appears to support the construct validity of PTSD. However, the very basis of this diagnosis has been criticized on a variety of fronts. Summerfield (2002), objecting to alleged political factors that gave the diagnosis of PTSD formal status as a psychiatric disorder (such as providing a reason to give Vietnam veterans state-funded treatment; see Koch et al., 2005, for a review), lamented:

> Psychiatrists serve neither society nor patients with psychiatric difficulties when they uncritically endorse the medicalisation of life (though they may well serve the pharmaceutical industry, with its vested interest in the medicalisation of the human predicament ...). It is academic shallowness and complacency that may permit sociocultural (and often political) values and expectations to be dressed up as medicopsychiatric facts. (p. 914)

In reality, virtually all psychiatric diagnoses are constructs borne in part of contemporary scientific consensus rather than concrete, biologically distinct and unchanging entities. For example, PTSD as a diagnostic construct has evolved over the years, and some have argued that its inclusion in the DSM is more a function of sociopolitical factors than of scientific discovery (Baldwin, Williams, & Houts, 2004; Scott, 1990). In addition, some authors (e.g., Koch et al., 2005, 2006) have noted that the very concept of PTSD requires further refinement and empirical study given a number of findings, including high rates of comorbidity (i.e., the concurrent presence of more than one mental health condition) between PTSD and other disorders (e.g., depression, specific phobias, and generalized anxiety disorder), strong prediction of development of PTSD by premorbid personality characteristics (especially neuroticism or negative affectivity), lack of consistently replicated laboratory and biological markers, and inconsistent symptom factor structure (for a review, see Rosen & Lilienfeld, 2008).

More broadly, it can be challenging to distinguish between such putatively separate entities as PTSD, depression, other anxiety disorders, chronic pain, and traumatic brain injury because of the substantial symptomatic and functional overlap among their diagnostic criteria and clinical presentation. Moreover, within forensic contexts, symptomatically complex claimants are more the norm than the exception. Taken together with the lack of evidence supporting the existence of natural boundaries between these "disorders," some authors have suggested that variations in symptoms may be continuous rather than discrete (e.g., Kendall & Jablensky, 2003). If so, then a dimensional approach to describing the presence and severity of symptoms (and associated psychological injuries) may be of greater utility, and forensic assessors should exercise caution in assuming that psychological injuries are true constructs that are either "present" or "absent" in a particular individual.

The high degree of comorbidity between PTSD and other disorders has led some to question the necessity and integrity of PTSD as a distinct disorder and propose rather that it is part of a larger construct such as negative affectivity (Bowman, 1999; Watson, 1999). Watson (1999), for instance, described anxiety disorders generally within a hierarchical model, with negative affectivity common to each, and each involving a unique construct as well. Recent research using taxometric procedures suggests that PTSD is underpinned by one or more dimensions rather than a discrete taxon (i.e., category in nature; Ruscio, Ruscio, & Keane, 2002).

In addition, we know that vastly more people in the population experience Criterion A stressors (the traumatic event that must be present in order to diagnose PTSD) than actually go on to develop PTSD. In summarizing this literature, Lee and Young (2001) reported that up to 93% of the population can be defined as having experienced a traumatic event, yet only 5–12% of the population ever develops PTSD. Some people might develop PTSD in response to a relatively minor traffic accident, whereas others can go through heavy combat, violent victimization, or even rape and not develop PTSD.

Complicating the picture is the strong possibility that many people who have *never* experienced a traumatic stressor could meet the other (i.e., symptom-based) criteria for PTSD (Rosen & Lilienfeld, 2008). For instance, Bodkin, Pope, Detke, and Hudson (2007) demonstrated that subjects presenting for treatment of depression were as likely to meet symptomatic criteria for PTSD when they had no history of exposure to traumatic stressors (as defined in DSM-IV), as when they did have such exposure. There are a number of potential explanations for this finding, including the possibility that symptoms of PTSD overlap with other mental health conditions such as depression, generalized anxiety, and specific phobia, as well as the possibility that many of these symptoms may be responsive to a wider range of nontraumatic psychosocial stressors. Still other research calls into question the claim that traumatic stressors are necessary for the development of PTSD symptoms. For example, in studies of nonclinical samples, Gold, Marx, Soler-Baillo, and Sloan (2005) and Mol and colleagues (2005) reported that participants who had experienced nontraumatic events, such as parental divorce, arrests, or serious relationship difficulties, were as likely or even more likely to exhibit PTSD symptoms as those who experienced traumatic events The astute reader will note the implications of this research for expert opinions on causality of PTSD in individual cases.

These observations have led some to posit that "individual differences are significantly more powerful than event characteristics in predicting PTSD" (Bowman, 1999, p. 28). In fact, as Bowman (1999) asserted, event characteristics contribute "relatively little variance" to the development of PTSD (p. 28). In addition, as Bowman explained, certain individual characteristics, such as beliefs about emotionality, are defined in part by group (i.e., culture) membership, leading to vastly different responses to similar events across cultures. As such, as Bowman noted, reports in the literature have observed seemingly discrepant outcomes, as 0% of approximately 500 Israeli children showing a traumatic disorder after being locked into sealed rooms during SCUD missile attacks, to 100% of 23 American children showing trauma after a bus hijacking. She suggested that cultural differences between Israelis and Americans accounted for this difference. As another example, there is epidemiological evidence that the prevalence of PTSD varies even across Western countries such as Australia and the United States, despite similar rates of trauma exposure (Creamer, Burgess, & McFarlane, 2001).

Can Science Address the Causal Nexus between Adverse Events and Psychological Injuries, and between Psychological Injuries and Subsequent Dysfunction?

Defining the Controversy

Although psychologists have developed well-validated tests and measures of current psychological functioning, that construct is just a small part of the equation in most legal contexts. More important is the juxtaposition of current functioning with past functioning (i.e., are claimants worse off than before the adverse event?) and the cause of any decline in functioning (i.e., was the decline caused by the alleged wrongful act?). Unfortunately, as

Greenberg, Otto, and Long (2003) aptly observed, "no instrument currently exists that can reliably assess what was the level and quality of a plaintiff's functioning or the capacity before a tortious event occurred, nor are there instruments that can reliably separate the effects of one prior trauma or experience from another" (p. 415).

Even if science could address the causal nexus between adverse events and psychological injuries, could science address the causal nexus between those psychological injuries and subsequent dysfunction? The legal question of import concerning dysfunction is the extent to which the claimant's psychological conditions impair his or her ability to work or function fully in other important areas of life, such as preferred recreations, socializing, activities of daily living, and intimacy. According to the American Medical Association (Cocchiarella & Andersson, 2001), *disability* involves some decrease in a person's ability to meet personal, social, or occupational demands *because of an impairment.* The forensic assessor's role is to determine the extent of any causal link between a mental health impairment (e.g., PTSD) and some functional disability (e.g., inability to work). Two issues are of note here. First, to what extent are psychological injuries (e.g., PTSD, depression) associated with functional disability (e.g., lowered economic performance, absenteeism from work, reduced efficiency at work)? Second, what domains of work or personal functioning need scrutiny in the assessment of individual disability claimants?

TRUSTWORTHINESS OF ASSESSMENT INFORMATION BASE

Assuming that reliable and valid assessment tools are available to help evaluate the relevant causal links in psychological injury cases, there might still be a controversy about their applicability to such cases. Because assessments of disability naturally focus on claimants with potential secondary gain, there is substantial controversy over the reliable assessment and meaning of symptom exaggeration or malingering. As such, even descriptions of *current* psychological functioning are potentially at jeopardy in the psychological injury context.

Research Relevant to the Controversy

ADDRESSING THE LINK BETWEEN THE ADVERSE EVENT AND SUBSEQUENT PSYCHOLOGICAL INJURIES

There is little controversy that traumatic events can sometimes trigger mental health problems. However, the post-hoc determination of a causal link between a specific event and subsequent mental health functioning is much less clear. As stated above, there are no tests, measures, or otherwise validated assessment protocols that are designed to do so. The matter is complicated by the law's requirement to factor competing causes into the determination of whether the adverse event is at least one of the material contributions to psychological injury. Furthermore, psychological measures cannot be used to infer past functioning, particularly when an intervening adverse event has occurred.

There really is no *direct* research on point. Although structured interviews of lifetime psychiatric functioning (e.g., "Has there *ever* been a time . . .") ostensibly could inform decisions about pre-event functioning, they are entirely reliant on self-report and hence are transparent to litigants in their intent. Assuming that such approaches are the best option, they remain limited in that they evaluate only diagnostic categories, as opposed to the full range of psychological functioning. Furthermore, they do not allow causal inferences to be made—that diminished psychological functioning is attributable to the event at question and not to other factors.

RELATING PSYCHOLOGICAL INJURIES TO DYSFUNCTION

We can say with reasonable confidence that psychological injuries are clearly related to reduced economic and other role functioning. This is the case for PTSD (e.g., see review by Fairbank, Ebert, & Zarkin, 1999) as well as for depression and panic disorder (e.g., Bilj & Ravelli, 2000; Matza, Revichi, Davidson, & Stewart, 2003). Longitudinal studies (e.g., Judd et al., 2000; Von Korff, Ormel, Katon, & Lin, 1992), which show that disability covaries with the severity of depressive and anxiety symptoms, support the hypothesis that psychological disorders are directly related to disability. More recent studies point to some disorder specificity, although a solid corpus of research has not yet accrued on the issue of specificity. For example, atypical major depression with hypersomnia appears to stand out by its association with more disability days than major depression, per se (Matza et al., 2003), and there is evidence that mood disorders are associated with impairment across a broader spectrum of daily activities, whereas anxiety disorders may have a greater impact on social functioning than on other areas (Spitzer et al., 1995). As well, there is some evidence that comorbidity increases the risk of work disability (Bilj & Ravelli, 2000).

However, there are substantial limitations to these conclusions. First, self-report disability measures are common in epidemiological research. Although some self-report measures are specific and concrete (e.g., asking respondents about number of days spent in bed), there are good reasons to believe that psychologically distressed individuals are overly pessimistic about their daily functioning (see review by Coyne & Gotlib, 1983). Thus, both epidemiological studies of the predictors of disability and individual assessments of disability claimants may overestimate functional disability based on individuals' pessimistic self-reports. As well, the studies mentioned above are limited in number. It is clear that much more research is necessary to provide a more convincing and detailed description of the relationship of psychological injuries to functional disability.

Second, the high rate of comorbidity among psychiatric diagnoses makes it hard to attribute disability to a specific diagnosis. For example, as many as 50% of PTSD cases simultaneously meet criteria for major depression (e.g., Blanchard & Hickling, 1996). Is it the depression, the PTSD, or the joint occurrence of the two that is associated with functional disability? Sometimes, this distinction does not matter, legally. If a tortious event produced two or three disorders, the tortfeasor (i.e., person found liable for having committed a tort) is liable for all of them. However, sometimes comorbidity has crucial legal implications. If depression predated a tortious event that led to PTSD, the tortfeasor is liable only for the postevent disability and loss attributable to the PTSD, and *not* the depression.

Third, there is a very strong relationship between mental and physical disorders (see reviews by Gnam, 2005; Schnurr & Green, 2004), and evidence indicates that increases in functional disability among individuals with comorbid physical and mental disorders is primarily associated with the additional mental disorder (e.g., Kessler, Ormel, Demler, & Stang, 2003). This finding suggests that disability claimants with chronic pain complaints are likely to suffer more substantial functional disability if they have comorbid mental health problems such as depression. Once again, much more research is needed in this area.

Fourth, there is substantial evidence that personality and interpersonal attributes in their own right are substantive predictors of disability leave. For example, personality characteristics of suspiciousness and hostility (Regehr, Goldberg, Glancy, & Knott, 2002), as well as interpersonal conflict at work and neuroticism (Appelberg, Romanov, Heikkilae, & Honkasalo, 1996), all predict work disability leave, sometimes more powerfully than do clinical conditions such as PTSD or depression. It is a telling statement about the early developmental stage of mental health disability research that no large-scale studies have yet examined relationships between a wide range of mental health variables (e.g., different clinical disorders as well as different personality traits) and disability in both occupational and personal domains.

TRUSTWORTHINESS OF INFORMATION BASE

Malingering is the intentional production of exaggerated mental health problems in order to obtain an identifiable external reward. This description involves several components: (1) the existence of some concrete external incentive for appearing distressed or disabled, (2) self-described problems or other behaviors that appear extreme compared to other claimants in a similar context, and (3) a specific internal motivation. The first of these superficially appears easiest to assess, although it presumes a homogeneity of motivation. To our knowledge, this presumption has never been tested.

The second component has been tested in a variety of settings. The base rate of malingering or symptom exaggeration is a subject of some debate for a number of reasons. First, there is no true gold standard for the determination of malingering against which one can compare assessment methods. Second, the base rate of malingering or symptom exaggeration in non-forensic samples is unknown (see Rogers, 1997). Thus, our knowledge of the frequency of malingering is often based on surveys of practitioners (e.g., Rogers, Sewell, & Goldstein, 1994). The latter authors found that experienced forensic assessors estimated nearly 16% of their forensic clients but only 7% of their nonforensic clients to be malingering. More recently, Mittenberg, Patton, Canyock, and Condit (2002), in a very large survey of neuropsychologists, found that approximately 30% of personal injury and disability claimants were thought to be malingering or exaggerating symptoms. Thus, there is apparently a high rate of symptom exaggeration/malingering in compensation-seeking samples, although the concept of malingering itself is somewhat hard to pin down empirically.

A common design for evaluating putative measures of malingering is to compare nonlitigants who are instructed either to fabricate symptoms or to respond honestly (see Rogers & Bender, 2003, for a review). Different variants of coached versus uncoached and different incentives to successfully malinger have been evaluated in these studies. These studies have good internal validity but questionable external validity, given that most such studies involve university students or other individuals outside of the true litigation context. However, malingering instruments have also been evaluated within known group designs, in which clinical subjects with or without litigation are compared. To summarize briefly, a number of different measures of symptom overendorsement (e.g., Minnesota Multiphasic Personality Inventory–2 [MMPI-2] Infrequency scale and its derivatives, MMPI-2 Fake Bad Scale; for a review, see Iverson & Lange, 2006), measures of atypical mental health symptoms (e.g., Structured Interview for Reported Symptoms [SIRS]; Rogers, Bagby, & Dickens, 1992), or tests of reduced effort (Tombaugh, 1997) can differentiate malingerers from honest responders in simulation designs and can also differentiate known groups of litigants from nonlitigants. Thus, it is clear that forensic assessors identify a relatively high rate (between 15 and 30% of cases) of potential malingering or symptom exaggeration within claimants, and that a number of assessment methods are available that can discriminate known groups with respect to their tendencies to overendorse mental health difficulties, show atypically low effort in cognitive tasks, or endorse atypical mental health symptoms. However, because there is no gold standard for malingering, research in this area leads to only tentative conclusions with respect to making judgments of malingering in individual cases.

Finally, the assessment and diagnosis of malingering involves the expert making a judgment about the claimant's "intent." This is probably the most fragile area in the assessment of malingering. It is not clear just how psychologists or other mental health professionals can empirically determine a person's intention. Forensic assessors may best be advised to avoid commenting on a claimant's intentions.

GAPS IN SCIENTIFIC KNOWLEDGE

Little Research Has Been Conducted with Ecologically Relevant Samples of Litigants

Knowledge continues to accumulate regarding the prevalence of particular stress-related mental health disorders and their conditional prevalence related to particular types of traumas/stressors (e.g., Breslau et al., 1991; Norris, 1992). Increasingly reliable techniques are being developed for the assessment of these conditions as they typically present in clinical and research contexts (e.g., Weathers, Ruscio, & Keane, 1999). However, our ability to draw accurate inferences from forensic assessments of these stress-related mental health conditions is limited by the fact that the overwhelming majority of research in this area has been conducted on convenience or treatment-seeking samples of individuals, without consideration of litigation or compensation status (Koch et al., 2005). This sampling bias is problematic because there is substantial evidence that personal injury litigation and compensation seeking are associated with elevated reports of emotional distress and disability (e.g., Frueh, Gold, & de Arellano, 1997). Thus, the generalizability of our current knowledge about the prevalence of mental health problems and assessment methods for such problems to a claimant population is unknown.

Similarly, the dearth of research from forensic contexts makes it difficult to know how to interpret client responses to commonly used self-report measures of symptomatology (e.g., PTSD Checklist—Civilian Version [PCL-C]; Blanchard, Jones-Alexander, Buckley, & Forneris, 1996). The norms for such instruments are based on treatment-seeking samples without consideration of compensation-seeking status. At a minimum, studies are needed that compare litigating and nonlitigating samples on their responses to psychological tests. Future research could also examine how common characteristics of claimants (e.g., multiple problems, chronic pain, and use of analgesics) may influence responses to self-report tests. Such research would increase the ecological validity of forensic assessments using such tests.

Standardized Methods for Addressing Cause Are Lacking

As described above, there are no validated measures or protocols for addressing the causal issues that lie at the heart of psychological injury claims. In fact, the current status of assessing the relationship between mental health conditions and functional disability may be accurately termed "prescientific." Many clinicians merely use the Global Assessment of Functioning (GAF) Scale from DSM-IV (American Psychiatric Association, 2000) as a proxy for estimating disability. This is problematic because the GAF confounds a dimension of psychiatric symptom severity (e.g., mild symptoms such as depressed mood with mild insomnia vs. serious symptoms such as suicidal ideation, severe obsessional rituals) with a dimension of functional impairment (e.g., "generally functioning pretty well" vs. "any serious impairment in social, occupational, or school functioning"). Such a confound (1) encourages the assessor to overestimate the relationship between symptoms and functional impairment and (2) prevents the assessor from considering any variables that mediate this relationship. To the extent that they rely on the GAF to estimate disability, professional opinions about disability are tautological ("He is sick, therefore he cannot work").

Developing a research base that could inform opinions on causal issues related to disability claims is a daunting task that would require large-scale prospective studies, with repeated measurements of psychological functioning, life events, dysfunction in all major life domains, response to treatment, and the potential mediators of the association between these factors. What we are left with is the "investigative interviewing" that Melton and colleagues (1997) recommend in many forensic assessment contexts: making logical inferences, based on interviews of examinees and collaterals and reviews of collateral documents, about the likelihood that the legally relevant adverse event was associated with a worsening in psychological functioning, and whether this worsening might relate to disability. A good first step for research would be the development of a reliable standardized protocol for such investigations. Questions of validity would be more difficult to pursue.

Unknown Vulnerability of Measures to Response Styles

Because structured interviews and symptom checklists typically have high face validity, using them may result in overestimations of distress in claimants motivated to emphasize their problems. For example, structured diagnostic interviews, such as the Clinician-Administered PTSD Scale (CAPS; Blake et al., 1998), require the interviewer to describe a particular problem or symptom and then ask the interviewee whether he or she has experienced that symptom. It is conceivable that this method of questioning could serve to "coach" the claimant to excessively endorse symptoms. More open-ended questioning without potentially "leading" questions might be less vulnerable to exaggeration. Unfortunately, more open-ended methods require a level of self-awareness and an ability to describe symptoms that may be lacking in many claimants. At this time, it is unknown how structured interviewing procedures are affected by the claims status of the interviewee and what adaptations to these procedures (e.g., requirements for detailed descriptions of claimants' unique experiences of such symptoms) may be necessary in order to yield the most valid information.

Compounding these difficulties, we do not understand the extent to which claimants' motivations for their personal injury or disability claims are homogeneous (unlikely, given the diversity of individual differences) or heterogeneous, and the extent to which these varied motivations (e.g., financial gain, seeking of therapy, seeking a subjective sense of justice, seeking revenge) might influence response styles. This basic research is important to better understand the motivational context in which claimants approach assessment appointments.

Additionally, tools for the assessment of malingering are still primarily limited to self-report measures of excessive endorsement of distress or other symptoms of mental illness (e.g., MMPI-2, F, Fp, Fake Bad scales) and tests of low effort within neuropsychological assessments. Although structured interviews for malingering (e.g., SIRS—Rogers et al., 1992; Miller Forensic Assessment of Symptoms Test [M-FAST]—Miller, 2001) have been developed, they have not yet been extensively evaluated with psychological injury claimants.

The Validity of Collateral Information Is Unknown

It is commonly assumed by forensic assessors that third-party information (e.g., collateral interviews, health or employment records) provides a means of "confirming" the presence of symptoms reported by the claimant and may in fact be a more valid source of information, given financial incentives for self-reported distress (Melton et al., 1997). Conceptually, however, collateral reports from family members may also be distorted by financial incentives. Moreover, health records may provide little help because mental disorders generally are underdetected in primary care (e.g., Tiemens, Von Korff, & Lin, 1999; Zimmerman & Mattia, 1999). Psychological injuries pose further complications because of their internal and subjective nature (e.g., someone may experience intrusive memories without observers noticing).

To date, little research exists either to support or refute the assumption that collateral sources provide more valid information than the claimant. A review of the literature reveals limited research on the concordance between self-report and third-party report with respect to commonly cited psychological injuries (cf. Calhoun et al., 2002; Gallagher, Riggs, Byrne, & Weathers, 1998, for a discussion of PTSD symptoms and related problems in combat veterans). More research is needed to support the presumed reliability, validity, and overall utility of collateral information in the forensic assessment of mental health conditions.

MYTHS AND MISCONCEPTIONS

Trauma Necessarily Leads to Distress and Dysfunction

Perhaps one of the most significant misconceptions held by the general public and mental health professionals is that certain traumatic life experiences will invariably be associated with severe psychological distress. This expectation may lead less informed assessors to conduct assessments with a confirmatory bias that seeks to "find" PTSD in the client. This misconception likely stems from earlier conceptualizations of PTSD that attributed the development of this disorder to "an event that is outside the range of usual human experience and that would be markedly distressing to almost anyone" (American Psychiatric Association, 1987). However, more recent research has revealed that exposure to life-threatening trauma appears to be common in the general public (e.g., Norris, 1992) and that only a minority of individuals exposed to traumatic events develop PTSD, with lifetime prevalence estimates around 8% (Breslau, Davis, Andreski, & Peterson, 1991).

Trauma Must Be Objectively Severe to Lead to PTSD

This, of course, is the corollary of the previous misconception. Bodkin and colleagues (2007) examined the validity of this presumption in a creative study. They took 103 sequential subjects seeking treatment for depression and examined the subjects' history of trauma as well as for symptoms of PTSD via the Structured Clinical Interview for DSM-IV (SCID-IV). Fifty-four of these subjects were rated by two independent raters as having experienced a Criterion A traumatic stressor, and 36 were rated as not having experienced any traumatic stressor. For subjects who had not experienced traumatic stressors, those PTSD symptom questions requiring reference to a traumatic event were asked instead about periods of experiencing "distressing thoughts, worries, or fears." Using this proxy for the reexperiencing symptom cluster, the authors were able to determine which subjects would meet symptomatic criteria for PTSD. Seventy-eight percent of subjects with rater-agreed traumatic event histories met symptomatic criteria for PTSD, and, more tellingly, 78% of subjects *without* traumatic event histories also met symptomatic criteria for PTSD. These authors summarized the implications of their findings as follows: "It appears that the symptom cluster currently attributed to PTSD may be a non-specific group of symptoms widely observed in patients with mood and anxiety disorders, regardless of trauma history" (p. 182).

Even among persons who have experienced a traumatic event, research underscores the point that the objective severity of the event is less important in terms of the development of PTSD than is the subjective severity (for a review, see Koch et al., 2006). That is, events in which physical injury was minor, but during which a person felt he or she might die, or experienced great fear, are more likely to lead to PTSD than objectively more serious events unaccompanied by intense fear.

Diagnosis of Psychological Impairment Is Equivalent to Disability

This is untrue for several reasons. First, following a trauma, individuals may suffer from psychological injuries in the form of emotional distress (e.g., anxiety, fear, anger, humiliation) that may not correspond to any particular diagnostic category but which may nevertheless interfere with daily functioning and therefore be considered grounds for compensation under the law (Koch et al., 2006). As well, Schutzwohl and Maercker (1999) reported that certain subthreshold PTSD cases were more distressed on psychological measures than were some people who met criteria for PTSD. Similarly, Buckley, Blanchard, and Hickling (1996) showed that people with a diagnosis of PTSD are not always more distressed than people without such a diagnosis.

As such, the presence of a diagnosis should not automatically lead to a conclusion of disability (i.e., inability to work). It is clear from a reading of the research on predictors of work disability that it is the outcome of a complex set of independent variables, including claimant variables such as personality traits (e.g., hostility), clinical conditions (e.g., PTSD), possibly subfacets of clinical conditions (e.g., fatigue from depression), problems in one's personal life (e.g., family stressors), workplace variables (e.g., social support), and societal variables (e.g., disability benefits). The number of variables known to predict disability status suggests that there will be diverse disability outcomes among different people within the same environment as well as diverse disability outcomes among people with the same diagnoses but living in different contexts.

Disability Is a Binary Variable

Forensic assessors are frequently asked by lawyers or insurance adjusters whether claimants are "disabled," showing some limited appreciation of the continuum and multidimensionality of disability. Disability likely is a multidimensional construct consisting of multiple domains of work and personal functioning (see Dillman, 2003) within which any single person may be influenced by a unique combination of factors. Individuals suffering some form of disability in the workplace can vary on multiple dimensions. As such, they may be "disabled" to perform certain tasks, but not others. In addition, degree of disability likely is continuously distributed, and hence parsing people into two groups—disabled or not—would appear artificial and likely reflects the more general tension between law and psychology to force inherently "gray" issues into black and white.

CONCLUSIONS

Scientifically Supported Uses of Psychological Science and Assessment Techniques

- Psychological evaluation of *current* mental health functioning, if accompanied by caveats pertaining to the limits of current testing of response styles in litigating samples.
- *Description* of claimant and collateral reports of *past* functioning, if accompanied by caveats pertaining to limits of this task.

• The use of well-validated measures of symptom overendorsement, such as the validity scales of the MMPI-2, limited to offering opinions about individual claimants' response set during assessment, and not to the offering of opinions with respect to the diagnosis of malingering, per se.

Scientifically Untested or Controversial Uses

• Offering conclusions about the effect of psychological injury on specific areas of disability in the future (e.g., being able to perform some but not other work tasks; precise estimates about the length of time during which a person may be unable to function in certain domains). The literature can support statements about the effect of psychological injuries on broad areas of future functioning (work, educational, familial). However, there is less information available on how this effect might manifest specifically in a given case, given the presence of any number of potential mediators that research has yet thoroughly to investigate.

Scientifically Unsupported Uses

• Any definitive conclusions that current functioning was *caused* by the legally contested adverse event.

• Any definitive statements about past psychological functioning derived from current psychological testing, as no instruments or assessment protocols exist that can do so.

• Diagnoses of malingering, absent conclusive evidence of intentionality.

• Offering prognoses about future psychological functioning or disability on the basis of mental health variables alone. Disability is not equivalent to diagnosis; some people who are diagnosed with a mental disorder can work and function reasonably well. Others cannot, and the difference often may lie with factors other than mental illness, per se (e.g., social support).

COMMUNICATING CONSENSUS AND CONTROVERSIES

Forensic experts must indicate to lawyers, insurance adjusters, and courts the following about the assessment of psychological injuries: First, structured interviews avoid many of the problems and biases associated with unstructured interviews. The use of self-report scales and inventories, although useful as additional sources of information, may be vulnerable to exaggeration or yea-saying biases. However, such scales may still offer some information to help detect aberrant response styles. The use of medical records and other collateral records should be done with an appreciation of the limitations of such data. In addition, the forensic assessor should ensure that lawyers, insurance adjusters, and courts are informed of the importance of conducting a broad-based assessment that takes into consideration previous personality characteristics and psychological functioning, as well as current comorbid conditions, given the relevance of these factors in predicting psychological injury as well as disability. They should also qualify the results of their assessments by noting the significant limitations of the current forensic literature with respect to the likelihood of developing psychological injury following certain types of traumas, the possible vulnerability of certain assessment methods to symptom exaggeration in compensation-seeking individuals, and the lack of norms from forensic samples for many of the commonly used symptom measures.

Second, it is also important that evaluators do not make definitive conclusions that the adverse event under legal dispute caused current and future psychological impairment. Rather, they should explain and integrate the descriptions of pre-event mental health functioning, current functioning, and describe any *possible* causes, including the event in question. Although it would be acceptable to opine about the relative importance of competing causes, whether the event in question was a legal cause (i.e., had at least a material contribution to the injuries) is a question for the trier of fact to answer.

Once the presence and severity of a psychological injury are established, the focus turns to examining the impact of that injury on an individual's functioning. Although anxiety and depressive disorders show a strong relationship to work-related disability, little research is available on evidence-based methods of linking mental health symptoms to work disability in individual cases. No well-researched disability assessment tools relevant to linking psychological disturbance to work disability have yet been developed. Furthermore, we have no actual research basis for concluding that *specific* psychological domains of wellness are a prerequisite for good work functioning. The empirical expert should inform the courts of the research literature relating mental health conditions to disability, as well as providing straightforward descriptions of the possible behavioral pathways through which individual claimants might either become disabled or—alternatively—those individual strengths, workplace environmental factors, or other variables that would argue for little or no functional disability in an individual claimant.

REFERENCES

American Psychiatric Association. (1987). *Diagnostic and statistical manual of mental disorders* (3rd ed., rev.). Washington, DC: Author.

American Psychiatric Association. (2000). *Diagnostic and statistical manual of mental disorders* (4th ed., text rev.). Washington, DC: Author.

Andreason, N. C. (1995). Posttraumatic stress disorder: Psychology, biology, and the Manichaean warfare between false dichotomies. *American Journal of Psychiatry, 152,* 963–965.

Appelberg, K., Romanov, K., Heikkilae, K., & Honkasalo, M.L. (1996). Interpersonal conflict as a predictor of work disability: A follow-up study of 15,348 Finnish employees. *Journal of Psychosomatic Research, 40,* 157–167.

Baldwin, S. A., Williams, D. C., & Houts, A. C. (2004). The creation, expansion, and embodiment of posttraumatic stress disorder: A case study in historical critical psychopathology. *Scientific Review of Mental Health Practice, 3,* 33–52.

Bilj, R. V., & Ravelli, A. (2000). Current and residual functional disability associated with psychopathology: Findings from the Netherlands Mental Health Survey and Incidence Study (NEMESIS). *Psychological Medicine, 30,* 657–668.

Blake, D. D., Weathers, F., Nagy, L. M., Kaloupek, D. G., Charney, D.S., & Keane, T. M. (1998). *Clinician-administered PTSD scale for DSM-IV.* Boston: National Center for Posttraumatic Stress Disorder.

Blanchard, E. B., & Hickling, E. J. (1996). *After the crash: Assessment and treatment of motor vehicle accident survivors.* Washington, DC: American Psychological Association.

Blanchard, E. B., Jones-Alexander, J., Buckley, T. C., & Forneris, C. A. (1996). Psychometric properties of the PTSD Checklist (PCL). *Behaviour Research and Therapy, 34,* 669–673.

Bodkin, J. A., Pope, H. G., Detke, M. J., & Hudson, J. I. (2007). Is PTSD caused by traumatic stress? *Journal of Anxiety Disorders, 21,* 176–182.

Bowman, M. L. (1999). Individual differences in posttraumatic distress: Problems with the DSM-IV model. *Canadian Journal of Psychiatry, 44,* 21–33.

Breslau, N., Davis, G. C., Andreski, P., & Peterson, E. L. (1991). Traumatic events and posttraumatic stress disorder in an urban population of young adults. *Archives of General Psychiatry, 48,* 216–222.

Buckley, T. C., Blanchard, E. B., & Hickling, E. J. (1996). A prospective examination of delayed onset PTSD secondary to motor vehicle accidents. *Journal of Abnormal Psychology, 105,* 617–625.

Calhoun, P. S., Beckham, J. C., Feldman, M. E., Barefoot, J. C., Haney, T., & Bosworth, H. B. (2002). Partners' ratings of combat veterans' anger. *Journal of Traumatic Stress, 15,* 133–136.

Cocchiarella, L., & Andersson, G. B. J. (2001). *Guides to the evaluation of permanent impairment* (5th ed.). Chicago: American Medical Association.

Coyne, J. C., & Gotlib, I. H. (1983). The role of cognition in depression: A critical appraisal. *Psychological Bulletin, 94,* 472–505.

Creamer, M., Burgess, P., & McFarlane, A. C. (2001). Post-traumatic stress disorder: Findings from the Australian National Survey of Mental Health and Well-being. *Psychological Medicine, 31,* 1237–1247.

Dillman, E. G. (2003). Impairment to earning capacity based on psychological findings. In I. Z. Schultz & D. O. Brady (Eds.), *Psychological injuries at trial* (pp. 342–356). Washington, DC: American Bar Association.

Douglas, K. S., Huss, M. T., Murdoch, L. L., Washington, D. O., & Koch, W. J. (1999). Posttraumatic stress disorder stemming from motor vehicle accidents: Legal issues in Canada and the United States. In E. J. Hickling & E. B. Blanchard (Eds.), *International handbook of road traffic accidents and psychological trauma: Current understanding, treatment, and law* (pp. 271–290). New York: Elsevier Science.

Eden, S. M. (2001). "I am having a flashback ... all the way to the bank": The application of the "thin skull" rule to mental injuries—*Poole v. Copland, Inc. North Carolina Central Law Journal, 24,* 180–189.

Fairbank, J. A., Ebert, L., & Zarkin, G. A. (1999). Socioeconomic consequences of traumatic stress. In P. A. Saigh & J. D. Bremner (Eds.), *Posttraumatic stress disorder: A comprehensive text* (pp. 180–198). Needham Heights, MA: Allyn & Bacon.

Frueh, B. C., Gold, P. B., & de Arellano, M. A. (1997). Symptom overreporting in combat veterans evaluated for PTSD: Differentiation on the basis of compensation-seeking status. *Journal of Personality Assessment, 68,* 369–384.

Gallagher, J. G., Riggs, D. S., Byrne, C. A., & Weathers, F. W. (1998). Female partners' estimations of male veterans' combat-related PTSD severity. *Journal of Traumatic Stress, 11,* 367–374.

Gnam, W. H. (2005). The prediction of occupational disability related to depressive and anxiety disorders. In I. A. Schultz & R. J. Gatchel (Eds.), *Handbook of complex occupational disability claims: Early risk identification, intervention, and prevention* (pp. 371–386). New York: Springer.

Gold, S. D., Marx, B. P., Soler-Baillo, J. M., & Sloan, D. M. (2005). Is life stress more traumatic than traumatic stress? *Journal of Anxiety Disorders, 19,* 687–698.

Greenberg, S. A., Otto, R. K., & Long, A. C. (2003). The utility of psychological testing in assessing emotional damages in personal injury litigation. *Assessment, 10,* 411–419.

Iverson, G. L., & Lange, R. T. (2006). Detecting exaggeration and malingering in psychological injury claims. In W. J. Koch, K. S. Douglas, T. L. Nicholls, & M. L. O'Neill (Eds.), *Psychological injuries: Forensic assessment, treatment, and law* (pp. 76–112). New York: Oxford University Press.

Judd, L. L., Akiskal, H. S., Zeller, P. J., Paulus, M., Leon, A. C., Maser, J. D., et al. (2000). Psychosocial disability during the long-term course of unipolar major depressive disorder. *Archives of General Psychiatry, 57,* 375–380.

Kendell, R., & Jablensky, A. (2003). Distinguishing between the validity and utility of psychiatric diagnoses. *American Journal of Psychiatry, 160,* 4–12.

Kessler, R. C., Ormel, J., Demler, O., & Stang, P. E. (2003). Comorbid mental disorders account for the role impairment of commonly occurring chronic physical disorders: Results from the National Comorbidity Survey. *Journal of Occupational and Environmental Medicine, 45,* 1257–1266.

Koch, W. J., Douglas, K. S., Nicholls, T. L., & O'Neill, M. L. (2006). *Psychological injuries: Forensic assessment, treatment, and law.* Oxford, UK: Oxford University Press.

Koch, W. J., O'Neill, M., & Douglas, K. S. (2005). Empirical limits for the forensic assessment of PTSD litigants. *Law and Human Behavior, 29,* 121–149.

Lee, D., & Young, K. (2001). Post-traumatic stress disorder: Diagnostic issues and epidemiology in adult survivors or traumatic events. *International Review of Psychiatry, 13,* 150–158.

Lynch v. Knight, 11 Eng. Rep. 854 (1861).

Matza, L. S., Revichi, D. A., Davidson, J. R., & Stewart, J. W. (2003). Depression with atypical features in the National Comorbidity Survey: Classification, description, and consequences. *Archives of General Psychiatry, 60,* 817–826.

Melton, G. B., Petrila, J., Poythress, N. G., & Slobogin, C. (1997). *Psychological evaluations for the courts: A handbook for mental health professionals and lawyers* (2nd ed.). New York: Guilford Press.

Miller, H.A. (2001). *M-FAST: Miller Forensic Assessment of Symptoms Test: Professional manual.* Odessa, FL: Psychological Assessment Resources.

Mittenberg, W., Patton, C., Canyock, E. M., & Condit, D. C. (2002). Base rates of malingering and symptom exaggeration. *Journal of Clinical and Experimental Neuropsychology, 24,* 1094–1102.

Mol, S. S. L., Arntz, A., Metsemakers, J. F. M., Dinant, G.-J., Vilters-Van Montfort, P. A. P., & Knottnerus, J. A. (2005). Symptoms of post-traumatic stress disorder after nontraumatic events: Evidence from an open population study. *British Journal of Psychiatry, 186,* 494–499.

Norris, F. H. (1992). Epidemiology of trauma: Frequency and impact of different potentially traumatic events on different demographic groups. *Journal of Consulting and Clinical Psychology, 60,* 409–418.

Regehr, C., Goldberg, G., Glancy, G. D., & Knott, T. (2002). Posttraumatic symptoms and disability in paramedics. *Canadian Journal of Psychiatry, 47,* 953–958.

Rogers, R. (Ed.). (1997). *Clinical assessment of malingering and deception* (2nd ed.). New York: Guilford Press.

Rogers, R., Bagby, R. M., & Dickens, S. E. (1992). *Structured interview of reported symptoms: Professional manual.* Odessa, FL: Psychological Assessment Resources.

Rogers, R., & Bender, S. D. (2003). Evaluation of malingering and deception. In A. M. Goldstein & I. B. Weiner (Eds.), *Handbook of psychology: Vol. 11. Forensic psychology* (pp. 109–129). Hoboken, NJ: Wiley.

Rogers, R., Sewell, K. W., & Goldstein, A. (1994). Explanatory models of malingering: A prototypical analysis. *Law and Human Behavior, 18,* 543–552.

Rosen, G. M., & Lilienfeld, S. O. (2008). Posttraumatic stress disorder: An empirical evaluation of core assumptions. *Clinical Psychology Review, 28,* 837–868.

Ruscio, A. M., Ruscio, J., & Keane, T. M. (2002). The latent structure of posttraumatic stress disorder: A taxometric investigation of reactions to extreme stress. *Journal of Abnormal Psychology, 111,* 290–301.

Schnurr, P. P., & Green, B. L. (Eds.). (2004). *Trauma and health: Physical health consequences of exposure to extreme stress.* Washington, DC: American Psychological Association.

Schutzwohl, M., & Maercker, A. (1999). Effects of varying diagnostic criteria for posttraumatic stress disorder are endorsing the concept of partial PTSD. *Journal of Traumatic Stress, 12,* 155–165.

Scott, W. J. (1990). PTSD in DSM-III: A case in the politics of diagnosis and disease. *Social Problems, 37,* 294–310.

Spitzer, R. L., Kroenke, K., Linzer, M., Hahn, S. R., Williams, J. B., deGruy, F. V., et al. (1995). Health-related quality of life in primary care patients with mental disorders: Results from the PRIME-MD 1000 Study. *Journal of the American Medical Association, 274,* 1511–1517.

Summerfield, D. (2002). ICD and DSM are contemporary cultural documents. *British Medical Journal, 324,* 914.

Tiemens, B. G., Von Korff, M., & Lin, E. H. B. (1999). Diagnosis of depression by primary care physicians versus a structured diagnostic interview: Understanding discordance. *General Hospital Psychiatry, 21,* 87–96.

Tombaugh, T. N. (1997). The Test of Memory Malingering (TOMM): Normative data from cognitively intact and cognitively impaired individuals. *Psychological Assessment, 9,* 260–268.

Von Korff, M., Ormel, J., Katon, W., & Lin, E. H. (1992). Disability and depression among high utilizers of health care: A longitudinal analysis. *Archives of General Psychiatry, 49,* 91–100.

Watson, D. (1999). Dimensions underlying the anxiety disorders: A hierarchical perspective. *Current Opinion in Psychiatry, 12,* 181–186.

Weathers, F. W., Ruscio, A. M., & Keane, T. M. (1999). Psychometric properties of nine scoring rules for the Clinician-Administered Posttraumatic Stress Disorder Scale. *Psychological Assessment, 11,* 124–133.

Zimmerman, M., & Mattia, J. I. (1999). Psychiatric diagnosis in clinical practice: Is comorbidity being missed? *Comprehensive Psychiatry, 40,* 182–191.

CHAPTER 13

Controversies in Child Custody Evaluations

William T. O'Donohue, Kendra Beitz, and Lauren Tolle

OVERVIEW OF TECHNIQUES AND CONTROVERSIES

Divorce rates have skyrocketed over the last 20 years. Statistics suggest that whereas in 1977 one-third of all marriages ended in divorce (Lyman & Roberts, 1985), more recently 50% of marriages end in divorce. The incidence of divorce is over 1 million cases each year, with the majority of these (60%) involving children under the age of 18 (National Center for Health Statistics of the United States, 1995).

Because of both the importance and complexity of child placement decisions and because of what appears to be obvious "psychological-behavioral" factors that typically fall outside the expertise of attorneys and judges involved, mental health professionals are increasingly being asked to provide recommendations to the courts on placement of children (Otto, 2000). The Guidelines of the American Psychological Association (1994) suggest that the overall reasons for psychologists to become involved is to provide "an additional source of information and an additional perspective not otherwise readily available to the court on what appears to be in a child's best interests, and thus can increase fairness of the determination the court must make" (American Psychological Association, 1994, p. 677).

The American Law Institute's (ALI) Principles of the Law of Family Dissolution (2002) highlights that the primary objective when determining custody placements is to serve the child's best interests. These best interests are fostered by parenting planning and agreement on custody arrangements and childrearing; maintaining continuity of existing parent–child attachments and meaningful contact with parents; placement of children in caretaking relationships with adults who love them, provide for their needs, and prioritize meeting their needs; along with limited exposure to conflict and violence.

States are nearly unanimous in their agreement that the best interests of the child involve joint custody (American Law Institute, 2002), and this view has been supported by empirical research indicating that better child outcomes postdivorce are associated with either joint custody or substantial contact with the noncustodial parent (Emery, 1999). Thus, joint custody or substantial contact with both parents should be the default value unless there are perturbing factors that render the child's best interests as having either no, minimal, or supervised contact with the parent associated with the perturbing factors. These factors include child abuse, poor attachment, poor parenting skills, significant emotional instability/mental disorder of the parent, environmental instability, and excessive conflict.

Does Divorce Negatively Affect Children? What Are the Buffering Variables?

Defining the Controversy

Studies that have examined children's adjustment after divorce have frequently suggested that children of divorced families have been found to fall within normal ranges in both psychological and cognitive functioning (Braver et al., 1993; Kelly, 1998; Whiteside & Becker, 2000). In contrast, literature also suggests that children from divorced families are at greater risk of adjustment problems than children from intact families (Kelly & Emery, 2003).

Research Relevant to the Controversy

A number of studies have examined children from divorced families in an attempt to answer this question. Several studies have concluded that children are adversely affected by divorce. Of course, it is important to note that research findings in this area are largely correlational in nature, and thus it is incredibly difficult, if not impossible, to infer causality (i.e., preexisting differences are not accounted for, studies cannot randomly assign children to divorced or intact families, etc.). We therefore caution the reader that this controversy is one that may remain unsolved, given the inherent methodological problems in drawing causal inferences. However, more longitudinal research is following children assigned to different custody arrangements (sole, 50/50 joint, maintaining proportion, etc.), with different kinds of children (ages, gender, special needs, attachment relationships), and with different kinds of parents (abusive, different mental health status, different levels of conflict). Needless to say, this is very complex and resource-intensive research. However, we must point out that very little research of this nature is being carried out currently.

DIVORCE AND POORER OUTCOMES

Numerous studies have been conducted that have found that children from divorced homes exhibit more behavioral problems, as compared to children from intact homes, and that these problems are often long term. Specifically, meta-analyses that examined 104 studies have revealed that individuals from divorced homes have poorer (1) psychological well-being (i.e., depression and low life satisfaction), (2) family well-being (defined as presence of marital dissatisfaction or divorce), (3) socioeconomic well-being (low educational attainment, low income, and low occupational prestige), (4) self-concept, (5) social competence, and (6) physical health problems than individuals from families whose parents remained married (Amato, 2000, 2001; Amato & Keith, 1991).

Several important longitudinal studies have examined the long-term well-being of children from divorced families. Strengths and limitations of these studies are discussed elsewhere (e.g., Ahrons & Tanner, 2003). Results from these studies, all of which followed individuals from divorced families and intact families for at least 20 years, found that individuals from divorced families were more likely to engage in "acting out" behaviors as adolescents (e.g., engaging in their first sexual experience earlier; earlier onset of drug use; longer time period of drug use at higher levels; impulsive, irresponsible, or antisocial behavior), less likely to experience academic accomplishments (fewer entered and completed college with a bachelor's degree; higher dropout rate), more likely to be pessimistic about marriage (less likely to marry; more difficulty in romantic relationships), more likely to divorce, more likely to experience depression, have difficulty at work, and report feeling less close to their biological parents, as compared to individuals from intact families (Amato, 2006; Hetherington & Kelly, 2002; Wallerstein & Lewis, 2004). It should be noted that Amato (2006) also found that offspring from intact, high-discord families experienced problems similar to individuals from divorced families, including greater discord in their own marriages, less social support, and lower levels of psychological well-being. However, they did not differ from intact, low-discord families in terms of educational attainment or relationship disruptions.

DIVORCE AND POSITIVE/NO-DIFFERENCE OUTCOMES

Finally, some have suggested that divorce can be associated with positive outcomes in children. Specifically, Arditti (1999, as cited in Amato, 2000) found that postdivorce daughters, in particular, developed close relationships with their mothers. In addition, some studies found that children were better off on multiple outcomes if parents in high-conflict marriages divorced rather than remain married (Amato & Booth, 1997, as cited in Amato, 2000; Amato, Loomis, & Booth, 1995). It should also be noted that many studies have found preexisting problem behaviors in children and problematic child–parent relationships, suggesting that divorce is not the only factor associated with problems (Amato, 2000).

In general, despite the overwhelming amount of literature that has found associations between children from divorced families and poorer psychological adjustment, socioeconomic achievement, higher marital dissatisfaction and higher divorce rates, poorer self-concept and social competence, as compared to children from intact families, given the methodological problems inherent in this research, it is not possible to conclude that these problems are solely due to divorce (Amato, 2000, 2001; Amato & Keith, 1991). Likewise, literature has found that children from intact families as well as children from high-discord, intact families are quite similar in well-being to children from divorced families on a number of outcomes (Amato, 2006; Hetherington & Kelly, 2002). In conclusion, although it appears that children from divorced families experience more long-term psychosocial problems than children from intact families, the definitive explanation is not available. Given that divorce is not likely to be eradicated, the pressing issue then becomes not whether or not it is bad, but what factors postdivorce are associated with poorer outcomes in children and how these might be mitigated; ideally, custody arrangements should take these buffering variables into account.

Relatively little literature has definitively demonstrated factors that are associated with better or poorer adjustment in children postdivorce. Nonetheless, certain factors of divorced families that are associated with long-term consequences in adulthood have been identified. These factors include attachment, parenting skills, parental conflict, environmental instability, and emotional instability.

Attachment. Healthy attachment to parents plays an important role in the functioning of children and adolescents (Taub, 1997). Separations from a caregiver to whom the child is attached are considered detrimental to development and are associated with problems with peer relationships, aggression, poor school performance, and low self-esteem (Ainsworth & Witting, 1969; Marcus & Betzer, 1996; O'Koon, 1997; Schneider & Younger, 1996). In addition, children who experience a high-quality relationship with their father were found to have better adjustment postdivorce. However, children whose fathers negatively influenced them (were absent or did not have a quality relationship with the child) were found to have poorer outcomes postdivorce (Amato & Gilbreth, 1999; Buchanan, Maccoby, & Dornbusch, 1996; Harper & Fine, 2006; Papp, Cummings, & Goeke-Morey, 2005; Whiteside & Becker, 2000).

Parenting Skills. Thomson, Hanson, and McLanahan (1994) reviewed a number of studies that demonstrated that the impact of changes in family structure (i.e., divorce/separation) on children is attenuated by healthy parenting. Parental warmth, parallel parenting, age-appropriate expectations, authoritative parenting, and supportive coparenting have all been found to be protective factors postdivorce (Gould, 1998; Hetherington, Cox, & Cox, 1981; Kelly & Emery, 2003; Lamborn, Mounts, Steinberg, & Dornbusch, 1991; Steinberg, 2001; Wallerstein & Kelly, 1980). In contrast, poorer adjustment (i.e., difficulties in cognitive, emotional, and social areas of the child's life) was found to be associated with disagreement and inconsistencies between parents, continued anger between parents, poor parental adjustment, and authoritarian or neglectful parenting (Wallerstein & Kelly, 1980; Whiteside & Becker, 2000). Parenting styles tend to be consistent over time (McNally, Eisenberg, & Harris, 1991), which is important to consider when making permanent child placements, as inept parental discipline has been associated with child aggression, delinquency, and an increased risk for child abuse (Novak, 1996).

Parental Conflict. One reason why divorce can be particularly stressful for children is that it is likely to be preceded, and often followed by, a period of parental conflict (Amato & Keith, 1991). It has been estimated that 25% of parents are in "high conflict" postdivorce (Maccoby & Mnookin, 1992). Parental conflict (e.g., hostility, violence, and other acts of marital aggression; acting deliberately subversively and using the child in ways to harm the other parent, such as telling the child to disobey the other parent or using the child as a conduit for punishing the other parent) is associated with deleterious effects on child and adolescent functioning (Emery, 1999; Gould, 1998; Hetherington et al., 1981; Otto, Buffington-Vollum, & Edens, 2003; Wallerstein & Kelly, 1980; Whiteside & Becker, 2000) and has been shown to be a stronger predictor of adjustment than family structure (Kot & Shoemaker, 1999). Also, when conflict is encapsulated (i.e., children are not placed in the middle) or mediated by paternal involvement and the parent–child relationship, children appear to function as well as those from no- or low-conflict families (Hetherington & Stanley-Hagan, 1999; Pruett, Williams, Insabella, & Little, 2003).

Environmental Instability. There has been a shift from family preservation as the presiding value in recognition of the fact that children who remain in unstable homes are at risk (Ballou et al., 2001). Environmental stability promotes child security (Bray, 1991, as cited in Gould, 1998). An "instable environment" may include factors such as inconsistency, extreme poverty, inadequate supervision, substance abuse, violence, and physical abuse. LeVine (1974) places economic goals second in the hierarchy of the universal functions of parenting, which include domains such as basic education. Economic stability is one of the most powerful predictors of postdivorce child functioning; unstable economic conditions tend to be associated with poorer housing, schools, neighborhoods, child care, health care, and less supportive parenting (Hetherington, 1989; Lamb, Sternberg, & Thompson, 1997; Novak, 1996; Thomson, Hanson, & McLanahan, 1994). Although the effects of poverty can be mitigated by various factors (e.g., the presence of an accepting, stimulating, and organized environment; Novak, 1996), extreme economic hardship (i.e., homelessness) is likely to adversely impact child functioning. The lack of child monitoring following divorce (which could be attributed to motivational deficits of the parent or the parent's own environmental demands, such as work schedule) (Hetherington, 1990, as cited in Novak, 1996) has been associated with child behavior problems, including delinquency (Patterson, DeBaryshe, & Ramsey, 1989). Finally, substance abuse, violence, and physical abuse cause family disruptions and negatively affect the well-being of children (Lamb et al., 1997; Sun, 2001). Specifically, excessive parental drug and alcohol abuse has been shown to be detrimental to the development of socialization and a variety of internalizing and externalizing problems (see Otto et al., 2003, for a review).

Emotional Instability. Emery (1999) suggests that four mental health problems among adults are of special concern to understanding the consequences of divorce: depression, antisocial behavior, major mental illness (i.e., schizophrenia or bipolar disorder), and personality disorders. Specifically, research suggests that parental depression, bipolar schizophrenia, or display of antisocial or problematic behaviors indicative of other personality disorders has been associated with a number of negative child outcomes, including adjustment problems, psychopathology, aggression, delinquency, and other externalizing problems (Emery, 1999; for a review, see Otto et al., 2003). Other researchers have noted that the relationship between psychopathology and children's functioning might not be causal (Jenuwine & Cohler, 1999). A diagnosis is not the primary concern; rather, the impact of parental psychological functioning on child development is the primary concern (Herman et al., 1997; Otto et al., 2003). When this link can be demonstrated, measurement of parental emotional stability is clinically relevant for determining child custody or placement.

Are There Valid and Useful Assessment Instruments for Custody Evaluations?

Defining the Controversy

Custody evaluations often include multiple constructs (e.g., attachment, abuse potential, parenting skills) that are discussed across different time periods (past, present, future); an assessment instrument might be adequate for one of these tasks or time periods but poor at another. Therefore it is important to be concerned about *validities*, rather than a single validity, during the custody evaluation, as there are a number of distinct inferences we want to make.

Research Relevant to the Controversy

Unfortunately, tests generally used in custody evaluations are problematic, making the quality of most inferences based on them questionable (Emery, Otto, & O'Donohue, 2005; O'Donohue & Bradley, 1999). In addition, it is questionable whether we *can* construct assessment strategies with reasonable validity and whether we *will* construct these. The prediction task is complex in that we may be asking a question involving a prediction about states of affairs a decade or more away. In addition, to our knowledge, there has been little recent progress and little ongoing development in assessment.

THE LACK OF RELEVANT, PSYCHOMETRICALLY SOUND MEASUREMENT INSTRUMENTS

Many reviewers have suggested that currently there is a dearth of psychometrically sound assessment instruments and strategies in this field (Emery et al., 2005; O'Donohue & Bradley, 1999; Otto, Edens, & Barcus, 2000). As Otto and colleagues (2000) noted, a common error is to use psychological tests that do not address psycholegal issues directly relevant to the child custody questions (e.g., parenting capacity, best interest of the child or the interaction between these), but rather simply measure a general construct (e.g., intelligence) that may be only indirectly related to more specific and relevant child custody issues. A national survey of mental health professionals conducting child custody evaluations found that 58% routinely used intelligence tests, 48% routinely used the Rorschach, and 37% routinely used the Thematic Apperception Test (Ackerman & Ackerman, 1997). (See Wood et al., Chapter 9, this volume, for an evaluation of these projective tests.) Grisso and Conlin (1984) has suggested that psychological tests specific to child custody issues need to be developed and psychometrically evaluated because

> Too often we rely on assessment instruments and methods that were designed to address *clinical* questions, questions of psychiatric diagnosis, when clinical questions bear only secondarily on real issues in many child custody cases. Psychiatric interviews, Rorschachs, and MMPIs might have a role to play in child custody assessment. But these tools were not designed to assess parents' relationships to children nor to assess parents' child rearing attitudes and capacities and *these* are often the central questions in child custody cases. (p. 484)

Some tests and test batteries have been specifically developed to measure constructs relevant to child custody evaluations. The most notable of these are the tests of Ackerman (Ackerman & Schoendorf, 1992) and Bricklin and Elliot (1991). However, they have been nearly universally criticized, and their psychometric properties are inadequate (Grisso, Borum, Edens, Moyle, & Otto, 2003). Table 13.1 summarizes problematic or missing psychometric

TABLE 13.1. Comparisons of Custody Evaluation Measures across American Psychological Association Standards for Educational and Psychological Testing

	Recommended	Required	BPS[e]	PORT[f]	PASS[g] and PPCP[b]	ASPECT[c]
Validity		✓				
• Construct related[d]	✓		? α not reported; convergence with other measures with questionable convergent validity; mixed findings for convergent validity; and questionable methodology[d]	? α not reported; convergent validity with other measures with questionable validity; and questionable methodology[d]	× Not reported[d]	? α ranges from .50 to .76, with some item–total correlations negatively correlated[d]
• Content related[d]	✓		? Content assessed is narrow and not adequate for comprehensive assessment[d]	? No coherent theory re relationship between human figure drawings and parenting[d]	? Content not linked to a model for parenting; adequacy and thoroughness of content not evaluated[d]	? Based on literature review for some but not all items; uses tests not designed for custody (i.e., MMPI)[d]
• Criterion related[d]	✓		? Predicted judges' decisions in 93% of 27 cases, but unclear whether or not judges' decisions were contaminated by receiving test results; judges' decisions not necessarily in best interest of child[d]	? Predicted judges' decision in 92% of 87 cases, but unclear whether or not judges' decisions were contaminated by receiving test results; judges' decisions not necessarily in best interest of child[d]	× Not reported[d]	? Predicted judges' decision 60–91% of time in 57 cases, but methodology is questionable; judges' decisions not necessarily in best interest or child[d]
• Differential prediction[d]	✓		× Not reported[d]	× Not reported[d]	× Not reported[d]	× 96.9% white and upper middle class[d]

Reliability					
• Test–retest[b]	✓	? Demonstrated in 12 cases over a short time frame, but in unpublished dissertations[a]	? Demonstrated in small sample with unclear methods and in an unpublished dissertation[a]	× Not reported[a]	× Not reported[a]
• Internal consistency[b]		× Not reported[a]	× Not reported[a]	× Not reported[a]	✓ α ranges from .50 to .76 with some item–total correlations negatively correlated[a]
Norms	✓	× No clearly delineated normative sample[a]	× Normative data not reported[a]	× Normative data not reported[a]	✓ Note: Norms are provided but sample is very homogeneous[c]
Manual/users' guide	✓	× Manual is provided, but research data are so abbreviated that it is not possible to evaluate adequacy of sample, methods, or results[a]	× Manual is provided, but studies conducted lack experimental rigor and suffer from methodological limitations[a]	× Manual is provided, but does not include psychometric data[a]	? Manual describes research data but data are questionable[a]

Note. ✓ = standard met; ×, standard not met; ?, weak/questionable evidence for meeting standard.

[a]American Educational Research Association, American Psychological Association, and National Council on Measurement in Education (1999); [b]Pedhazer and Schmelkin (1991); [c]Ackerman and Schoendorf (1992); [d]Grisso, Borum, Edens, Moyle, and Otto (2003); [e]Bricklin (1990a); [f]Bricklin (1989); [g]Bricklin (1990b); [h]Bricklin and Elliott (1991).

properties and test features for the most commonly used measures for determining child custody or placement. The information provided in Table 13.1
and literature presented above both demonstrate that several measures currently used in custody evaluations lack the reliability and validity necessary
to complete methodologically sound evaluations.

GAPS IN KNOWLEDGE

Despite the fact that custody evaluations have been conducted for decades,
many issues have been left unresolved. Given the ambiguity involved in the
"best interest" guidelines for custody evaluators, many of these appear to
have been left to individual evaluators to resolve on their own—with likely
little consistency across the field. Included in this section is a discussion of
several of these.

What Constructs Should Be Assessed in a Custody Evaluation?

As Tolstoy said, "Happy families are all alike; every unhappy family is
unhappy in its own way." This issue of a guiding assessment model has
both nomothetic and idiographic dimensions. That is, which constructs
should be assessed in each child custody evaluation? And, due to the
unique circumstances in any particular case, which additional constructs
should be assessed given the case's idiosyncrasies? The field has no generally accepted theory that identifies relevant constructs (O'Donohue &
Bradley, 1999).

How Should Disparate Data Be Examined and Used
in the Ultimate Questions?

If depression and attachment are determined to be relevant to custody
decisions, how do these two constructs relate, and interrelate, to custody
outcomes? First, if the mother is significantly depressed after she discov-
ers her husband's affair, but her husband is blissfully happy with his
new girlfriend, how, if at all, do these two dynamics impact custody
arrangements (i.e., how is her current depression related to her long-term
parenting capacity or the child's best interests; how is his unfaithful-
ness or possibly mild antisocial behavior related to these?). Second, if the
mother's depression does affect her attachment to her children, is this
then more relevant to custody arrangements? Third, what if the mother

initially responds well to some sort of depression treatment, and attachment seems to be improving to the youngest children but not the oldest? One can begin to see the complexities of the multiple constructs that usually emerge in these evaluations. However, there is no clear system in which to move from values of variables to statements that are more relevant to custody arrangements.

Need for Better Testing Criteria and Measures in Child Custody Cases

Three organizations have adopted guidelines for conducting child custody evaluations (summarized in Table 13.2). These guidelines (though with some disagreement) conclude that psychological tests should target factors such as emotional stability, environmental stability, attachment, parenting skills, and conflict. However, the field either lacks such measures or current measures are not adequately responsive to the underlying *psycholegal* issues at play in custody settings. Heilbrun (1995) gives eight criteria that tests should meet in order to be used in a child custody evaluation: The test must (1) be commercially available; (2) have a published manual describing development, psychometric properties, and procedures for administration; (3) be peer-reviewed in professional journals; (4) have ongoing research exploring its usefulness (validity); (5) have test–retest reliability that is at least .80; (6) be relevant to the legal issues or to a psychological construct underlying a legal issue; (7) be administered in a standardized fashion; and (8) have measures of response style.

We now examine existing measures that address the potentially buffering factors discussed in the first controversy, as these are relevant to child adjustment, and several have empirical support, though they may not necessarily have been designed for use in custody evaluations. The need for these measures is also discussed.

Measuring Attachment

Both the American Academy of Child and Adolescent Psychiatry (Herman et al., 1997) and ALI's Principles of the Law of Family Dissolution (American Law Institute, 2002) recommend assessing parent–child attachment when defining the "best interest of the child." Additionally, many state statutes require the court to include the strength of the parent–child bond when making placement and custody decisions (Hall, Pulver, & Cooley, 1996). Currently, there are inadequate assessments for measuring parent–child attachment and thus a much needed area of research.

TABLE 13.2. Comparisons of Guidelines for Custody Evaluations

Domains	APA	AFCC	AACAP
Assessment of child's needs (including psychological and developmental), parents' ability to meet these needs, and parents' abilities to provide for child's future needs (AACP adds physical and educational needs as well)	✓	✓	✓
Parenting abilities or lack thereof	✓		✓
Capacity to provide a stable, loving home	✓		
Misconduct or inappropriate behavior that negatively influences child (e.g., substance use/abuse)	✓		✓
Parent psychopathology as it impacts the child or the ability to parent	✓		✓
Wishes of the child	✓		✓
Assessment of strengths, vulnerabilities, and needs of all other family members		✓	
Wishes and interests of the parents		✓	
Parent–child attachment			✓
Parent alienation			✓
Gender issues			✓
Sibling relationships			✓
Parents' physical health that could adversely impact child			✓
Parents' work schedules and subsequent impact on child needs			✓
Parents' financial situation and subsequent impact on child			✓
How family members resolve conflict			✓
Social support networks for child that might be affected by custody arrangement			✓
Cultural and ethnic influences that may play a role in child growth and development			✓
Impact of parents' ethics and value systems on the child			✓
Significance of religious issues and impact on child			✓
Assessment modes			
Multiple methods, including (but not limited to) clinical interviews, direct observation, and/or psychological assessments	✓		✓
Collateral information, including (but not limited to) other reports (e.g., from schools, health care providers, child care providers, agencies, and institutions) and interviewing other individuals (e.g., family, friends)			✓
Interview stepparents or potential stepparents			✓

Note. APA, American Psychological Association (1994); AFCC, Association of Family and Conciliation Courts (1995); AACAP, American Academy of Child and Adolescent Psychiatry (1997).

Measuring Parenting Skills

A number of currently available paper-and-pencil tests measure parenting skills. For example, the Child-Rearing Practices Report (CRPR; Block, 1965) is a questionnaire with excellent psychometric properties (Locke & Prinz, 2002) that assesses both ineffective and effective parenting practices. The Alabama Parenting Questionnaire (APQ; Shelton, Frick, & Wooton, 1996) is another questionnaire with good psychometric properties (Locke & Prinz, 2002) that assesses monitoring/supervision, consistency of discipline, corporal punishment, and other discipline-related practices. It should be noted, however, that these questionnaires, in addition to others (see Locke & Prinz, 2002, for a review), were *not* developed for the purpose of determining child custody, and more specifically, for screening for egregious parenting. Parenting questionnaires that have been designed to be used in custody evaluations (i.e., Gould, 1999) lack psychometric data. The need for such a measure with sound psychometric properties is evident.

Measuring Parental Conflict

A number of paper-and-pencil measures are currently available for measuring conflict. The Conflict Tactics Scale (CTS; Strauss, 1979) is a widely used self-report measure designed to assess how people behave during conflict with others. The Family Environment Scale (FES; Moos & Moos, 1994) is a self-report measure that contains a subscale designed to measure conflict as well. The Personal Assertion Analysis (PAA; Hedlund & Lindquist, 1984) is designed to measure how people behave during interpersonal interactions, including behaviors such as conflict avoidance and aggression during conflict. None of these measures were specifically designed for use in custody evaluations. Additionally, existing scales of parental conflict do not include validity scales to assess response styles, such as social desirability/lying. The need for such a measure with sound psychometric properties is evident.

Measuring Environmental Stability

A number of paper-and-pencil measures are currently available for measuring family environment/environmental stability. The Family Adaptation and Cohesion Scales–III (FACES-III) is a measure of family structure, including family cohesion and adaptability (Olson, Portner, & Lavee, 1985).

The Family Assessment Measure–III assesses a number of domains related to family environment, including involvement, roles, and values (FAM-III; Skinner, Steinhauer, & Santa-Barbara, 1995). The Family Environment Scale (FES; Moos & Moos, 1994) is a self-report measure that is designed to measure family environment as well. None of these measures was specifically designed for use in custody evaluations. Additionally, existing scales of environmental stability do not include validity scales to assess response styles, such as social desirability/lying. The need for such a measure with sound psychometric properties is evident.

Measuring Emotional Stability

In order to measure all aspects of emotional stability that could be relevant to child custody, an assessment of all Axis I and II disorders in the fourth edition of the *Diagnostic and Statistical Manual of Mental Disorders* (DSM-IV; American Psychiatric Association, 1994) may be necessary. This includes an assessment of psychotic, mood, anxiety, somatoform, factitious, dissociative, sexual and gender identity, eating, sleeping, impulse control, adjustment, and personality disorders; all of the subcategories within each; and all of the diagnostic criteria for each subcategory. Additionally, if parental psychopathology is raised as a concern in a custody dispute, a number of existing validated self-report instruments (e.g., Beck Depression Inventory–2—Beck, 1996) and structured interviews (SCID-I—First, Spitzer, Gibbon, & Williams, 1997; SCID-II—First, Gibbon, Spitzer, Williams, & Benjamin, 1997) can be administered. Whereas mental health professionals have training in administration and interpretation of such measures, they may lack expertise in evaluating when parental psychopathology is relevant to child custody or placement.

How Far Should the Custody Evaluation Go?

Should a custody evaluation it make specific recommendations (e.g., visitations every other weekend) or just state psychological findings relevant to these decisions and allow the judge to make the ultimate decisions? Melton (1978) and others have generally recommended always leaving the ultimate decisions to the legal entities. However, there is at least a clinical lore that judges do not like making custody decisions and would prefer—sometimes in their order for the evaluation—that the evaluator make explicit recommendations.

How Should Factual Disputes That Arise in Custody Evaluations Be Resolved?

For example, if deviant pornography is found on the family computer and the wife claims it is the husband's and the husband's claims it is the wife's, how is this relevant factual dispute to be handled in the custody evaluation? Given that mental health professionals are not experts in resolving this kind of issue, does the evaluator write a report with contingent recommendations?

How Are Value Issues That Emerge in Custody Evaluations Resolved?

Science can determine causal relationships but it cannot determine the ultimate value of the effects. Is the absence of religious participation a bad, good, or neutral factor? Is this a relativistic issue, in that it depends on something else, and if so, on what does it legitimately depend? There are often difficult tradeoffs to be weighed. If a parent works many hours, there can be a tradeoff between financial status for the family and time with the child. For instance, this harder work could result in poorer attachment but better-educated children (they could afford better private schools). Is this a worse or better outcome than a better parent–child attachment and a more poorly educated child? Questions of sexuality are notoriously value laden and often arise in child custody evaluations. Is a parent's homosexual lifestyle a problem? Is the parent's pornography use (and with certain types of pornography, say, bestiality) relevant and a problem? Is the parent's low sexual desire or asexuality a problem? O'Donohue and Bradley (1999) recommended explicating these value questions and explained their concern that in many custody evaluations, the evaluator's value positions are hidden in his or her recommendations and treated as "psychological fact" as opposed to a value.

There is a large research agenda related to these controversies. We recommend that family attorneys, judges, psychologists, and child advocates convene to develop consensus regarding some of the conceptual questions, such as which variables should be measured and how different value issues should be handled in a custody evaluation. Then psychologists should develop assessment strategies to better measure these (e.g., attachment). Algorithms also need to be decided upon to blend this disparate information. Finally, quality improvement methods should be developed and used to make sure that standards are being implemented across a variety of custody evaluations and that these, as a whole, can improve over time (O'Donohue & Fisher, 2006).

MYTHS AND MISCONCEPTIONS

Myth 1: There is a Reasonably Well-Established Standard for Conducting Child Custody Evaluations

As previously described, some guidelines exist, but these are quite vague. There has been no study of the interrater reliability of custody evaluations (Emery et al., 2005; O'Donohue & Bradley, 1999; Otto et al., 2000). Thus, the extent to which evaluators would arrive at the same conclusion is unknown. In addition, the extent to which evaluators would use the same methods is also unknown. There appears to be a large amount of unwanted variability in the questions asked, the methods pursued, the way information is processed, and the kinds of conclusions reached. This multisided problem is due, in part, to the following factors: (1) the vagueness and complexity of the constructs of interest, such as "child's best interest" or "parenting capacity"; (2) the idiosyncratic nature of each case; (3) lack of knowledge about variables that contribute to a child's well-being in the context of divorce; (4) lack of adequate psychometrics, especially predictive validity, of our instruments; (5) the variability in state law; and (6) the predilections and skill of evaluators.

Myth 2: Custody Evaluators Can Settle Factual Disputes

Often there are key factual questions on the table (e.g., Does Mr. X physically abuse his wife, as she claims?), and evaluators need to be cautious in their reasoning on these matters. Generally, we have no special expertise in deciding such questions, which raise issues of standards of evidence. We recommend writing a report with contingent recommendations (e.g., "If it is the case that Mr. X has physically abused his wife, as she reports, then ... ").

Myth 3: Parent Alienation Syndrome (PAS) Is a Well-Researched and Accepted Phenomenon

PAS (Emery et al, 2005; O'Donohue & Bradley, 1999) almost exclusively arises in custody disputes. It is characterized as the "programming" of a child by one parent to denigrate the other and the child's own contribution to the vilification of the target parent (Gardner, 2001). The assumption regarding PAS is that the child's disdain for the target parent is unjustified and negatively impacts the parent–child relationship. Whether this syndrome actually exists is questionable, given the empirical evidence. Gould (1998) suggests that syndrome or not, it is important to evaluate the negative influences a parent can have on the child that adversely affects the child's relationship with the other parent.

CONCLUSIONS

Scientifically Unsupported Uses

Because there is a wide amount of variability in what constitutes a custody evaluation (e.g., questions addressed, assessments used, idiographic issues such as alleged abuse, ages of children), it is impossible to address the question of whether "custody evaluations" meet standards of legal admissibility. In addition, we would claim that the key task in the usual custody evaluation is a predictive one: What arrangements over time for this child (or these children) are in his or her (or their) best interests? Specialized tests that are often used in custody evaluations (the Ackerman–Schoendorf Scales for Parent Evaluation of Custody [ASPECT]; Bricklin's measures) do not have known predictive validity regarding this question, and current evaluative data on these measures suggest that they perform quite poorly. As such, their use is not supported.

Scientifically Supported Uses

At times, questions can be asked that are relevant to custody evaluations that mental health professionals can validly answer. These tend to pertain to the evaluation of current psychological or psychiatric functioning. Questions such as "Does this child have any special needs related to his or her mental health?"; "Does this parent have a mental health diagnosis that can impact on the child's best interests?"; "Are there remediable mental health problems that affect the child's best interests and what is the prognosis of these?" are questions that mental health professionals can currently address that can help the court.

In addition, the psychologist *as an educator* can review the research (briefly cited above) about divorce and allow the court to understand what is known about the impact of divorce on children, subject to the caveat issues about the difficulty of inferring causality.

Scientifically Controversial or Largely Untested Uses

As mentioned above, tests and measures should show predictive *validities* (as different time periods may be of interest); again these validities are complicated by contextual variables (e.g., What is the quality of the predictive inference of this test for a 3-year-old Asian American girl with two younger siblings, an alcoholic father, a depressed mother, but very supportive, yet ailing, grandparents?). Although there are numerous tests or measures with generally sound psychometric properties for the purpose of evaluating current functioning (as reviewed above), these measures tend to lack evaluation of their predictive validity within custody contexts. These kinds of studies are difficult to conduct (as is all longitudinal research). Thus, currently a skeptical answer can be given about otherwise reliable and valid assessment methods and measures: Our measures and our custody evaluations have untested predictive validity in custody contexts (O'Donohue & Bradley, 1999). Because they have demonstrated psychometric properties in other contexts, their use here is described as untested, or controversial, rather than explicitly unsupported.

COMMUNICATING CONSENSUS AND CONTROVERSIES

As noted above, there are no theories that identify the constructs to measure in child custody evaluations. O'Donohue, Beitz, and Cummings (2008) have attempted to rectify this situation and suggest that five major factors could play a role. These factors could mitigate substantial involvement with one parent and also lead to poorer adjustment in children and include: (1) poor attachment; (2) poor parenting skills, including abuse or neglect; (3) emotional instability/mental disorder of the parent; (4) environmental instability; and (5) excessive conflict. Given that science has assisted in identifying these five factors as potentially predictive of child adjustment in custody decisions, it is important for custody evaluators to inform the court via their reports to address consistently these factors, and to test them using empirically supported methods. Custody evaluators should educate the courts as to where each parent falls along these parameters, allowing the ultimate decision to be guided more objectively by science than by a custody evaluator's clinical judgment.

The determination of what constitutes a quality, or even an adequate, child custody evaluation is still unknown. Laws vary across states, which makes standardization or generalization difficult. The wording of relevant laws is often unclear: For example, it is not clear how to unpack the phrase "best interests of the child," the most common construct in state statutes. In addition, there is little relevant psychological research that answers questions regarding what constructs ought to be measured in custody evaluations. We propose one model. The psychometric adequacy of many psychological tests for the kinds of inferences made in child custody exams is also poor. In addition, there are questions about how to weigh various factors and even how far the mental health professional should go in making recommendations. How to resolve value issues or factual disputes that may arise in these evaluations is also unclear. Professionals working with attorneys or testifying in court should be clear about the limitations of knowledge in this area.

REFERENCES

Ackerman, M. T., & Ackerman, M. C. (1997). Custody evaluation practices: A survey of experienced professionals (revisited). *Professional Psychology: Research and Practice, 28,* 137–145.

Ackerman, M. T., & Schoendorf, K. (1992). *Ackerman–Schoendorf Scales for Parent Evaluation of Custody manual.* Los Angeles: Western Psychological Services.

Ahrons, C. R., & Tanner, J. L. (2003). Adult children and their fathers: Relationship changes 20 years after parental divorce. *Family Relations, 52,* 340–351.

Ainsworth, M. D., & Witting, B. A. (1969). Attachment and exploratory behavior of one-year olds in a strange situation. In B. M. Foss (Ed.), *Determinants of infant behavior IV* (pp. 111–136). London: Methuen.

Amato, P. R. (2000). The consequences of divorce for adults and children. *Journal of Marriage and the Family, 62,* 1269–1287.

Amato, P. R. (2001). Children of divorce in the 1990s: An update of the Amato and Keith (1991) meta-analysis. *Journal of Family Psychology, 15*(3), 355–370.

Amato, P. R. (2006). Marital discord, divorce, and children's well-being: Results from a 20-year longitudinal study of two generations. In A. Clarke-Stewart & J. Dunn (Eds.), *Families count: Effects on child and adolescent development* (pp. 179–202). New York: Cambridge University Press.

Amato, P. R., & Gilbreth, J. G. (1999). Nonresident fathers and children's well-being: A meta-analysis. *Journal of Marriage and the Family, 61*(3), 557–573.

Amato, P. R., & Keith, B. (1991). Parental divorce and the well-being of children: A meta-analysis. *Psychological Bulletin, 110,* 26–46.

Amato, P. R., Loomis, L. S., & Booth, A. (1995). Parental divorce, marital conflict and offspring well-being during early adulthood. *Social Forces, 73,* 895–915.

American Academy of Child and Adolescent Psychiatry. (1997). Practice parameters for child custody evaluation. *Journal of the American Academy of Child and Adolescent Psychiatry, 36*(10S), 57S–68S.

American Educational Research Association, American Psychological Association, & National Council on Measurement in Education. (1999). *Standard for educational and psychological testing.* Washington, DC: American Educational Research Association.

American Law Institute. (2002). *Principles of the law of family dissolution: Analysis and recommendations.* Newark, NJ: LexisNexis.

American Psychiatric Association. (1994). *Diagnostic and statistical manual of mental disorders* (4th ed.). Washington: Author.

American Psychological Association. (1994). Guidelines for child custody evaluations in divorce proceedings. *American Psychologist, 49,* 677–680.

Association of Family and Conciliation Courts. (1995). *Model standards for child custody evaluation.* Madison, WI: Author.

Ballou, M., Barry, J., Billinghan, K., Boorstein, B. W., Butler, C., Gershber, R., et al. (2001). Psychological model for judicial decision making in emergency child placement. *American Journal of Orthopsychology, 71,* 416–425.

Beck, A. T. (1996). *Beck Depression Inventory–2 (BDI-II).* San Antonio, TX: Psychological Corp.

Block, J. (1965). *The child-rearing practices report (CRPR): A set of Q items for the description of parental socialization attitudes and values.* Unpublished manuscript, Institute of Human Development, University of California, Berkeley.

Braver, S. L., Wolchik, S. A., Sandler, I. N., Sheets, V. L., Fogas, B., & Bay, R. C. (1993). A longitudinal study of noncustodial parents: Parents without children. *Journal of Family Psychology* 7(1), 9–23.

Bray, J. H. (1991). Psychosocial factors affecting custodial and visitation arrangements. *Behavioral Sciences and the Law, 9*(4), 419–437.

Bricklin, B. (1989). *Perception-of-Relationships Test manual.* Furlong, PA: Village Publishing.

Bricklin, B. (1990a). *Bricklin Perceptual Scales manual.* Furlong, PA: Village Publishing.

Bricklin, B. (1990b). *Parental Awareness Skills Survey manual.* Furlong, PA: Village Publishing.

Bricklin, B., & Elliot, G. (1991). *Parent perception of child profile (PPCP).* Furlong, PA: Village Publishing.

Buchanan, C. M., Maccoby, E. E., & Dornbusch, S. M. (1996). *Adolescents after divorce.* Cambridge, MA: Harvard University Press.

Emery, R. E. (1999). *Marriage, divorce, and children's adjustment: Developmental clinical psychology and psychiatry* (2nd ed.). Thousand Oaks, CA: Sage.

Emery, R. E., Otto, R. K., & O'Donohue, W. T. (2005). A critical assessment of child custody evaluations: Limited science and a flawed system. *Psychological Science in the Public Interest, 6*(1), 1–29.

First, M. B., Gibbon, M., Spitzer, R. L., Williams, J. B. W., & Benjamin, L. S. (1997). *User's guide for the Structured Clinical Interview for DSM-IV Axis II per-*

sonality disorders (SCID-II). Washington, DC: American Psychiatric Association.

First, M. B., Spitzer, R. L., Gibbon, M., & Williams, J. B. W. (1997). *Structured Clinical Interview for DSM-IV Axis I disorders (SCID-I)*. Washington, DC: American Psychiatric Association.

Gardner, R. A. (2001). Should courts orders PAS children to visit/reside with the alienated parent?: A follow-up study. *American Journal of Forensic Psychology, 19*(3), 61–106.

Gould, J. W. (1998). *Conducting scientifically crafted child custody evaluations*. Thousand Oaks, CA: Sage.

Gould, J. W. (1999). A paradigm for the forensic evaluation of child custody determination. *Family and Conciliation Courts Review, 37*(2), 135–158.

Grisso, T., Borum, R., Edens, J. F., Moyle, J., & Otto, R. K. (2003). Evaluating competencies: Forensic assessments and instruments (2nd ed.). In R. Roesch (Series Ed.), *Perspectives in law and psychology* (Vol. 16, pp. 229–307). New York: Kluwer Academic/Plenum Press.

Grisso, T., & Conlin, M. (1984). Procedural issues in the juvenile justice system. In N. Reppucci, L. Weithorn, E. Mulvey, J. Monahan, & R. Price (Eds.), *Mental health, law and children* (pp. 171–193). Beverly Hills, CA: Sage.

Hall, A. S., Pulver, C. A., & Cooley, M. J. (1996). Psychology of the best interest standard: Fifty state statutes and their theoretical antecedents. *American Journal of Family Therapy, 24,* 171–180.

Harper, S. E., & Fine, M. A. (2006). The effects of involved nonresidential fathers' distress, parenting behaviors, interparental conflict, and the quality of father–child relationships on children's well-being. *Fathering, 4*(3), 286–311.

Hedlund, B. L., & Lindquist, C. U. (1984). The development of an inventory for distinguishing among passive, aggressive, and assertive behaviors. *Behavioral Assessment, 6*, 379–390.

Heilbrun, K. (1995). Child custody evaluation: Critically assessing mental health experts and psychological tests. *Family Law Quarterly, 29*, 63–78.

Herman, S. P., Duanne, J. E., Ayres, W., Arnold, V., Benedek, E., Benson, R. S., et al. (1997). Practice parameters for child custody evaluation. *Journal of the American Academy of Child and Adolescent Psychiatry, 36*, 57S–69S.

Hetherington, E. M. (1989). Coping with family transitions: Winners, losers, and survivors. *Child Development, 60*, 1–14.

Hetherington, E. M., Cox, M., & Cox, R. (1981). Effects of divorce on parents and children. In M. Lamb (Ed.), *Nontraditional families* (pp. 35–38). Hillsdale, NJ: Erlbaum.

Hetherington, E. M., & Kelly, J. (2002). *For better or for worse: Divorce reconsidered*. New York: Norton.

Hetherington, E. M., & Stanley-Hagan, M. (1999). The adjustment of children with divorced parents: A risk and resiliency perspective. *Journal of Child Psychology and Psychiatry, 40,* 129–140.

Jenuwine, M. J., & Cohler, B. J. (1999). Major parental psychopathology and child custody. In R. M. Galatzer-Levy & L. Kraus (Eds.), *The scientific basis of child custody decisions* (pp. 285–318). New York: Wiley.

Kelly, J. B. (1998). Marital conflict, divorce, and children's adjustment. *Child and Adolescent Psychiatric Clinics of North America, 7,* 259–271.

Kelly, J. B., & Emery, R. E. (2003). Children's adjustment following divorce: Risk and resilience perspectives. *Family Relations, 52,* 352–362.

Kot, L., & Shoemaker, H. M. (1999). Children of divorce: An investigation of the developmental effects from infancy through adulthood. *Journal of Divorce and Remarriage, 31,* 161–178.

Lamb, M. E., Sternberg, K. J., & Thompson, R. A. (1997). The effects of divorce and custody arrangements on children's behavior, development, and adjustment. *Family and Conciliation Courts Review, 35,* 393–404.

Lamborn, S. D., Mounts, N. S., Steinberg, L., & Dornbusch, S. M. (1991). Patterns of competence and adjustment among adolescents from authoritative, authoritarian, indulgent, and neglectful homes. *Child Development, 62,* 1049–1065.

LeVine, R. A. (1974). Parental goals: A cross-cultural view. *Teachers College Record, 76,* 226–239.

Locke, L. M., & Prinz, R. J. (2002). Measurement of parental discipline and nurturance. *Clinical Psychology Review, 22*(6), 895–929.

Lyman, R. D., & Roberts, M. C. (1985). Mental health testimony in child custody litigation. *Law and Psychology Review* 9(15), 15–34.

Maccoby, E. E., & Mnookin, R. H. (1992). *Dividing the child: Social and legal dimensions of child custody.* Cambridge, MA: Harvard University Press.

Marcus, R. F., & Betzer, P. D. S. (1996). Attachment and antisocial behavior in early adolescence. *Journal of Early Adolescence, 16,* 229–248.

McNally, S., Eisenberg, N., & Harris, J. D. (1991). Consistency and change in maternal child-rearing practices and values: A longitudinal study. *Child Development, 62,* 190–198.

Melton, G. B. (1978). The psychologist's role in juvenile and family law. *Journal of Clinical Child Psychology, 7,* 189–192.

Moos, R. H., & Moos, B. S. (1994). *Family environment scale manual* (3rd ed.). Palo Alto, CA: Consulting Psychologists Press.

National Center for Health Statistics of the United States. (1995). Estimated number of children involved in divorces and annulments. *Monthly Vital Statistics Report, 43*(9), 12.

Novak, G. (1996). *Developmental psychology: Dynamic systems and behavior analysis.* Reno, NV: Context Press.

O'Donohue, W., Beitz, K., & Cummings, N. (2008). A model for constructs relevant to child custody evaluations. *Journal of Forensic Psychology Practice, 7*(4), 125–139.

O'Donohue, W., & Bradley, A. (1999). Conceptual and empirical issues in child custody evaluations. *Clinical Psychology: Science and Practice, 6,* 310–322.

O'Donohue, W. T., & Fisher, J. E. (2006). Introduction. In J. E. Fisher, W. T. O'Donohue, & T. William (Eds.), *Practitioner's guide to evidence-based psychotherapy* (pp. 1–23). New York: Springer Science + Business Media.

O'Koon, J. (1997). Attachment to parents and peers in late adolescence and their relationship with self-image. *Adolescence, 32,* 471–482.

Olson, D. H., Portner, J., & Lavee, Y. (1985). *FACES III.* St. Paul: Department of Family Science, University of Minnesota.

Otto, R. K. (2000). The use of psychological testing in child custody evaluations. *Family and Conciliation Courts Review, 38,* 312–340.

Otto, R. K., Buffington-Vollum, J. K., & Edens, J. F. (2003). Child custody evaluation. In A. M. Goldstein & I. B. Weiner (Eds.), *Handbook of psychology: Vol. 11. Forensic psychology* (pp. 179–208). New York: Wiley.

Otto, R. K., Edens, J. F., & Barcus, E. H. (2000). The use of psychological testing in child custody evaluations. *Family and Conciliatory Courts Review, 38,* 312–340.

Papp, L. M., Cummings, E. M., & Goeke-Morey, M. C. (2005). Parental psychological distress, parent–child relationship qualities, and child adjustment: Direct, mediating, and reciprocal pathways. *Parenting: Science and Practice 5*(3), 259–283.

Patterson, G. R., DeBaryshe, B. D., & Ramsey, E. (1989). A developmental perspective on antisocial behavior. *American Psychologist, 44,* 329–335.

Pedhazer, E. J., & Schmelkin, L. P. (1991). *Measurement, design, and analysis: An integrated approach.* Hillsdale, NJ: Erlbaum.

Pruett, M. K., Williams, T. Y., Insabella, G., & Little, T. D. (2003). Family and legal indicators of child adjustment to divorce among families with young children. *Journal of Family Psychology 17*(2), 169–180.

Schneider, B. H., & Younger, A. J. (1996). Adolescent–parent attachment and adolescents' relations with their peers: A closer look. *Youth and Society, 28,* 95–108.

Shelton, K., Frick, P., & Wooton, J. (1996). Assessment of parenting practices in families of elementary school-age children. *Journal of Clinical Child Psychology 25,* 317—329.

Skinner, H. A., Steinhauer, P. D., & Santa-Barbara, J. (1995). *FAM-III manual.* Toronto: Multi-Health Systems.

Steinberg, L. (2001). We know some things: Parent–adolescent relationships in retrospect and prospect. *Journal of Research on Adolescence, 11,* 1–19.

Strauss, M. A. (1979). Measuring intrafamily conflict and violence: The Conflict Tactics (CT) Scales. *Journal of Marriage and the Family, 41,* 75–88.

Sun, Y. (2001). Family environment and adolescents' well-being before and after parents'marital disruption: A longitudinal analysis. *Journal of Marriage and Family, 63,* 697–713.

Taub, D. (1997). Autonomy and parental attachment in traditional-age undergraduate women. *Journal of College Student Development, 38*(6), 645–654.

Thomson, E., Hanson, H. L., & McLanahan, S. S. (1994). Family structure and child well-being: Economic resources vs. parental behaviors. *Social Forces, 73*(1), 221–242.

Wallerstein, J. S., & Kelly, J. B. (1980). Effects of divorce on the visiting father-child relationship. *American Journal of Psychiatry, 137*(12), 1534–1539.

Wallerstein, J. S., & Lewis, J. M. (2004). The unexpected legacy of divorce: Report of a 25-year study. *Psychoanalytic Psychology, 21,* 353–370.

Whiteside, M. F., & Becker, B. J. (2000). Parental factors and the young child's postdivorce adjustment: A meta-analysis with implications for parenting arrangements. *Journal of Family Psychology 14*(1), 5–26.

CHAPTER 14

Controversies in Evaluating Competence to Stand Trial

Norman G. Poythress and Patricia A. Zapf

Adjudicative competence (also called "competence to stand trial," "competence to proceed," or "fitness to proceed") relates to the legally mandated abilities that a criminal defendant must possess in order to participate in adjudicatory proceedings. The minimum standard for adjudicative competence is that the defendant have "sufficient present ability to consult with his attorney with a reasonable degree of *rational* understanding and a *rational* as well as *factual* understanding of proceedings against him" (*Dusky v. United States*, 1960, p. 403, emphasis added). Because of threats to the fairness and accuracy of proceedings that involve an incompetent defendant, proceedings against a defendant who lacks these minimum abilities must be suspended until such time as he or she is able to competently participate.

Because the legally recognized premises for incompetence lie in the domain of mental impairment, the courts routinely rely on the evaluations and testimony of mental health professionals to inform decisions about adjudicative competence. In this context it is not sufficient for a defendant to have impaired mental abilities; adjudicative competence determinations ultimately depend on whether, and the extent to which, impaired mental functioning adversely affects (loosely, "causes") the functional legal abilities implied by *Dusky*. This chapter focuses on controversies in the conceptualization of adjudicative competence and the clinical techniques for conducting competence assessments for the courts.

CONTROVERSIES IN ADJUDICATIVE COMPETENCE ASSESSMENTS

We address two controversies related to adjudicative competence assessments, focusing primarily on assessment methodology and the relative strengths and weakness of idiographic versus nomothetic evaluation methods. Although this controversy is not specific to the assessment of competence to stand trial, recently developed measures that emphasize nomothetic information have enlivened this particular debate. We also address a more substantive issue—the role of decisional competence (Bonnie, 1992, 1993)—in the conceptualization and evaluation of adjudicative competence.

Idiographic and Nomothetic Approaches to Assessing Competence-Related Abilities

A number of tools to facilitate clinical assessments of adjudicative competence have been developed; these have been reviewed in detail elsewhere (Grisso, 2003; Melton, Petrila, Poythress, & Slobogin, 2007). What we have termed the *idiographic approach* involves the use of a predetermined menu of topics that the clinician is encouraged to pursue using a semistructured interview (SSI). Exemplars of this approach include the Competency to Stand Trial Assessment Instrument (CAI; Laboratory of Community Psychiatry, 1973), the Interdisciplinary Fitness Interview (IFI; Golding, Roesch, & Schreiber, 1984; see also IFI-R; Golding, 1993), and the Fitness Interview Test—Revised (FIT-R; Roesch, Zapf, & Eaves, 2006). What we have termed *nomothetic measures* are those more structured instruments that involve highly standardized administration and reference to relevant offender group norms for interpretation of scores. Exemplars of nomothetic measures include the MacArthur Competence Assessment Tool—Criminal Adjudication (MacCAT-CA; Poythress et al., 1999) and the Evaluation of Competency to Stand Trial—Revised (ECST-R; Rogers, Tillbrook, & Sewell, 2004).

SSIs function as an *aide memoir* by identifying domains of legal functioning for inquiry; otherwise, they impose relatively little structure or discipline on the assessment process. Within each domain clinicians are free to develop their own questions; they are also free to explore various legal domains in greater or lesser detail and to go outside the framework of the measure to explore additional substantive areas of their own choosing. SSI measures typically utilize an ordinal scale for recording the clinician's judgment of the defendant's impairment (if any) with respect to each issue that is probed. The CAI, for example, employs a 5-point rating scale of incapacity: 1 = total, 2 = severe, 3 = moderate, 4 = mild, 5 = none. Such numerical ratings typically are not aggregated in any arithmetic way (e.g., summed or averaged), nor are they interpreted as "scores" in light of normative data on how a reference group of defendants may have performed when evaluated using this measure. Rather, they reflect the examiner's judgment of the adequacy of this defendant's responses to whatever set of questions the examiner chose to pose on this occasion. Thus, SSIs focus on the individual and his or her unique (i.e., *idiographic*) responses, which are interpreted according to the subjective standards of the clinician as to adequacy of the defendant's skill or performance.

In contrast, the nomothetic approach to adjudicative competence assessment involves the administration of a highly structured instrument that standardizes inquiries with respect to a limited set of functional legal abilities. Depending on the measure, items may be scored, as with SSIs, using clinical judgment ratings (ECST-R; MacCAT-CA Appreciation measure), or they may be structured as actual performance tasks (MacCAT-CA Understanding and Reasoning measures), in which case responses are scored for accuracy against *a priori*, consensus-based criteria. To illustrate, the Mac-CAT-CA Understanding scale assesses a defendant's knowledge of general, legally prescribed features of adjudicatory procedures and the responsibilities of legal actors. Item 5 asks the defendant to describe the responsibilities of a judge at a jury trial. Credit is given for responses that identify any of four judicial functions: instructing the jury, ruling on challenges to admissibility of evidence, maintaining order and ensuring procedure is followed, and imposing a sentence. A defendant's score on item 5 is added to the scores on seven other Understanding scale items to yield a single numerical index that relates to the *factual understanding* criterion in *Dusky*.

What primarily distinguishes nomothetic measures from idiographic ones is that the scores are interpreted in reference to the performance of groups of offenders who previously have completed the measures. The "meanings" assigned to an individual's Understanding scale score range from "minimal or no impairment," to "mild impairment," to "clinically significant impairment," and provide a normative indication of the present defendant's abilities to understand the legal proceedings, as compared to previous defendants who have been judged to be "competent" or "incompetent." Other things being equal (which is *not* necessarily the case), "minimal or no impairment" carries the message that, "as assessed using this particular measure, this defendant's capacity is more like that of other competent defendants than that of incompetent defendants," whereas "clinically significant impairment" indicates that in prior studies, the observed level of impaired functioning was much more strongly associated with adjudicative incompetence.

Foundational and Decisional Competence

Although *Dusky* distinguishes three abilities needed for adjudicative competence—rational understanding of proceedings, factual understanding of proceedings, rational assistance of counsel—the criteria are broad and not elaborated with precision. A review of the adjudicative competence literature prior to 1992 reveals that attempts to elaborate the *Dusky* criteria have focused largely on issues such as "capacity to understand the charges, the purpose of the criminal process and the adversary system, especially the role of the defense counsel; capacity to appreciate one's situation as a defendant in a criminal prosecution; and ability to recognize and relate pertinent information to counsel concerning the facts of the case" (Bonnie, 1992, p. 297).

Bonnie's (1992, 1993) reformulation of the competence construct distinguishes this traditional view of competence, which he labeled "foundational competence" or "competence to assist counsel," from the notion of "decisional competence." *Foundational competence* relates to an array of abilities that *any* defendant must have in order to participate in adjudicatory proceedings; in contrast, *decisional competence* focuses on the specific, contextual demands of a defendant's case and the particular decisions that he or she would be expected to make. Most relevant are those decisions that implicate the waiver of a constitutionally guaranteed right (e.g., to waive Fifth Amendment Rights and testify; to plead guilty), about which the law requires a degree of autonomous participation by defendants. Impaired capacity for a particular decision (e.g., whether to plead guilty) would not necessarily render a defendant incompetent if that decision were not salient in his or her case (e.g., defense was planning to go to trial) or if legally acceptable alternative decision-making procedures might be used. Thus, Bonnie argues that competence should be viewed as two separate but related constructs that allow for a useful explanatory framework for the existing features of settled law, clarification of those areas of the law that are unsettled, and a theoretical foundation for defining the psycholegal abilities required of a defendant within each of these constructs.

Decisional competence is controversial in two respects. Most importantly, because the *Dusky* criteria do not explicitly mention decisional issues, the role of decisional competence vis-à-vis more traditional constructions of adjudicative competence must be clarified. A key issue is whether it is part of (encompassed by) the *Dusky* criteria or sufficiently distinct from it that an independent judicial determination is required. Second, regardless of how the first issue is resolved, the legal recognition of decisional competence at any level potentially has implications for the assessments that mental health professionals conduct. Arguably, the capacity for autonomous decision making implicates a degree of analytic ability (e.g., weighing alternatives) that goes beyond the basic abilities required to take the role of a defendant and assist counsel.

RESEARCH RELEVANT TO THE CONTROVERSIES

In this section and the next, we elaborate on the controversies noted above, consider extant research relevant to the controversies, and note gaps in literature regarding these issues. We first consider the relative strengths and weaknesses of idiographic and nomothetic approaches. As will be seen, to a considerable extent the strengths of the SSI approach mirror the limitations of the nomothetic assessment approaches, and vice versa.

Strengths and Weaknesses of the SSI Approach

One strength of the idiographic approach is the breadth of coverage permitted by the use of SSIs. The available SSIs delineate broad domains of inquiry (e.g., 13 for the CAI, 5 for the IFI-R, 16 for the FIT-R) with numerous subheadings under each that broaden the potential scope of inquiry. Furthermore, the clinician can go beyond the framework of the measure to assess factors not explicit in the menu of topics, thus enabling the assessment of issues that may arise only infrequently (e.g., competence to waive counsel). With SSIs the clinician also has the flexibility to pose questions in any fashion that he or she believes will facilitate the assessment. This flexibility is particularly helpful with defendants who have mental impairment that differentially affects the extent to which they are able to respond to certain kinds of inquiries (e.g., recall vs. recognition formats). The flexibility of this approach also enables the clinician to probe in detail the defendant's belief structure (rational thinking) regarding the legal system in general and specific issues that are unique to *this* defendant's legal circumstances.

These strengths of SSIs also come, however, with potential limitations. The minimum structure for clinical inquiries means that two examiners evaluating the same defendant, even if they use the same SSI, might ask different numbers of questions about a given issue (e.g., understanding of court proceedings) or employ questions of radically different difficulty level—either of which might affect their perceptions of the defendant's capacities. Furthermore, the absence of explicit criteria for scoring a defendant's responses may increase the variance in the clinical ratings assigned. It may be enough for one examiner to give a high rating if the defendant knows that his charges are "serious" and could result in "being locked up." A different examiner might require greater precision and expect the defendant to describe the charge as "a felony first degree" for which the consequences are "8–10 years in prison" in order to earn a high rating.

Specifically with respect to the assessment of "factual understanding," the use of clinical ratings is arguably an inferior way to index capacity. Factual understanding may best be conceived as the defendant's *knowledge* (distinguished from beliefs) of the design features of the adjudicatory process and the responsibilities of its participants—features about which there is a high degree of consensus and which vary little, if at all, from one defendant to another. For example, the important legally prescribed duties of a judge, jury, or attorney are consistent across cases and can be enumerated and articulated with reasonable precision; similarly the constitutional rights surrendered in pleading guilty are essentially the same for one defendant as for another; and so forth. Reasonably rigorous tests of this type of legal knowledge can be constructed and used to index capacity in a fashion that is less susceptible to the vagaries of clinical ratings.

An additional limitation of the available SSI instruments is the subjectivity of clinical interpretations with respect to indices that might be derived by combining multiple-item ratings. On the CAI, for example, one might combine ratings from items 3 (Quality of relating to the attorney), 4 (Planning of legal strategy), and 10 (Capacity to disclose facts to attorney) in order to speak generally to the issue of "Capacity to assist counsel." Given the 1 (total incapacity) to 5 (no impairment) rating scale for each item on this instrument, a defendant's score could range from 3 to 15. No research data have been gathered to suggest interpretive meanings for such scores. The meaning of an extreme score (a 3 or a 15) might be easy on its face, but only the clinician's subjective opinion could provide a basis for the meaning of a score of 7, or 9, or 12.

Strengths and Weaknesses of the Nomothetic Approach

Nomothetic instruments are designed specifically to reduce sources of variance associated with examiner idiosyncrasies and to provide an empirical referent for interpreting indices of capacity. A fixed set of questions, determined at the point of test construction to reasonably sample the domain of inquiry, is asked and probed in largely the same fashion by any clinician who uses the measure. Item scoring is guided by explicit criteria that reflect consensus-based judgments as to the adequacy of the response. These structural features reduce the extent to which examiners' behavior (i.e., selection of questions, subjective criteria for scoring) influences the score assigned. A court may differ in its judgment of the array of issues that, ideally, should have been queried in a particular case. A court also might accord differential importance to performance on any one item in comparison to another (e.g., on nomothetic measures each item is commonly accorded equal weight). But to the extent that the clinician's judgments or conclusions about the defendant's capacities are conditioned on responses to a standard set of questions that were scored against explicit criteria, the behaviors that underlie the clinical judgments are relatively transparent.

The normative interpretation of scale indices adds a further degree of consistency and transparency to the more global conclusions that a clinician may offer. Where normative data have been developed, the statistical basis that underlies the interpretation of any particular score can be examined and the extent to which a score is more reflective of competent versus incompetent performance in the reference offender population can be inspected. Whether or not the trier of fact finds such normative interpretations to be compelling, their use reduces the likelihood of courts having to try to fathom the basis for clinical conclusions proffered merely on the basis of "my professional opinion."

Nomothetic instruments have limitations as well. One limitation already noted is the limited domains that such measures tap. Legal competence is an "open construct," meaning that it is broad, complex, and not subject to being defined precisely by a limited or circumscribed set of criteria upon which all can agree. Thus, at the outset of instrument construction, choices have to be made about the breadth and depth of inquiry; once those choices are made and the research upon which scoring and interpretation are based has been completed, the content of nomothetic measures is fixed. Unlike SSIs, which give the clinician relatively free rein as to content, nomothetic measures lack the flexibility to permit a broader scope of inquiry than their developers conceived. For example, although the MacCAT-CA includes items that assess aspects of a defendant's comprehension of the guilty plea process, nothing in the instrument addresses issues related to other decisional competence issues. The MacCAT-CA also does not systematically tap other cognitive (e.g., memory) or communicative (e.g., speech coherency) factors potentially relevant to competence determinations. Nomothetic measures cannot be used to assess performance domains that have not been built into them; therefore they cannot be used as "stand alone" assessments of competence-related abilities. Inevitably, other data collection in the form of additional tests or SSI is needed to assess issues unique to a given case or that stand outside the design structure of nomothetic instruments.

Nomothetic approaches may be particularly well suited for assessing defendants' legal knowledge relevant to factual understanding, but more limited for assessing rational understanding. As indicated above, it is the relatively fixed corpus of legal information that is similar across cases—such as the design features of the legal system, the prescribed roles of legal actors, and the broad parameters of formalized procedures such as guilty plea agreements—that best lends itself to assessment using performance-based items for which consensus-based scoring criteria can be developed. In contrast, defendants' belief structures are much more likely to be idiosyncratic across cases, particularly when impairment, ranging from implausible to outright delusional thinking, is associated with offense-related behaviors that are likely to be highly case specific. This factor poses challenges to the nomothetic approach because of the difficulty in creating standardized inquiries that accommodate the diversity of issues about which defendants may harbor idiosyncratic beliefs. Although the MacCAT-CA Appreciation measure and similar measures provide some structured clinical data about implausible/delusional thinking with respect to a limited set of issues, at this point in time the clinical investigation of defendants' rational understanding necessarily requires the more flexible SSI approach.

As noted elsewhere in the text, nomothetic measures such as the MacCAT-CA should not be used as stand-alone measures of competence. The MacCAT-CA manual instructs users to interview defendants about their specific charges and allegations independent of the administration of the instrument itself.

Legal and Empirical Findings Regarding Decisional Competence

As noted above, Bonnie distinguished foundational from decisional competence, the latter being particularly concerned with decisions that implicate the waiver of a constitutionally guaranteed right (e.g., to waive Fifth Amendment Rights and testify; to plead guilty) about which the law requires a degree of autonomous participation by defendants. The Supreme Court case most on point to this distinction is *Godinez v. Moran* (1993), a case in which the Court considered whether there should be a different/higher standard of competence for pleading guilty or waiving the right to assistance of counsel than for standing trial. The Supreme Court rejected the Ninth Circuit's analysis that a higher standard (different from *Dusky*; that is, one of capacity for "reasoned choice" among the alternatives available to him or her) for waiving a constitutional right ought to apply. Instead, the majority in *Godinez* held that the standards for waiving counsel, pleading guilty, and standing trial were to be considered the same and that the *Dusky* standard would suffice as the constitutional minimum for each situation. Delivering the opinion for the majority, Justice Thomas wrote:

> While the decision to plead guilty is undeniably a profound one, it is no more complicated than the sum total of decisions that a defendant may be called upon to make during the course of a trial.... We can conceive of no basis for demanding a higher level of competence for those defendants who choose to plead guilty. If the *Dusky* standard is adequate for defendants who plead not guilty, it is necessarily adequate for those who plead guilty. Nor do we think that a defendant who waives his right to the assistance of counsel must be more competent than a defendant who does not, since there is no reason to believe that the decision to waive counsel requires an appreciably higher level of mental functioning than the decision to waive other constitutional rights. (*Godinez v. Moran*, 1993, pp. 398–399)

The interpretation of *Godinez* has been controversial among legal scholars. Some have interpreted this decision as setting a low bar for adjudicative competence, requiring only that defendants perform satisfactorily with respect to the specific abilities set out in *Dusky*. Others have interpreted *Godinez* as having recognized decisional abilities as implicit, if not explicit, aspects of competence (albeit still encompassed by *Dusky*) and therefore critical focal points for assessment within the appropriate context in which the competence issue arises. As Justice Blackmun argued in the dissenting opinion, competence cannot be considered in a vacuum divorced from its specific context. Rather, competence evaluations must be "specifically tailored to the context and purpose of a proceeding" (*Godinez v. Moran*, 1993, p. 413)—and, we believe, should include an assessment of the defendant's decision-making abilities within the context of his or her specific case.

There is relatively little research that is directly on point to inform the wisdom of the different interpretations of *Godinez* regarding decisional competence; however, the limited empirical data currently available suggest that clinicians' judgments about adjudicative competence may vary depending on whether decision-making abilities are explicitly assessed. Research using a prototype measure that eventually evolved into the MacCAT-CA provided the data that are most salient. The study involved a sample of 70 defendants who had been adjudicated as incompetent, hospitalized for competence restoration treatment, and rated independently by clinical staff upon admission as exhibiting either "moderate" or "gross" impairment in competence-related abilities. Of these 70 defendants, 52 (74.6%) met research criteria for "impaired" capacity on the prototype measures of abilities related to trial participation (i.e., understanding legal charges; the roles of attorneys, judge, jury; the nature of sentencing). An additional 11 defendants met research criteria for "impaired" capacity *only on decisional competence measures* related to the decision to plead guilty or the decision to waive a jury in favor of a bench trial (Poythress, Bonnie, Monahan, Otto, & Hoge, 2002, p. 101, Table 4.5). From a clinical assessment perspective, these defendants would have been "false negatives" but for the detection of significantly impaired performance on research tools designed explicitly to assess decisional competence capacities.

Other research, however, raises concerns that current instrumentation and clinical practice may not facilitate the elicitation of decisional competence information (or, if obtained, then used). Using confirmatory factor analysis, Zapf, Skeem, and Golding (2005) examined the various potential competing factor structures of the MacCAT-CA: the three-factor structure defined by the three MacCAT-CA measures, a two-factor structure defined by Bonnie's distinction between foundational and decisional abilities, and various mixed models that attempted to combine the three- and two-factor structures. These researchers found support for the three-factor structure conforming to the three MacCAT-CA measures noted above (Understanding, Reasoning, and Appreciation); however, the two-factor model that distinguished foundational abilities from decisional abilities was not supported. Thus, although the MacCAT-CA includes items relevant to one key decisional issue (to waive the right to trial and instead plead guilty), these particular items do not constitute a discrete index to which examiners might refer in addressing a defendant's decisional competence abilities.

Some of the SSIs specify domains of inquiry that relate to decisional competence issues. For example, the CAI includes items for rating the ability to plan legal strategy (including possible guilty plea) and capacity for testifying relevantly (which would entail waiving the Fifth Amendment right against self-incrimination). Similarly, the IFI-R and FIT-R include discrete sections devoted to the considerations of pleading guilty and waiving counsel. However, a study of real-world competence evaluations revealed that the modal examiner addressed foundational abilities to the exclusion of decisional ones (Skeem, Golding, Cohn, & Berge, 1998), despite the fact that (1) the CAI was the most frequently used assessment tool in the sample, and (2) all clinicians in the study had participated in training that emphasized assessment using the IFI-R.

Collectively these studies suggest that although decisional competence abilities may be important determinants of capacity, triers of fact are probably not receiving such information to inform their decisions. The MacCAT-CA does not provide a discrete index of decisional competence abilities, and forensic examiners using (or at least trained in the use of) SSIs that provide a focus on decisional capacities appear to (largely) ignore these issues in their reports (if not also their assessments). Together with studies that have found rates of agreement between examiners' opinions regarding competence and court competence adjudications in excess of 95% (suggesting that the courts defer to examiners in determining the issue of competence; Cox & Zapf, 2004; Zapf, Hubbard, Cooper, Wheeles, & Ronan, 2004), these studies suggest that Bonnie's decisional competence construct, although conceptually sound, is likely having minimal impact in current practice. Newer nomothetic measures that focus more explicitly, if not exclusively, on decisional competence capacities may be needed; alternatively, a heightened awareness of the importance of the construct and a more disciplined approach to competence assessment is indicated for users of SSIs.

GAPS IN KNOWLEDGE ABOUT TECHNIQUES

For a book that addresses *Psychological Science in the Courtroom*, an obvious point of relevance is the extent to which there is scientific support for the various assessment procedures under discussion. It is beyond the scope of this chapter to undertake a measure-by-measure critique of various tools (SSIs and others) developed for use in adjudicative competence assessments (but see Grisso, 2003; Melton et al., 2007; Zapf & Viljoen, 2003); however, we note briefly the kinds of scientific data regarding the reliability (consistency) and validity (accuracy) that might be most relevant for courts to use in judging the scientific foundation for various procedures.

Notably, this discussion is most relevant to jurisdictions that follow admissibility guidelines articulated by the U.S. Supreme Court in *Daubert v. Merrell Dow Pharmaceuticals, Inc.* (1993), which challenged judges to evaluate expert testimony, broadly speaking, on the strength of the scientific evidence supporting the procedures used by the expert to derive his or her findings.

In jurisdictions that follow the "general acceptance" rule for admissibility, perhaps little more is required than that the expert assert, with some claim of professional consensus, that the procedures(s) used are accepted by the majority of his or her peers.

There is scant scientific evidence for the reliability and validity of many of the adjudicative competence measures referenced in this chapter. For some measures, such as the IFI or CAI, few studies of their reliability or validity have been published in refereed scientific journals. Some of the published studies, although well designed, have been of such limited scope that generalizing the findings may pose a concern (e.g., the lone empirical study of the IFI was based on a sample of 77 defendants and 8 clinicians, none of whom were psychiatrists, from a single jurisdiction). In addition, it is difficult to evaluate some SSI measures because the "scores" or "ratings" generated using the measure are not commonly aggregated into indices that relate to discrete *Dusky*-pertinent abilities. Consequently, much of the literature on the reliability of clinician judgments about competence has focused on agreement between examiners as to whether the defendant was, categorically, "competent" or "incompetent."

Studies that focus on examiners' categorical agreements are of limited value because, even when agreement rates are high, it is often impossible to discern the subjective calculus used by the clinicians to integrate the data into a categorical outcome. High levels of categorical agreement may result from factors other than the reliability of the measures used to structure data collection—for example, research samples may include very extreme cases that make for "easy" calls, or examiners may employ implicit decision rules (e.g., defendants with active psychotic symptoms are "incompetent," others are "competent") that promote reliable (although perhaps not highly valid) judgments. Absent evidence of interexaminer agreement regarding the specific information collected using SSIs, it is difficult to defend any claims that the measures themselves yield reliable results.

This does not mean that SSIs measures are necessarily unreliable, nor does it mean that this general approach to competence assessment cannot yield scientifically respectable models of adjudicative competence. However, much of the information needed to systematically assess reliability is presently lacking. To move these measures beyond the status of providing primarily anecdotal information and to demonstrate more robustly their scientific properties, research is needed that investigates the extent to which different examiners using the same SSI (1) solicit similar amounts and kinds of information with respect to each item or domain of inquiry, (2) assign similar ratings of (in)capacity for each item or index, and (3) draw similar clinical inferences about the defendant's level of (in)capacity with respect to discrete *Dusky* capacities (including decisional competence).

There is also a dearth of research investigating the validity of SSIs, and the challenges to research in this area are substantial. The few "validity" studies to date have focused on the concordance between clinicians' categorical judgments ("competent" vs. "incompetent") and actual legal determinations. For a variety of reasons, this is a flawed criterion. As noted above, there is ample empirical evidence that judges readily defer to, and routinely rubber-stamp, examiners' opinions (Cox & Zapf, 2004; Zapf et al., 2004) rather than forming independent legal judgments that could potentially provide a valid criterion.

There are also conceptual, measurement, and legal reasons that dichotomous outcomes offer a poor criterion for evaluating the validity of adjudicative competence measures. Although adjudicative competence as a *legal* construct is a dichotomous one, the clinical and research models for assessing competence-related abilities, whether based on ordinal clinical ratings (SSIs) or performance scores on "tests" of capacity (some nomothetic measures), involve dimensional data. Other features of adjudicative competence as a legal construct preclude any scientifically rigorous translation of clinical and research dimensional data into categorical outcomes. For example, competence criteria are articulated using qualifiers (e.g., *sufficient* present ability; *reasonable degree* of rational understanding) that facilitate flexible legal decision making but which defy scientific operationalization. Furthermore, categorical legal competence determinations may depend, in part, on other nonscientific considerations, such as case complexity or social and political considerations (e.g., the extent to which the court determines a need to move a high-profile case forward in order to get closure and restore community stability) that (at least presently) cannot be measured in any rigorously scientific fashion.

This analysis suggests that to establish the validity of adjudicative competence measures investigators should not focus on the measures' capacity to "predict" (in a statistical sense) categorical adjudicative competence status. Rather, what is needed are studies that demonstrate convergent findings across measures, at the level of items or scales designed to index comparable competence-related abilities. Another potentially useful approach illustrated, to some degree, in the research by Golding and colleagues (1984) would be to identify blue-ribbon panels of experts who are highly familiar with and trained in the research and clinical conceptualizations of competence that underpin a particular instrument. These panels' independent assessments (at the item, scale, or index level) of the competence abilities of a particular research sample could then serve as a criterion against which to compare the assessment results of a cadre of adequately trained clinicians who evaluated the same defendant sample using that instrument.

There is somewhat more evidence pertaining to the reliability and validity of nomothetic measures than for many SSIs. Instruments such as the MacCAT-CA and the ECST-R have been the subject of better-funded and/ or more systematic empirical investigations. The performance characteristics of these measures have been reported in numerous articles in peer-reviewed journals, and quantitative indices relating to the reliability and validity of these measures are available for examination (and cross-examination) both in the literature and in the professional manuals.

With respect to the current gaps in our knowledge regarding the available competence assessment instruments, perhaps most significant is that these instruments assist clinicians in collecting data that are either idiographic *or* nomothetic in nature but do not allow for the merging of these two types of information. Idiographic information is a necessity in any competence evaluation in order to access and accommodate features and issues that are unique to the individual case. Nomothetic data, although not an absolute necessity, provides potentially valuable normative information as to this defendant's standing in comparison to other defendants in terms of competence-related abilities. The merging of idiographic with nomothetic information would allow for a determination regarding where this particular defendant stands in comparison to other defendants in terms of his or her competence-related abilities evaluated in a case-specific, contextualized manner. To date, there have not been any empirical investigations regarding the incremental utility of using nomothetic methods in an idiographic evaluation, nor have there been any empirical comparisons, using either a standard multitrait multimethod framework or comparisons with a "blue-ribbon panel of experts" (or other similar sound criterion), of the available nomothetic and idiographic methods.

Regarding future instrument development, specifically with respect to the assessment of the defendant's ability to provide rational assistance to counsel, the development of a new instrument (or a revision of a current one), wherein the content of the questions is idiographic in nature but the structure and format of the instrument would allow for nomothetic comparisons, would provide evaluators with the opportunity to conduct idiographic evaluations but to also compare the defendant in a normative way to a body of other defendants. Thus, the merging of these two types of information would allow evaluators to provide the courts with an integrated view of the defendant's functioning, both in terms of how this defendant compares to other defendants as well as how he or she is able to perform within the context of the specifics of his or her actual case.

There is also a need for studies that focus specifically on decisional competence issues. Some issues, such as deciding to waive right to counsel or the right to jury trial, simply have not been studied systematically using any of these assessment procedures. Further instrument development and evaluation of procedures for assessing these decisional competence issues are needed.

Finally, it may be possible, with the assistance of legal consultants, for researchers to devise an index of case complexity that might enable them in some fashion to take the potential moderating effect of this factor into account, in their derivation of interpretive norms. That is, at different levels of case complexity, a score on any given competence index (e.g., the Mac-CAT-CA Appreciation measure or the ECST-R Rational Assisting Counsel scale) might have a different nomothetically derived meaning, depending on the comparison group of defendants (e.g., high vs. low case complexity) used to generate the norms applicable in a particular case. Given the great diversity of complexity across criminal cases, the magnitude and cost of the research project(s) needed to develop norms that would be sensitive to case complexity would be substantial. Nevertheless, this area represents a gap in current knowledge that could be addressed, in principle, through further empirical investigation.

MYTHS AND MISPERCEPTIONS

Myth 1: Forensic Examiners Can Determine Legal Competence

Despite considerable progress in both the conceptualization of competence (e.g., Bonnie, 1992) and in the development of more legally informed clinical instrumentation for assessing competence-related abilities, there remain differences of opinion both within and across discipline boundaries concerning the proper role of the forensic examiner in competence evaluations. Legal scholars continue to criticize judges who

> relinquish to mental health professionals their responsibility for deciding the defendant's competency to stand trial. . . . Mental health professionals are not

expert in deciding whether the defendant has a "sufficient" ability to consult with his or her attorney or has a "reasonable" degree of rational understanding. Those decisions are legal policy decisions appropriately within the province of the judge. (Morris, Haroun, & Naimark, 2004, p. 243)

At the same time, research suggests that judges defer to the opinions of forensic examiners in large numbers of cases (Cox & Zapf, 2004), and surveys reveal the beliefs and attitudes of sitting judges that mental health professionals

are more qualified (through their specific training) to answer the question of competency than are judges or other legal professionals. One judge, in particular, indicated his frustration when mental health professionals will not speak to the ultimate issue. He indicated that his job would be "much easier" if the mental health professional would "simply state whether the defendant is competent or not." (Zapf et al., 2004, p. 35)

This is but a single instance of the long-standing debate as to whether, as a general matter, mental health professionals should offer opinions that embrace ultimate legal issues. In the context of the present analysis, the fact that contemporary measures such as the MacCAT-CA may label a defendant's performance on a scale or measure as in the (nomothetically determined) "clinically impaired" range raises the additional concern that clinicians, judges, or attorneys may inappropriately view such interpretations as categorically dispositive of the competence question. Thus, perhaps more than ever it is incumbent on users of these measures to respect the limitations on clinical models of adjudicative competence and to emphasize that the information they provide, either in reports or in testimony, is only advisory to the ultimate decision made by the trier of fact.

Myth 2: Competence Is a Static State

The idea that competence is a fixed or stable state, either across time or across potentially changing contextual demands of a particular case, is an inaccurate conceptualization of this construct; competence varies with time and with situation. Competence status may change across time because the acuity of a mentally ill defendant's symptoms may fluctuate as a function of quality of treatment, the stress of lengthy delays to adjudication, or natural fluctuations associated with the disorder.

Bonnie's articulation of the decisional competence construct has made more salient the notion that the specific abilities required of a defendant may vary with the kinds of decisions that his or her case demands—and that these decisions may change as a function of changing defense strategy. As Justice Blackmun noted in the dissenting opinion in *Godinez*, "a person who is 'competent' to play basketball is not thereby 'competent' to play the violin. Competency for one purpose does not necessarily translate to competency for another purpose" (*Godinez v. Moran*, 1993, p. 413). This instability has two important implications for the current discussion. First, as has been previously noted, competence assessments must be conducted within the context in which the issue arises and thus must take into consideration all (or as many as forseeably possible) issues and decisions relevant to the specific competence context. An important corollary is that when the competence context changes, so too must the evaluation (i.e., not necessarily the "standard" for competence—recall the holding in *Godinez*—but, rather, the focus of the inquiries). Second, the dynamic nature of competence directly violates one of the assumptions underlying psychological test construction (see Roesch, Hart, & Zapf, 1996), and so we must consider the impact of this variability when using nomothetic assessment instruments.

Myth 3: Competence Assessments Optimally Yield Categorical Findings

Clinically, each of the individual abilities required for a defendant to be considered competent within a particular context can be considered along a continuum, whereby a given individual may be able to perform the ability to a greater or lesser degree. Evaluators may form ordinal judgments or provide nomothetic characterizations of the relative strengths and weakness of an individual defendant with respect to each of the specific abilities required in a particular situation (e.g., appears to be able to factually understand the nature of the proceedings; appears to show impairment with respect to her ability to appreciate her role as a defendant; appears to have difficulty understanding the various plea options). It is this series of characterizations or judgments that, ideally, informs the decision of the trier of fact. As noted earlier, courts may disagree with these judgments or characterizations in light of other available data or because they weight differently the particular factors or findings that underpin a clinical finding. Furthermore, adjudicative competence is ultimately a socially constructed status that includes not only clinical qua scientific information about a defendant's abilities, but also legal (e.g., case complexity) and social policy considerations that do not lend themselves to clinical or scientific appraisal. There is no ultimate criterion for competence and no gold standard against which to compare decisions regarding an individual's competence status. Evaluators must consider these issues when being pressed to arrive at an "ultimate opinion" regarding a defendant's competence status.

CONCLUSIONS

We have discussed a number of concerns and limitations in recently developed measures of adjudicative competence. We laud the advances in instrumentation for assessing competence-related abilities, including the recent measures that utilize nomothetic data to help benchmark a defendant's (in) capacities in normative terms. These advances notwithstanding, limitations in the scope and reach of these forensic assessment tools and the socially constructed nature of the competence inquiry militates against mental health professionals offering categorical conclusions about a defendant's competence. Clinicians should aspire to provide a careful delineation of the defendant's relative strengths and weaknesses with respect to the competence abilities that can be assessed systematically, and a candid and careful description of specific idiographic data that may facilitate the trier of fact in reaching its own, independent categorical determination of a defendant's competence.

In terms of the admissibility of these competence assessment measures, we believe that both the idiographic and the nomothetic measures would meet both the relevancy test as well as the general acceptance or *Frye* test. In addition, we believe that the measures themselves would hold up under a *Daubert* inquiry as long as the evaluator used these measures in an appropriate fashion. That is, as long as the measure(s) constituted only one piece of data upon which the evaluation was based and the data from the measure were considered appropriately and weighted accordingly in light of all other data sources that comprised the evaluation.

Scientifically Supported, Unsupported, and Controversial Uses of Competence Measures

Scientifically Supported Uses

- Incorporating the results of idiographic assessment measures in competence evaluations
- Incorporating the results of nomothetic assessment measures in competence evaluations
- Using either idiographic or nomothetic measures (or both) in delineating the specific competence-related abilities and deficits of an individual

Scientifically Unsupported Uses

- Combining clinical ratings from multiple items or "scales" on idiographic measures and interpreting the scores as being indicative of competence or incompetence
- Using nomothetic measures as the sole basis for an opinion regarding competence without a case-specific idiographic inquiry
- Combining scores on nomothetic measures to create a dichotomous indication of competence or incompetence

Controversial Uses

- Relying solely on data from idiographic assessment instruments in coming to an opinion regarding a defendant's current competence status

COMMUNICATING CONSENSUS AND CONTROVERSIES

In terms of communicating the areas of consensus and controversy delineated above, forensic evaluators should be careful to focus their written reports and testimony regarding a defendant's competence in terms of specific competence-related abilities and by giving specific examples of the relevant abilities and deficits of the particular defendant. In this way, evaluators can guard against misinterpretations regarding the nomothetically determined categorical levels of performance indicated by second-generation measures of competence. To reiterate a point made above, it is incumbent on users of these measures to be clear about what they can and cannot do in terms of identifying a defendant's capacities.

Evaluators' opinions regarding competence to stand trial, whether they be opinions regarding the ultimate legal issue or opinions regarding the defendant's abilities and deficits with respect to specific competence-related abilities, need be formed on the basis of all available data. Performance on competence assessment instruments constitutes only one piece of this data. Thus, evaluators need to be clear in their communications with the courts regarding the abilities of *this* defendant, in light of *these* charges, working with *this* defense counsel, and within the context of *this particular* case. Idiographic illustration of the defendant's specific abilities and deficits will greatly assist in the normative interpretation of assessment results provided by measures of adjudicative competence.

REFERENCES

Bonnie, R. J. (1992). The competence of criminal defendants: A theoretical reformulation. *Behavioral Sciences and the Law, 10,* 291–316.

Bonnie, R. J. (1993). The competence of criminal defendants: Beyond *Dusky* and *Drope. University of Miami Law Review, 47,* 539–601.

Cox, M. L., & Zapf, P. A. (2004). An investigation of discrepancies between mental health professionals and the courts in decisions about competency. *Law and Psychology Review, 28,* 109–132.

Daubert v. Merrell Dow Pharmaceuticals, Inc., 509 U.S. 579 (1993).

Dusky v. United States, 362 U.S. 402 (1960).

Godinez v. Moran, 113 S. Ct. 2680 (1993).

Golding, S. L. (1993). *Interdisciplinary Fitness Interview—Revised: A training manual.* Salt Lake City: State of Utah Division of Mental Health.

Golding, S. L., Roesch, R., & Schreiber, J. (1984). Assessment and conceptualization of competency to stand trial: Preliminary data on the Interdisciplinary Fitness Interview. *Law and Human Behavior, 8,* 321–334.

Grisso, T. (2003). *Evaluating competencies: Forensic assessments and instruments* (2nd ed.). New York: Kluwer Academic/Plenum Press.

Laboratory of Community Psychiatry, Harvard Medical School. (1973). *Competency to stand trial and mental illness* (DHEW Publication No. ADM77–103). Rockville, MD: Department of Health, Education, and Welfare.

Melton, G. B., Petrila, J., Poythress, N. G., & Slobogin, C. (2007). *Psychological evaluations for the courts: A handbook for mental health professionals and lawyers* (3rd ed.). New York: Guilford Press.

Morris, G. H., Haroun, A. M., & Naimark, D. (2004). Assessing competency competently: Toward a rational standard for competency-to-stand-trial assessments. *Journal of the American Academy of Psychiatry and Law, 32,* 231–245.

Poythress, N. G., Bonnie, R. J., Monahan, J., Otto, R., & Hoge, S. K. (2002). *Adjudicative competence: The MacArthur studies.* New York: Kluwer.

Poythress, N. G., Nicholson, R., Otto, R. K., Edens, J. F., Bonnie, R. J., Monahan, J., et al. (1999). *Professional manual for the MacArthur Competence Assessment Tool—Criminal Adjudication.* Odessa, FL: Psychological Assessment Resources.

Roesch, R., Hart, S. D., & Zapf, P. A. (1996). Conceptualizing and assessing competency to stand trial: Implications and applications of the MacArthur treatment competence model. *Psychology, Public Policy, and Law, 2,* 96–113.

Roesch, R., Zapf, P. A., & Eaves, D. (2006). *Fitness Interview Test—Revised: A structured interview for assessing competency to stand trial.* Sarasota, FL: Professional Resource Press.

Rogers, R., Tillbrook, C. E., & Sewell, K. W. (2004). *Evaluation of Competency to Stand Trial—Revised: Professional manual.* Lutz, FL: Psychological Assessment Resources.

Skeem, J. L., Golding, S. L., Cohn, N., & Berge, G. (1998). Logic and reliability of evaluations of competence to stand trial. *Law and Human Behavior, 22,* 519–547.

Zapf, P. A., Hubbard, K. L., Cooper, V. G., Wheeles, M. C., & Ronan, K. A. (2004). Have the courts abdicated their responsibility for determination of competency to stand trial to clinicians? *Journal of Forensic Psychology Practice, 4,* 27–44.

Zapf, P. A., Skeem, J. L., & Golding, S. L. (2005). Factor structure and validity of the MacArthur Competence Assessment Tool—Criminal Adjudication. *Psychological Assessment, 17,* 433–445.

Zapf, P. A., & Viljoen, J. L. (2003). Issues and considerations regarding the use of assessment instruments in the evaluation of competency to stand trial. *Behavioral Sciences and the Law, 21,* 351–367.

PART V

COURTROOM SENTENCING

RISK AND REHABILITATION

CHAPTER 15

Violence Risk Assessment

CORE CONTROVERSIES

Kirk Heilbrun, Kevin S. Douglas, and Kento Yasuhara

Violence risk assessment is an area that has received considerable attention during the last two decades, reflecting in part a growing societal concern about the impact of violent crime and violent behavior. It has also received much scientific and professional attention. The question of whether someone will behave violently within the specified future arises in a broad range of legal decisions, including civil commitment, criminal sentencing, juvenile transfer and commitment, and hospital release decision making. It is also important in decisions involving criminal diversion, workplace violence risk, and national security. It should come as no surprise, therefore, that researchers, scholars, and professionals have been involved in a number of advances in violence risk assessment during the last two decades, including research with more clearly operationalized variables and sensitive outcomes (e.g., Monahan et al., 2001), the development of specialized tools (e.g., the Classification of Violence Risk [COVR], Monahan, Steadman, Robbins, et al., 2005; the Historical–Clinical–Risk Management–20 [HCR-20], Webster, Douglas, Eaves, & Hart, 1997; the Level of Service/Case Management Inventory [LS/CMI], Andrews, Bonta, & Wormith, 2004; Violence Risk Appraisal Guide [VRAG], Harris, Rice, & Quinsey, 1993; Quinsey, Harris, Rice, & Cormier, 2006), and clearer risk communication (Heilbrun, Dvoskin, Hart, & McNiel, 1999; National Research Council, 1989).

There has also been important debate regarding scientific questions and how scientific findings can be translated into practice in the last two decades. This chapter addresses two primary areas that have been controversial in the area of violence risk assessment. (We emphasize the point that this chapter addresses the topic of violent behavior and violent offending, but not the broader topic of general offending.) The first pertains to the relative validity of actuarial versus "structured professional judgment" (SPJ) models of risk assessment. This controversy is a contemporary iteration of the long-standing actuarial–clinical prediction debate (Meehl, 1954). Second, we consider the role of group-based nomothetic data in making predictions in an individual case. These two issues do not exhaust the domain of controversies in risk assessment, by any means. For instance, there has been ongoing discussion and debate concerning the role of risk management in the larger process of risk assessment (e.g., Douglas & Skeem, 2005; Heilbrun, 1997). Given that Chapter 16 of this book focuses on risk-reducing interventions, we will not discuss this topic as a primary area. Furthermore, the association between mental illness and violence remains unsettled (e.g., contrast the "pro" vs. "con" conclusions drawn by Silver, 2006, and Quinsey, Harris, Rice, & Cormier, 1998, respectively). However, psychosis is a single (potential) risk factor; we have decided to focus on the larger risk assessment process, rather than on any one single risk factor. We briefly discuss some of these issues under "Gaps in Knowledge."

OVERVIEW OF TECHNIQUES AND CONTROVERSIES

Actuarial versus Nonactuarial Risk Assessment

Actuarial prediction involves identifying predictors on an empirical (or theoretical) basis and validating them against known outcomes, employing fixed decision rules that combine predictor variables in a predefined way. This method reduces the error associated with unstructured judgment in predicting a specific outcome, although it is limited to this outcome (and hence cannot incorporate aspects of violence such as severity, imminence, duration, or frequency unless they have been incorporated into the definition of outcome; see Borum, 1996; Hart, 2001). Since violence is a phenomenon that is often underreported, "known outcomes" are an important consideration in the accuracy of such actuarial prediction. Currently the research strategy that allows investigators to most accurately gauge whether violent behavior has occurred involves using a combination of self-report, collateral observation, and official records (Monahan et al., 2001). This strategy is neither controversial nor the focus of this section. We note the necessity of two fundamental assumptions within actuarial prediction approaches: that both predictors and outcomes can be operationalized reliably, and that the validity of actuarially derived predictors depends in part on the accurate measurement of outcome.

It is important to define our terms and briefly to describe the larger context of the actuarial versus clinical prediction issue (Grove & Meehl, 1996; Meehl, 1954), so that it is clear what controversy we do (and do not) perceive in the risk assessment field. The terms "actuarial" and "clinical" are used as Meehl (1954) and colleagues (Grove & Meehl, 1996; Grove, Zald, Lebow, Snitz, & Nelson, 2000) have suggested. They described actuarial prediction as "a formal method" that "uses an equation, a formula, a graph, or an actuarial table to arrive at a probability, or expected value, of some outcome" (Grove & Meehl, 1996, p. 294). The actuarial approach, then, is defined by a routinized or mechanical combination of risk factors that have been validated against known outcomes.

The clinical prediction procedure, on the other hand, has been described as an "informal, 'in the head,' impressionistic, subjective conclusion, reached (somehow) by a human clinical judge" (Grove & Meehl, 1996, p. 294). Although some (Sawyer, 1966) have rightly pointed out that discretion can enter the decision-making task at numerous stages (i.e., selection of risk factors; measurement of risk factors; combination of risk factors), the most common conceptualization of the defining element of actuarial prediction is the mechanistic, reproducible combination of predictive factors.

Research over the last 50 years has shown convincingly that actuarial prediction is typically moderately more accurate than clinical prediction, as defined earlier (Ægisdóttir et al., 2006; Grove et al., 2000). This finding applies in the violence prediction field as well. Mossman (1994) conducted a meta-analysis of 58 datasets involving the prediction of violence. Although clinical predictions were more accurate than chance (area under the receiver operating curve [AUC] = .67), they were less accurate than the average AUC for all studies (.78), for cross-validated discriminant function predictions (.71), or for behavior-based predictions (.78). Ægisdóttir and colleagues (2006) concluded that in the violence prediction arena, statistical prediction is 17% more accurate than clinical prediction. (An AUC is an index of predictive strength. It ranges from 0 to 1, with .50 indicating zero predictive utility, and 1 indicating perfect positive prediction. It represents the probability that a person who is positive on the outcome—here, violence—will have a higher score on the predictive measure than a person who is negative on the outcome.)

Why, then, is the statistical-versus-clinical prediction issue controversial in the risk assessment field? It might be observed that actuarial measures, in addition to being modestly more accurate than clinical judgment, are typically more practical once the actuarial measure has been developed and validated. This observation, of course, would apply more readily to circumstances in which many judgments are being made (e.g., civil commitment, parole) than it would to contexts in which more intensive investment of resources is necessary (e.g., conditional release of insanity acquittees; ongoing supervision and risk management of offenders).

Another reason for this continued controversy involves the emergence of a structured, though non-actuarial, approach to risk assessment, initially developed in response to concerns about some of the initial actuarial risk assessment instruments. Instruments developed under the SPJ approach could in principle be used in an actuarial fashion (as described above), although were not intended to (see below). It is also important to point out that SPJ instruments were developed as a potentially reasonable, empirically defensible approach to risk assessment that did not have some of the perceived weaknesses of extant actuarial instruments or of unstructured clinical prediction. In developing the SPJ approach and concomitant instruments, the point was not to show that nonactuarial prediction, *generally*, could possess comparable predictive validity relative to actuarial prediction. Such a comparison would require certain "ground rules," such as use of the same information base and cross-validated actuarial predictive estimates (Grove et al., 2000). As such, we agree with the meta-analytic findings (discussed above), based on such ground rules, that actuarial prediction, as a general approach, is modestly more accurate than clinical prediction. The point, rather, was to develop a violence risk assessment procedure that addressed some of the perceived weaknesses of existing actuarial violence prediction instruments. If this approach was comparably valid to actuarial violence prediction instruments, despite incorporating different information, then it would be considered acceptable. Readers should keep this point in mind when reading the remainder of the chapter.

The SPJ model was developed in response to the following potential disadvantages of extant actuarial instruments: (1) they tend to offer static, unchanging estimates of risk, not allowing any modification of the risk estimate based on treatment or changing circumstances; (2) they offer precise numeric estimates of risk (e.g., 76%) without showing that such estimates cross-validate to new samples; (3) they tend to exclude treatment-relevant risk factors (criminogenic needs, or dynamic risk factors) that hold promise for risk reduction, despite research indicating that the targeting of such factors in intervention reduces recidivism (see Andrews et al., 2004); and (4) they are relevant to legal questions focusing only on prediction, but less applicable when the law assumes the potential for change in risk of violence toward others. In this chapter we focus primarily on actuarial and structured professional judgment approaches to risk assessment. We should point out that these two approaches to risk assessment share some features (most notably, the types of risk factors included on them, the use of operational definitions and coding rules, and the ways in which they have been evaluated), which we discuss later in this chapter. They are sufficiently distinct (i.e., in methods of item selection; methods of item integration) to describe separately—but their methodological "common ground" may help to explain why both have emerged as leading approaches in contemporary risk assessment.

SPJ measures originally were conceived as professional guidelines for the assessment of risk that could inform risk management and treatment. However, their developers recognized the perils of a purely unstructured, clinical approach. Structure was imposed by requiring the explicit coding of 20–30 specified risk factors on a 3-point scale (present, possibly/partially present, absent), each operationally defined, and each derived from the larger empirical literature. Numeric estimates of risk can be misleadingly precise when a single number is not presented with accompanying confidence intervals. (For instance, "50%" may represent the midpoint of a 95% confidence interval from .48 to .52, or the midpoint of a 95% confidence interval from .10 to .90, or a mean not accompanied by calculated confidence intervals. These three scenarios cannot be distinguished when only "50%" is presented as an estimate of the risk of future conduct). Similarly, precise numeric estimates often do not generalize across samples, a point we discuss later. Rather than reaching a numeric conclusion, SPJ evaluators are asked to rate each case as low, moderate, or high risk by assuming (1) the more risk factors present that are *individually relevant to a person's violent behavior*, the higher the risk; and (2) the greater the degree of intervention required to stem the risk of violence, the higher the risk. The SPJ model requires evaluators both to indicate the presence of a risk factor and specify the importance of that risk factor to understanding a given person's proneness to violence. Consider the example of substance use, a well-validated risk factor. For some people, it is strongly related to violence risk; for others, it is not. The "judgment" part of SPJ requires evaluators to decide for whom it is relevant (and to what extent) and for whom it is not.

SPJ methods do not require the algorithmic combination of risk factors to reach a risk judgment, nor do they offer numeric estimates of risk (for clinical purposes). Instead, they have evaluators consider the nomothetically supported evidence (through the coding of operationalized risk factors) for what type and intensity of treatment and management are indicated in a given case, based on the presence of empirically supported, specified risk factors in that case. Hence, SJP methods are intended to (1) identify the most relevant risk factors present in a given case, and (2) relate these to the indicated treatment or management strategies.

Nonetheless, measures must be evaluated. Befitting the requirements of the test standards jointly derived and adopted in 1999 by the American Educational Research Association (AERA), the American Psychological Association (APA), and the National Council on Measurement in Education (NCME), the empirical evaluation of psychological measures should parallel their intended clinical use(s). For SPJ measures, this means that their final judgment of low, moderate, and high risk—a nonactuarial index of risk—must be shown empirically to differentially identify persons as such. The core controversy involves the development and use of nonactuarial decision-making instruments, despite meta-analytic evidence that shows actuarial prediction to be reliably (though modestly) more accurate than nonactuarial methods.

Individual-Level Actuarial Predictions Based on Nomothetic Data

Despite being derived nomothetically, actuarial instruments are typically used to make decisions about single cases. In this section we discuss an important empirical consideration in the application of actuarially derived predictions to individual cases. It has long been recognized that there are "tough, unresolved philosophical problems connected with the application of frequencies to individual cases" (Meehl, 1973, p. 234). This discussion has particular relevance for legal decision making, as most of the decisions made about those involved in criminal or civil litigation do require the application of evidence to a single case.

Actuarial prediction of violence is typically communicated in one of two ways: through language involving *probability* (e.g., "There is a 10% likelihood that this individual will be violent" or "This individual is at low risk of violence, with low defined as fewer than 13% of individuals behaving violently") or *frequency* (e.g., "Of 100 such individuals, 10 will be violent") (see, e.g., Slovic & Monahan, 1995). This is the strength of actuarial prediction when properly employed—the identification of levels of risk in a way that facilitates accurate decision making over a large number of cases—and communication in this manner underscores this strength (Heilbrun et al., 1999).

But the applicability of such group-derived probability figures to an individual case depends on the margin of error. When such margins are relatively narrow, estimates based on the representative probability figure can apply well; when margins are wide, this probability figure is less precise and therefore less meaningful. We address this particular point in consideration of a recent paper making this very point (Hart, Michie, & Cooke, 2007)— that many actuarial instruments have such wide margins of error that concluding that an individual falls into a given risk category is less meaningful than it would be with a narrower confidence interval. Hart and colleagues argue that some actuarial risk assessment instruments are too error-prone at the individual level to offer meaningful guidance to practitioners— although we would note that this argument could be applied to any measure for which the risk judgment is quantified and confidence intervals are calculated. We illustrate our discussion by considering actuarial prediction tools with relatively narrow and wide margins of error, respectively.

RESEARCH RELEVANT TO CONTROVERSIES

Actuarial versus Nonactuarial Risk Assessment

Most research on SPJ instruments considers whether numeric total or subscale scores predict violence. This is a necessary step in their validation because it tests (1) whether the risk factors, as defined on the instruments, actually predict violence, and (2) the general proposition that the more risk factors that are present, the higher the likelihood that a person will act violently (Douglas & Kropp, 2002). However, because SPJ instruments were not intended to derive risk estimates strictly from numeric scores, a further step in their evaluation is necessary—whether the final risk judgments of low, moderate, and high risk, themselves based on the risk factors present in a given case, also predict violence (Douglas & Kropp, 2002).

At the time of writing this chapter, there were 10 published studies focusing on the question of whether final SPJ risk judgments predict violence. Of these 10 published studies, eight showed that SPJ judgments are predictive of recidivistic violence (Catchpole & Gretton, 2003; de Vogel & de Ruiter, 2005, 2006; de Vogel, de Ruiter, van Beek, & Mead, 2004; Douglas, Ogloff, & Hart, 2003; Douglas, Yeomans, & Boer, 2005; Enebrink, Långström, & Gumpert, 2006; Kropp & Hart, 2000). Two of 10 studies failed to provide support for the predictive validity of SPJ judgments (Sjösted & Långström, 2002; Viljoen et al., 2008). It should be noted that in one of two studies (Sjösted & Långström, 2002), *none* of the four risk assessment measures (three actuarial, one SPJ) predicted the main outcome of interest.

Five studies have tested incremental validity of the SPJ judgments relative to the numeric or actuarial use of the instruments upon which they are based. In each of these five studies, the SPJ judgment added incrementally to the predictive power of the numeric use of the given instrument (de Vogel & de Ruiter, 2006; Douglas et al., 2003, 2005; Enebrink et al., 2006; Kropp & Hart, 2000). In others, the SPJ judgment was significantly more predictive of outcome than actuarial predictions based on other, actuarial measures (de Vogel & de Ruiter, 2005, 2006; de Vogel et al., 2004; Douglas et al., 2003, 2005). For instance, in one study (de Vogel et al., 2004), the Sexual Violence Risk–20 (SVR-20; Boer, Hart, Kropp, & Webster, 1997), SPJ judgment AUC of .83 (r = .60) with sexual recidivism was statistically significantly larger than the AUC for an actuarial measure, the Static-99 (Hanson & Thornton, 1999) (AUC = .66; r = .30). In another study (Douglas et al., 2003), the HCR-20 SPJ judgment was significantly more predictive of violence than the Psychopathy Checklist—Revised (PCL-R; Hare, 2003), used actuarially, in multivariate analyses that directly compared the two (see also de Vogel & de Ruiter, 2005; Douglas et al., 2005). Other research (Douglas et al., 2005) has reported that both the SPJ judgment and a separate actuarial instrument (in this study, the VRAG) entered multivariate analyses as independent predictors of outcome, indicating that both the SPJ and actuarial risk judgments in this study offered unique predictive power beyond the other. In the one study that has investigated it (Enebrink et al., 2006), SPJ judgments were more accurate than either actuarial judgments or unstructured clinical predictions.

These studies suggest that structured data, when combined using professional judgment rather than a "formula," predict violence at least as well as actuarial predictions using either the specified risk factors on the SPJ tools (combined in actuarial fashion) or separate actuarial tools. Most of the studies that have formally compared the SPJ judgment to some form of actuarial prediction have reported that they add incrementally to the latter or produce significantly higher effect sizes. As Garb (2003) noted, mental health professionals who are careful in what information they consider and how they make judgments can be reliable and valid in such judgments. However, the SPJ approach has been criticized for failing to offer numeric estimates of risk (see Quinsey et al., 1998, 2006). As we discuss next, however, efforts to derive such probability estimates have themselves yielded mixed results, especially upon cross-validation. To be meaningful, actuarial estimates of violence risk must be successfully cross-validated and relatively stable across samples.

It is clear that actuarial instruments can produce moderate-to-large effect sizes in predicting violent behavior. In a recent meta-analysis of 48 studies (Blair, Marcus, & Boccaccini, in press), three popular actuarial risk assessment instruments (the VRAG; the Sex Offender Risk Appraisal Guide [SORAG]—Quinsey, Rice, & Harris, 1995; the Static-99—Hanson & Thornton, 1999), had, on average, moderate correlations with violence (averaged $r = .31$, range = .28–.34). The predictive accuracy was highest for the development samples ($r = .44$ for the VRAG; $r = .46$ for the SORAG; $r = .33$ for the Static-99), second highest in cross-validation studies by the developing authors (VRAG $r = .36$; SORAG $r = .35$), and lowest for cross-validation studies conducted by authors not involved in the development of the instrument (VRAG $r = .30$; SORAG $r = .29$; Static-99 $r = .27$). It is important, however, to evaluate actuarial instruments as they are intended to be used. Most such instruments provide probability estimates as a function of the risk category into which a given person falls. One important question is whether such probability estimates generalize reasonably across samples.

The evidence for stability of probability estimates across samples is mixed. Even considering the most sophisticated actuarial prediction instrument for violent behavior among individuals released into the community after psychiatric hospitalization—the COVR (Monahan, Steadman, Appelbaum, et al., 2005)—differing levels of probability estimates have been reported upon cross-validation. For instance, in the derivation sample, 76% of the "high-risk" group was violent postdischarge, compared to only 1% of the "low-risk" group. The associated AUC was .88. This is clearly very strong prediction. In a cross-validation study using the same methodological parameters as the derivation sample, however, the low-risk group's actual recidivism rate was 9%, and the high-risk group's was 35%. The associated AUC was .63 (Monahan, Steadman, Robbins, et al., 2005). In a modified follow-up procedure that deviated somewhat from the derivation parameters (i.e., slightly longer follow-up; slightly different definition of violence), the low-risk group's recidivism remained at 9%, and the high-risk group's was 49%. The associated AUC was .70. To some extent, these differing levels can be explained by the expected shrinkage between derivation and cross-validation samples. However, the MacArthur Risk study was quite large and well designed, underscoring the challenges facing those who would develop actuarial measures but do not have the capacity to collect data from 1,000+ participants across three sites, using multiple measures of outcome.

Mills, Jones, and Kroner (2005) tested the robustness of probability estimates derived from both the Level of Service Inventory—Revised (LSI-R) and VRAG in an independent sample of 207 correctional offenders. Their general conclusion is informative, particularly because both of these measures were designed to be used in the type of sample upon which the research is based:

> The results of this study do not support the generalizability of the original probabilities associated with the prediction bins, although the LSI-R bins performed much better than the VRAG bins. Overall, the original LSI-R probabilities tend to underestimate the likelihood of general reoffending and the original VRAG probabilities tend to overestimate the likelihood of violent reoffending. Furthermore, this study does not support the use of the initial validation probability bins of either instrument with our sample. (p. 579)

They further noted that showing a statistically meaningful association between an actuarial risk assessment instrument and outcome in a new sample is insufficient to demonstrate cross-validated *clinical utility*. For such clinical utility to be supported, the research must demonstrate that the indices that are actually intended to be used in practice—here, estimated probabilities associated with certain score ranges on the instruments—show robustness across samples. In the Mills and colleagues (2005) study, expected and observed probabilities (using the VRAG as an example) varied minimally in some score categories (expected vs. observed probabilities in categories 1–4, respectively, were 0% vs. 0%, 8% vs. 0%, 12% vs. 15%, and 17% vs. 18%) and substantially in others (expected vs. observed probabilities in categories 5, 8, and 9, respectively, were 35% vs. 15%, 76% vs. 48%, and 100% vs. 33%).

In other research, greater stability between expected and observed probabilities has been reported. For instance, Harris, Rice, and Cormier (2002) reported a cross-validation of the VRAG on an independent sample of 347 male forensic patients. They reported a correlation of $r = .98$ between observed and expected probabilities. Even with a correlation approaching perfect, however, there was one category in which the observed and expected probabilities differed by 17%, underscoring the importance of considering both overall correlation between observed and expected and within-category differences in the appraisal of stability of probability estimates.

A reasonable conclusion about well-developed and validated actuarial instruments is that persons who score in higher risk categories are more likely to be violent than persons who score in lower risk categories. Attaching precise probability estimates is more problematic, unless the supporting research clearly demonstrates that such probability estimates generalize robustly across samples upon cross-validation. We have discussed the observed range of recidivism probabilities across studies, suggesting that some tools are not as precise as specific numerical estimates might convey.

Individual-Level Actuarial Predictions Based on Nomothetic Data

In an important discussion of the "margins of error" associated with actuarial prediction, Hart and colleagues (2007) noted that actuarial tools often identify relative categories or levels of risk. Such categories are bounded by upper and lower limits, expressed in terms of "95% confidence intervals." For such categories to be most meaningful, their upper and lower bounds should not overlap with immediately adjacent categories. In addition, the narrower the range between upper and lower bounds within categories, the more meaningful the conclusion that an individual's score is in a given category.

This issue bears directly on the precision with which predictions can be made. There are at least three ways to communicate the results of actuarial prediction in probability terms when such probabilities are expressed in categories (e.g., 1–9, or "very low," "low," "moderate," "high," or "very high"). One way is to give the category without the associated probability or confidence interval—certainly the least desirable approach to communicating risk if the probability is available, as it should be using actuarial procedures. A second approach involves citing the category and associated probability level, but without the 95% confidence interval (e.g., "Mr. Jones's score places him in the moderate risk category; individuals in this category have a 27% probability of being arrested for a violent offense over the next year"). The third approach is most precise in conveying both probability and the limits of this estimate. It involves conveying the category, associated probability, and 95% confidence intervals within which the cited probability lies. For example: "Mr. Jones's score places him in the moderate risk category. With 95% confidence, this category describes a 23–31% likelihood of rearrest for a violent offense within the next year, with the best estimate being 27%."

Hart and colleagues (2007) also addressed applicability of confidence intervals to individual cases using Wilson's formula (Wilson, 1927) and argued that the resulting confidence intervals are so large as to render the use of precise probability estimates at the individual level untenable. However, inserting $N = 1$ into the confidence interval formula may not be a meaningful application of the formula, as the authors themselves acknowledge, and others (Harris & Rice, 2007; Mossman, 2007) have noted as well. There is no dispute that the size of confidence intervals is inversely related to the size of the sample—a coin flipped 10,000 times will have a very narrow confidence interval around the probability of "heads" (.50), while a coin flipped 10 times will have a much larger confidence interval. This is the "hard philosophical question" about applying group data to individuals, however. Both probability estimates and confidence intervals are important to convey in order to gauge the precision of the results of numeric risk appraisals.

This observation is important. For instance, when 95% confidence intervals are applied to the categories of the VRAG and Static-99, there is some overlap between immediately adjacent categories. This overlap makes the distinction between some categories less precise and meaningful than the distinctions between other, more extreme categories. The VRAG has a total of nine risk categories, and each of the nine categories showed some degree of overlap with the immediately adjacent category. However, the distinction between low risk (e.g., categories 1–3) and high risk (e.g., categories 8–9) is entirely nonoverlapping. By contrast, the 5 categories described by the COVR (Monahan, Steadman, Appelbaum, et al., 2005) are entirely nonoverlapping within 95% confidence intervals.

The combination of overlapping categories with larger confidence intervals suggests particular caution when using even strong actuarial tools such as the VRAG and Static-99 on an individual basis. The application of actuarial tools is more clearly indicated for group-based decisions (e.g., assigning particularly intensive treatment to all high-risk individuals). When used individually, there is nothing that can be done to compensate for the larger confidence intervals associated with the single case. However, actuarial results are more likely to be meaningful when used to reflect extreme and distinct groups (e.g., high vs. low risk) than less extreme, more overlapping groups.

GAPS IN KNOWLEDGE

Actuarial versus Structured Professional Judgment Risk Assessment

Why Does SPJ "Work"?

The available research supports the proposition that SPJ judgments perform as well as actuarial judgments, at least those derived from extant risk assessment instruments. There are several possible explanations for this proposition, though none has been studied empirically.

The simplest explanation is that actuarial and SPJ procedures are more similar than they are distinct. Consider three relevant dimensions to risk assessment: (1) whether relevant variables have been identified and clearly operationalized, (2) whether such variables are collected in a way that permits numerical coding, and (3) whether scored variables are combined according to a previously established formula. Both actuarial and SJP tools use variables that have been identified and operationalized, although they may differ on the approach to identifying such variables. The VRAG and the COVR, for instance, use variables identified through the empirical analysis of variables in a large dataset, whereas the HCR-20 employs variables identified more broadly in the literature as theoretically and empirically related to risk. Both actuarial and SPJ tools also promote the coding of variables into interval or ordinal categories that can be measured for reliability. Where these approaches differ is in their combination of scored items. Actuarial approaches use total scores; SPJ approaches use broad judgments based on the evaluator's appraisal of the meaning of the risk factors and protective factors that have been considered and appraised. Assuming that developers of SPJ tools select robust risk factors that have been consistently demonstrated to be related to crime or violence, it is perhaps not surprising that the potentially higher reliability of actuarial measures (at least those derived from careful empirical analysis of a dataset and cross-validated through comparable means in other datasets) is offset by the greater flexibility of SPJ in focusing appraisals to the individual case.

There are three additional possible explanations as well. First, it could be that SPJ judgments allow evaluators to incorporate additional information, beyond that upon which the actuarial estimate is based. In Grove and colleagues' (2000) meta-analysis, this was true for most studies in which clinical prediction outperformed actuarial prediction. However, in Ægisdóttir and colleagues' (2006) meta-analysis, it was not. It should be noted that an unequal information base violates rules for fair comparisons between actuarial and clinical prediction. However, the intent of SPJ was not to study the actuarial–clinical prediction debate per se.

Second, it is possible that the flexibility of SPJ procedures permits idiographic optimization of nomothetically supported risk factors within a given case, and does so within a "structured enough" framework to permit adequate reliability and validity. A third possibility extends the second: SPJ instruments may facilitate the recognition of patterns or interactions of risk factors in individual cases, and hence facilitate informed theorizing about risk at the individual level.

A further and related question is whether building such features (i.e., individual relevance of risk factors; additional case-relevant information not captured by the actuarial instrument's preset list of risk factors; recognition of individual patterns or interactions of risk factors) into an actuarial framework would then result in the actuarial procedure being more accurate than SPJ judgments. This is certainly possible, and would be consistent with orthodox thinking on actuarial approaches. However, research has not yet addressed such possibilities. Indeed, before such research could be conducted, research would first need to address why SPJ judgments "work."

Under What Circumstances Are Actuarial Judgments of Risk Likely to Be Most Robust?

To date, violence risk researchers have not identified the conditions under which actuarial algorithms or equations are highly likely to be generalizable, or robust across samples. The stability of actuarial estimates across samples can vary as a function of numerous sample and study features. In principle, the closer the cross-validation sample to the calibration sample in terms of participants and study design, the better the algorithm should perform in the cross-validation sample. Yet even across similar settings and methods (Monahan, Steadman, Appelbaum, et al., 2005; Monahan, Steadman, Robbins, et al., 2005), algorithms have not always performed comparably to derivation samples.

Moderation by Gender or Race

There is simply not enough research on whether risk assessment measures—whether SPJ or actuarial—work comparably for men and women, people of differing ethnic and racial backgrounds, and people from different countries. Some instruments were developed for use only with men (most instruments designed for use with sexual offenders) and hence should not be used with women. Other instruments were developed solely with male samples (i.e., VRAG), and evidence does not support their use with women (Harris et al., 2002). Some of the limited research available suggests that the HCR-20 performs comparably for men and women (Nicholls, Ogloff, & Douglas, 2004). However, other research (de Vogel & de Ruiter, 2005) has found that its SPJ judgments perform comparably between men and women, but its numeric scores may not. In a recent review of research on the use of the LSI system with women (Holtfreter & Cupp, 2007), the authors concluded that although these instruments show comparable, though somewhat lower, predictive accuracy for women than men, there were notable differences in terms of mean levels, and the specific risk factors that seemed to be important across gender.

In terms of ethnicity, country of origin, and race, there are very limited data. For commonly used instruments such as the VRAG, the LSI-R, the LS/CMI, and the HCR-20, there is no discernable difference in accuracy as a function of the country in which research has been conducted (although there also is no meta-analytic evidence on point yet). Within North America, there is surprisingly little research on the potential moderating role of race or ethnicity. Fujii, Tokioka, Lichton, and Hishinuma (2005) reported comparable predictive utility of the HCR-20 across European American, Native Hawaiian, and Asian American patients, despite some differences in terms of which specific factors were related to violence across groups. Långström (2004) reported that although the Static-99 and Rapid Risk Assessment for Sex Offence Recidivism (RRASOR) were predictive of sexual and non-sexual violent recidivism among sexual offenders in a Swedish sample with European ancestry, they were not predictive among offenders with African or Asian roots. Schlager and Simourd (2007) reported low (near-zero) predictive accuracy of the LSI-R for Hispanic and African American offenders. Bonta (1989) reported comparable performance of the LSI for Aboriginal and non-Aboriginal offenders, although some of the subscales showed differential predictive utility across groups. In a sample of 532 offenders, Whiteacre (2006) reported more classification errors (false positives, false negatives, overall classification accuracy) for the prediction of institutional infractions for African American offenders relative to European American or Hispanic offenders.

The issue of predictive bias as a function between gender, race, or ethnicity is not settled. Even among the studies that do compare groups, formal moderation analyses (Baron & Kenney, 1986) typically are not reported, hence making the interpretation of differences difficult. There is some suggestion that even if levels of predictive accuracy are comparable, there may be different pathways to violence for some groups relative to others. Research could profitably address this issue, as it has important implications beyond risk assessment (particularly for understanding and managing violence among subgroups of persons).

Is Mental Illness a Risk Factor for Violence?

In many risk assessment contexts (particularly civil commitment), there is a question of whether a person's risk for violence is linked to his or her mental illness. Despite the presence of literally hundreds of studies that address this question, it remains unclear whether mental illness is indeed a risk factor for violence. The "gap in knowledge," then, involves the circumstances (if any) under which mental illness is related to violence. In a meta-analysis of 204 studies on the relationship between psychosis and violence, Douglas, Guy, and Hart (2008) reported that psychosis was associated with a 50–70% increase in the odds of violence. However, the strength of the association differed drastically as a function of several moderators. In particular, studies conducted on samples from the community had much higher odds ratios (~3.5) than studies conducted on those in hospitals and correctional facilities (~1.5). Studies that compared people with psychosis to people with primarily externalizing disorders had much smaller odds ratios (~0.85) compared to studies in which the comparison was to people with primarily internalizing disorders (~2.2). Similarly, the comparison of people with psychosis to people with no known mental disorder resulted in a larger odds ratio (~3.7), compared to studies that contrasted people with psychosis to people with (any) nonpsychotic mental disorder (~1.5). Studies that measured psychosis at the level of symptom produced larger odds ratios (~2.1) than those that were conducted at the level of diagnosis (~1.3–1.7). This was particularly the case for positive (~2.3) compared to negative (~1.3) symptoms.

Individual-Level Actuarial Predictions Based on Nomothetic Data

A number of specialized tools are used to classify risk for violence or criminal offending. Almost without exception, these tools do not have associated confidence intervals published in their manuals. The COVR constitutes an exception, and serves as a good example of how the development and psychometric properties of an actuarial tool should be described in order to address the questions raised in this section. Confidence intervals are described for the development of the COVR (see Monahan, Steadman, Appelbaum, et al., 2005, pp. 30, 37). In addition, these confidence intervals do not overlap, making the distinction between immediately adjacent risk groups more meaningful.

There are two important gaps in our knowledge about how actuarial tools can be applied to single cases. The first is the size of the confidence intervals and the extent to which they overlap, calculated on a "group" basis—both of which are apparently absent for all published actuarial tools except the COVR. The second involves the limits of precision for nomothetically derived actuarial measures when applied to single cases. The calculation of individual case confidence intervals describes the predictive precision when actuarial results are applied to a single case. This calculation is apparently unknown (or at least unpublished) for all of these tools.

MYTHS AND MISPERCEPTIONS

In the remainder of this chapter we integrate the two primary controversies that we have identified. We do so because some of the misperceptions, scientifically supported/unsupported uses, and conclusions are applicable to both.

Estimates of Risk Are Static or Do Not Change Over Time

Some actuarial risk instruments (e.g., VRAG) offer a single probability of violence that is applied over a lengthy period of time. This presumes that a given person has, say, a 63% chance of violence over some period of time, say, 10 years. Recent conceptual work in the risk and violence fields has called for attention to dynamic (changeable) risk (Douglas & Skeem, 2005), or risk *state* as opposed to risk *status* (Skeem & Mulvey, 2002). As Dvoskin and Heilbrun (2001) stated:

> An individual's risk [state] may be seen as changing over time and in response to interventions, as contrasted with the single, unchanging risk [status] estimate yielded under the prediction model by actuarial tools that use static (unchangeable through planned intervention) risk factors. (p. 8)

Risk *state* pertains to intraindividual changes in risk over time. That is, what factors increase or diminish a given individual's risk for violence at different times in his or her life? At certain times, a person might be at great risk for violence (e.g., when intoxicated, noncompliant with medication, and homeless), and other times that *same* person would be at low risk for violence (e.g., when sober, treatment compliant, and safely housed). Risk *status* pertains to interindividual differences in risk. That is, what risk factors distinguish the risk posed by people who share a common elevation or pattern of risk factors relative to people who do not share these risk factors? Although there is no consensus in the field (see Quinsey et al., 2006, for criticisms of dynamic risk), many commentators endorse the view that if dynamic risk factors (or criminogenic needs) change, then the probability of risk changes accordingly. As such, offering a single probability estimate oversimplifies what is likely to be a much more complex waxing and waning of the likelihood of violence over time.

There is empirical support for this proposition. *Indirect* support comes from dozens of studies showing that many risk factors for violence have been shown to (1) change over time, and (2) relate to violence (see Douglas & Skeem, 2005, for a review). These are largely disparate bodies of research, however (i.e., many studies show that levels of anger wax and wane over time, whereas another set of studies shows that anger tends to predict violence), which is why such evidence is only indirect. However, several studies show a direct link between changes in certain risk factors and concomitant changes in the probability of violence (Andrews, Bonta, & Wormith, in press; Andrews & Robinson, 1984; Hanson & Harris, 2000; Hanson, Harris, Scott, & Helmus, 2007; Hudson, Wales, Bakker, & Ward, 2002; Mulvey et al., 2006; Skeem et al., 2006). As such, there is empirical support for the proposition that a person's level of risk changes over time, in response to changes in risk factors.

Actuarial Prediction Is Invariably Superior to Any Other Form of Risk Assessment

There is no question that actuarial prediction is consistently and modestly more accurate than *unstructured* clinical judgment. This was Meehl's (1954) conclusion over 50 years ago, and it appears as warranted today as it was then (Ægisdóttir et al., 2006; Grove et al., 2000). But the questions of future violence risk as framed by social science researchers and by the law may differ, at times substantially. Legal decisions usually focus on single cases, raising considerations of the generalizability and ecological validity of some research on actuarial prediction as it applies to the law. To put it simply: If judges wanted to know only how likely it was that defendants would behave in ways researchers defined as violent, within the outcome periods used in such research, and from populations that were the subject of such research, then the adoption of exclusively actuarial approaches in forensic assessment of violence risk might be indicated. But legal decisions often strive to incorporate contingent aspects of violence risk (e.g., differing outcome periods; severity, imminence, and frequency of potential violence) and risk factors that can be controlled (e.g., living circumstances, availability of means for and potential victims of violence; job status/financial support; social support; substance abuse) that would be very difficult to incorporate into actuarial assessment. It would not be impossible, as illustrated by one such actuarial tool. The development of the COVR, supported by many years of MacArthur Foundation funding, was facilitated by the use of classification tree analysis, permitting the simultaneous consideration of multiple variables (Monahan et al., 2001), and it comes closest to an actuarial strategy that permits a wide range of relevant variables to be considered prospectively. But this strategy is extraordinarily time-consuming and labor-intensive, and is not practical except under very unusual circumstances. When actuarial prediction is based on a tool that has been developed with a more limited sample, has not been extensively cross-validated, and may therefore not generalize well to individuals outside a limited jurisdiction, it seems clear that it should not be accorded the same influence as tools that do have such features in their development.

CONCLUSIONS

Actuarial strategies developed from small samples and insufficiently validated may have wide margins of error. This margin of error for a 95% confidence interval, which is closely related to the precision of the prediction and the confidence with which it can be communicated, is wider for individual cases and small groups than it is for larger groups. Predictions about a given individual using such actuarial strategies are less likely to characterize accurately his or her violence risk if the probability is cited but these two caveats are not included in the communication.

Scientifically Supported Uses

- Conclusions that persons scoring higher on validated actuarial risk assessment instruments or rated as higher risk on validated SPJ instruments are at greater risk for violence than those scoring lower on these instruments.
- Actuarial prediction strategies for group-based predictions, with large derivation and validation samples, using mean probability and including margin of error.
- Use of extreme risk categories as more informative and less subject to limits of overlapping confidence intervals.
- Indication that application of group-based data to an individual case or small number of cases will result in wider confidence intervals than application to a large number of cases.

Scientifically Unsupported Uses

- Actuarial prediction strategies without large derivation and validation samples.
- Actuarial prediction strategies applied to populations that are not part of the derivation and validation samples.
- Conclusions that a given *individual* has an X probability of violence in the future, without the context of confidence intervals and the caution about less certainty in the individual case.

Scientifically Controversial and/or Largely Untested Uses

- Actuarial prediction strategies with large derivation and validation samples using mean probability but not citing margin of error and its increased uncertainty when applied to single cases.
- The assumption that there are reliable, known probability estimates that are robust across samples, even at the group level.

COMMUNICATING CONSENSUS AND CONTROVERSIES

Actuarial prediction strategies, when appropriately derived and validated, are powerful tools for enhancing the accuracy of predictions. When actuarial strategies are not based on appropriate derivation and validation procedures, however, their accuracy is likely to be poorer and less clear. Since poorly derived and validated actuarial strategies still retain the "actuarial cachet," their use may mislead the consumer into concluding that they are more accurate than they actually are. The appropriate use of actuarial strategies in a forensic context in which a prediction is requested involves using tools that have been derived and validated on appropriately large samples, and communicating in terms of probability or frequencies, while concurrently citing the margin of error, emphasizing the usefulness of extreme categories, and describing the increased uncertainty when group-based data are applied to single cases.

If evaluators report precise probability estimates, they should also report the known confidence intervals and the implications of the confidence intervals for the accuracy of the estimate. If there are no known confidence intervals, however, then evaluators should not communicate a precise numerical estimate of risk because the precision of such an estimate cannot be evaluated. Evaluators who communicate in categorical terms (e.g., high, moderate, and low risk) should be prepared to discuss the well-supported finding (for both actuarial and SJP studies) that such categories distinguish among risk levels reasonably well. Furthermore, *evaluators should report the full range of observed probabilities published in all cross-validation studies for the actuarial risk category into which the evaluee falls.* Evaluators may choose to report the range of observed recidivism rates from published SPJ studies, as well, with the clear caveat that these are not intended to represent any given individual's risk, but rather were reported to test the basic proposition that persons rated as higher risk are at higher risk than those rated as moderate or low risk.

REFERENCES

Ægisdóttir, S., White, M. J., Spengler, P. M., Maugherman, L. A., Cook, R. S., Nichols, C. N., et al. (2006). The meta-analysis of clinical judgment project: Fifty-six years of accumulated research on clinical versus statistical prediction. *The Counseling Psychologist, 34*(3), 341–382.

Andrews, D. A., Bonta, J., & Wormith, J. (2004). *The Level of Service/Case Management Inventory user's manual.* North Tonawanda, NY: Multi-Health Systems.

Andrews, D. A., Bonta, J., & Wormith, J. (in press). The Level of Service (LS) assessment of adults and older adolescents. In R. K. Otto & K. S. Douglas (Eds.), *Handbook of violence risk assessment.* New York: Routledge.

Andrews, D. A., & Robinson, D. (1984). *The Level of Supervision Inventory: Second report.* A report to Research Services (Toronto) of the Ontario Ministry of Correctional Services. Toronto: Ministry of Correctional Services.

Baron, R. M., & Kenny, D. A. (1986). The moderator–mediator variable distinction in social psychological research: Conceptual, strategic, and statistical considerations. *Journal of Personality and Social Psychology, 51*(6), 1173–1182.

Blair, P. R., Marcus, D. K., & Boccaccini, M. T. (2008). Is there an allegiance effect for assessment instruments?: Actuarial risk assessment as an exemplar. *Clinical Psychology: Science and Practice, 15*, 263–279.

Boer, D., Harts, S., Kropp, R., & Webster, C. (1997). *Manual for the Sexual Violence Risk–20: Professional guidelines for assessing risk of sexual violence.* Vancouver, BC, Canada: British Columbia Institute on Family Violence and Mental Health, Law, and Policy Institute, Simon Fraser University.

Bonta, J. (1989). Native inmates: Institutional response, risk, and needs. *Canadian Journal of Criminology, 31*, 49–62.

Borum, R. (1996). Improving the clinical practice of violence risk assessment: Technology, guidelines, and training. *American Psychologist, 51*, 945–956.

Catchpole, R. E. H., & Gretton, H. M. (2003). The predictive validity of risk assessment with violent young offenders: A 1-year examination of criminal outcome. *Criminal Justice and Behavior, 30,* 688–708.

de Vogel, V., & de Ruiter, C. (2005). The HCR-20 in personality disordered female offenders: A comparison with a matched sample of males. *Clinical Psychology and Psychotherapy, 21,* 226–240.

de Vogel, V., & de Ruiter, C. (2006). Structured professional judgment of violence risk in forensic clinical practice: A prospective study into the predictive validity of the Dutch HCR-20. *Psychology, Crime, and Law, 12,* 321–336.

de Vogel, V., de Ruiter, C., van Beek, D., & Mead, G. (2004). Predictive validity of the SVR-20 and Static-99 in a Dutch sample of treated sex offenders. *Law and Human Behavior, 28,* 235–251.

Douglas, K. S., Guy, L. S., & Hart, S. D. (2008). *Psychosis as a risk factor for violence to others: A meta-analysis.* Manuscript submitted for publication.

Douglas, K. S., & Kropp, P. R. (2002). A prevention-based paradigm for violence risk assessment: Clinical and research applications. *Criminal Justice and Behavior, 29,* 617–658.

Douglas, K. S., Ogloff, J. R. P., & Hart, S. D. (2003). Evaluation of a model of violence risk assessment among forensic psychiatric patients. *Psychiatric Services, 54,* 1372–1379.

Douglas, K. S., & Skeem, J. L. (2005). Violence risk assessment: Getting specific about being dynamic. *Psychology, Public Policy, and Law, 11,* 347–383.

Douglas, K. S., Yeomans, M., & Boer, D. P. (2005). Comparative validity analysis of multiple measures of violence risk in a general population sample of criminal offenders. *Criminal Justice and Behavior, 32,* 479–510.

Dvoskin, J. A., & Heilbrun, K. (2001). Risk assessment and release decision-making: Toward resolving the great debate. *Journal of the American Academy of Psychiatry and the Law, 29,* 6–10.

Enebrink, P., Långström, N., & Gumpert, C. H. (2006). Predicting aggressive and disruptive behavior in referred 6- to 12-year-old boys: Prospective validation of the EARL-20B risk/needs checklist. *Assessment, 13,* 356–367.

Fujii, D. E. M., Tokioka, A. B., Lichton, A. I., & Hishinuma, E. (2005). Ethnic differences in prediction of violence risk with the HCR-20 among psychiatric inpatients. *Psychiatric Services, 56,* 711–716.

Garb, H. (2003). Clinical judgment and mechanical prediction. In A. M. Goldstein & I. B. Weiner (Eds.), *Handbook of psychology: Vol. 11. Forensic psychology* (pp. 27–42). Hoboken, NJ: Wiley.

Grove, W. M., & Meehl, P. E. (1996). Comparative efficiency of informal (subjective, impressionistic) and formal (mechanical, algorithmic) prediction procedures: The clinical–statistical controversy. *Psychology, Public Policy, and Law, 2,* 293–323.

Grove, W. M., Zald, D. H., Lebow, B. S., Snitz, B. E., & Nelson, C. (2000). Clinical versus mechanical prediction: A meta-analysis. *Psychological Assessment, 12,* 19–30.

Hanson, R. K., & Harris, A. J. R. (2000). Where should we intervene?: Dynamic predictors of sexual offense recidivism. *Criminal Justice and Behavior, 27*, 6–35.

Hanson, R. K., Harris, A. J. R., Scott, T., & Helmus, L. (2007). *Assessing the risk of sexual offenders on community supervision: The Dynamic Supervision Project.* Corrections Research User Report 2007-05. Ottawa: Public Safety Canada.

Hanson, R. K., & Thornton, D. (1999). Static-99: Improving actuarial risk assessments for sex offenders. Ottawa: Department of the Solicitor General of Canada.

Hare, R. (2003). *The Hare Psychopathy Checklist—Revised: 2nd Edition.* Toronto: Multi-Health Systems.

Harris, G. T., & Rice, M. E. (2007). Characterizing the value of actuarial violence risk assessments. *Criminal Justice and Behavior, 34*, 1638–1658.

Harris, G. T., Rice, M. E., & Cormier, C. A. (2002). Prospective replication of the *Violence Risk Appraisal Guide* in predicting violent recidivism among forensic patients. *Law and Human Behavior, 26*, 377–394.

Harris, G. T., Rice, M., & Quinsey, V. (1993). Violent recidivism of mentally disordered offenders: The development of a statistical prediction instrument. *Criminal Justice and Behavior, 20*, 315–335.

Hart, S. (2001). Assessing and managing violence risk. In K. Douglas, C. Webster, S. Hart, D. Eaves, & J. Ogloff (Eds.), *HCR-20 violence risk management companion guide* (pp. 13–25). Burnaby, BC, Canada: Mental Health, Law, & Policy Institute, Simon Fraser University, and Department of Mental Health Law and Policy, Florida Mental Health Institute, University of South Florida.

Hart, S., Michie, C., & Cooke, D. (2007). The precision of actuarial risk assessment instruments: Evaluating the "margins of error" of group versus individual predictions of violence. *British Journal of Psychiatry, 190*, S60–S65.

Heilbrun, K. (1997). Prediction vs. management models relevant to risk assessment: The importance of legal context. *Law and Human Behavior, 21*, 347–359.

Heilbrun, K., Dvoskin, J., Hart, S., & McNiel, D. (1999). Violence risk communication: Implications for research, policy, and practice. *Health, Risk, and Society, 1*, 91–106.

Holtfreter, K., & Cupp, R. (2007). Gender and risk assessment: The empirical status of the LSI-R for women. *Journal of Contemporary Criminal Justice, 23*, 363–382.

Hudson, S. M., Wales, D. S., Bakker, L., & Ward, T. (2002). Dynamic risk factors: The Kia Marama evaluation. *Sexual Abuse: A Journal of Research and Treatment, 14*, 103–119.

Kropp, P. R., & Hart, S. D. (2000). The Spousal Assault Risk Assessment (SARA) guide: Reliability and validity in adult male offenders. *Law and Human Behavior, 24*, 101–118.

Långström, N.(2004). Accuracy of actuarial procedures for assessment of sexual offender recidivism risk may vary across ethnicity. *Sexual Abuse: A Journal of Research and Treatment, 16*, 107–120.

Meehl, P. (1954). *Clinical versus statistical prediction: A theoretical analysis and a review of the evidence*. Minneapolis: University of Minnesota Press.

Meehl, P. (1973). Why I do not attend case conferences. In P. E. Meehl *Psychodiagnosis: Selected papers* (pp. 225–302). Minneapolis: University of Minnesota Press.

Mills, J. F., Jones, M. N., & Kroner, D. G. (2005). An examination of the generalizability of the LSI-R and VRAG probability bins. *Criminal Justice and Behavior, 32*, 565–585.

Monahan, J., Steadman, H., Appelbaum, P., Grisso, T., Mulvey, E., Roth, L., et al. (2005). *Classification of Violence Risk: Professional manual*. Lutz, FL: PAR.

Monahan, J., Steadman, H., Robbins, P. C., Appelbaum, P., Banks, S., Grisso, T., et al. (2005). Prospective validation of the multiple iterative classification tree model of violence risk assessment. *Psychiatric Services, 56*, 810–815.

Monahan, J., Steadman, H., Silver, E., Appelbaum, P., Robbins, P. C., Mulvey, E., et al. (2001). *Rethinking risk assessment: The MacArthur study of mental disorder and violence*. New York: Oxford University Press.

Mossman, D. (1994). Assessing predictions of violence: Being accurate about accuracy. *Journal of Consulting and Clinical Psychology, 62*, 783–792.

Mossman, D. (2007). Avoiding errors about "margins of error." *British Journal of Psychiatry, 191*, 561.

Mulvey, E. P., Odgers, C., Skeem, J., Gardner, W., Schubert, C., & Lidz, C. (2006). Substance use and community violence: A test of the relation at the daily level. *Journal of Consulting and Clinical Psychology, 74*, 743–754.

National Research Council. (1989). *Improving risk communication*. Washington, DC: National Academy Press.

Nicholls, T. L., Ogloff, J. R. P., & Douglas, K. S. (2004). Assessing risk for violence among female and male civil psychiatric patients: The HCR-20, PCL: SV, and McNiel & Binder's VSC. *Behavioral Sciences and the Law, 22*, 127–158.

Quinsey, V., Harris, G., Rice, M., & Cormier, C. (1998). *Violent offenders: Appraising and managing risk*. Washington, DC: American Psychological Association.

Quinsey, V., Harris, G., Rice, M., & Cormier, C. (2006). *Violent offenders: Appraising and managing risk* (2nd ed.). Washington, DC: American Psychological Association.

Quinsey, V., Rice, M., & Harris, G. (1995). Actuarial prediction of sexual recidivism. *Journal of Interpersonal Violence, 10*, 85–105.

Sawyer, J. (1966). Measurement and prediction, clinical and statistical. *Psychological Bulletin, 66*, 178–200.

Schlager, M. D., & Simourd, D. J. (2007). Validity of the Level of Service Inventory—Revised (LSI-R) among African American and Hispanic male offenders. *Criminal Justice and Behavior, 34*, 545–554.

Silver, E. (2006). Understanding the relationship between mental disorder and violence: The need for a criminological perspective. *Law and Human Behavior, 30*, 685–706.

Sjöstedt, G., & Långström, N. (2002). Assessment of risk for criminal recidivism among rapists: A comparison of four different measures. *Psychology, Crime, and Law, 8*, 25–40.

Skeem, J. L., & Mulvey, E. (2002). Monitoring the violence potential of mentally disordered offenders being treated in the community. In A. Buchanan (Ed.), *Care of the mentally disordered offender in the community* (pp. 111–142). New York: Oxford University Press.

Skeem, J. L., Schubert, C., Odgers, C., Mulvey, E., Gardner, W., & Lidz, C. (2006). Psychiatric symptoms and community violence among high-risk patients: A test of the relationship at the weekly level. *Journal of Consulting and Clinical Psychology, 74*, 967–979.

Slovic, P., & Monahan, J. (1995). Probability, danger, and coercion. *Law and Human Behavior, 19*, 4965.

Viljoen, J. L., Scalora, M., Cuadra, L., Bader, S., Chávez, V., Ullman, D., et al. (2008). Assessing risk for violence in adolescents who have sexually offended: A comparison of the J-SOAP-II, J-SORRAT-II, and SAVRY. *Criminal Justice and Behavior, 35*, 5–23.

Webster, C., Douglas, K., Eaves, D., & Hart, S. (1997). *HCR-20: Assessing risk for violence* (Version 2). Burnaby, BC, Canada: Mental Health, Law, and Policy Institute, Simon Fraser University.

Whiteacre, K. W. (2006). Testing the Level of Service Inventory—Revised (LSI-R) for racial/ethnic bias. *Criminal Justice Policy Review, 17*, 330–342.

Wilson, E. (1927). Probable inference, the law of succession, and statistical inference. *Journal of the American Statistical Association, 22*, 209–212.

CHAPTER 16

Appropriate Treatment Works, but How?

REHABILITATING GENERAL, PSYCHOPATHIC, AND HIGH-RISK OFFENDERS

Jennifer L. Skeem, Devon L. L. Polaschek,
and Sarah Manchak

Does the provision of psychosocial treatment to criminal offenders meaningfully increase public safety? If so, is this true even of offenders at highest risk of recidivism, including those with psychopathic traits or with repeated violent behavior? These questions have attracted intense and long-standing debate in both academic and public policy circles. In this chapter we distill the state of the science on whether treatment reduces recidivism risk for general offenders and for high-risk offenders; outline current gaps in knowledge; and articulate conclusions about scientifically supported, unsupported, and controversial uses of treatment with both offender groups. We focus on psychosocial treatment, particularly contemporary treatment that targets multiple changeable risk factors for recidivism in adult offenders (rather than educational, vocational, faith-based, and related programs). We define here as *general offenders* those with varied index offenses, criminal histories, and estimated risk of recidivism. We define *high-risk offenders* as a subset of general offenders who have more serious, diverse, and numerous past offenses and a high estimated risk of recidivism. Given that there is less controversy about whether appropriate treatment reduces general offenders' risk of recidivism, we devote greater attention to informing the debate about the treatment of high-risk offenders.

CORE ISSUES AND CONTROVERSIES

Does Treatment Reduce Recidivism Risk for General Offenders?

Defining the Controversy

In the field of corrections there has long been tension between the goals of protecting community safety ("control") and promoting offender rehabilitation ("care"). Indeed, three models of correctional supervision can be differentiated based on the extent to which they focus on control (surveillance model), care (treatment model), or both (hybrid model) (Skeem & Manchak, 2008). For nearly a quarter of a century, chiefly for sociopolitical reasons well-documented elsewhere, surveillance has been the dominant model of supervision in the United States. Recently, the hybrid model has gained ascendance in some agencies as evidence for the effectiveness of some correctional treatment programs has grown. Symbolic of this movement is Governor Schwarzenegger's renaming of one of the largest correctional systems in the Unites States, the "California Department of Corrections *and Rehabilitation*," and creation of a strike team to implement a multi-billion-dollar measure to "shift our approach to rehabilitating prisoners" (Maile, 2007). Across the nation, stakeholders have become interested in results-driven policies and "evidence-based" criminal justice programs (Aos, Miller, & Drake, 2006).

This wave of optimism about the potential for treatment to reduce offenders' risk of recidivism is not universal. First, believers and skeptics alike share a serious concern about "correctional quackery," observing that most treatment programs—as *implemented* by correctional agencies—do not apply evidence-based principles of practice (Farabee, 2005; Latessa, Cullen, & Gendreau, 2002). Second, at least one skeptic is concerned that a "powerful bias in academic circles" (Farabee, 2005, p. xvi) leads researchers to "spin" the results of methodologically flawed studies to support the rehabilitative zeitgeist.

Based on a summary of poor practices and research, Farabee (2005) argued that correctional rehabilitation efforts should be abandoned and surveillance increased to reduce recidivism. Although the topic exceeds the scope of this chapter, there is compelling experimental evidence that increased surveillance actually *increases* parolees' risk of rearrest if it is unaccompanied by rehabilitative efforts (see Skeem & Manchak, 2008). As Byrne and Taxman (2006) observe, "It is the recent failure of conservative crime control strategies to demonstrate effectiveness that has been one of the main reasons that 'treatment' has reemerged as a key feature of the latest wave of federal initiatives" (pp. 10–11). Here, we set aside the surveillance model to focus on the hybrid model.

Research Relevant to the Controversy

Given our focus on correctional models that include rehabilitation efforts, *does* psychosocial treatment meaningfully reduce offenders' risk of recidivism? The answer provided by meta-analyses of thousands of studies is, "It depends." First, much depends on the extent to which the treatment program in question follows a standard set of principles—principles that are outlined by the "risk–needs–responsivity" model (RNR; Andrews, Bonta, & Hoge, 1990). There are no "RNR" programs per se. Instead, treatment programs differ in the extent to which they follow these principles. Meta-analytic studies show that offenders are less likely to recidivate when programs target higher- rather than lower-risk cases and match the intensity of supervision and treatment services to their level of risk for recidivism (*risk* principle), match modes of service to their abilities and styles (*responsivity* principle), and target their criminogenic needs, or changeable risk factors for recidivism (*need* principle; e.g., Andrews et al., 1990; Andrews & Bonta, 1998; Lowenkamp, Latessa, & Smith, 2006). With respect to the latter point, the effectiveness of programs is associated with the number of criminogenic needs they target (e.g., antisocial peer associations, positive attitudes toward crime), relative to noncriminogenic needs (i.e., disturbances that impinge on an individual's functioning, e.g., anxiety or poor self esteem; Andrews et al., 1990). The effect size is notable: Providing treatment that follows RNR principles reduces an offender's risk of recidivism by 24–53%, relative to making no rehabilitative efforts (Andrews et al., 1990; Andrews & Bonta, 1998).

Second, beyond prototypic RNR characteristics, the effectiveness of rehabilitation programs depends on the model of treatment applied, with cognitive-behavioral techniques such as cognitive restructuring and relapse prevention performing better than behavior modification techniques alone (e.g., token economies; Pearson, Lipton, Cleland, & Yee, 2002). However, there appear to be few differences in effectiveness among specific brands of cognitive restructuring, such as "Reasoning and Rehabilitation" (Aos et al., 2006; Landenberger & Lipsey, 2005). In fact, based on analyses of 58 experiments and quasi-experiments that controlled for design problems, Landenberger and Lipsey (2005) found that there were no differences among brand name and generic cognitive models. However, treatment was significantly more effective when it was intensive (more hours provided), included individual sessions (not just group treatment), and focused on anger control. After controlling for design problems (e.g., exclusion of treatment dropouts), cognitive programs reduced an offender's recidivism risk by 25–50% (average to maximum effect), relative to making no rehabilitative efforts.

Third—and presently least well researched—specific aspects of the interpersonal process between therapists and offenders during program delivery also predict outcome. According to one meta-analysis (Dowden & Andrews, 2004), therapist behaviors that are predictive of outcome include conveying an enthusiastic, warm, and personally respectful style, making program rules clear and exerting authority without being authoritarian, frequently praising offenders for prosocial behavior, and structuring offender learning into concrete, graded steps. Moderate-to-large correlations resulted when programs incorporated some of these characteristics, compared to none. In a more recent study of a specialty mental health supervision program, Skeem, Eno Louden, Polaschek, and Camp (2007) found that officer–probationer relationships significantly protected against future probation violations and revocation when they were characterized by caring, fairness, trust, and an authoritative (not authoritarian) style.

Fourth, as the preceding points suggest, the effectiveness of the rehabilitation program depends on the quality with which it is implemented. For example, in the meta-analysis described earlier, the quality of the treatment—indexed by such features as provider training, implementation monitoring, and provision of treatment in research rather than practice contexts—strongly predicted recidivism reduction (b =.40; Landenberger & Lipsey, 2005). Lowenkamp and colleagues (2006) recently examined the relation between program integrity and program effectiveness, based on a matched sample of over 6,000 parolees who were, or were not, treated in 1 of 38 community residential treatment programs upon prison release, and were then followed for 2 years to track recidivism. Based on site visits, the authors coded the extent to which each program assessed clients and focused on higher-risk offenders; delivered cognitive interventions that focused on criminogenic needs; attended to the qualifications, skills, and values of staff; and evaluated their own effectiveness. Overall, treated parolees were *more* likely to return to prison than their matched, untreated counterparts (d = −.43). However, this disappointing result likely reflected the fact that most programs (63%) were classified as "unsatisfactory" in adherence; indeed, only one program (3%) was classified as "satisfactory." Program integrity scores were moderately associated with program effectiveness, or parolees' likelihood of avoiding recidivism ($r = .42$).

This body of research indicates that (1) program integrity relates substantially to program effectiveness, and (2) the vast majority of correctional programs lack program integrity, and many amount to little more than "quackery" (Latessa et al., 2002). This conclusion lends credence to Farabee's (2005) concern that most programs, as implemented, are unlikely to be effective. Nevertheless, tools are now available to monitor adherence to evidence-based principles of correctional rehabilitation (Lowenkamp et al., 2006). These tools may help bridge the chasm between science and practice, allowing effective treatment to reach more offenders.

Farabee's (2005) other concern was that researchers tend to spin the results of methodologically flawed studies to support the rehabilitative zeitgeist. To what extent does the effectiveness of hybrid programs depend on the methodological rigor of the studies designed to evaluate them? Extant research suggests that design flaws may inflate—but do not fully account for—estimates of hybrid programs' effectiveness. On one hand, based on analysis of 68 studies rated for methodological rigor on a 5-point scale, Weisburd, Lum, and Petrosino (2001) found that the study's degree of internal validity was moderately inversely associated with effect size estimates ($r = -.30$), with the 15 experimental studies manifesting an average effect size of zero. However, the studies included in this analysis were "criminal justice interventions" that extended well beyond offender rehabilitation programs to include a variety of crime prevention programs. In a meta-analysis of 14 randomized experiments that evaluated offender rehabilitation programs, Farrington and Welsh (2005) found that even a heterogeneous group of programs significantly reduced recidivism risk ($d = .14–.16$). Moreover, in a meta-analysis of cognitive and behavioral therapies, Pearson and colleagues (2002) found *larger* effects for studies of higher methodological quality (M $r = .21$ vs. .11 for "excellent" and "poor" studies, respectively). Based on the meta-analysis of cognitive therapies described earlier, Lowenkamp and colleagues (2006) found that six variables capturing methodological rigor, including design (i.e., randomized, matched, or neither), were unassociated with recidivism effect size. Although studies were more likely to find an effect when they excluded treatment "dropouts" from analysis, Lowenkamp and colleagues still found substantial effects for cognitive therapies on recidivism, after controlling for this design problem.

In our view, without spin, research indicates that psychosocial treatment significantly reduces offenders' risk of recidivism. This reduction is particularly likely when (1) there is substantial integrity in implementing the treatment program, (2) providers establish caring, "firm but fair" relationships with offenders, (3) cognitive-behavioral techniques are applied to address changeable risk factors for recidivism, and (4) general principles of the RNR model are followed.

The RNR risk principle dictates that intensive services should be provided to higher-risk offenders. For example, treatment programs for high-risk offenders are significantly more effective than those focused on low-risk offenders ($b = .27$; Lowenkamp et al., 2006). For a variety of reasons, placing low-risk offenders in intensive programs is not simply inefficient; it can increase their risk of recidivism (Andrews et al., 1990). Thus, the most intensive rehabilitation programs should be reserved for offenders who are at high risk of recidivating. But is there a "high-risk point" at which an offender simply cannot be redeemed? This question brings us to our second controversy.

Pushing the Envelope: Does Treatment Reduce Recidivism Risk for Psychopathic and Other High-Risk Offenders?

Defining the Controversy

The risk principle distinctly is at odds with the field's pervasive therapeutic pessimism about offenders with psychopathy. This pessimism is easily summarized. The prevailing view is that those with psychopathic traits are inalterably dangerous predators. The prognosis for effectively treating a patient with psychopathy "is practically zero. The main therapeutic task is to protect the family, the therapist and society from such a patient" (Kernberg, 1998, p. 377).

So where is the controversy? Despite its extremity, this view rests on little or no compelling empirical evidence. The pessimistic view has been "so deeply ingrained in the culture of mental health and legal professionals alike that few objective efforts ... have actually examined the treatability of psychopaths" (Zinger & Forth, 1998, p. 256). However, accumulating evidence has cast doubt on the notion that psychopathic individuals are hopeless cases that must be incapacitated: Instead, they may be high-risk cases in need of intensive treatment to reduce their recidivism risk.

It is important to define what we mean by "psychopathic." Prototypically, psychopathy is defined by interpersonal and affective features of emotional detachment (e.g., "lovelessness," callousness, low anxiety proneness, remorselessness, deceitfulness; e.g., Cleckley, 1976; McCord & McCord,

1964). Operationally, however, psychopathy often is studied as—and sometimes mistakenly equated with—scores on the Psychopathy Checklist—Revised (PCL-R; Hare, 2003) and its derivatives, the Youth Version (PCL:YV; Forth, Kosson, & Hare, 2003) and Screening Version (PCL:SV; Hart, Cox, & Hare, 1995). The PCL-R captures some features of emotional detachment (old "Factor 1"), but was developed with adult male offenders and affords considerable coverage to past involvement in violent, criminal, and other socially deviant behavior (old "Factor 2"). Although this operationalization of psychopathy may be viewed as problematic (Skeem & Cooke, in press), we focus here on the treatment amenability of "PCL psychopathic" offenders, who typically manifest both psychopathy *and* past violent and other criminal behavior. We adopt this focus because (1) research is available on treatment outcome, as a function of PCL scores (including Factor 1 scores, which can be isolated as a proxy for prototypic psychopathy), and (2) compared to prototypic psychopathic offenders, PCL psychopathic offenders likely are at greater risk of recidivism, given their past criminal behavior (see Skeem & Cooke, in press), and may therefore better fit the RNR risk principle. Although Cleckley (1976) viewed tendencies toward violence and major crime as something "independent, to a considerable degree, of the other manifestations which we regard as fundamental" to psychopathy (p. 262), Hare (1996) described PCL psychopaths as "intraspecies predators" who will use "impulsive and cold-blooded violence to attain their ends" (p. 1). Compared to Cleckley's psychopath, Hare's predator may embody more fear and therapeutic pessimism.

PCL psychopaths likely overlap substantially with a larger class of high-risk offenders, who we define as offenders with relatively serious, diverse, or numerous past offenses and a high estimated risk of recidivism. There is some evidence for this notion. First, in a sample of 53 men assigned to an intensive treatment program for high-risk offenders, Polaschek (2007) found that the group's average score on the PCL:SV was at the 90th percentile (near the scale's maximum), even though many were not viewed as prototypically psychopathic in the "emotionally detached" sense. Second, Wong, Gordon, and Gu (2007) found that profiles of dynamic risk factors for 65 PCL-R psychopathic offenders were similar in shape and elevation to those of 203 high-risk violent offenders referred to a specialty treatment program. The profiles consisted of such variables as criminal attitudes, violence cycle, and substance abuse. Third, based on a sample of 206 offenders, Kroner, Mills, and Reddon (2005) found that PCL-R scores were strongly correlated with scores on three actuarial risk assessment tools (e.g., $r = .77$ with LSI-R). Moreover, they found that four tools, created by randomly selecting items

from the PCL-R and the three actuarial tools, performed as well as the original scales in predicting new convictions and revocations. What overlapping,
risk-relevant features do all of these measures tap? A factor analysis of over
1,500 offenders' scores on the tools suggested that the PCL-R and actuarials
all captured criminal history, a persistent antisocial lifestyle, and, to a lesser
extent, psychopathic personality features and alcohol/mental health issues.
All four factors were predictive of new convictions and revocations.

Despite such suggestions of group overlap, there appears to be less therapeutic pessimism about high-risk offenders than about PCL psychopaths.
Indeed, as shown later, several treatment programs have been developed
specifically for high-risk offenders. Are these programs effective? In the next
section we review evidence on the treatment of PCL psychopathic offenders
and then other high-risk offenders.

Research Relevant to the Controversy

PCL PSYCHOPATHIC OFFENDERS

There is compelling conceptual support for the notion that psychosocial
treatment would have little impact on prototypically psychopathic individuals. After all, a large body of psychotherapy research indicates that the
quality of the therapeutic alliance is the strongest controllable predictor
of symptom improvement, explaining more variance in outcome than the
specific techniques applied (e.g., cognitive, behavioral, interpersonal; Martin, Garske, & Davis, 2000). For offenders, a strong therapeutic alliance
or a healthy dual-role relationship helps to protect against future violent
offending (Brown & O'Leary, 2000) and probation violations and revocation (Skeem et al., 2007). Given that the prototypic psychopath lacks the
emotional capacity for meaningful attachment, how could he establish an
effective bond with a treatment provider ... particularly when he may also
be manipulative, deceitful, and domineering?

Despite these logical links, there is no compelling evidence that the
criminal behavior of offenders with high scores on the PCL is impervious
to treatment. Setting aside treatment *outcome* for the moment, there is evidence that PCL psychopathic offenders tend to (1) misbehave during treatment, (2) make relatively slow treatment progress, and (3) receive relatively
low doses of treatment. Such facts may come as no surprise to those who
have worked clinically with these individuals. First, PCL scores have been
shown to predict (albeit weakly, $r \approx .10-.20$) within-treatment misbehavior,
including treatment nonadherence, drug use, verbal abuse, violence, and

breaking other institutional rules (Alterman, Rutherford, Cacciola, McKay, & Boardman, 1998; Richards, Casey, & Lucente, 2003; Skeem, Douglas, Edens, Poythress, & Lilienfeld, 2005).

Second, with respect to treatment progress, PCL scores predict slower response to treatment (Morrissey, Mooney, Hogue, Lindsay, & Taylor, 2007; Salekin, 2002; Skeem, Monahan, & Mulvey, 2002). Sometimes PCL scores predict marginally lower "end-of-treatment" improvement ratings made by clinicians or researchers (Ogloff, Wong, & Greenwood, 1990; Rogers, Jackson, Sewell, & Johansen, 2004; Skeem et al., 2005; cf. Alterman et al., 1998; Caldwell, McCormick, Umstead, & Van Rybroek, 2007). However, in the two studies that have included repeated measures of symptoms and behavior, PCL scores have *not* predicted pretreatment to posttreatment changes in substance-abuse-related life problems (Alterman et al., 1998), aggression (Caldwell et al., 2007), and rule compliance (Caldwell et al., 2007). This finding preliminarily suggests that psychopathic offenders are as likely as other offenders to manifest change during treatment. Whether that change is attributable to treatment per se is unclear, given that neither study involved an untreated control group. Nevertheless, together, this research suggests that psychopathic individuals require intensive treatment, just like individuals with other embedded personality patterns (Pilkonis & Frank, 1988) and offenders with other bases for high recidivism risk (Andrews et al., 1990). Improvement occurs, but it may take time.

Third, PCL scores significantly predict premature termination and short treatment duration. Although the relationship often is weak ($r \cong -.10$ to $-.24$; e.g., Alterman et al., 1998; Richards et al., 2003; Skeem et al., 2005), psychopathic offenders sometimes receive as little as half the amount of treatment as their nonpsychopathic counterparts (Ogloff et al., 1990). It is ironic that psychopathic offenders require intensive treatment (see above), but are likely to receive even less treatment than lower-risk offenders. Some studies of the relation between PCL psychopathy and treatment outcome—which rarely take treatment length into account—may simply be rediscovering the risk principle rather than uncovering findings unique to PCL psychopaths. One clear avenue to poor treatment outcome is provision of insufficient treatment.

In sum, these studies indicate that psychopathic individuals are difficult to treat and often do not receive much treatment—points that few would contest. The studies do not, however, indicate that psychopathic individuals fail to respond to treatment. So, what of treatment outcome? Is the pain of retaining and treating psychopathic individuals worth it? Unfortunately, only a handful of quasi-experimental studies, and no experiments, have examined the relation between PCL scores and treatment response. In this review we set aside the larger body of uncontrolled research showing that pretreatment PCL scores predict posttreatment recidivism because these studies tell us nothing about whether treatment *reduces* psychopathic individuals' risk of recidivism. Instead, we highlight the few adequately powered quasi-experimental studies that have been conducted, as they are much more informative about this issue.

One study often is cited to support the notion that treatment "makes psychopaths worse." Rice, Harris, and Cormier (1992) retrospectively evaluated a now-defunct therapeutic community (TC) at a forensic hospital in Canada that was designed in the 1960s for offenders with mental disorders. The authors matched on age, index offense, and criminal history over 100 offenders who were treated for 2 years or more in this program with untreated offenders who typically served a prison sentence. They used institutional files to retrospectively rate these offenders on the PCL-R ($M = 19$) and a variety of records to determine whether offenders recidivated over an average follow-up period of 10 years. Recidivism was defined as a new charge, a parole revocation, or return to the hospital for behavior that the researchers believed might have resulted in a new charge.

Using the entire matched sample of 140 offenders who had an opportunity to recidivate, Rice and colleagues (1992) found no differences between treated and untreated offenders in general or violent recidivism. Having found no overall effect for the TC, the authors focused on the 46 treatment-matched PCL-R psychopaths (PCL-R total ≥ 25). Relative to their untreated controls, psychopaths treated in this TC were equally likely to recidivate generally (89% vs. 81%, respectively), and *more* likely to recidivate violently (55% vs. 78%, respectively). Similar results were found when the authors abandoned their matched design and compared a larger sample of treated ($n = 53$) with untreated ($n = 29$) psychopaths. Despite the TC's limited or negative impact on psychopaths, it appeared to have a positive effect on nonpsychopaths. Compared with untreated nonpsychopaths ($n = 90$), unmatched treated nonpsychopaths ($n = 116$) were *less* likely to recidivate, both generally (58% vs. 44%) and violently (39% vs. 22%). Thus, PCL psychopathy status interacted with treatment status (TC/prison) to predict recidivism.

It would be inappropriate to draw causal conclusions from this retrospective study because it was not randomized, observed differences between comparison groups were not statistically controlled, and the influence of any differences in postrelease supervision (e.g., conditional release) were not considered. Still, what *might* the results of this study mean? Perhaps they mean that "treatment makes psychopaths worse." The authors speculated that treatment in this TC taught offenders socioemotional skills that helped nonpsychopaths behave prosocially but served to "embolden [psychopaths] to manipulate and exploit others" (Harris & Rice, 2006, p. 556). The idea is that psychopaths acquired an ability to "read people" that they applied "in novel ways to commit violent crime" (Rice et al., 1992, p. 409). These new skills somehow made psychopaths more adept at committing, and getting caught for, a violent crime.

In our opinion, the results are more likely to mean that subjecting high-risk offenders to intensive, radical, involuntary treatment makes them more likely to recidivate violently than leaving them alone. PCL psychopaths spent about as much time as nonpsychopaths in this TC (M = 62 vs. 71 months), but probably had important nonshared experiences there. First, this 1960s TC used extreme "defense altering" techniques. For example, offenders were required to spend up to 2 weeks in nude encounter groups in a "total encounter capsule," where they were fed through tubes in the walls, in order to "achieve true communication and discover their essential nature" (Harris, Rice, & Cormier, 1994, p. 285). Given their rigid defenses, psychopathic offenders apparently were particularly likely to be administered LSD, alcohol, and other drugs to disrupt their glibness, aloofness, and hostility, increase their anxiety, and make them "chemically cooled out and dependent" and therefore more accessible to their peers and treatment (Harris et al., 1994, p. 288). Substance use is a well-validated risk factor for violence (e.g., Monahan et al., 2001). Second, the TC was involuntary: Offenders could not opt out or drop out. If they refused to participate, they were referred to a disciplinary subprogram "until they complied with program requirements" (Rice et al., 1992, p. 402). Relative to their nonpsychopathic counterparts, PCL psychopaths in this TC were significantly more likely to be written up for misbehavior, to be placed in seclusion, and to be referred multiple times to the disciplinary subprogram (Rice et al., 1992). Each of these TC variables was, in turn, significantly predictive of recidivism in the general sample (and not statistically controlled, when examining the relation between psychopathy and recidivism). These findings are in keeping with the general literature, which suggests that punitive surveillance strategies (Skeem & Manchak, 2008) and inappropriate psychosocial treatment (Lilienfeld, 2007) can be iatrogenic.

One study produced results that differ from, but have been likened to, those of Rice and colleagues (1992). Hare, Clark, Grann, and Thornton (2000) described the preliminary results of a nonrandomized, nonmatched control study of 278 male offenders from seven English prisons. Key methodological and analytic details were omitted. For example, the authors report no PCL-R interrater reliability data, acknowledge that they could not determine how much treatment inmates received and whether this differed as a function of PCL-R scores, and do not describe whether and how the treatment group differed from the control group. PCL-R ($M = 17$) ratings were completed as part of the admission process, and 55 of the 278 offenders were deemed psychopathic (PCL-R ≥ 25). Two-year reconviction rates were analyzed as a function of inmates' participation in one or more of several treatment programs, "most of which were short term and involved anger management and social skills training" (p. 635).

After controlling for age and criminal history, the authors found that PCL-R psychopathy did *not* moderate the effect of treatment on reconviction for a general or violent crime. PCL psychopaths responded to treatment no differently than nonpsychopaths. For reasons that are not explained, the authors dichotomized offenders based on a score of 9 on old Factor 1, and then conducted uncontrolled analyses to compare the groups. Hare and colleagues (2000) found that treatment had no effect on low Factor 1 offenders, but was associated with higher rates of general recidivism for high Factor 1 offenders.

It is difficult to determine what to make of this study, given that treatment had no effect for all other groups examined (PCL-R psychopaths; PCL-R nonpsychopaths; low Factor 1 offenders). One possibility is that treatment uniquely provided high Factor 1 offenders with "new insights into human vulnerability" (Hare, 1993, p. 197) that made them more likely to get reconvicted. This seems implausible, however, given that the authors found similar effects for educational and vocational programs (how would a math class teach an offender socioemotional skills?). Another possibility is that Factor 1 offenders were gifted at manipulating rehabilitation-oriented professionals into believing that they had made good progress and at securing release too early. This too seems doubtful. Although one early uncontrolled study (Seto & Barbaree, 1999) suggested that sex offenders with high PCL-R scores who exhibited good behavior in treatment were particularly likely to recidivate, more sophisticated analyses of those data indicate that the original conclusion was incorrect. As Barbaree (2005) notes, "The strength of inferences made and the degree of attention paid to the Seto and Barbaree (1999) finding were at odds with the strength of the data presented" (p. 1128). "To reiterate ... there is no evidence in our data ... that psychological treatment caused psychopaths to reoffend at a higher rate" (p. 1129). The Hare and colleagues (2000) data also provide no evidence that PCL-R psychopaths respond differently to treatment than nonpsychopaths.

We hope that future reports will attempt to replicate (and explain) their Factor 1 effect.

The three remaining studies paint a more optimistic picture of treatment outcome for PCL psychopaths. First, based on a prospective, multisite study of 381 male offenders, Skeem and colleagues (2005) examined the relation between PCL-R scores ($M = 22$) coded within weeks of admission and subsequent (1) within-treatment behavior and end-of-treatment status (based on discharge records and clinician ratings), and (2) risk of general recidivism within 1 year (based on FBI records). Offenders were mandated to residential substance abuse treatment programs that lasted an average of 6 months, emphasized the building of skills to avoid substance abuse, and were structured such that offenders earned their way through levels of treatment that involved increasing privileges and responsibility.

In wholly nontechnical terms, the results suggest that treating psychopathic offenders is painful for treatment providers but may be well worth it. PCL-R scores weakly, but significantly, predicted within-treatment misbehavior (e.g., violence, unexcused absences, medication refusal) and clinicians' perceptions that offenders had made limited progress in mastering the skills needed to overcome drug problems (Skeem et al., 2005). Nevertheless, PCL-R scores were unrelated to objective and subjective ratings of offenders' status at the end of treatment (e.g., attainment of the highest program level). More importantly, PCL-R scores did not moderate the effect of treatment intensity on risk of general recidivism (eta = $-.19$). In a logistic regression with general recidivism as the outcome, there was no interaction between PCL-R scores and days of treatment, after entering the main effect of PCL-R scores, days of treatment, and treatment site. Similar effects were found with old Factor 1 scores, violent recidivism, and other variations on predictors and outcomes.

Perhaps offenders who receive more treatment are less likely to recidivate than those who receive less treatment, regardless of the effects of treatment per se. Or, perhaps there is a more modest treatment effect for highly psychopathic offenders. To test these possibilities, Skeem and colleagues (2005) focused on 115 highly psychopathic offenders (PCL-R $\geq$ 25) and completed a propensity score analysis to control for the effect of nonrandom assignment to "low" versus "high" doses of substance abuse treatment (based on a median split of days in treatment). The propensity score condensed 11 key variables (e.g., demographics, symptoms, criminal versatility) into one score that predicted the probability of assignment to the high-treatment group. Given evidence that this score rendered the treatment assignment process "strongly ignorable," we conditioned the treatment estimate on propensity scores in a logistic regression analysis. The results indicate that, after controlling for the treatment assignment process, psychopathic offenders who received higher doses of substance abuse treatment were about three times less likely to recidivate than those who received lower doses of treatment.

These results are echoed by the results of two other quasi-experimental studies involving different populations, treatment approaches, and research designs. First, Caldwell and colleagues (2007) evaluated the effectiveness of an intensive treatment program for serious youthful offenders, based on a sample of 141 youths with pronounced PCL:YV scores ($\geq$ 28) and extreme histories of institutional infractions and violence (e.g., half had hospitalized or killed victims). The PCL:YV and other risk assessment tools were reliably rated at baseline, and offenders were followed for about 2 years after release to track recidivism rates. Relative to the "treatment as usual" condition, the intensive treatment program involved more resources (e.g., higher clinician-to-offender ratio; average 45 weeks of programming) and a different philosophy for treating high-risk, violent youthful offenders (less emphasis on sanctions; more emphasis on gradually eroding antagonistic bonds with authority figures to overcome defiant attitudes). Although the groups did not differ in their rates of general recidivism, high-risk youths who participated in an intensive treatment program were 2.7 times *less* likely to recidivate violently in the community, compared with those who participated in treatment as usual. This was the case after controlling for the treatment assignment process, baseline PCL:YV scores, and supervision status upon release. As the authors note, youths "with more psychopathic features present more challenging treatment candidates. Nevertheless, these data suggest, at a minimum, that there is a subgroup of youths with pronounced psychopathic features who can respond to appropriate treatment of sufficient duration" (Caldwell et al., 2007, p. 584).

Second, based on relatively intensive longitudinal data from the MacArthur Violence Risk Assessment Study (MVRAS, N = 871), Skeem and colleagues (2002) found that PCL:SV psychopathy did not moderate the effect of psychiatric treatment as usual in reducing adult patients' risk of violence in the community. After patients were assessed in a psychiatric hospital, they were followed in the community for 1 year after discharge. Patients and collateral informants were interviewed every 10 weeks to assess the number of outpatient treatment sessions they had attended (as assessed by self-report) and whether they had been involved in a serious violent incident (as assessed by self-report, collateral report, and records). Treatment typically involved psychotherapy, psychotropic medication management, or a combination thereof. General MVRAS results indicated that involvement in intensive outpatient treatment in one 10-week period (7 or more sessions vs. 0–6 sessions) significantly reduced the likelihood of patient violence during the next 10-week period, even after using propensity scores to control for the nonrandom process of assignment to intensive treatment (Monahan et al., 2001). Skeem and colleagues replicated and extended this finding with PCL:SV psychopathic patients, with over 100 variables eligible for inclusion in propensity scores. After controlling for the effects of treatment assignment, high-scoring PCL:SV patients who received intensive treatment during the first follow-up period were 3.6 times less likely to be violent during the second follow-up period than those who received less frequent sessions. In the larger sample, PCL:SV scores (including Factor 1 scores) did not interact with treatment involvement to predict violence. Psychopathic patients were as likely as nonpsychopathic patients to benefit from adequate doses of treatment as usual in the community, in terms of violence reduction.

As is the case with all extant studies of psychopathy and treatment outcome, causal conclusions cannot be drawn from these three studies because they were not randomized controlled trials. Propensity score analyses were applied in each study to better approximate experimental conditions, but it is possible that the treatment and control groups differed on an unobserved feature beyond the many variables represented in propensity scores. Still, the consistency of the results across study designs, treatment programs (substance abuse, correctional, psychiatric), and populations (adults, youths, offenders, patients) is striking. When a finding holds across a "heterogeneity of irrelevancies," or variation in persons, settings, treatments, and measures that are presumed irrelevant, the validity of the knowledge claim earns more compelling support (see Shadish, 1995).

In that vein, the results of these three studies are consistent with the results of Salekin's (2002) earlier meta-analysis of 42 studies that involved a broad range of treatments, populations, and measures of psychopathy. Across studies, the average proportion of patients who benefited from treatment minus the proportion of patients who benefited without treatment was 62% ($p < .01$). This review included some methodologically limited studies and a few studies in which psychopathy was too loosely defined. Still, regardless of the way in which the investigators defined psychopathy, psychopathic individuals showed some improvement with treatment (e.g., PCL-R psychopaths = 57% success rate). The type of treatment (e.g., cognitive > therapeutic communities) and its duration were strongly related to its effectiveness for psychopathic individuals, variously defined.

The results of this meta-analysis combined with the recent research described earlier cast serious doubt on the view that PCL psychopathic individuals are hopeless cases to be incapacitated. Perhaps, at least for the moment, we should put aside PCL scores and their attendant assumptions to provide these individuals with intensive, targeted, appropriate intervention on the basis of their RNR factors.

OTHER RESEARCH ON HIGH-RISK OFFENDERS

A small body of research has—perhaps inadvertently—done just that: ignored the baggage associated with the label "psychopathy" and instead asked research questions consistent with the RNR principles. For example, if providing low-intensity treatment to high-risk offenders has little or no effect on recidivism (e.g., Friendship, Blud, Erikson, Travers, & Thornton, 2003), how much treatment is actually needed for high-risk offenders? In an unusually illuminating study of over 600 offenders, Bourgon and Armstrong (2005) evaluated outcomes at the Rideau Centre in Canada, where the aim was to match program intensity (three levels: 100, 200, and 300 hours) to offenders' risk of recidivism and number of criminogenic needs. Not all men completed the recommended program duration, and an untreated comparison group was available. The cognitive-behavioral therapy (CBT) program targeted such criminogenic needs as substance abuse and anger control and focused on both attitudes and skill development. Offenders were followed for 1 year after release to track whether they were reincarcerated. The authors' general findings were consistent with the risk principle, in that substantial reductions in reincarceration rates were found for all levels of risk (assessed using a well-validated tool) *if* offenders received the recommended "dose" of treatment. Of most interest is the effect of program intensity on high-risk/high-need offenders' rates of reincarceration. When these offenders received the 300 hours of programming recommended, they were less likely to be returned to custody (38%) than when they completed only 100 hours of programming (62%) or went untreated (59%).

The Rideau program is unusual in its focus on providing intensive treatment to *general* high-risk offenders. The few evaluated programs at the 300-hour end of the spectrum tend to target sex offenders or violent offenders. The content of these programs often focuses on putative differences in criminogenic needs, compared to other offenders. For violent offenders, these differences in criminogenic needs may be more apparent than real, given that (1) general high-risk offenders tend to have histories of at least one violent offense (e.g., Bourgon & Armstrong, 2005), (2) dynamic risk factors for violence are—if anything—better predictors of *general* recidivism than violent recidivism (Wong & Gordon, 2006), and (3) intensive programs designed for violent offenders can have general recidivism effects (e.g., Polaschek, 2008, see below).

There are several violent offender–focused programs that follow the risk principle: providing intensive treatment for high-risk offenders. One such program is Montgomery House, a community residential CBT-based program in New Zealand. Berry (2003) case-matched 82 mainly Maori program completers and noncompleters with untreated offenders to evaluate the impact of this program, following them over an average of 17 months. Even with a conservative intent-to-treat analysis, violent offenders assigned to treatment were significantly less likely to be reconvicted for a violent offense than their matched peers, who were not assigned to treatment.

Another New Zealand program for high-risk violent men is the Violence Prevention Unit, at Rimutaka Prison, where prisoners undertake about 300 hours of CBT aimed at reducing their likelihood of violent and general recidivism. "High risk" is defined as a more than 40% estimated risk of returning to prison (i.e., risk of reconviction for a serious offense) over a 5-year period. Some 82 high-risk program starters were matched with untreated controls in risk-relevant variables and then followed for a 3.5 year period. During the follow-up, 62% of program completers, 72% of their untreated controls, 71% of noncompleters, and 75% of their untreated controls were reconvicted for violence (Polaschek, 2008). Phi for the treated group was .11, indicating an "average" treatment effect that compared favorably to the mean phi for correctional interventions overall (McGuire, 2004).

Two reports examine outcomes for high-risk violent prisoners in Canada. The first report focuses on the Violence Prevention Program (VPP; Cortoni, Nunes, & Latendresse, 2006), an internationally accredited 190-hour CBT program that—like the Rimutaka program above—focuses on a raft of criminogenic needs. This study had a large sample, a matched untreated sample, and statistically controlled analyses for prior treatment. At 1-year follow-up postrelease, 8.5% of treatment completers, 24.5% of noncompleters, and 21.8% of matched comparisons had been reconvicted for violent offences. Similar patterns of results were obtained for parole revocation and other indices of recidivism.

In the second report, Di Placido, Simon, Witte, Gu, and Wong (2006) evaluated the Regional Psychiatric Centre (RPC) in Saskatchewan for high-intensity CBT rehabilitation; mainly, the 6- to 8-month-long aggressive behavior control program. The authors investigated rates of reconviction over a 2-year period in four groups of high-risk (estimated recidivism risk ≥ 67%) male offenders who had entered the RPC: treated and untreated gang members, and treated and untreated nongang members (n = 40 per group). Given that the "untreated" samples contained both assessed-only referrals and treatment noncompleters, this study may overestimate treatment effects. Nevertheless, the untreated sample was closely matched to the treated sample on risk and other recidivism-relevant variables. Each group had an average of three prior violent convictions. Relative to the untreated sample, offenders who completed treatment were significantly less likely to be reconvicted of any offense (violent or nonviolent), but were not significantly less likely to be reconvicted of a violent offense per se (perhaps because of limited statistical power). Differences in reconviction for any offense at 2 years (n = 135) were: treated and untreated gang members, 50% versus 65%, and treated and untreated nongang members, 58% versus 69%. Although the program appears effective with both groups, the inclusion of treatment dropouts in the comparison groups limits confidence in the findings.

In conclusion, little is known about whether intensive programs targeting high-risk violent offenders can reduce risk. Published outcome studies on programs with this profile are almost nonexistent, but the results of all four studies discussed here are promising (Berry, 2003; Bourgon & Armstrong, 2005; Cortoni et al., 2006; Polaschek, 2008), and initiatives underway in several countries promise to provide more relevant data in the next few years.

CHIEF GAPS IN KNOWLEDGE

General Offenders

The first and most pronounced gap in knowledge about the treatment of general offenders involves the mechanisms by which appropriate treatment works. What characteristics change in general offenders as a function of treatment? Do programs oriented toward RNR reduce dynamic risk factors for crime that, in turn, reduce recidivism risk? If so, which dynamic risk factors are most efficient to target? Do programs that apply cognitive restructuring or a general CBT approach actually change offenders' antisocial thinking and increase their prosocial skills? What role does the quality of the relationship between provider and offender play in effecting change? The biggest challenge here is to develop reliable and valid measures that can link purported mechanisms of change to recidivism outcomes (see Polaschek & Collie, 2004).

The second major gap in knowledge about the treatment of general offenders pertains to the generalizability of treatment effects. Do such factors as gender, ethnicity, and mental disorder moderate the effect of well-implemented RNR and cognitive-behavioral programs on recidivism risk? Given that offenders with mental disorder are particularly likely to fail community supervision, even when provided with "state-of-the-art" mental health treatment, it will be particularly important to determine whether well-validated correctional treatment programs reduce these offenders' risk of recidivism (see Skeem & Manchak, 2008).

PCL Psychopathic and Other High-Risk Offenders

First, research is needed to examine the extent to which well-implemented, intensive (300+ hours), cognitive-behavioral programs that adhere to RNR principles reduce recidivism risk for psychopathic offenders. To date, no published, rigorous studies of high-risk offenders have included both the PCL and risk assessment tools and examined the effect of *appropriate* treatment on recidivism. Such studies are needed to test directly the extent to which (1) PCL psychopathic offenders are high-risk general offenders, and (2) state-of-the-art treatment for high-risk offenders reduces PCL psychopathic offenders' recidivism risk. To date, relevant studies of adult psychopathic offenders have examined only the effect of therapeutic communities (Rice et al., 1992), low-intensity cognitive programs (Hare et al., 2000), and "treatment as usual" for psychiatric (Skeem et al., 2002) or substance abuse problems (Skeem et al., 2005). Unfortunately, high-risk offender programs typically do not examine PCL psychopathy and its relation to treatment response.

Second, the gaps in knowledge about general offenders apply to high-risk offenders as well. Intensive treatment appears to reduce recidivism risk for high-risk offenders, but the mechanism by which it does so is unclear. For example, although there is evidence that psychopathic individuals' substance abuse, aggression, and rule compliance change with treatment (Alterman et al., 1998; Caldwell et al., 2007), it is unclear whether psychopathic traits per se change with treatment (but see Rogers et al., 2004).

Third, we do not know how effective treatment would be if it (1) fit the abilities and styles of PCL psychopaths (in RNR terms, was "responsive" to these offenders), or (2) explicitly targeted and attempted to change risk-relevant psychopathic features. As noted earlier, the treatment programs studied to date have not been designed for psychopathic individuals; instead, the treatment programs targeted other conditions (e.g., substance abuse), ignoring psychopathy. Treatment programs for high-risk offenders may implicitly take PCL psychopathic individuals' responsivity needs into account, by, for example, using state-of-the-art treatment engagement strategies. However, it is possible that a different *type* of treatment approach, directly tailored to psychopathic individuals, would be even more effective. Dialectical behavior therapy (DBT) was developed for borderline personality disorder, another difficult-to-treat condition, and has been shown in experimental research to reduce therapy dropout rates and suicide attempts by half, compared to treatment provided by expert clinicians (Linehan et al., 2006). DBT seeks to build such borderline-relevant skills as distress tolerance and emotion regulation. An analogous program could be developed for psychopathy. For example, Suedfeld and Landon (1978) discussed the possibility of developing "arousal modification" treatments to help psychopathic individuals satisfy their need for stimulation in a prosocial manner, perhaps by building vocational and avocational skills to match their job and leisure interests. To date, however, there have been no rigorous evaluations of psychopathy-specific treatment programs. The optimal type and dose of treatment for these individuals remain to be determined.

Although "300 or more" sessions have been identified as helpful for high-risk offenders, the optimal type of treatment arguably has not been identified for these individuals, either. One major gap in knowledge here is whether it is possible to disaggregate the larger group of high-risk offenders into more homogeneous groups with shared criminogenic needs that can be targeted in focused treatment programs.

MYTHS AND MISCONCEPTIONS

Offenders Cannot Be Rehabilitated

The notion that offenders cannot be rehabilitated is a misconception. As shown in the opening section of this chapter, an ever-increasing body of evidence suggests that appropriate psychosocial treatment significantly reduces offenders' risk of recidivism and defines the principles and form of appropriate treatment.

Treatment Resources Should Be Reserved for the Willing and the Changeable

It is also a misconception that correctional treatment resources should be reserved for low-risk, willing, or otherwise "easy-to-treat" offenders. As earlier, a large body of research indicates that maximum reductions in recidivism occur when the intensity of services is matched to the offenders' level of risk. Small changes in high-risk offenders may well yield greater returns in recidivism reduction than small-to-medium changes in low- to medium-risk offenders. Rather than being excluded from rehabilitation efforts, high-risk offenders should receive intensive doses of appropriate treatment, and programs should see it as their obligation to meet the responsivity needs of these offenders (Beyko & Wong, 2005). A number of promising strategies for increasing treatment motivation for offenders are available and could be incorporated into treatment efforts (see McMurran, 2002).

Treatment Teaches Psychopaths Skills That Make Them Worse

There has been speculation, but no evidence, that treatment teaches psychopathic individuals socioemotional skills that increase their likelihood of committing and getting caught for crime. This speculation largely is based on the unreplicated results of one study, which showed that PCL psychopathic offenders who received intensive treatment in a radical program were more likely to recidivate violently (but not generally) than those who were simply imprisoned (Rice et al., 1992). Recent research suggests that PCL psychopaths respond to intensive treatment provided in conventional programs with reductions in risk of violence and recidivism (e.g., Skeem et al., 2005). Whether their socioemotional skills increase or decrease with treatment is unknown.

CONCLUSIONS ABOUT THE "STATE OF THE SCIENCE"

General Offenders

With mixed offender samples, there is empirical support for the use of interventions that (1) broadly adhere to the RNR principles and specifically target empirically validated changeable risk factors for recidivism; (2) are cognitive-behavioral in form and content (i.e., target skills and attitudes; use structured methods of modeling, rehearsal, and positive reinforcement); (3) are provided by individuals who establish caring, "firm but fair" relationships with offenders; and (4) are implemented with integrity.

Unsupported interventions include (1) intensive surveillance, boot camps, or other "get tough" approaches without rehabilitation components (for reviews, see Aos et al., 2006; Skeem & Manchak, 2008); (2) humanistic interventions that focus on purported offender needs that are not linked to recidivism risk (e.g., self esteem); and (3) interventions that otherwise violate RNR principles (e.g., provide intensive treatment to low-risk offenders).

Untested and controversial interventions include humanistic or positive psychology approaches that shift intervention foci away from risk management and toward addressing purported underlying universal needs (e.g., the original Good Lives Model [GLM]; Ward & Stewart, 2003). There currently are no published outcome data on GLM-based programs.

PCL Psychopathic and Other High-Risk Offenders

For high-risk offenders there is tentative empirical support for intensive intervention that broadly adheres to the same principles validated for general offenders.

Unsupported intervention approaches include (1) those unsupported with general offenders (no matter how intensive, programs based on correctional quackery remain ineffective; e.g., Rice et al., 1992), and (2) those that approach PCL psychopaths as a distinct group who should be denied treatment because of special treatment-resistant characteristics. Extant evidence suggests that PCL scores may better be viewed as another dimensional indicator of risk than a tool for distinguishing a unique class of untreatable offenders.

Untested and controversial approaches include those that target specialist offending in high-risk offenders, given that there is little evidence of specialization either in offending career or in criminogenic needs for high-risk offenders.

General Conclusions

These are exciting times to be engaged with research and practice in offender rehabilitation. There is a more significant body of scientific knowledge on what works with general offenders now than at any time in the past. In some jurisdictions this knowledge base has begun to erode several decades of increasingly punitive correctional agendas. We can say with some confidence that rehabilitation can increase community safety.

Also promising is the fledgling science on treatment endeavors with those most committed to a life of crime. History shows that high-risk offenders—particularly those labeled as psychopaths—are not the first caste of untreatables psychotherapists have created without first examining whether our assumptions were borne out empirically. There is no doubt that such offenders can be unpleasant to treat, but are they as unresponsive as we thought? Perhaps not.

Yet even with general offenders, knowledge of the mechanisms involved in rehabilitative change, risk reduction, and desistance remain largely unknown. With high-risk offenders, there is simply a need for more carefully designed program outcome studies, and as with general offenders, investigations must follow of what changes and how. There is much still to do.

REFERENCES

Alterman, A., Rutherford, M., Cacciola, J., McKay, J., & Boardman, C. (1998). Prediction of 7 months methadone maintenance treatment response by four measures of antisociality. *Drug and Alcohol Dependence, 49*(3), 217–223.

Andrews, D., & Bonta J. (1998). *The psychology of criminal conduct*. Cincinnati, OH: Anderson.

Andrews, D., Bonta, J., & Hoge, R. (1990). Classification for effective rehabilitation: Rediscovering psychology. *Criminal Justice and Behavior, 17*(1), 19–52.

Aos, S., Miller, M., & Drake, E. (2006). *Evidence-based adult corrections programs: What works and what does not*. Olympia: Washington State Institute for Public Policy.

Barbaree, H. (2005). Psychopathy, treatment behavior, and recidivism: An extended follow-up of Seto and Barbaree. *Journal of Interpersonal Violence, 20*(9), 1115–1131.

Berry, S. (2003). Stopping violent offending in New Zealand: Is treatment an option? *New Zealand Journal of Psychology, 32*(2), 92–100.

Beyko, M., & Wong, S. (2005). Predictors of treatment attrition as indicators for program improvement not offender shortcomings: A study of sex offender treatment attrition. *Sexual Abuse: A Journal of Research and Treatment, 17*, 375–389.

Bourgon, G., & Armstrong, B. (2005). Transferring the principles of effective treatment into a "real world" prison setting. *Criminal Justice and Behavior, 32*(1), 3–25.

Brown, P., & O'Leary, D. (2000). Therapeutic alliance: Predicting continuance and success in group treatment for spouse abuse. *Journal of Consulting and Clinical Psychology, 68*(2), 340–345.

Byrne, J., & Taxman, F. (2006). Crime control strategies and community change: Reframing the surveillance vs. treatment debate. *Federal Probation, 70*(1), 3–12.

Caldwell, M., McCormick, D., Umstead, D., & Van Rybroek, G. (2007). Evidence of treatment progress and therapeutic outcomes among adolescents with psychopathic features. *Criminal Justice and Behavior, 34*(5), 573–587.

Cleckley, H. (1976). *The mask of sanity* (5th ed.). St. Louis, MO: Mosby.

Cortoni, F., Nunes, K., & Latendresse, M. (2006). *An examination of the effectiveness of the Violent Prevention Program* (No. R-178). Ottawa, ON, Canada: Correctional Service of Canada.

Di Placido, C., Simon, T., Witte, T., Gu, D., & Wong, S. (2006). Treatment of gang members can reduce recidivism and institutional misconduct. *Law and Human Behavior, 30*(1), 93–114.

Dowden, C., & Andrews, D. (2004). The importance of staff practice in delivering effective correctional treatment: A meta-analytic review of core correctional practice. *International Journal of Offender Therapy and Comparative Criminology, 48*(2), 203–214.

Farabee, D. (2005). *Rethinking rehabilitation: Why can't we reform our criminals?* Washington, DC: AEI Press, American Enterprise Institute for Public Policy Research.

Farrington, D., & Welsh, B. (2005). Randomized experiments in criminology: What have we learned in the last two decades? *Journal of Experimental Criminology, 1,* 1–29.

Forth, A. E., Kosson, D. S., & Hare, R. D. (2003). *The Psychopathy Checklist: Youth Version.* Toronto: Multi-Health Systems.

Friendship, C., Blud, L., Erikson, M., Travers, L., & Thornton, D. M. (2003). Cognitive-behavioral treatment for imprisoned offenders: An evaluation of HM Prison Service's cognitive skills programmes. *Legal and Criminological Psychology, 8,* 103–114.

Hare, R. D. (1993). *Without conscience: The disturbing world of the psychopaths among us.* New York: Simon & Schuster.

Hare, R. D. (1996). Psychopathy and antisocial personality disorder: A case of diagnostic confusion. *Psychiatric Times, 13*(2). Retrieved April 23, 2006, from *www.psychiatrictimes.com/p960239.html.*

Hare, R. D. (2003). *The Hare Psychopathy Checklist—Revised* (2nd ed.). Toronto: Multi-Health Systems.

Hare, R. D., Clark, D., Grann, M., & Thornton, D. (2000). Psychopathy and the predictive validity of the PCL-R: An international perspective. *Behavioral Sciences and the Law, 18*(5), 623–645.

Harris, G. T., & Rice, M. E. (2006). Treatment of psychopathy: A review of empirical findings. In C. J. Patrick (Ed.), *Handbook of psychopathy* (pp. 555–572). New York: Guilford Press.

Harris, G. T., Rice, M. E., & Cormier, C. (1994). Psychopaths: Is a therapeutic community therapeutic? *Therapeutic Communities: International Journal for Therapeutic and Supportive Organizations, 15*(4), 283–299.

Hart, S., Cox, D., & Hare, R. (1995). *The Hare Psychopathy Checklist: Screening Version.* Toronto: Multi-Health Systems.

Kernberg, O. (1998). The psychotherapeutic management of psychopathic, narcissistic, and paranoid transferences. In T. Millon, E. Simonsen, M. Birket-

Smith, & R. D. Davis (Eds.), *Psychopathy: Antisocial, criminal, and violent behavior* (pp. 372–392). New York: Guilford Press.

Kroner, D., Mills, J., & Reddon, J. (2005). A coffee can, factor analysis, and prediction of antisocial behavior: The structure of criminal risk. *International Journal of Law and Psychiatry, 28*(4), 360–374.

Landenberger, N., & Lipsey, M. (2005). The positive effects of cognitive-behavioral programs for offenders: A meta-analysis of factors associated with effective treatment. *Journal of Experimental Criminology, 1*(4), 451–476.

Latessa, E., Cullen, F., & Gendreau, P. (2002). Beyond correctional quackery: Professionalism and the possibility of effective treatment. *Federal Probation, 66,* 43–50.

Lilienfeld, S. O. (2007). Psychological treatments that cause harm. *Perspectives on Psychological Science, 2,* 53–70.

Linehan, M. M., Comtois, K. A., Murray, A. M., Brown, M. Z., Gallop, R. J., Heard, H. L., et al. (2006). Two-year randomized controlled trial and follow-up of dialectical behavior therapy versus therapy by experts for suicidal behaviors and borderline personality disorder. *Archives of General Psychiatry, 63,* 757–766.

Lowenkamp, C., Latessa, E., & Smith, P. (2006). Does correctional program quality really matter?: The impact of adhering to the principles of effective interventions. *Criminology and Public Policy, 5*(3), 201–220.

Maile, B. (2007). *Governor Schwarzennegger creates strike teams to implement historic prison reform plan.* Retrieved December 2, 2008 from *gov.ca.gov/indexphp?/press-release/6197.*

Martin, D., Garske, J., & Davis, K. (2000). Relation of therapeutic alliance with outcome and other variables: A meta-analytic review. *Journal of Consulting and Clinical Psychology, 68*(3), 438–450.

McCord, W., & McCord, J. (1964). *The psychopath: An essay on the criminal mind.* Princeton, NJ: Van Nostrand.

McGuire, J.(2004). *Understanding psychology and crime: Perspectives on theory and action.* Maidenhead, UK: Open University Press.

McMurran, M. (2002). *Motivating offenders to change: A guide to enhancing engagement in therapy.* Chichester, UK: Wiley.

Monahan, J., Steadman, H., Silver, E., Appelbaum, P., Robbins, P., Mulvey, E., et al. (2001). *Rethinking risk assessment: The MacArthur study of mental disorder and violence.* New York: Oxford University Press.

Morrissey, C., Mooney, P., Hogue, T., Lindsay, W., & Taylor, J. (2007). Predictive validity of the PCL-R for offenders with intellectual disability in a high security hospital: Treatment progress. *Journal of Intellectual and Developmental Disability, 32*(2), 125–133.

Ogloff, J., Wong, S., & Greenwood, A. (1990). Treating criminal psychopaths in a therapeutic community program. *Behavioral Sciences and the Law, 8*(2), 181–190.

Pearson, F., Lipton, D., Cleland, C., & Yee, D. (2002). The effects of behavioral/cognitive behavioral programs on recidivism. *Crime and Delinquency, 48*,(3), 476–496.

Pilkonis, P., & Frank, E. (1988). Personality pathology in recurrent depression: Nature, prevalence, and relationship to treatment response. *American Journal of Psychiatry, 145*(4), 435–441.

Polaschek, D. L. L. (2007). *Rimutaka Violence Prevention Unit Evaluation Report IV. Interim report on prospective evaluation: Intermediate measures of treatment change.* Wellington, New Zealand: New Zealand Department of Corrections.

Polaschek, D. L. L. (2008). *High-intensity rehabilitation for violent offenders in New Zealand: Reconviction outcomes for high- and medium-risk prisoners.* Manuscript submitted for publication.

Polaschek, D. L. L., & Collie, R. (2004). Rehabilitating serious violent adult offenders: An empirical and theoretical stocktake. *Psychology, Crime, and Law, 10*(3), 321–334.

Rice, M., Harris, G., & Cormier, C. (1992). An evaluation of a maximum security therapeutic community for psychopaths and other mentally disordered offenders. *Law and Human Behavior, 16*(4), 399–412.

Richards, H., Casey, J., & Lucente, S. S. (2003). Psychopathy and treatment response in incarcerated female substance users. *Criminal Justice and Behavior, 30*(2), 251–276.

Rogers, R., Jackson, R., Sewell, K., & Johansen, J. (2004). Predictors of treatment outcome in dually-diagnosed antisocial youth: An initial study of forensic inpatients. *Behavioral Sciences and the Law, 22*(2), 215–222.

Salekin, R. (2002). Psychopathy and therapeutic pessimism: Clinical lore or clinical reality? *Clinical Psychology Review, 22*, 79–112.

Seto, M., & Barbaree, H. (1999). Psychopathy, treatment behavior, and sex offender recidivism. *Journal of Interpersonal Violence, 14*(12), 1235–1248.

Shadish, W. (1995). The logic of generalization: Five principles common to experiments and ethnographies. *American Journal of Community Psychology, 23*(3), 419–428.

Skeem, J. L., & Cooke, D. (in press). Is antisocial behavior essential to psychopathy?: Conceptual directions for resolving the debate. *Psychological Assessment.*

Skeem, J. L., Douglas, K., Edens, J., Poythress, N., & Lilienfeld, S. (2005, March). *Whether and how antisocial and psychopathic traits moderate the effect of substance abuse treatment.* Paper presented at the American Psychology-Law Society conference, San Diego, CA.

Skeem, J. L., Eno Louden, J., Polaschek, D., & Camp, J. (2007). Assessing relationship quality in mandated community treatment: Blending care with control. *Psychological Assessment, 19*, 397–410.

Skeem, J. L., & Manchak, S. (2008). Back to the future: From Klockar's model of effective supervision to evidence-based practice in probation. *Journal of Offender Rehabilitation, 47*, 220–247

Skeem, J. L., Monahan, J., & Mulvey, E. (2002). Psychopathy, treatment involvement, and subsequent violence among civil psychiatric patients. *Law and Human Behavior, 26*(6), 577–603.

Ward, T., & Stewart, C. (2003). Good lives and the rehabilitation of sexual offenders. In T. Ward, D. Laws, & M. Hudson (Eds.), *Sexual deviance: Issues and controversies* (pp. 21–44). Thousand Oaks, CA: Sage.

Weisburd, D., Lum, C., & Petrosino, A. (2001). Does research design affect study outcomes in criminal justice? *Annals of the American Academy of Political and Social Science, 578,* 50–70.

Wong, S., & Gordon, A. (2006). The validity and reliability of the Violence Risk Assessment Scale: A treatment-friendly violence risk assessment tool. *Psychology, Public Policy, and Law, 12,* 279–309.

Wong, S., Gordon, A., & Gu, D. (2007). Assessment and treatment of violence-prone forensic clients: An integrated approach. *British Journal of Psychiatry, 190*(Suppl. 49), S66–S74.

Zinger, I., & Forth, A. (1998). Psychopathy and Canadian criminal proceedings: The potential for human rights abuses. *Canadian Journal of Criminology, 40*(3), 237–276.

PART VI

CONCLUDING THOUGHTS AND FUTURE DIRECTIONS

Finding Common Ground between Scientific Psychology and the Law

John P. Petrila

In 1978 Morse wrote what still stands as one of the most trenchant critiques of the use of mental health professionals as experts in legal disputes. Morse asserted that such testimony did not rest on a sufficient scientific foundation to merit judicial acceptance as "expert." He also argued forcefully that too often mental health professionals exerted undue influence over decisions that were fundamentally of a moral nature. He concluded that, at best, mental health professionals should serve as specially trained fact witnesses and that they should "refrain from drawing social and moral conclusions about which they are not expert" (Morse, 1978, p. 392).

Bonnie and Slobogin (1980), in response, argued that mental health professionals were qualified to offer observations and conclusions that went beyond the expertise of the typical layperson. They concluded that the courts should be more generous in permitting such testimony than Morse would allow, with the proviso that mental health professionals carefully delineate the limits of their expertise and not invade the province of judge or jury. Melton and colleagues adopt a similar view, while cautioning that mental health professionals should not testify on legal questions without knowledge of available research specific to the issue at hand (Melton, Petrila, Poythress, & Slobogin, 2007; see also Slobogin, 2006). In practice, the courts are much closer to the views of Bonnie, Slobogin, and others than they are to those of Morse.

Morse wrote at a time when "expert" testimony from mental health professionals existed in a virtual empirical vacuum. For example, in a seminal review of available research, Monahan (1981) concluded that empirical evidence at the time substantiated earlier claims that clinical predictions of future violence were no better (and, in fact, were sometimes worse) than "flipping coins in the courtroom" (Ennis & Litwak, 1976).

The preceding chapters in this volume demonstrate that the state of knowledge has advanced considerably since Monahan's review and the emergence of psychology and law as a discrete field. The growth in research has been accompanied by an explosion of assessment instruments designed to structure inquiries into a number of core psychology and law questions. At least some of those instruments have been subjected to rigorous studies on reliability and validity (Grisso, 2002). At the same time a series of decisions by the U.S. Supreme Court has conferred explicit authority on the courts to more aggressively police the admission of testimony offered as "expert" (see Faigman & Monahan, Chapter 1, this volume, for a review). Subsequent to the Court's decisions two commentators concluded that "the years ahead will be difficult ones for experts whose opinions rest on shaky empirical foundations" (Faigman & Monahan, 2005, p. 633).

Given these developments one might reasonably ask whether Morse's concerns about the empirical base for testimony have continuing relevance. Perhaps we have reached a point in the maturation of psychology and law where rigorous research, available both to expert witnesses and to newly empowered, scientifically sophisticated jurists, can assure that expert testimony is admitted only when appropriate. However, although the preceding chapters give cause for optimism in some areas, they also make clear that advances in relevant science have been more limited than some might acknowledge. Indeed, it might be argued that more than 30 years after Morse's critique, the number of legal issues on which mental health professionals provide nonscientifically based testimony has actually *increased* rather than declined.

The chapters in this volume also illustrate a broader point about psychology and law by what they do *not* cover. The best science in the field has emerged in response to specific questions posed in specific legal cases: Is the defendant competent? Is this eyewitness's testimony reliable? Is the defendant likely to pose a future risk to third parties? These are important questions and demand the most informed expert testimony possible. However, one might argue that the growing sophistication of psychology and law as a specialty has been accompanied by a growing narrowness of focus. Psychological testimony can have immense consequences for an individual in a legal proceeding, including imposition of the ultimate sanction in capital cases. Yet psychology and law should be more than the sum of a set of increasingly assured answers to a set of questions posed by the judicial system. For example, as noted below, most individuals with mental illnesses who may pose a risk to third parties spend most of their lives in community settings, yet the management and treatment of these individuals in that context have been virtually absent from psychology and law inquiry. It is fair to conclude, from this volume, that there is little law today in "psychology *and* law," though as Haney noted decades ago, there is much "psychology *in* law" (Haney, 1980).

The rest of this chapter examines the "state of the science" as revealed by the preceding chapters; examines the consequences of not knowing as much as perhaps we think we know; and concludes with some observations about the need to assure that efforts to answer a few important questions posed by the law do not isolate the field from broader developments in law, policy, and science.

SOME THOUGHTS ON THE PRESENT STATE OF THE FIELD

1. *We have more scientific knowledge to inform clinical testimony than ever, but less than we think we have.* There is no question that there have been significant research advances on core questions posed by legal decision makers. The preceding chapters provide a comprehensive review of much of that knowledge. Some of the advances are on fundamental issues where there was little useful scientific knowledge less than three decades ago. For example, Heilbrun, Douglas, and Yasuhara (Chapter 15, this volume) point out that the development of actuarial and structured professional judgment models has greatly improved the accuracy of risk assessments, particularly when compared to unstructured clinical assessments.

At the same time, they also make clear that these new models, while performing substantially better than pure clinical assessment, still have wide margins of error *when applied to the individual*. While the risk of such errors has long been acknowledged by those developing the models, the emergence of a solid body of research demonstrating that structured assessment is far superior to unstructured assessment has led many to conclude that structured risk assessments are "good enough" in legal proceedings where the individual's liberty (and sometimes, life) is at issue.

However, what if such judgments are not as good when applied to the individual as we now consider them to be? Discussions of the "ecological fallacy" in the social sciences (i.e., drawing an inference about an individual based on observed characteristics of the group in which the individual falls) go back at least to 1950 (Robinson, 1950) and continue today (King, Rosen, & Tanner, 2004). Does testimony regarding future risk presented by an individual fall prey to the ecological fallacy? A recent paper discussed by Heilbrun and colleagues in Chapter 15 of this volume (Hart, Michie, & Cooke, 2007) asserts that the use of probability estimates at the individual level is simply empirically unsupported, an assertion that inevitably leads to a conclusion that the margin of error is too wide to permit the use of such testimony. One paper constitutes little more than an alternative hypothesis in this case, and certainly the conclusions and methods used by Hart and colleagues will face sharp challenge (see, for example, Harris & Rice, 2008). Yet this is precisely the type of debate the field needs, on both scientific and legal/moral grounds. For it seems clear that if Hart et al. are correct, they raise a fundamental challenge not only to structured risk assessment but to any number of areas where psychology and law have begun making individual judgments based on group probabilities. The current state of risk assessment may be "good enough" for legal decision making, in part because of its demonstrated superiority to unstructured assessment. Yet we need to continue to probe the issue, rather than simply assume that the science has advanced adequately because it has addressed previous shortcomings in expert testimony.

There have also been important research developments in other critical areas of long-standing import, for example, the issue of competence to stand trial. Given these developments, it might be assumed that an adequate research base exists so that researchers can turn to the development of knowledge in other, less explored areas. After all, competence to stand trial is one of the foundational issues in the development of psychology and law, has been the focus of scholarly attention for more than four decades (e.g., see Robey, 1965), and has been the subject of increasingly sophisticated and well-funded research studies since the 1990s (Poythress, Bonnie, Monahan, Otto, & Hoge, 2002). However, as Poythress and Zapf (Chapter 14, this volume) note, "There is scant scientific evidence for the reliability and validity of many ... adjudicative competence measures." The fact that many measures lack a demonstrated scientific foundation calls into question whether such measures should be used in practice.

Given the gaps in the science that informs competence assessments, perhaps it should not be surprising that there is virtually no research base for many of the emerging issues on which mental health professionals provide (or would like to provide) "expert" testimony. For example, Redlich and

Meissner (Chapter 6, this volume) conclude that "current police interrogation methods and practice represent little more than an art, much less a science," and Lynn and colleagues (Chapter 4) find that "claims made by the proponents of forensic hypnosis are overblown." Koch, Nader, and Haring (Chapter 12) state unequivocally that "there are no validated measures or protocols for addressing the causal issues that lie at the heart of psychological injury claims"; as to the state of research on another common forensic topic, "despite the fact that custody evaluations have been conducted for decades, many issues have been left unresolved . . . [and] many of these appear to have been left to individual evaluators to resolve on their own—with likely little consistency across the field" (O'Donohue, Beitz, & Tolle, Chapter 13).

There is no question that impressive strides have been made in developing a research base relevant to at least some of the issues that forensic examiners are asked to address. However, it also seems beyond dispute that from a scientific perspective, we have only begun to scratch the surface. It is worth remembering, as Kocsis notes, that "satisfaction with a technique does not necessarily equate with its accuracy" (Chapter 11, this volume). In short, improving practice through research is not the same as assuring that practice is actually scientifically sound; making expert testimony better does not necessarily assure that it is good enough.

2. *One of the most salutary developments in the field has been the creation of research-based assessment tools. However, even the best instrument does not automatically convert bad practice into good.* Historically, forensic assessments of core issues such as competence to stand trial and responsibility at the time of the offense were anchored in clinical diagnoses. When a forensic examiner (or legal decision maker) found a person incompetent or not responsible, the person almost always had also been found to have a psychotic disorder. Over time, based on research and growing awareness that diagnosis usually had little to do with resolution of a legal question, there was a major effort to disentangle legal concepts from diagnosis and to create instruments that anchored the assessment in the issues embedded in the law. As a result, an impressive number of instruments has been developed that enables the examiner to differentiate the forensic examination from a more standard clinical inquiry. Over the years, the number of tools and the legal issues they purport to address have multiplied rapidly (for the best extant review, see Grisso, 2002).

There is little question that the use of at least some of these instruments can improve practice and result in more reliable and valid conclusions than unstructured clinical judgment. In some specialized situations, there has been wide adoption of reliable and validated instruments. For example, at least 30 state correctional systems in the United States have adopted the Level of Service Inventory—Revised (LSI-R) as a standard tool for making classification and discharge decisions involving prisoners (Corrections Transition Policy Group, 2006). The Massachusetts Youth Screening Instrument–2 (MAYSI-2), a brief screening tool designed to screen for mental health needs of youths in juvenile detention settings, has been the subject of extensive study (Vincent, Grisso, Terry, & Banks, 2008) and has been adopted for use in various contexts (e.g., juvenile detention, probation) by 41 states.

However, adoption of even the best instruments has been mixed, particularly among general practitioners who do not specialize in forensic examinations but who have made forensic work part of their practice. Monahan (2008), for example, concludes from a review of available research that the majority of clinicians performing risk assessments continue to rely on unstructured clinical judgment, despite clear evidence that unstructured assessments are less reliable than structured assessments. Nicholson and Norwood (2000), in a meta-review of studies on actual forensic practice, concluded: "If the truth is what it is, not what it should be, we must acknowledge that the practice of forensic psychological assessments falls far short of its promise" (p. 40). Lally (2003) found good consensus among forensic diplomates regarding the acceptability of a number of instruments in forensic work. Diplomates, however, are forensic *specialists*; it appears that general practitioners continue, in many cases, to rely on outdated techniques.

There is also evidence that clinicians who rely on instruments in conducting examinations may reach for instruments that are unrelated to the task at hand. For example, a study of 1,357 reports submitted by examiners evaluating youths' competence to proceed in delinquency proceedings in Florida found that of the six instruments most commonly used, only one had been normed for use with children (Christy, Douglas, Otto, & Petrila, 2004). The sole normed instrument was Grisso's Comprehension of *Miranda* Rights Instrument, something not particularly relevant to the Florida competence test. In all, examiners used 118 instruments, nearly all completely unrelated to the statutory criteria forming the basis for the examination. One can understand why a clinician would look to an instrument as an anchor for a forensic exam, but the use of unvalidated, unreliable, and irrelevant instruments is worse than simply using unstructured clinical judgment, because it can give the legal decision maker the belief that the examination had some scientific basis.

Forensic practice has not been the only area where research has had a mixed impact on practice. The Institute of Medicine, in a much cited report in 2001, concluded that on average it took 17 years for new knowledge to be incorporated into practice by health care professionals. Therefore, it is probably unsurprising that many forensic examiners have been unaffected by the most recent research findings; it is worth remembering that even for those areas of psychology and law where the research base is richest, it is barely two decades old. It may be that broader acceptance of appropriate instruments by nonspecialists will come over time, but the use of inappropriate instruments is a continuing source of concern for the field (Otto & Heilbrun, 2002).

3. *Although cautious optimism may be justified regarding the eventual impact of science on practice, the apparent spread of unsubstantiated claims of expertise in emerging areas of forensic practice is a continuing problem.* This volume provides a number of examples where mental health professionals purport to provide expert testimony to the courts despite the near complete absence of any research substantiating the claims to expertise. These include, but are not limited to, profiling, hypnosis, and what Davis and Loftus (Chapter 3, this volume) refer to as the "hypothesis of repression itself and the conditions under which it is most likely to occur (if at all)." The courts have been generally vigilant about barring proffered testimony on some of these issues, for example, profiling, based on concerns that such testimony may unduly sway jurors to assume that a "profile" proves that the individual on trial is guilty. On the other hand, litigation regarding repressed memory has been lengthy, contentious, and in many ways unsettled on the ultimate question of the law's view of the reliability and validity of such evidence.

Despite the lack of a scientific foundation, and despite judicial resistance, mental health professionals continue to present themselves as "expert" in situations where available research simply does not substantiate the claim. There are undoubtedly many reasons for this practice; the preceding chapters offer some insight. One is public enthusiasm for certain issues that is vastly disproportionate to the available data. For example, Davis and Loftus note the vast disparity between the state of the science and public acceptance of claims based on repressed memory, and Kocsis cites a number of surveys showing that police agencies find profiling useful in focusing an investigation (though much less so in identifying a particular offender). Broad public acceptance may create a market for consultation in an area such as profiling that in turn attracts those fashioning themselves as "profilers." In notorious cases, profiling receives enormous media attention, which may reinforce public perceptions that it is credible. And in certain cases, individuals become celebrities and make apparently unsubstantiated claims that their writing "helps us learn how to anticipate potential violent behavior before it's too late" (*www.johndouglasmindhunter.com/bio.php*). Over time, such topics become part of graduate education, and students enter the professional world hoping to earn a living as a profiler. This is not a model of professional development based on good science.

Another reason for bad practice is bad technique—a potential issue in any area of forensic examination. In controversial areas of practice, the problem can be exacerbated by examiner conduct that interferes with or contaminates the examination itself. For example, an area of particular concern is the manner in which interviews are sometimes conducted with children, where leading (and misleading) questions can result in reports of abuse that, in fact, may be the product of the questions posed by the examiner (Bruck & Ceci, Chapter 7, this volume; also Redlich & Meissner, Chapter 6, this volume, on police interrogation techniques and false confessions).

In more established areas of research, there are often wide gaps between public perception and research findings. For example, Cutler and Wells, in their review of eyewitness identification issues (Chapter 5, this volume), note that there are several very important areas where expert testimony is scientifically supported and can be helpful to the legal system. At the same time, they conclude that "the gaps in the research on eyewitness identification prevent the expert from providing the court with the information it most needs," which is whether a given eyewitness identification is correct or incorrect. They point out, however, that judges may press for an expert opinion on this latter issue, despite the lack of scientific support for such opinions. Many experts will resist responding to the question; others may not.

Finally, and perhaps paradoxically, the growing popularity of forensic practice may contribute to unsubstantiated and confusing claims of expertise in some settings. Many individuals who enter forensic practice have been well trained. However, there are also many individuals who act as a forensic examiner only occasionally, and there are also individuals who have gone into forensic practice to escape market pressures that have made the private practice of psychology increasingly difficult. This is not a new problem (Grisso, 1987), though it may have intensified in recent years. In response, as Otto and Heilbrun (2002) point out, the field has evolved into a specialty, with certification and practice standards only the most visible examples. However, as the number of full and part-time forensic examiners increases, so do marketing opportunities for vendors, particularly in the development of assessment instruments. As noted above, good instruments can improve practice. On the other hand, a bad instrument can make bad practice even worse, by creating the impression that the examination using the instrument has some scientific value. There are clear standards for determining whether an assessment tool has been validated (Heilbrun, 1992; Otto, Edens, & Barcus, 2000). Unfortunately, in an increasingly market-driven environment, such standards are too often ignored.

4. *Repetition (and broad acceptance) of a hypothesis does not convert the hypothesis into scientific fact.* Each of the preceding chapters does an excellent job of describing the state of the science. As noted, there have been major strides in a number of areas, but as each chapter makes clear, there is still much work to be done in adding to the scientific foundation of forensic practice.

Part of a continuing challenge is testing certain hypotheses that become part of the received wisdom, hypotheses often prefaced with the phrase "everybody knows." In the 1980s, "everybody knew" that mental health professionals could not predict risk; that hypothesis was tested and turned out to be generally true. However, what followed was an enormous amount of research that resulted in a reshaping of the question (from violence prediction to risk assessment) and the development of methods to inform clinical practice. As a result, the statement "everybody knows" that mental health professionals have nothing to offer on the question of future risk is heard far less often.

Today, "everybody knows" that psychopaths cannot be treated. In a recent review, Harris and Rice (2006) state the received wisdom this way:

> We believe that there is no evidence that any treatments yet applied to psychopaths have been shown to be effective in reducing violence or crime.... The reason ... is that psychopaths are fundamentally different from other offenders and that there is nothing "wrong" with them in the manner of a deficit or impairment that therapy can "fix." (p. 568)

This received wisdom has assumed the force of an immutable principle in many quarters. Certainly, treatment of certain populations, in general, can be difficult: As Skeem, Polaschek, and Manchak make clear in Chapter 16 (this volume), there are philosophical, scientific, and clinical impediments to assuming that treatment can reduce recidivism in *any* correctional population. However, they also conclude that "the notion that offenders cannot be rehabilitated is a misconception" and that "an ever-increasing body of evidence suggests that appropriate psychosocial treatment significantly reduces offenders' risk of recidivism.... "

What then of those who are called psychopaths? The notion that such individuals are untreatable (and that treatment "makes them worse") permeates clinical practice and is accepted as a matter of fact (or faith) in many judicial proceedings. But is it the case that every study has demonstrated, beyond doubt, that this is scientifically true? The answer to this question today is simply no.

The evidence that treatment can result in reduced risk for violence and recidivism among psychopaths is still sparse, but it exists (Skeem et al., Chapter 16, this volume; Edens, Skeem, & Kennealy, Chapter 8, this volume). This does not mean definitively that treatment ameliorates violence risk in all circumstances, nor does it mean that existing treatment modalities are the best treatment that can be designed. However, it *does* mean that the therapeutic nihilism that dominates psychological and legal decision making regarding psychopathy is unwarranted from a scientific perspective. The "fact" that psychopaths do not possess any deficits that can be remedied by therapy is a working hypothesis, not a scientifically established psychological law.

The question of treatability is not simply an interesting research issue. To call someone a "psychopath" in a legal setting appears to trump any other fact or characteristic about that person and pushes the legal decision maker in the direction of more severe punishment (Edens, Colwell, Desforges, & Fernandez, 2005). In addition, rehabilitative options may be withheld because of judicial certainty that the person cannot be treated. The result is the creation of a "caste of untreatables" (Skeem & Petrila, 2003) who are consigned reflexively to punitive rather than rehabilitative dispositions.

Finally, the power of the label "psychopath," combined with the received wisdom regarding untreatability, makes this an area where the forensic examiner may effectively, if unknowingly, make the moral judgment reserved for the court simply by calling the person a psychopath. Given this possibility, the examiner must be particularly cautious regarding not only the manner in which testimony is presented but also the types of legal proceedings in which psychopathy is presented. As Edens and colleagues report in this volume, there are certain important legal issues for which the construct has little validation; in those areas, use of the term may be completely unwarranted or, at a minimum, require careful explanation of the limits of the construct in that particular setting.

5. *Researchers and clinicians cannot assume that the courts will appropriately exercise their authority to police admissibility.* If the courts used their authority to routinely block proffered expert testimony that suffered from the problems noted in this chapter, there might be less cause for concern. However,

as McAuliff and Groscup note (Chapter 2, this volume), the two existing studies on the issue of judges' scientific gatekeeping abilities suggest that many judges lack the scientific knowledge to assess validity, an issue that, under *Daubert*, is an important component of the admissibility decision. This is not surprising, of course, because most judges (and lawyers) are not scientifically trained. McAuliff and Groscup conclude that jurors are also ill-equipped to judge science, and that traditional techniques for challenging expert testimony (e.g., cross-examination) are insufficient to safeguard the courts against junk science.

Although most judges lack formal scientific training, it appears that post-*Daubert* courts have raised the bar to the admissibility of scientific evidence. One review (Vickers, 2005) concluded that lawyers challenge expert testimony more frequently and that judges exclude such testimony more often since *Daubert*. In Vickers's view, this reflects a broader attitudinal shift among judges and lawyers more than a strict application of the text of *Daubert*; she believes that the decision caused lawyers and judges to become more attuned to the issue of junk science generally and that this shift has resulted in more challenges to evidence that historically might have been admitted. In her view, the result has been somewhat mixed. Evidence without merit has been excluded in some cases. On the other hand, she is concerned that the bar has been raised much higher than is warranted, eroding the liberal rules of admissibility that have long governed, causing sound evidence to be excluded.

Faigman and Monahan (Chapter 1, this volume) illustrate this concern in their discussion of *People v. Miller* (2005). In this case a California appellate court exempted clinically based predictions of future violence under the state's Sexually Violent Predator Act from a preliminary admissibility hearing while indicating that opinions based on actuarial instruments would have to undergo such a hearing. According to Faigman and Monahan, "in effect, the California rule means that expert opinion with little or no scientific basis is readily admitted, but opinion that is based on scientific text must survive [the admissibility hearing] gauntlet." They describe this outcome as "particularly perverse" because of the wide gap in validity between judgments based on empirically structured risk assessment tools and those emerging from unstructured clinical judgment.

In other contexts one might wish for more aggressive scrutiny of psychological evidence that is often taken at face value. For example, syndrome evidence would seem ripe for challenge. It has been suggested that judges admit some syndromes with arguably questionable scientific underpinning— for example, battered women syndrome and rape trauma syndrome—based on the fact that prior courts admitted the evidence rather than on an independent review of the underlying science (Dixon & Dixon, 2003). Other research appears to support the conclusion that *Daubert* and its progeny have had little impact on the admissibility of such evidence (Dahir et al., 2005).

It is unrealistic to expect judges (and jurors) to reach the scientifically appropriate decision in all cases in which expert psychological testimony is offered. This basic reality suggests that clinicians (and researchers) must first police themselves. If that does not occur, the results can be devastating in situations where civil liberties and due process are at stake, something discussed in more detail below.

SOME THOUGHTS ON THE FUTURE

The state of psychological science in the courtroom is better than it has ever been. Certainly the overall trajectory since the late 1980s has been positive. There is more scholarly research on important issues than ever, forensic practice has never been more popular, and the emphasis on creating standards for practice is a necessary and important development. Much of the best research described in the preceding chapters focuses on core criminal justice issues, for example, competence to stand trial, future risk, and the accuracy of eyewitness testimony. At the same time, there is some danger that as the field continues to mature, it will become increasingly detached from important developments in science, policy, and law because the field of psychology and law has evolved primarily in response to specific legal questions posed to resolve individual cases. However, there are broader policy and law issues that go largely unaddressed as psychology and law drills deeper and deeper into a handful of specific questions. A number of examples illustrate this concern.

1. *The impact on the field of psychology and law of scientific findings from other fields needs to be considered more explicitly.* Scientists in other fields are reporting work that, on its face, would appear to be of great significance to psychology and law researchers and legal decision makers. In 2002, an article in *Science* reported the results of a study seeking to determine why some maltreated children grew up to become violent whereas others did not. Whether certain children are likely to engage in criminal and violent behavior in the future has been an issue in psychology and law, articulated most recently in a debate regarding the applicability of psychopathy to adolescents. This study examined the potential ameliorating affect of a particular gene on potential violence; the investigators reported their findings in this way:

We studied a large sample of male children from birth to adulthood to determine why some children who are maltreated grow up to develop antisocial behavior, whereas others do not. A functional polymorphism in the gene encoding the neurotransmitter-metabolizing enzyme monoamine oxidase A (*MAOA*) was found to moderate the effect of maltreatment. Maltreated children with a genotype conferring high levels of *MAOA* expression were less likely to develop antisocial problems. These findings may partly explain why not all victims of maltreatment grow up to victimize others, and they provide epidemiological evidence that genotypes can moderate children's sensitivity to environmental insults. (Caspi et al., 2002, p. 851)

A small percentage of individuals (12%) with a low activity *MAOA* genotype and a history of being maltreated accounted for 44% of the research cohort's convictions for violent offenses, and 85% of these individuals committed some type of antisocial behavior.

In a more recent study, the same research team examined children with a diagnosis of attention-deficit/hyperactivity disorder to determine why a subgroup of such children engaged in antisocial behavior. They concluded that children with "valine/valine homozygotes had more symptoms of conduct disorder, were more aggressive, and were more likely to be convicted of criminal offenses compared with methionine carriers" (Caspi et al., 2008, p. 203).

The authors do not claim in either case to have "solved" the problem of what causes antisocial behavior through a gene test. Nor is the suggestion here that genetic and other factors will provide a "one-size-fits-all" explanation for causation; in fact a metareview several years ago by the National Institute of Mental Health (1999) concluded that, at that point, there was no research showing a causative link between a particular gene or combination of genes and mental illness. However, findings such as those noted here ultimately may have implications for the prevention and management of violence, through the identification of an at-risk cohort of individuals. The use of genetic testing to identify at-risk cohorts (whether for illness or behavior) is a very complex topic raising significant legal, ethical, and clinical issues; in at least some circumstances, those issues have implications for the study of psychology and law.

2. *The implications of psychology and law research for community treatment, and the implications of advancements in community treatment for psychology and law research, should be a major focus in the future.* As Skeem and colleagues (Chapter 16, this volume) illustrate, considerable attention has been paid to treatment in correctional settings. Emerging research has extended that focus to community correctional settings; for example, the impact of spe-

cial forms of probation on treatment adherence by probationers (Skeem & Manchak, 2008).

At the same time, most individuals with serious mental illnesses are in the community, including those who may present a risk to third parties. In community settings, nonspecialist clinicians account for many forensic examinations and, as important, most of the treatment. Given this fact, it is essential that the field of psychology and law begin to better inform community care, particularly in managing risk; conversely, it is essential that advances in community treatment better inform the psychology and law field. Two examples may illustrate this point.

First, it seems clear that some risk assessment tools may assist in managing risk in community settings because of the domains they consider. Risk assessment tools that include dynamic and contextual factors that may serve as protective factors against future risk to third parties are especially important (for a review, see Heilbrun et al., Chapter 15, this volume). In extending the inquiry beyond static factors, these instruments permit a more nuanced look at the individual by considering factors that might be controlled not only in the assessment but in the management of risk. However, as noted earlier, these tools appear to have had little impact, to date, on assessment practice in the community (Monahan, 2008); not using the tools may have an impact on risk *management*, since one of the essential merits of these tools is the focus on dynamic factors that, if controlled through treatment, may reduce dangerous behavior. In other words, whereas risk *assessment* increasingly relies on structured inquiries tied to factors empirically associated with dangerous behavior, risk *management* is often a comparatively unstructured affair.

At the same time, psychology and law could consider more closely those advances in community treatment that do appear to reduce risk. For example, in juvenile justice, multisystemic therapy has proved effective in reducing antisocial behavior in juvenile offenders (Henggeler, Schoenwald, Borduin, Rowland, & Cunningham, 1998). As a result, its use has been extended in community settings, where it has been shown to reduce costs compared with treatment as usual (Sheidow et al., 2004). Linehan has done pioneering and empirically validated work in devising treatments for individuals with borderline personality disorders (Linehan, 1993). Skeem's examination of probation has begun to integrate literature on the therapeutic relationship with community correctional literature (Skeem & Manchak, 2008). However, there is much essential work to be done in this arena, since one of the primary goals of community-based mental health treatment is reducing the likelihood of future risk, and the reduction of future risk, not simply its assessment, should form the core of a psychology and law agenda.

3. *In its focus on specific questions posed by the legal system, psychology and law research has not addressed important areas of inquiry that have broader policy and legal implications.* There are occasions when psychology and law research plays a major role in highly visible judicial decisions. One famous recent example is the decision by the U.S. Supreme Court outlawing the death penalty for defendants charged with offenses committed before 18 years of age (*Roper v. Simmons*, 2005). In his opinion for the majority, Justice Kennedy relied, in part, on an article by Steinberg and Scott (2003), which linked adolescent developmental maturity to the legal principle of proportionality in imposing punishment; Justice Kennedy used the comparative lack of developmental maturity among adolescents, as well as research into adolescent brain development, as part of his rationale for his conclusion that the purposes of the death penalty would not be served when imposed in response to crimes committed by adolescents.

However, there are legal and policy issues that the psychology and law field has only lightly brushed, at best. For example, there is no mention in the preceding chapters of the risk of future harm to self. Yet in Florida, one of the few states with a data system that contains all petitions resulting in an examination to determine if the person meets civil commitment standards, 58% of forms specifying that harm was the reason for the petition indicated that it was harm to self only; another 21% were for harm to self and to others, whereas only 7% was for harm to others alone (Christy, 2007). These data suggest that risk to self is a far more important issue, at least in the context of civil commitment in Florida, than is risk to third parties, yet psychology and law research focuses almost exclusively on risk to others. The statutory criteria for civil commitment in every state require consideration of the appropriateness of less restrictive alternatives to hospitalization, and research on the management of risk to self could assist in such decisions. More broadly, research on the management (and treatment) of individuals who pose both a risk to self and others would be instructive; are there differences, for example, between individuals judged to be a risk to both self and others and those judged to be a risk only to self? If so, what are those differences, and how might they inform decisions about managing the person's care in community settings?

There is also little in the preceding chapters about co-occurring (substance abuse and mental illness) disorders, though co-occurring disorders are common among arrested and incarcerated populations. One of the most important contributors to future violence is substance abuse, which, when combined with mental illness, is far stronger as a factor than mental illness alone (e.g., Steadman et al., 1998). That finding, and its implications, emerged from psychology and law research. What has been less discussed are the implications of such findings for civil commitment policies, more generally. Civil commitment laws focus principally on mental illness as the underlying disorder, with companion laws in many states permitting commitment based on substance abuse (Hafemeister & Amirshahi, 1992). If substance abuse is one of the most significant variables in dangerous behavior among individuals with a co-occurring mental illness, do civil commitment laws that focus attention primarily on mental illness focus on the population most at risk? Should civil commitment policy be reexamined to assure that civil commitment laws take into account co-occurring disorders, with individuals committed to integrated care?

Finally, there is virtually nothing in the preceding chapters about elder issues. Elders are the fastest growing segment of the population in many Western countries, and their problems spill over into legal settings in both criminal and civil contexts. Psychology and law has given this part of the population little attention, with the exception of the issue of competence.

There are many reasons a field focuses on some issues rather than others. Future risk is an obvious concern that cuts across both civil and criminal law; psychology and law researchers responded to a specific question in this area as to whether mental health professionals could add anything "expert" to legal decision making. Competence is also a core issue that arises in many legal settings.

Yet, at some point, it is reasonable to ask whether a particular area of inquiry requires the sheer amount of attention it draws. A handful of issues (psychopathy and eyewitness testimony are two examples) draw much of the scholarly attention devoted to psychology and law. It is not surprising that a comparatively small number of issues command what some consider a disproportionate amount of attention. These issues are important and interesting. In addition, the study of psychology and law, as with most academic fields, is built on a model in which students tend to follow the interests of their major professors in choosing dissertation topics. As a result, interest in those areas tends to perpetuate itself. This is not necessarily a bad thing, since it provides the intellectual capacity to examine an issue in depth and over time. However, it is reasonable to ask at what point the attention becomes disproportionate to the return.

4. *Questions of civil liberties and individual rights need to remain an essential focus of psychology and law scholars and practitioners.* Finally, a renewed and sustained interest in civil liberties and individual rights should be integral to the study and practice of psychology and law in the future. It is worth noting that as psychology and law emerged as a discrete field, mental health

law was primarily rights-oriented. Constitutional principles were used successfully to narrow the reach of civil commitment, extend rights regarding consent to treatment to people with serious mental illnesses, and to improve the standard of care provided in state psychiatric facilities—then the most frequently used venue for long-term confinement of people with serious mental illnesses (for a review, see Appelbaum, 1994). In general, the direction of social change was toward the expansion of civil rights, and psychology and law research into future risk, into competence, into other areas, complemented the direction of the law by refining clinical decision making that affected individual rights.

Today, however, the social/legal climate is very different. Rights-oriented litigation has receded as a tool, at least in the United States, as the U.S. Supreme Court has become more conservative and stepped back sharply from the use of constitutional law to expand individual rights; the effect on mental health law has been dramatic (Petrila, 2001). Rehabilitation as an ideal has evaporated in juvenile and adult criminal justice systems, and the "war on terrorism" has resulted in expanded executive authority over practices such as preventive detention and the erosion of due process rights.

In psychology and law, these trends manifest themselves most clearly in judicial proceedings that apply sexually violent predator (SVP) statutes. Such statutes permit the indefinite confinement of individuals convicted of sexual offenses after the end of a prison term (Fitch, 2003). The U.S. Supreme Court has upheld the constitutionality of these laws and, in doing so, has laid the jurisprudential foundation for the use of expanded civil commitment criteria in general (Dorsett, 1998). While individuals are committed under SVP statutes indefinitely and possibly for life, a relaxed judicial climate regarding oversight of governmental actions has meant little scrutiny of institutional confinement, where little if any treatment is provided (Janus & Logan, 2003).

Given the consequences for the individual, and for public safety, this is an area where clinical testimony should be at its most expert. Tools exist; many risk assessment tools have been developed specifically for use in assessing future risk in cases of sexual offending. Yet, the evidence suggests that in practice, testimony in such cases often exaggerates the scientific foundation of the expert opinion on future dangerousness; courts fail to bar questionable testimony; and the assumption that certain classes of individuals are untreatable has permeated judicial and clinical decision making (Prentky, Janus, Barbaree, Schwartz, & Kafka, 2006). In other words, in individual cases, one can find many of the practices that are most dangerous to individual liberty: inattentive judicial gatekeeping, substandard clinical practice, and the relabeling of a hypothesis as fact. The result is an erosion of due process, abetted by bad clinical practice.

Psychology and law researchers and forensic practitioners cannot unilaterally uphold individual liberties and rights and simultaneously protect public safety. Such responsibilities fall ultimately to the legal system. But overstated claims and bad clinical practice can be harmful to individual rights (and to public safety) in a legal/social climate in which traditional legal safeguards have been dramatically diminished.

SUMMARY

At its best, the field of psychology and law has produced increasing knowledge on a number of core legal questions that affect hundreds of thousand of individuals a year. Practice, at least among specialists, has become more rigorous, and the emergence of forensic practice as a specialty has been a positive development on the whole. This volume provides the best available snapshot of psychological sciences in the courtroom at an important point in the development of the field. It captures what we know, what we do not know, and what we might want to know. In the aggregate, it provides evidence that the field has come a long way from where it began barely three decades ago. It also provides the invaluable service of suggesting where the field should go in the future.

REFERENCES

Appelbaum, P. (1994). *Almost a revolution: Mental health law and the limits of change.* New York: Oxford University Press.

Bonnie, R., & Slobogin, C. (1980). The role of mental health professionals in the criminal process: The case for informed speculation. *Virginia Law Review, 66,* 427–522.

Caspi, A., McClay, J., Moffitt, T. E., Mill, J., Martin, J., Craig, I. W., et al. (2002). Role of genotype in the cycle of violence in maltreated children. *Science, 297,* 851–854.

Caspi, A., Langley, K., Milne, B., Moffitt, T., O'Donovan, M. Owen, M. J., et al. (2008). A replicated molecular genetic basis for subtyping antisocial behavior in children with attention-deficit/hyperactivity disorder. *Archives of General Psychiatry, 65,* 203–210.

Christy, A. (2007). *Special report of Baker Act data.* Tampa: University of South Florida, Louis de la Parte Florida Mental Health Institute, Baker Act Reporting Center.

Christy, A., Douglas, K. S., Otto, R. K., & Petrila, J. (2004). Juveniles evaluated incompetent to proceed: Characteristics and quality of mental health professionals' evaluations. *Professional Psychology: Research and Practice, 35*, 380–388.

Corrections Transition Policy Group. (2006). *Final report to Governor-Elect Jon S. Corzine*. Retrieved September 12, 2008, from *www.njstatelib.org/digit/r424/r4242006c.pdf*.

Dahir, V., Richardson, J., Ginsburg, G., Gatowski, S., Dobbin, S., & Merlino, M. (2005). Judicial application of *Daubert* to psychological syndrome and profile evidence: A research note. *Psychology, Public Policy, and Law, 11*, 62–82.

Dixon, J., & Dixon, K. (2003). Gender-specific clinical syndromes and their admissibility under the federal rules of evidence. *American Journal of Trial Advocacy, 27*, 25–65.

Dorsett, K. A. (1998). *Kansas v. Hendricks*: Marking the beginning of a dangerous new era in civil commitment. *DePaul Law Review, 48*, 113–159.

Edens, J. F., Colwell, L., Desforges, D. M., & Fernandez, K. (2005). The impact of mental health evidence on support for capital punishment: Are defendants labeled psychopathic more deserving of death? *Behavioral Sciences and the Law, 23*, 603–625.

Ennis, B. J., & Litwak, T. R. (1974). Psychiatry and the presumption of expertise: Flipping coins in the courtroom. *California Law Review, 62*, 693–752.

Faigman, D., & Monahan, J. (2005). Psychological evidence at the dawn of the law's scientific age. *Annual Review of Psychology, 56*, 631–659.

Fitch, W. L. (2003). Sexual offender commitment in the United States: Legislative and policy concerns. *Annals of the New York Academy of Sciences, 989*, 489–501.

Grisso, T. (1987). The economic and scientific future of forensic assessment. *American Psychologist, 42*, 831–839.

Grisso, T. (2002). *Evaluating competencies: Forensic assessments and instruments*. New York: Springer.

Hafemeister, T., & Amirshahi, A. (1992). Civil Commitment for Drug Dependency: The Judicial Response. *Loyola Law Review, 26*, 401.

Haney, C. (1980). Psychological and legal change: On the limits of a factual jurisprudence. *Law and Human Behavior, 4*, 147–200.

Harris, G. T., & Rice, M. E. (2006). Treatment of psychopathy: A review of empirical findings. In C. J. Patrick (Ed.), *Handbook of psychopathy* (pp. 555–572). New York: Guilford Press.

Harris, G. T., & Rice, M. E. (2008). *Abandoning evidence-based risk appraisal in forensic practice: Comments on "Precision of actuarial risk assessment instruments."* Retrieved September 21, 2008, from *www.mhcp-research.com/hmcrespond.htm*.

Hart, S. D., Michie, C., & Cooke, D. J. (2007). Precision of actuarial risk assessment instruments. *British Journal of Psychiatry, 190*(Suppl. 49), S60–S65.

Heilbrun, K. (1992). The role of psychological testing in forensic assessment. *Law and Human Behavior, 16*, 257–272.

Henggeler, S. W., Schoenwald, S. K., Borduin, C. M, Rowland, M. D., & Cunningham, P. B. (1998). *Multisystemic treatment of antisocial behavior in children and adolescents*. New York: Guilford Press.

Institute of Medicine. (2001). *Crossing the quality chasm: A new health system for the 21st century*. Washington, DC: Author.

Janus, E. S., & Logan, W. A. (2003). Substantive due process and the involuntary confinement of sexually violent predators. *Connecticut Law Review, 35,* 319–384.

King, G., Rosen, O., & Tanner, M. (2004). *Ecological inferences: New methodological strategies*. New York: Cambridge University Press.

Lally, S. (2003). What tests are acceptable for use in forensic evaluations?: A survey of experts. *Professional Psychology: Research and Practice, 34,* 225–232.

Linehan, M. M. (1993). *Cognitive-behavioral treatment of borderline personality disorder*. New York: Guilford Press.

Massachusetts Youth Screening Instrument–2. (2008). Retrieved September 14, 2008, from *www.maysiware.com/MAYSI2Statewide.htm*.

Melton, G. B., Petrila, J., Poythress, N. G., & Slobogin, C. (2007). *Psychological evaluations for the courts: A handbook for mental health professionals and lawyers* (3rd ed.). New York: Guilford Press.

Monahan, J. (1981). *Predicting violent behavior: An assessment of clinical techniques*. Thousand Oaks, CA: Sage.

Monahan, J. (2008). Structured risk assessment of violence. In R. Simon & K. Tardiff (Eds.), *Textbook of violence assessment and management* (pp. 17–33). Washington, DC: American Psychiatric Association.

Morse, S. (1978). Law and mental health professionals: The limits of expertise. *Professional Psychology, 9,* 389–399.

National Institute of Mental Health. (1999). Report of the National Institute of Mental Health's Genetics Workgroup. *Biological Psychiatry, 45,* 559–602.

Nicholson, R. A., & Norwood, S. (2000). The quality of forensic psychological assessments, reports, and testimony: Acknowledging the gaps between promise and practice. *Law and Human Behavior, 24,* 9–44.

Otto, R. K., Edens, J. F., & Barcus, E. H. (2000). The use of psychological testing in child custody evaluations. *Family and Conciliation Courts Review, 38,* 312–340.

Otto, R. K., & Heilbrun, K. (2002). The practice of forensic psychology: A look toward the future in light of the past. *American Psychologist, 57,* 5–18.

People v. Miller, WL 768749 (Cal. App. 4 Dist. 2005).

Petrila, J. (2001). From constitution to contracts: Mental disability law at the turn of the century. In L. Frost & R. Bonnie (Eds.), *The evolution of mental health law* (pp. 75–100). Washington, DC: American Psychological Press.

Poythress, N. G., Bonnie, R. J., Monahan, J., Otto, R., & Hoge, S. K. (2002). *Adjudicative competence: The MacArthur studies*. New York: Kluwer.

Prentky, R. A., Janus, E., Barbaree, H., Schwartz, B. K., Kafka, M. P. (2006). Sexually violent predators in the courtroom: Science on trial. *Psychology, Public Policy, and Law, 12,* 357–386.

Robey, A. (1965). Criteria for competency to stand trial: A checklist for psychiatrists. *American Journal of Psychiatry, 122,* 616–623.

Robinson, W. S. (1950). Ecological correlations and the behavior of individuals. *American Sociological Review, 15,* 351–357.

Roper v. Simmons, 534 U.S. 551 (2005).

Sheidow, A., Bradford, W., Henggeler, S., Rowland, M., Halliday-Boykins, C., Schoenwald, S., et al. (2004). Treatment costs for youths receiving multisystemic therapy or hospitalization after a psychiatric crisis. *Psychiatric Services, 55,* 548–554.

Skeem, J., & Manchak, S. (2008). Back to the future: From Klockars' model of effective supervision to evidence-based practice in probation. *International Journal of Offender Rehabilitation, 47,* 220–247.

Skeem, J., & Petrila, J. (2003). An introduction to the special issues on juvenile psychopathy: Informing the debate. *Behavioral Sciences and the Law, 21,* 689–694.

Slobogin, C. (2006). *Proving the unprovable: The role of law, science, and speculation in adjudicating culpability and dangerousness.* New York: Oxford University Press.

Steadman, H. J., Mulvey, E. P., Monahan, J., Robbins, P., Appelbaum, P. S., Grisso, T., et al. (1998). Violence by people discharged from acute psychiatric inpatient facilities and by others in the same neighborhoods. *Archives of General Psychiatry, 55,* 393–401.

Steinberg, L., & Scott, E. (2003). Less guilty by reason of adolescence: Developmental immaturity, diminished responsibility, and the juvenile death penalty. *American Psychologist, 58,* 1009–1018.

Vickers, A. L. (2005). *Daubert,* critique and interpretation: What existing studies tell us about the application of *Daubert. University of San Francisco Law Review, 45,* 109–147.

Vincent, G. M., Grisso, T., Terry, A., & Banks, S. (2008). Sex and race differences in mental health symptoms in juvenile justice: The MAYSI-2 national meta-analysis. *Journal of the American Academy of Child and Adolescent Psychiatry, 47*(3), 282–290.

Index

Page numbers followed by *n* indicate note, *t* indicate table.

Abductive inference, 60
Accuracy of a technique, criminal profiling and, 247–251
Actuarial profiling, compared to criminal profiling, 246
Actuarial risk assessment
  based on nomothetic data, 338–339, 343–344, 348–349
  communicating findings from, 352–353
  myths and misconceptions regarding, 350–351
  overview, 351–352
  research regarding, 344–349
  violence risk assessment, 334–338
Adjudicative competence
  communicating findings from evaluations for, 327
  foundational and decisional competence, 312–313
  myths and misconceptions regarding, 323–326
  overview, 309–310, 326–327
  See also Competency to stand trial evaluations
Admissibility standards
  child witnesses and, 166–167
  competency to stand trial evaluations and, 326
  control question test (CQT) and, 236
  criminal profiling and, 254–258
  distinguishing science from nonscience, 17–18
  expert testimony and, 100–101
  Federal Rules of Evidence and, 6–15
  future considerations regarding, 21–23
  general acceptance test and, 4–6
  interrogation and, 142–143
  judging of reliability factors, 30–36
  juror credulity and, 19–21
  overview, 3–4, 396–398
  recovered memories and, 71–73, 75*n*
  relevancy test and, 15–17
  research regarding eyewitness identification and, 104–106
  Rorschach Inkblot Test and, 217
  validity and reliability and, 12–15
  See also Daubert v. Merrell Dow Pharmaceuticals, Inc. (1993); *Frye v. United States* (1923)
Adolescents
  divorce and, 286
  Rorschach Inkblot Test and, 211–212
African Americans, Psychopathy Checklist—Revised (PCL-R) and, 188–189
Age regression, hypnosis and, 86–87
Aggression, Rorschach Inkblot Test and, 215. *See also* Violence risk assessment
Alabama Parenting Questionnaire (APQ), 297
Alexander v. Smith & Nephew (2000), 9
American Law Institute (ALI) test of insanity, 11
American Polygraph Association, 229, 233
American Society of Clinical Hypnosis (ASCH), 81, 84, 90
Anecdotal data
  criminal profiling and, 246–247
  false and repressed memories, 61
Anger control treatment, 361
Antisocial behavior, 399

Antisocial personality disorder
  Psychopathy Checklist—Revised (PCL-R) and,
    176–177
  Rorschach Inkblot Test and, 208–209, 218
Anxiety disorders, Rorschach Inkblot Test and,
    208–209, 217–218
Assessment
  custody evaluations and, 290–294, 292t–293t,
    295–298, 296t
  instruments of, 391–393, 394–395
  repressed memories and, 58–59
  See also Assessment of psychological injuries;
    Assessment of risk
Assessment of psychological injuries
  communicating findings from, 278–279
  myths and misconceptions regarding, 275–277
  overview, 263–272, 277–278
  posttraumatic stress disorder (PTSD) and,
    264–267
  research regarding, 272–275
  See also Trauma
Assessment of risk
  control question test (CQT) and, 237–238
  future directions of, 400
  juror credulity and, 20–21
  Psychopathy Checklist—Revised (PCL-R) and,
    193, 364–365
  See also Violence risk assessment
Attachment
  assessment of, 295
  custody evaluations and, 294–295
  divorce and, 288
Attention-deficit/hyperactivity disorder, 399
Attorneys, 32–33

Battered women syndrome, 397–398
Beck Depression Inventory–2, 298
Behavioral Analysis Interview (BAI)
  overview, 126
  research regarding, 129
Betrayal trauma theory, 69–70
Bias
  accuracy of eyewitness identification and,
    103–105, 108–110
  admissibility standards regarding recovered
    memories and, 72–73
  criminal profiling and, 248
  in deception detection, 130–131
  expert testimony and, 115–116
  hypnosis and, 93–94
  interrogation and, 126–127, 140
  interviews with child witnesses and, 150–154
  racial, 103–105, 108–110
  therapeutic assessment and, 58–59
Bipolar disorder, 208
Borderline personality disorder, 208
Brain fingerprinting, 227–228. See also Guilty
  knowledge test (GKT)

Child abuse accommodation syndrome, 15–17
Child maltreatment, 399
Child sexual abuse
  admissibility standards regarding recovered
    memories and, 71–73
  false memories of, 56
  repressed memories and, 62–70
  suggestive interviewing and, 154–158
  See also Recovered memories; Repressed
    memories
Child sexual abuse accommodation syndrome
  (CSAAS), 154–158
Child witnesses
  myths and misconceptions regarding, 159–164
  overview, 149–158, 165–166
  research regarding, 164–167
Child-Rearing Practices Report (CRPR), 297
Children
  projective drawings and, 204
  Rorschach Inkblot Test and, 211–212
  See also Child sexual abuse; Child witnesses
Children's Apperception Test (CAT), 204
Civil commitment policy, 402
Civil liberties, 402–404
Classification of Violence Risk (COVR)
  overview, 333, 341, 351
  research regarding, 345, 348–349
Clinician-Administered PTSD Scale (CAPS), 274
Cognitive restructuring, 360–361
Cognitive treatment, 360–361
Cognitive-behavioral therapy (CBT)
  high-risk offenders and, 373–375
  research regarding, 375–377
  See also Treatment
Collateral information, 275
Commitment laws, 402
Comorbidity
  disability and, 269–270
  posttraumatic stress disorder (PTSD) and, 266
Compelling evidence, recovered memories and,
  60
Competency to Stand Trial Assessment
  Instrument (CAI)
  overview, 310, 313–314, 323
  research regarding, 318–319, 320
Competency to stand trial evaluations
  communicating findings from, 327
  controversies regarding, 310–319
  myths and misconceptions regarding, 323–326
  overview, 309–310, 326–327, 390–391
  research regarding, 313–323
  See also Adjudicative competence
Complete Polygraph Handbook, The (Abrams, 1989),
  238
Comprehensive System for the Rorschach
  with children and adolescents, 212
  diagnosis and, 208–209
  overview, 203–204

Comprehensive System for the Rorschach *(cont.)*
  research regarding, 207–208
  science and, 216–218
Conduct disorder, Rorschach Inkblot Test and, 208–209
Confessions
  peer review and, 140–141
  presumption of guilt and, 126–128
  See also False confessions
Confessions, false
  future research regarding, 135–136
  interrogation and, 124–125, 131–133
  myths and misconceptions regarding, 136–141
  overview, 141–143
  Reid Technique of investigative interviewing and, 127–128
  research regarding, 128–133
Confidence intervals
  actuarial prediction strategies and, 352–353
  Psychopathy Checklist—Revised (PCL-R) and, 193
Confirmation bias, interrogation and, 126–127, 140
Conflict Tactics Scale (CTS), 297
Confrontation phase of interrogation, 127
Consumer satisfaction surveys, criminal profiling and, 247
Continuing education for judges and attorneys regarding scientific judgments, 46–48
Control question test (CQT)
  communicating findings from, 238–239
  myths and misconceptions regarding, 232–236
  overview, 225–227, 236–238
  research regarding, 229–232
Correctional supervision, 359
Court-appointed experts, 45–46
Criminal investigations
  bias and, 130–131
  criminal profiling and, 245–246, 254
  hypnosis and, 93–94
Criminal investigative analysis, 256. *See also* Criminal profiling
Criminal personality traits, Rorschach Inkblot Test and, 209–210
Criminal profiling
  admissibility of, 254–258
  myths and misconceptions regarding, 253–254
  overview, 245–246, 258, 393–394
  research regarding, 246–253
  science and, 246–251
Cross-examination
  expert testimony and, 110
  hypnosis and, 85–86, 91
  improving judgments of validity and, 38–40
  juror credulity and, 20
  overview, 41–48
  validity and, 33
Custody and isolation phase of interrogation, 127

Custody cases
  communicating findings from custody evaluations, 302–303
  myths and misconceptions regarding, 300–301
  overview, 284–294, 292t–293t, 301–302
  research regarding, 294–300, 296t
  Rorschach Inkblot Test and, 205, 210–211, 215, 218

Daubert v. Merrell Dow Pharmaceuticals, Inc. (1993)
  adjudicative competence and, 319–320
  admissibility standards and, 3–4, 105, 397
  child witnesses and, 166–167
  competency to stand trial evaluations and, 326
  control question test (CQT) and, 236–238
  criminal profiling and, 256
  evidence-based practice and, 23
  expert testimony and, 119
  Federal Rules of Evidence and, 6–15
  future considerations and, 21–22
  legacy of, 27–28
  overview, 6–15, 26
  in practice, 8–15
  scientific reasoning ability and, 28–30
Deception detection
  communicating findings from, 238–239
  future research regarding, 134
  interrogation and, 129
  myths and misconceptions regarding, 232–236
  overview, 141–142, 224–229, 236–238
  presumption of guilt and, 126–128, 130–131
  research regarding, 229–232
  See also Polygraphs
Decisional competence
  overview, 312–313
  research regarding, 316–319, 323
  See also Adjudicative competence
Deductive reasoning, 17–18
Depression
  custody evaluations and, 294–295
  disability and, 270
  Rorschach Inkblot Test and, 208–209
Developmental stages
  future research regarding, 399
  suggestive interviewing of child witnesses and, 159–164, 164–165
Diagnosis
  posttraumatic stress disorder (PTSD), 264–267
  Psychopathy Checklist—Revised (PCL-R), 176–177
  Rorschach Inkblot Test and, 208–209
Diagnostic and Statistical Manual of Mental Disorders (DSM-IV-TR)
  custody evaluations and, 298
  posttraumatic stress disorder (PTSD) in, 264
  Psychopathy Checklist—Revised (PCL-R) and, 176–177

Diagnostic labels, prejudice and, 184–185
Disability
    communicating findings regarding, 278–279
    comorbidity and, 269–270
    malingering and, 271–272
    myths and misconceptions regarding, 276–277
    posttraumatic stress disorder (PTSD) and, 268
    research regarding the assessment of, 272–275
Disclosure
    interviews with child witnesses and, 157–158
    repressed memories and, 69–70
Discovery requirements, 117–118
Dissociation
    myths and misconceptions regarding, 70–71
    repressed memories and, 62–63, 69
Distorted Form
    diagnosis and, 208, 209
    overview, 206–207
Divorce, affects of on children, 285–290. See also Custody cases
"Documented" victims, false and repressed memories and, 62
Draw-a-Person (DAP) test, 204
Dusky v. United States (1960)
    adjudicative competence and, 309, 311–313, 320–321
    compared to Godinez v. Moran (1993), 317
Dysfunction, psychological injury and, 269–270

Ecological validity
    hypnosis and, 88–89
    overview, 29, 389–390
Education, 47–48
EEGs, guilty knowledge test and, 227–228
Emotional instability
    assessment of, 298
    divorce and, 290
Environmental instability
    assessment of, 297–298
    divorce and, 289–290
Error rate
    criminal profiling and, 252
    Daubert Court and, 12, 13–14
Evaluation of Competency to Stand Trial—Revised (ECST-R), 310–311, 323
Event-related potential (ERP), guilty knowledge test and, 227–228
Evidence, child sexual abuse and, 64
Evidence, compelling, 60
Evidence, expert
    admissibility standards and, 3–4
    distinguishing science from nonscience, 17–18
    Federal Rules of Evidence and, 6–15
    judging of the validity of, 30–36
    opposing experts, 41–48
    See also Expert testimony
Evidence-based practice, 22–23

Exner norms
    with children and adolescents, 212
    research regarding, 214–215
    Rorschach Inkblot Test and, 207–208
Expert evidence
    admissibility standards and, 3–4
    distinguishing science from nonscience, 17–18
    Federal Rules of Evidence and, 6–15
    judging of the validity of, 30–36
    opposing experts, 41–48
    See also Expert testimony
Expert testimony
    admissibility standards regarding, 72–73, 100–101
    content of, 117–118
    court-appointed experts, 45–46
    criminal profiling and, 254–255
    cross examinations and, 38–40
    current state of the field of, 389–398
    eyewitness identification and, 100–101
    false confessions and, 125
    future considerations regarding, 21–22
    jurors and, 19–21, 138–139
    myths and misconceptions regarding, 111, 138–139
    opposing experts, 37–38
    overview, 118–119, 387–389, 396–398
    presentation of, 114–118
    psychopathic label and, 183–184
    relevancy test and, 15–17
    research regarding, 101–110, 104t
    science and, 111–114, 393–395
External validity
    expert testimony and, 101
    interrogation and, 131–132
    overview, 29
    See also Validity
Eyewitness identification
    accuracy of, 106–108
    expert testimony regarding, 100–101
    myths and misconceptions regarding, 111
    overview, 118–119
    presentation of, 114–118
    research regarding, 101–110, 104t
    science and, 111–114
    show-up identifications, 116
    suspect-bias factors and, 115–116
    See also Memory

Factual disputes, in custody cases, 299, 300
Factual understanding, adjudicative competence and, 311
False confessions
    future research regarding, 135–136
    interrogation and, 124–125, 131–133
    myths and misconceptions regarding, 136–141
    overview, 141–143

False confessions *(cont.)*
   Reid Technique of investigative interviewing
     and, 127–128
   research regarding, 128–133
False memories
   of childhood sexual abuse, 56
   compared to the rate of accurate recovered
     memories, 57–58
   compelling evidence and, 60
   hypnosis and, 87–88
   overview, 74
   procedural guidelines for hypnosis and, 90–91
   scientific tests of, 60–62
   See also Memory; Recovered memories;
     Repressed memories
False reports, suggestive interviewing of child
   witnesses and, 162–164
Family Adaptation and Cohesion Scales–III
   (FACES-III), 297–298
Family Assessment Measure–III (FAM-III), 298
Family Environment Scale (FES), 297, 298
Federal Bureau of Investigation (FBI)
   criminal profiling and, 246–247
   guidelines for hypnosis from, 90
Federal Rules of Evidence
   court-appointed experts, 45–46
   criminal profiling and, 256
   overview, 6–15, 26
   in practice, 8–15
Fit, 11
Fitness Interview Test—Revised (FIT-R)
   overview, 310, 313–314
   research regarding, 318–319
Forensic examiners, competency to stand trial
   evaluations and, 323–324
Forensic hypnosis
   age regression, 86–87
   compared with other recall techniques, 88
   ecological validity and, 88–89
   false memories and, 87–88
   myths and misconceptions regarding, 91–92
   overview, 80–82, 93–94, 94–95, 391
   procedural guidelines for, 90–91
   research regarding, 82–91
   scientific knowledge regarding, 91
   witness accuracy and, 82–84, 85–86
Forgetting, problems with testing the hypothesis
   of repressed memories and, 62–70
Foundational competence, 312–313. *See also*
   Adjudicative competence
Free-recall questions, interviews with child
   witnesses and, 158
Frye v. United States (1923)
   admissibility standards and, 3–4
   competency to stand trial evaluations and, 326
   criminal profiling and, 256
   distinguishing science from nonscience and,
     17–18
   expert testimony and, 118–119

   general acceptance test, 4–6
   juror credulity and, 19
   See also General acceptance test

Gender
   Psychopathy Checklist—Revised (PCL-R) and,
     188
   risk assessment and, 346–347
General acceptance test
   criminal profiling and, 256
   Daubert Court and, 12, 14–15
   judging of reliability factors and, 30–36
   overview, 4–6
   See also Frye v. United States (1923)
General Electric Co. v. Joiner (1997)
   Daubert Court and, 21
   Federal Rules of Evidence and, 7
   legacy of, 27–28
Genetic factors, future research regarding, 399
Gist processing, 160–161
Global Assessment of Functioning (GAF) scale, 273
Godinez v. Moran (1993), 316–318, 325
Guilt, presumption of
   future research regarding, 135
   interrogation and, 126–128
   research regarding, 130–131
Guilty knowledge detection
   communicating findings from, 238–239
   myths and misconceptions regarding, 232–236
   overview, 224–229, 236–238
   research regarding, 229–232
   See also Guilty knowledge test (GKT);
     Polygraphs
Guilty knowledge test (GKT)
   overview, 227–229
   research regarding, 229–232
   See also Guilty knowledge detection

Hall v. Baxter Healthcare Corp (1996), 21
Handbook of Forensic Rorschach Assessment (Gacono &
   Evans, 2008), 204
High-risk offenders
   overview, 358–359
   Psychopathy Checklist—Revised (PCL-R) and,
     364–365
   treatment and, 358–375, 376–377
Historical–Clinical–Risk Management–20 (HCR-20)
   overview, 333
   race and, 347
House–Tree–Person (HTP) test, 204
Hybrid model of correctional supervision, 359
Hypnosis
   age regression, 86–87
   compared with other recall techniques, 88
   ecological validity and, 88–89
   false memories and, 87–88
   myths and misconceptions regarding, 91–92
   overview, 80–82, 93–94, 94–95, 391
   procedural guidelines for, 90–91

research regarding, 82–91
scientific knowledge regarding, 91
witness accuracy and, 82–84, 85–86
Hypnotic age regression, 86–87
Hypothesis testing
compared to therapeutic practices, 58–59
overview, 395–396
repressed memories and, 58–59, 62–70

Identification tests
overview, 112–113
suspect-bias factors and, 115–116
See also Eyewitness identification
Idiographic approach to assessment
adjudicative competence and, 310–312
research regarding, 322
Impulsivity, evaluation of, 218
Incest, repressed memories and, 69–70
Individual rights, 402–404
Inductive reasoning, *Logerquist v. McVey* (2000)
and, 17–18
Instability, environmental
assessment of, 297–298
divorce and, 289–290
Intelligence, Rorschach Inkblot Test and, 208
Interdisciplinary Fitness Interview (IFI)
overview, 310, 313–314
research regarding, 318–319, 320
Internal validity
attorneys and, 33
expert testimony and, 101
interrogation and, 131–132
jurors and, 33–34
overview, 29
See also Validity
Interrogation of suspects
admissibility standards and, 142–143
future research regarding, 135–136
myths and misconceptions regarding, 136–141
overview, 124–125, 141–143, 391
police interrogation, 125–126
polygraphs and, 230
presumption of guilt and, 126–128
research regarding, 128–136
techniques of, 127–128, 131, 133
Interviewer bias, interviews with child witnesses
and, 150–154
Interviews
compared to interrogations, 126
interviews with child witnesses and, 150–154
Reid Technique of investigative interviewing,
127–128
suggestive interviews with child witnesses,
150–154
Investigations
bias and, 130–131
criminal profiling and, 245–246, 254
hypnosis and, 93–94
Ipse dixit, juror credulity and, 20

Joint custody, 285. *See also* Custody cases
Judges
admissibility standards and, 397–398
improving judgments of validity and, 45–48
validity and, 30–32
Junk science, safeguards against, 36–41
Juror credulity, 19–21
Jurors
expert testimony and, 138–139
improving judgments of validity and, 41–45
instructions for, 40–41
myths and misconceptions regarding, 138–139
research regarding, 104–106
validity and, 33–36
Juveniles
diagnostic labels and, 184–186
interrogation and, 133
predictive validity of the PCL-R and, 182–183
Psychopathy Checklist: Youth Version
(PCL:YV), 176, 182–183, 186–189
Rorschach Inkblot Test and, 211–212

Kelly–Frye test, 16–17
Kinetic Family Drawing (KFD), 204
Kumho Tire Ltd. v. Charmichael (1999)
admissibility standards and, 105
Federal Rules of Evidence and, 7
legacy of, 27–28

Labeling
psychopathic label and, 183–186
Rorschach Inkblot Test and, 212
Law enforcement, hypnosis and, 93–94
Law school, scientific training and, 47–48
Leading questions
in assessment, 58–59, 274
hypnosis and, 82–84
interviews with child witnesses and, 150–154
Level of Service Inventory—Revised (LSI-R)
overview, 342, 392
race and, 347
Level of Service/Case Management Inventory (LS/CMI)
overview, 333
race and, 347
Lie detection. *See* Deception detection
Lineup tests
overview, 112–113
suspect-bias factors and, 115–116
Logerquist v. McVey (2000), 17–18
Lynch v. Knight (1861), 264

MacArthur Competence Assessment Tool—
Criminal Adjudication (MacCAT-CA)
overview, 310–311, 315–316
psychopathy and, 371–373
research regarding, 317–318

Malingering
    disability and, 271–272
    overview, 278
    research regarding, 274
Massachusetts Youth Screening Instrument–2
    (MAYSI-2), 392
Memory
    hypnosis and, 80–82
    Logerquist v. McVey (2000) and, 17–18
    myths and misconceptions regarding, 70–71
    overview, 393
    See also Eyewitness identification; False
        memories; Recovered memories; Repressed
        memories
Mental illness
    interrogation and, 133
    physical disorders and, 270
    Rorschach Inkblot Test and, 208–209
    substance use and, 401–402
    treatment and, 400
    violence risk assessment and, 347–348
    See also Psychopathy
Mental impairment, 133
Miller Forensic Assessment of Symptoms Test
    (M-FAST), 274
Minimization phase of interrogation, 127
Minnesota Multiphasic Personality Inventory–2
    (MMPI-2), 271–272
Misleading questions
    assessment of psychological injury and, 58–59,
        274
    hypnosis and, 82–84
    interviews with child witnesses and, 150–154
M'Naughten test, 11
Mood disorders, Rorschach Inkblot Test and,
    217–218

Narcissistic personality disorder, Rorschach
    Inkblot Test and, 208–209
Nomothetic approach to assessment
    adjudicative competence and, 310–312
    research regarding, 322
    strengths and weaknesses of, 314–316
    violence risk assessment, 338–339
Nonactuarial risk assessment, 334–338
Note taking by jurors, 43–44

Open-ended questions, 274
Operational utilitarian argument, criminal
    profiling and, 248–249
Opinion in testimony
    distinguishing science from nonscience, 17–18
    juror credulity and, 19–21

Parent alienation syndrome (PAS), 300–301
Parental conflict
    assessment of, 297
    divorce and, 288–289

Parental suitability, Rorschach Inkblot Test and, 218
Parenting skills
    assessment of, 297
    divorce and, 288
Pathology, Rorschach Inkblot Test and, 206–208
Peer review and publication
    confessions and, 140–141
    Daubert Court and, 12, 14
    interrogation and, 140
People v. Kelly (1976), 19
People v. McDonald (1984), 19
People v. Miller (2005)
    overview, 397
    relevancy test and, 16
People v. Venegas (1998), 19
Personal Assertion Analysis (PAA), 297
Personal injury cases, Rorschach Inkblot Test
    and, 205
Personality, disability and, 270
Personality disorders, Rorschach Inkblot Test
    and, 208
Physical disorders, mental illness and, 270
Pleading effect, 109
Police interrogation
    future research regarding, 135–136
    myths and misconceptions regarding, 138,
        139–141
    overview, 125–126
    research regarding, 131–133
    See also Interrogation of suspects
Police investigations
    bias and, 130–131
    criminal profiling and, 245–246, 254
    hypnosis and, 93–94
Polygraphs
    communicating findings from, 238–239
    general acceptance test and, 6
    myths and misconceptions regarding, 232–236
    overview, 224–229, 236–238
    research regarding, 229–232
    See also Deception detection; Guilty knowledge
        detection
Posttraumatic stress disorder (PTSD)
    assessment of, 263–272
    myths and misconceptions regarding, 276–277
    overview, 264–267
    relevancy test and, 15–17
    Rorschach Inkblot Test and, 205, 208–209,
        215, 217–218
    See also Assessment of psychological injuries;
        Trauma
Predictions of violence. *See* Violence, predictions of
Predictive utility, Psychopathy Checklist—
    Revised (PCL-R), 177, 179–181
Predictive validity
    overview, 29
    Psychopathy Checklist—Revised (PCL-R),
        181–183

Rorschach Inkblot Test and, 209–210
violence risk assessment and, 351–352
Prejudice, psychopathic label and, 183–186
Prejudicial effect, Psychopathy Checklist—
     Revised (PCL-R), 177
Principles of the Law of Family Dissolution, 285
Profiling, criminal
    admissibility of, 254–258
    myths and misconceptions regarding, 253–254
    overview, 245–246, 258, 393–394
    research regarding, 246–253
    science and, 246–251
Projective drawings
    overview, 204
    use of in forensic settings, 212–214
Projective techniques
    communicating findings from, 218–219
    controversies regarding, 205–214
    myths and misconceptions regarding, 215–216
    overview, 202–205
    research regarding, 206–215
    science and, 216–218
Proof
    admissibility standards regarding recovered
         memories and, 71–73
    child sexual abuse and, 64
    repressed memories and, 64
Psychological expertise
    content of expert testimony and, 117
    Daubert Court and, 12–15
    See also Expert testimony
Psychological injuries, assessment of
    communicating findings from, 278–279
    myths and misconceptions regarding, 275–277
    overview, 263–272, 277–278
    posttraumatic stress disorder (PTSD) and,
         264–267
    research regarding, 272–275
    See also Trauma
Psychopathy
    custody evaluations and, 298
    myths and misconceptions regarding, 189–191,
         377–378, 395–396
    overview, 175–176, 191–193, 363–364
    psychopathic label and, 183–186
    research regarding, 186–189
    Rorschach Inkblot Test and, 209–210, 215,
         218
    treatment and, 190, 365–373, 376–380
    See also Mental illness
Psychopathy Checklist—Revised (PCL-R) and
    Psychopathy Checklist: Youth Version
    (PCL:YV)
    communicating findings from, 192–193
    controversies regarding, 177–186
    myths and misconceptions regarding, 189–191
    overview, 176, 176–177, 191–193, 364
    predictive validity of, 182–183

research regarding, 177–186, 186–189
treatment and, 365–373
Psychosis, Rorschach Inkblot Test and, 208
Psychosocial treatment. *See* Treatment
Psychotic disorders, Rorschach Inkblot Test and,
     208, 209
PTSD Checklist—Civilian Version (PCL-C), 273

Qualifications of experts, 10–11
Questions asked of witnesses. *See* Leading
     questions; Misleading questions

Race
    accuracy of eyewitness identification and,
         103–105, 108–110
    Psychopathy Checklist—Revised (PCL-R) and,
         188–189
    risk assessment and, 346–347
Racial profiling, compared to criminal profiling,
     246
Rape trauma syndrome, 397–398
Rapid Risk Assessment for Sex Offence
     Recidivism (RRASOR), 347
Recidivism
    communicating findings from risk assessments
         and, 353
    myths and misconceptions regarding, 377–378
    predictive validity of the PCL-R and, 181–183
    psychopathy and, 190, 365–373, 396
    Psychopathy Checklist—Revised (PCL-R) and,
         364–365
    Rorschach Inkblot Test and, 209–210, 215, 218
    treatment, 358–375
    treatment and, 377–378
    violence risk assessment and, 340, 347
Recovered memories. *See also* Memory; Repressed
    memories
    admissibility standards regarding, 71–73, 75*n*
    court testimony and, 73–74
    hypnosis and, 82–84
    overview, 55–56, 74, 393
Rehabilitation
    effectiveness of, 361–362
    myths and misconceptions regarding, 377–378
    risk–needs–responsivity (RNR) model and, 360
    treatment and, 358–375
    See also Treatment
Reid Technique of investigative interviewing
    overview, 127–128
    research regarding, 129
Relevance, 3–4, 11, 15–17
Reliability
    assessment of psychological injury and, 268
    competency to stand trial evaluations and,
         319–323
    Daubert v. Merrell Dow Pharmaceuticals, Inc.
         (1993) and, 27–28
    judging of, 30–36

Reliability *(cont.)*
  overview, 12–15
  polygraphs and, 230–232
  Psychopathy Checklist—Revised (PCL-R),
      177–178
  therapeutic assessment and, 58–59
Reports
  child witnesses and, 166–167
  content of, 117–118
Repressed memories
  admissibility standards regarding, 70–73, 75*n*
  court testimony and, 73–74
  juror credulity and, 19–20
  Logerquist v. McVey (2000) and, 17–18
  myths and misconceptions regarding, 70–71
  overview, 55–60, 74, 393
  problems with testing the hypothesis of, 62–
      70
  relevancy test and, 15–17
  scientific tests of, 60–62
  See also Memory; Recovered memories
Rights, individual, 402–404
Risk assessment
  control question test (CQT) and, 237–238
  future directions of, 400
  juror credulity and, 20–21
  Psychopathy Checklist—Revised (PCL-R) and,
      193, 364–365
  See also Violence risk assessment
Risk management, 400
Risk reduction, 400
Risk–needs–responsivity (RNR) model of
      treatment
  overview, 360, 363
  Psychopathy Checklist—Revised (PCL-R) and,
      364
  research regarding, 375–377
  science and, 378–380
Roberts Apperception Test (RAT), 204
Rorschach Inkblot Test
  with children and adolescents, 211–212
  communicating findings from, 218–219
  controversies regarding, 205–214
  custody evaluations and, 210–211, 291
  myths and misconceptions regarding, 215–216
  overview, 202–205
  predictive validity of, 209–210
  research regarding, 206–215
  science and, 216–218

Schizophrenia, Rorschach Inkblot Test and, 208
Schizotypal personality disorder, Rorschach
      Inkblot Test and, 208
Science
  custody evaluations and, 299–300
  deception detection and, 237–238
  distinguishing from nonscience, 17–18
  expert testimony and, 111–114, 393–395

false memories and, 60–62
Federal Rules of Evidence and, 26
future directions of, 398–404
improving judgments of validity and, 36–41,
      41–48
projective techniques and, 216–218
repressed memories and, 60–62
Science court, 46
Scientific advisors, 46
Scientific method, *Logerquist v. McVey* (2000) and,
      17–18
Scientific reasoning ability
  jurors and, 43–45
  overview, 28–30
Scientific training, for judges and attorneys,
      46–48
Self-centeredness, Rorschach Inkblot Test and,
      218
Self-harm, 401
Self-report inventories
  disability and, 269–270
  overview, 202–203
Semistructured interview
  adjudicative competence and, 310–311
  posttraumatic stress disorder (PTSD) and, 265
  research regarding, 318–319, 320–321
  strengths and weaknesses of, 313–314
Sex Offender Risk Appraisal Guide (SORAG), 341
Sex offender treatment, 237–238. *See also*
      Treatment
Sexual abuse, childhood
  admissibility standards regarding recovered
      memories and, 71–73
  false memories of, 56
  repressed memories and, 62–70
  suggestive interviewing and, 154–158
  See also Recovered memories; Repressed
      memories
Sexual abuse, repressed and recovered memories
      of. *See* Child sexual abuse; Recovered
      memories; Repressed memories
Sexual Violence Risk–20 (SVR-20), 340
Sexuality, custody evaluations and, 299
Sexually violent predators
  civil liberties and, 403
  psychopathic label and, 184
Sexually Violent Predators Act
  expert testimony and, 10
  People v. Miller (2005) and, 16
Show-up identifications, 116
Social fact testimony, 111–112
Social framework testimony, 111–112
Society for Personality Assessment, Rorschach
      Inkblot Test and, 215
SPJ approach to risk assessment
  communicating findings from, 353
  overview, 336–338, 351–352
  research regarding, 344–349

Stability, environmental
  assessment of, 297–298
  divorce and, 289–290
State v. Hurd (1981), 90–91
Statement Validity Analysis (SVA), 134
Static-99
  overview, 344
  race and, 347
Structured Clinical Interview for DSM-IV
    (SCID-IV)
  custody evaluations and, 298
  trauma and, 276
Structured Interview for Reported Symptoms
    (SIRS), 271–272
Structured interviews
  custody evaluations and, 298
  psychological injury and, 274
  trauma and, 276
Structured Professional Judgment (SPJ) risk
    assessment. *See* SPJ approach to risk
    assessment
Subjective forgetting method, false and repressed
    memories and, 61–62
Substance use
  mental illness and, 401–402
  psychopathy and, 368
Suggestibility in hypnosis, 87–88. *See also*
    Hypnosis
Suggestive interviews
  child witnesses and, 150–154, 154–158
  myths and misconceptions regarding, 159–164
Summaries of testimony, improving judgments of
    validity and, 44
Surveillance model of correctional supervision, 359
Suspect-bias factors, 115–116, 119
Symptom checklists, psychological injury and, 274
Symptoms of psychiatric disorders, Rorschach
    Inkblot Test and, 208–209
Syndrome evidence, 397–398

Testimony, 117–118. *See also* Expert testimony
Testimony, expert. *See* Expert testimony
Thematic Apperception Test (TAT)
  custody evaluations and, 291
  overview, 203–205
  science and, 217
  use of in forensic settings, 212–214
Therapeutic practices
  goals of therapy versus scientific methodology,
    58–59
  repressed memories and, 57, 58–59
  See also Treatment
Therapist testimony, admissibility standards
    regarding recovered memories and, 72–73.
    See also Expert testimony
Therapists, rehabilitation and, 361
Thought disorder, Rorschach Inkblot Test and,
    208

Training
  in deception detection, 130
  for judges and attorneys regarding scientific
    judgments, 46–48
Trauma
  myths and misconceptions regarding, 275–276
  repressed memories and, 56–57, 63–65
  See also Assessment of psychological injuries;
    Posttraumatic stress disorder (PTSD)
Treatment
  control question test (CQT) and, 237–238
  future directions of, 399–400
  myths and misconceptions regarding, 377–378,
    395–396
  overview, 358–375
  psychopathy and, 190, 365–373, 395–396
  research regarding, 375–377
  science and, 378–380
  See also Therapeutic practices
Treatment model of correctional supervision,
    359
"Truth serums," 92

United States v. Roldan-Zapata (1990), 9
United States v. Telfaire (1972), 40–41

Validity
  assessment of psychological injury and, 268,
    275
  competency to stand trial evaluations and,
    319–323
  criminal profiling and, 247–251
  custody evaluations and, 301–302
  Daubert v. Merrell Dow Pharmaceuticals, Inc.
    (1993) and, 28–30
  Federal Rules of Evidence and, 8
  fit inquiry and, 11
  general acceptance test and, 4–6
  hypnosis and, 88–89
  improving judgments of, 36–41
  interrogation and, 131–132
  judging of, 30–36
  juror credulity and, 19–21
  overview, 12–15
  polygraphs and, 229–230, 233–234
  Rorschach Inkblot Test and, 217–218
  therapeutic assessment and, 58–59
  violence risk assessment, 340
Violence, predictions of
  relevancy test and, 15–17
  violence risk assessment, 334–338
  See also Violence risk assessment
Violence Prevention Program (VPP), 374
Violence Risk Appraisal Guide (VRAG)
  gender and, 346
  overview, 333, 341, 344, 349
  race and, 347
  research regarding, 345

Violence risk assessment
  communicating findings from, 352–353
  Kelly–Frye test and, 17
  myths and misconceptions regarding, 349–351
  overview, 333–339, 351–352
  predictive validity of the PCL-R and, 181–183
  psychopathy and, 396
  research regarding, 344–349
  Rorschach Inkblot Test and, 209–210, 215, 218
  See also Risk assessment

Weisgram v. Marley (2000), 8
Wilson v. Phillips (1999), 19–20

Witness accuracy, hypnosis and, 82–84
Witness confidence, hypnosis and, 85–86
Witness identification
  accuracy of, 106–108
  expert testimony regarding, 100–101
  myths and misconceptions regarding, 111
  overview, 118–119
  presentation of, 114–118
  research regarding, 101–110, 104*t*
  science and, 111–114
  show-up identifications, 116
  suspect-bias factors and, 115–116
  See also Memory